THE LITERARY THING

THE LITERARY THING

history, poetry, and the making of a modern cultural sphere

Rosinka Chaudhuri

OXFORD
UNIVERSITY PRESS

OXFORD
UNIVERSITY PRESS

Oxford University Press is a department of the University of Oxford. It furthers the University's objective of excellence in research, scholarship, and education by publishing worldwide. Oxford is a registered trademark of Oxford University Press in the UK and in certain other countries

Published in India by
Oxford University Press
YMCA Library Building, 1 Jai Singh Road, New Delhi 110001, India

First published in 2014

ISBN-13: 978-0-19-808966-7
ISBN-10: 0-19-808966-X

Typeset in Adobe Garamond Pro 11/13
by Sai Graphic Design, New Delhi 110055

For Amit

I follow the smoke like a path I might take,
And I enjoy, at a sensitive and suitable moment,
Liberation from all speculation
And the awareness that metaphysics is a consequence of being out of sorts.

Fernando Pessoa, 'Tobacco Shop,' trans. Keith Bosley, in
A Centenary Pessoa (Manchester: Carcanet Press, 1995), p. 95

Contents

Preface

When I first presented this research project at the Centre for Studies in Social Sciences, Calcutta (CSSSC), I had conceived of it as a companion volume to my D.Phil. on English poetry in India in the nineteenth century. *Gentlemen Poets in Colonial Bengal: Emergent Nationalism and the Orientalist Project* (a title that militated against the trend of giving books names such as *Writing the Nation*) had just been published, and I wanted to take that work forward by turning to Bengali writing in the same period. As far as this book's title is concerned, it remains only to acknowledge Pierre Macherey, from whose essay, 'The Literary Thing', published in *Diacritics* in 2008 and discussed extensively in the Introduction here, it is taken. In no sense did the book remain a companion volume to my first book, though, as both research preoccupations and research methods evolved in very different directions.

The book has been almost ten years in the writing, charting its own course while other projects, such as *Derozio, Poet of India: The Definitive Edition, The Indian Postcolonial*, and *Freedom and Beef Steaks: Colonial Calcutta Culture* were completed and published in this period. This has meant that it has grown arbitrarily in the course of my career at the CSSSC, benefiting enormously from both the academic environment within it and the stimulation of conversation with the like-minded outside of it. The people I discussed this book with the most incessantly in the first category are certainly Gautam Bhadra and Partha Chatterjee; Gautam-da's fine instincts towards the literary and immense fund of knowledge in the historical have defined the direction many arguments in the book have taken, while much else within it has benefited not only from Partha-da's analytical and observational acumen, but also his infinite patience with the minutiae of research, from diacritical marks to library holdings. Outside of the Centre, I should first and foremost mention Arvind Krishna Mehrotra for his insightful contributions to conversations on poetry; also Peter D. McDonald, Sunetra Gupta, and Elleke Boehmer, friends since student days, and all at Oxford at this time. Brian Hatcher, David Curley, Michael Dodson, Bruce Robertson, Dan White, Mary Ellis Gibson, and William Radice have been occasional interlocutors over the years on this and related subjects. Raj Chandavarkar invited me to both give a talk and publish an occasional paper from a chapter at the Centre for South Asian Studies, Cambridge, in 2005 when it was still in Laundress Lane; to his memory and to Chris Bayly's continuing encouragement and generosity, I am grateful. Dipesh Chakrabarty is neither not of the CSSSC nor entirely of it—for his involved engagement with some sections of this book, and his ready responses to all and any queries, I am much indebted. But to me, more astonishing than anybody else with time and generosity was Ranajit Guha, who allowed neither time difference nor health issues to impede his style, reading, and commenting at length over the telephone on material sent to him by post.

My colleagues—past and present—at the CSSSC have provided invaluable support, friendship, and camaraderie, so essential to any congenial intellectual environment; for this I would like to thank especially Tapati Guha Thakurta, who has always thrown up relevant questions, apart from turning the visual archives at the Centre into an informing principle in my research generally, as well as Sibaji Bandyopadhyay, for his individual help with Bengali material. Manabi Majumdar, Dwaipayan Bhattacharya, Keya Dasgupta, and Bodhisattva Kar, closest on this corridor; and Janaki Nair, Lakshmi Subramaniam, Pradip Bose, Udaya Kumar, P.K. Datta, Manas Ray, Anirban Das, Rajarshi Dasgupta, Priya Sangameswaran, and Prachi Deshpande, all added and continue to add to the texture of daily life through discussion and debate, much of it at the canteen lunch table; Anjan Ghosh was integral to the ethos here, and will always be missed. The librarian, Siddhartha Ray, and the library staff, especially Sanchita and Jayati (not to forget Kali babu, even long after he retired), and the Archives office, especially Abhijit, Kamalika, and Ranjana, deserve unending gratitude, as do my students over the years. The

National Library, Kolkata, would have been a sealed book without Ashim Mukherjee and Swati Ghosh, and its splendid current Director General, our friend Swapan Chakrabarty, long may he prosper. The British Library was instrumental in the publication of my book *Derozio, Poet of India* in 2008, but much of what I put in there has, of course, informed the course of this book too.

My record of usually reluctant conference-going has nevertheless acquired weight and girth through the years. Working backwards over time, I would like to thank people who have heard portions of the book and enriched it with their comments in this long period. Chapters or sections from the book have been presented at the Nehru Memorial Museum and Library, Delhi, for which thanks to Amiya P. Sen; at the Crafts of World Literature conference at Oxford, thanks to Jarad Zimbler and Ben Etherington; at the English Department at King's College, London, thanks to Ruvani Ranasingha; as many as three times, I realize, at the Centre of South Asian Studies, University of Cambridge, thanks to Chris Bayly's continued support; at the Centre of 'Civilisations, Cultures, Littératures Et Sociétés', University of Paris-Sorbonne, thanks to Alexis Tadie and Laetitia Zecchini; at the Postcolonial Writing and Theory Seminar, University of Oxford, thanks to Elleke Boehmer; at an International Conference on 'Rabindranath Tagore in the World' at the Institute of Development Studies, Kolkata, thanks to Amiya Bagchi; at a workshop on 'Translation, Migration, and Modernity: South Asia and Beyond' at Newcastle University, thanks to Neelam Srivastava; at SOAS, University of London, as part of the South Asia History Seminar, thanks to Sunil Kumar and Shabnum Tejani; at a two-day conference on History and Teleology in Berlin, where I benefited from the comments of Dipesh Chakrabarty and Sanjay Subrahmanyam; at the European Conferences on Modern South Asian Studies at Lund and Manchester, thanks to William Radice; at a Sahitya Akademi conference hosted by the English Department at Visva-Bharati University, Santiniketan, thanks to Somdatta Mondol; at the Centre for Historical Studies, Jawaharlal Nehru University, thanks to Neeladri Bhattacharya, and at the Department of History, Delhi University, thanks to Sunil Kumar. Through the years, honouring a hoary tradition, chapters have also been regularly presented at the staff seminars of the CSSSC, as well as at the New Cultural Histories Conference organized by the CSSSC in

2010, while many encounters at its Cultural Studies Workshops have no doubt permeated the interstices of my thinking on many related issues.

Lastly, as always, comes family. Thanks are due to my parents, Ruba and Ranjan Khastgir, and parents-in-law, Bijoya and Nages Chandra Chaudhuri, especially the former, whose love of Bengali writing was infectious and enlivening. Also, for this book, my aunt, Anjali Ghosh, who first brought me to Bengali literature in the unrewarded hours of my schooldays, and my uncle, Kamal Ghosh, for making me part of their family at that time. To Radha I can only offer consolation that maybe later if she reads this book she will forgive me the interminable hours she has spent trailing around lecture halls; and to Amit, who informs my understanding of the literary thing in every way, and for whom anything I say here will be too little, my gratitude for his support.

Note on transliteration

In transliterating Bengali words the Bengali Romanization table from the Library of Congress has been used, with the exception of content within quotation marks, where the original spellings within the quote have been retained, and, of course, proper nouns. The only departure has been that the implicit vowel *a* that is mandatory after all consonants and consonant clusters in transliteration has generally not been used at the end of a word unless pronounced. Titles of Sanskrit works have been represented in their Bengali pronunciation. Bracketed Bengali words have also been liberally inserted both to clarify and highlight words and connections that are difficult to translate, and to link the translated portion more closely to the Bengali text. Also, the Indian custom of referring to authors by their first names instead of their surnames has been generally followed.

Introduction

The world—and even the world of artists—is full of people who can go to the Louvre, walk rapidly, without so much as a glance, past rows of very interesting, though secondary, pictures, to come to a rapturous halt in front of a Titian or a Raphael—one of those that have been most popularised by the engraver's art; then they will go home happy, not a few saying to themselves, 'I know my Museum.' Just as there are people who, having once read Bossuet and Racine, fancy that they have mastered the history of literature.

Fortunately from time to time there come forward righters of wrong, critics, amateurs, curious enquirers, to declare that Raphael, or Racine, does not contain the whole secret, and that the minor poets too have something good, solid and delightful to offer; and finally that however much we may love general *beauty, as it is expressed by classical poets and artists, we are no less wrong to neglect* particular *beauty, the beauty of circumstance and the sketch of manners.*

—Charles Baudelaire[1]

What is at stake is not to portray literary works in the context of their age, but to represent the age that perceives them—our age—in the age during which they arose. It is this that makes literature into an organon of history; and to achieve this, and not to reduce literature to the material of history, is the task of the literary historian.

—Walter Benjamin[2]

[1] Charles Baudelaire, 2008, 'The Painter of Modern Life', in Jonathan Mayne (tr. and ed.), *The Painter of Modern Life and Other Essays*, London: Phaidon Press, p. 1.

[2] Walter Benjamin, 1999, *Selected Writing, Vol. 2 (1927–34)*, Cambridge, Mass.: Harvard University Press, p. 464.

Both Ideas About the Thing and the Thing Itself

This series of studies is intended to be neither a history of Bengali poetic practice, nor a history of representations, but a succession of discrete cross-sectional examinations of moments in time in the history of 'poetry'—the quotation marks have a certain importance. My aim was not to write a history of poetic practices, tracing their successive forms, their evolution, and their dissemination; nor was it to analyse the specific forms, styles, or philosophical ideas through which these practices have been represented. Mediated through the quite recent and banal notion of 'modernity', the chapters in this book attempt to interrogate the history, aesthetic theory, or politics behind the poetry—in order to stand detached from it, bracketing its familiarity in order to analyse the theoretical and practical contexts within which it has been practised and published. Modern Bengali poetry itself did not appear until the middle of the nineteenth century, a fact that should be neither underestimated nor over-interpreted .... The use of poetry was established in connection with other phenomena: the development of diverse fields of knowledge and the establishment of a set of rules and norms—in part traditional, in part new—which found support in religious, political, pedagogical, and literary institutions; and in changes in the way individuals were led to assign meaning and value to their conduct, their duties, their pleasures, their feelings and sensations, their dreams. In short, it was a matter of seeing how 'poetry' came to be constituted in modern Indian societies, an experience that caused individuals to recognize themselves as subjects of a 'modernity', which was accessible to very diverse fields of knowledge and linked to a system of rules and constraints. What I planned, therefore, was a contingent history of the experience of modernity in poetry, where experience is understood as the correlation between fields of knowledge, types of normativity, and forms of subjectivity in a particular culture.[3]

[3] With apologies to Michel Foucault's introduction to *The Use of Pleasure*. The original passage reads:

> This series of studies is intended to be neither a history of sexual behaviours nor a history of representations, but a history of 'sexuality'—the quotation marks have a certain importance. My aim was not to write a history of sexual behaviours,

The preceding passage is a reworking of the introductory paragraph of Michel Foucault's *The Use of Pleasure*, the second volume of his *History of Sexuality*, with changes made to replace key words and phrases with ones that answer the cause of this book; the correspondences of the objectives set out in relation to his study of sexuality and that of this book's interrogation of a critical discourse on the literary were startling and obvious at the same time to a degree where its use became irresistible in the force of its applicability. In defence it might be possible to mention the well-known fact that Walter Benjamin's 'greatest intention', as mentioned by Hannah Arendt in her introduction to *Illuminations*, 'was to produce a work consisting entirely of quotations';[4] an extremity to which it would be near impossible to aspire. Nevertheless, a second quotation further serves the purpose of outlining the parameters defining this study. In an interview between Tariq Ali and Edward Said published in the *New Left Review* in 2003, Said had emphasized yet again what he conceived his life's work to have been about:

---

tracing their successive forms, their evolution, and their dissemination; nor was it to analyse the scientific, religious, or philosophical ideas through which these behaviours have been represented. I wanted first to dwell on that quite recent and banal notion of 'sexuality': to stand detached from it, bracketing its familiarity, in order to analyse the theoretical and practical context with which it has been associated. The term itself did not appear until the beginning of the nineteenth century, a fact that should be neither underestimated nor over-interpreted. … The use of the word was established in connection with other phenomena: the development of diverse fields of knowledge …; the establishment of a set of rules and norms—in part traditional, in part new—which found support in religious, judicial, pedagogical, and medical institutions; and changes in the way individuals were led to assign meaning and value to their conduct, their duties, their pleasures, their feelings and sensations, their dreams. In short it was a matter of seeing how an 'experience' came to be constituted in modern Western societies, an experience that caused individuals to recognize themselves as subjects of a 'sexuality', which was accessible to very diverse fields of knowledge and linked to a system of rules and constraints. What I planned, therefore, was a history of the experience of sexuality, where experience is understood as the correlation between fields of knowledge, types of normativity, and forms of subjectivity in a particular culture (Michel Foucault, 1987, *The History of Sexuality, Volume 2: The Use of Pleasure*, translated from French by Robert Hurley, London: Penguin, pp. 3–4).

[4] Hannah Arendt, 1992, 'Introduction to Walter Benjamin', in Walter Benjamin, *Illuminations*, London: Fontana Press, p. 9.

> It confirmed my sense that the study of literature was essentially a historical task, not just an aesthetic one. I still believe in the role of the aesthetic, but the 'kingdom of literature'—'for its own sake'—is simply wrong. A serious historical investigation must begin from the fact that culture is hopelessly involved in politics. My interest has been in the great canonical literature of the West—read, not as masterpieces that have to be venerated, but as works that have to be grasped in their historical density, so they can resonate ....[5]

An affirmation, after Said, that the 'study of literature' (in itself a phrase gone out of currency) is essentially a historical task, and asserting, additionally, that literariness or the aesthetic is itself historical and a force in history, must lead us to contemplate that other phrase that is of importance in the preceding statement: 'I still believe in the role of the aesthetic ....' An invocation of Foucault at the top of a piece of writing can automatically lead readers to assume exactly the opposite, and despite the well-worn criticism of Said's impossible mission to reconcile Foucauldian discourse theory with Auerbachian high humanism, it is the precise cohabitation of a new amalgam of those irreconcilables that the present study will at least partly be concerned with.

The imponderable value of the literary to critical discourse on literature is given pre-eminence in this study of cultural turning points in the history of Bengali literature so that we might investigate the place of the aesthetic in the composition of a literary culture without denuding it of its significance and aura, or, for that matter, of its historicity.[6] The focus, whether in Saidian postcolonial analysis or traditionally, has been on the 'great' writers of the past; however, the

[5] Edward Said, 2003, *New Left Review*, No. 24, Second Series, November–December, p. 62.

[6] I have used the term 'Bengali' rather than 'Bangla' throughout this book. 'Bangla' is the Bengali word for Bengali, and is used in Bangladesh to denote its official language, which is why the UN and its agencies also use 'Bangla' for the language of Bangladesh. However, 'Bengali' is still the official term in India and is used by the Census of India and in all Indian universities. Although 'Bangla' is often used nowadays in English prose to refer to the Bengali language, the practice seems both unnecessary and inflected with compulsions of political correctness. Crucially, I have also preferred 'Bengali' in order to be true to the spirit of the language in which this book is written.

emphasis here will mostly be on the minor poets rather than on the grand diachronic sweep of the canon, on the detail or the moment in time rather than on the march of history. While endorsing Said's claim regarding the political nature of literature, the concerns of this study (contrary to Said's lifelong contrapuntal readings of the great works of the Western canon) will be in the local and the marginal—doubly distanced not only because the works dealt with here from the nineteenth-century Bengali literary sphere were locationally marginal in the context of metropolis and empire, but because the figures discussed here (most, not all) have generally been regarded as being in the minor key even in the culture to which they were specific. The emphasis here, therefore, will be on demonstrating the importance of the less important to the constitution of a literary culture in particular and to the cultural sphere at large. The debates generated around the works dealt with in this book, the issues involved in their formulation of a literary culture for Bengal (rather than simply for 'Bengali literature'), and the political implications of the cultural space of literature in this period are read here, to reiterate Said, then, 'as works that have to be grasped in their historical density, so they can resonate'.

The period that is dealt with in this book, from when Iswar Gupta, the most famous poet in Bengal in the years preceding the great rebellion, started his career at the *Saṃbād Prabhākar* in 1831 as a nineteen-year old, to when Rabindranath wrote his first successful poems, also nineteen years old, around 1881, constructing his craft and his sensibility in a form distinct from his predecessors, is a fifty-year period that is fundamental to any understanding of the premises upon which modern Bengali literature and culture were founded. It was a unique period, as every period necessarily is, but it was also one in which an answer to the question of the shape of the Indian modern in part lies. The nineteenth century in Bengal has been celebrated and then reviled as a period of renaissance or false renaissance, and it is now time perhaps to move beyond those sterile parameters to an alternative understanding of the interactive, living, and cataclysmic nature of events. Names such as those of Hemchandra Bandyopadhyay or Akshaychandra Sarkar, Nabinchandra Sen or Rangalal Bandyopadhyay, or even the sixteen-year-old Rabindranath, were connected immediately to politics in a way that resists domestication, and which, because of their minority status, are not easily assimilable into 'great literature', allowing us, crucially, to address a brief era just prior and contiguous to the formation of 'high' canonical Bengali literature. Michael Madhusudan Datta, readily the 'great' poet among his peers, on the other hand, marks the space of 'deterritorialization' of a colonized writer in this context in his inhabitation of a space which had no access to power, which could have no real way out, which in relation to the universal, had no hope of taking centrestage.[7] In their location, all these writers are always irremediably connected to the political, and their active solidarity is therefore form-giving for modern Bengali culture or, indeed, for the shape of the putative Indian modern. The leap here from the Bengali to the Indian is not presumptuous or developmentalist; until we recognize that every regional Indian language crafted for itself, at this time, important relationships with the national, the cosmopolitan, and the modern in ways that were uniquely influential in constituting the particularities of Indian modernity at large, the discourse on India's many-hued modernity will never gain the multivalence it requires in order to function productively.

Apart from the fact that the figures dealt with in this book are mostly 'minor poets' in the canon, although crucial to the determination of the shape of literary and cultural discourse in their time, the other occupant of minority status as far as the subject matter of this book is concerned is, of course, the genre of poetry. The neglect of poetry and its study today is almost equally proportionate to its importance in

[7] Deleuze and Guattari (1986), commenting on Kafka and the Jewish literature of Warsaw and Prague, famously construct 'deterritorialization' as the condition of possibility within which a minor literature functions. Their thesis, currently over-familiar in the postcolonial arena, while useful in as much as it allows for the reconceptualization of a territory so far colonized by discussions on narrative and nation, is not the sense in which the word 'minor' has been used in the context of some of the poets dealt with here. The deterritorialization of Kafka's language was crucially informed by both its modernist indeterminacy and its location with regard to German and Czech speakers, giving a new reading of the category 'minor' and its location. The concerns of this study, however, are with certain 'minor poets' in the sense in which Baudelaire used it in *The Painter of Modern Life* rather than with what 'a minority constructs within a major language', which might perhaps be more applicable to Indian writing in English in the nineteenth century. (Gilles Deleuze and Felix Guattari, 1986, *Kafka: Toward a Minor Literature*, translated by Dana Polan, Minneapolis: University of Minnesota Press, p. 16.)

the nineteenth-century public sphere; no discussion of modernity in the world of letters in the late nineteenth century anywhere, whether London or Calcutta, can dispense with an understanding of the function of poetry and its criticism and the manner in which it was constitutive of the modern cultural sphere. Yet current discussions on the development of modern literary genres and aesthetic conventions in nineteenth-century Bengal have tended to ignore the seminal role of poetry, perhaps because of its relative neglect in the modern day in formulating the cultural imagination of Indians.

In academic discourse, the coming together of the birth of the novel, the concept of history, and the idea of the nation-state under the sign of the modern has led to an excess of concern with the manner in which the nation was brought into being, facilitating, thereby, a disregard for the structures of literary modernity as they shaped a new cultural consciousness, and a collective blindness towards the forceful intervention of poetry and song within those parameters.[8] Thus, while Meenakshi Mukherjee edited *Early Novels in India*, a Sahitya Akademi volume consisting of critical perspectives on the genre of the regional novel and its relation to the Indian nation, no such corresponding volume exists on regional poetry, which has seen very little critical work in English on the subject.[9] Dipesh Chakrabarty, a critic unusually sensitive to the literary in the domain of the social sciences, paradoxically elides any mention of it in a chapter devoted to poetry in his book *Provincializing Europe*, when he takes his argument about the division between the prosaic and the poetic in Tagore

[8] Sugata Bose makes this point in a footnote while discussing Partha Chatterjee's work, saying:

> Poetry has not received the same attention as prose from students of nationalism. The novel was arguably *the* literary vehicle that transmitted the content and forms of 'Western' nationalism to colonial settings. Poems and songs, despite borrowings of Western forms, represented alternative modes of expression that might suggest a different accent on the question of derivation in particular and the languages of nationalism in general. ('Nation as Mother: Representations and Contestations of "India" in Bengali Literature and Culture', in Sugata Bose and Ayesha Jalal (eds), *Nationalism, Democracy and Development: State and Politics in India* 1997, Delhi: Oxford University Press, p. 69, fn 29.)

[9] Meenakshi Mukherjee (ed.), 2002, *Early Novels in India*, Delhi: Sahitya Akademi.

further to conclude (without mentioning the seminal role of poetry) that 'The new prose of fiction—novels and short stories—was thus seen as intimately connected to questions of political modernity'.[10] Similarly, Partha Chatterjee, in his introduction to *The Nation and Its Fragments*, discusses the shaping of critical discourse in colonial Bengal in relation to drama, the novel, and even art, but ignores completely the fiercely contested and controversial processes by which modern Bengali poetry and literary criticism were formulated. 'The desire to construct an aesthetic form that was modern and national', to use his words, 'was shown in its most exaggerated shape', it is my contention, not in the Bengal school of art in the 1920s, as he claims, but long before that in the poetry of Rangalal Bandyopadhyay, Hemchandra Bandyopadhyay, Madhusudan Datta, and Nabinchandra Sen, and in the literary criticism and controversy surrounding their work in the nineteenth century.[11]

The 'modern' and the 'national' are not naturally contiguous terms as they are made to appear in this formulation, and much of the wilful shutting out of the literary and cultural imaginings that shaped most dialogues in this period has come about because of the manner in which these two words have appeared to be almost welded together in current cultural studies discourse. Prying open that space between those two terms, however, this book attempts to demonstrate that political modernity in the colonial years was fundamentally built upon the cultural imagination of the regional public, which, in turn, was formed in close correspondence with global issues of literature and history and the many local controversies and eruptions in society around individual poems examined for sedition, plays performed or proscribed, novels written and rewritten, and critical writings whose polemics formulated ideas of identity anew. We are only just, perhaps, exiting an era of obsession with the nation and the novel, both subsumed under categories of narration in the last twenty years in a manner detrimental to any understanding of the operation of literature outside of those parameters.

[10] Dipesh Chakrabarty, 2001, *Provincializing Europe: Postcolonial Thought and Historical Difference*, Delhi: Oxford University Press, p. 151.

[11] Partha Chatterjee, 1995, 'Introduction', *The Nation and Its Fragments*, New Delhi: Oxford University Press.

As far as the focus on the regional is concerned, the attempt here is to turn towards a sense of location, not in hermeneutical textual terms, but as a political vantage point of study and criticism. This book, then, cannot have a grand theme in the manner that is so popular among important Indian thinkers, historians, or social and political scientists; consequently, it is not about the idea of India, or imagining India, or producing India—in fact, there is no 'India' here except as it is located in the regional, the particular, the individual, and the ordinary. If the country comes up repeatedly in the discourse of some of the poets or critics who write in the nineteenth century, that is because they envisioned the local and the regional also as the national and the 'Indian', conflating the two registers without self-consciousness, the 'nation' projected outward from 'Bengal'. There is no great political or historical continuity that threads the chapters here together; no one teleological project to join the particularities of each situation into a meta-narrative of nation or modernity, no 'grand synthesis of unprecedented scope' then, either attempted or accomplished in these pages.[12]

The History of Literary History

Almost exactly parallel to and contiguous with developments in the Western hemisphere, two well-developed lineages in the study of literature in India over the nineteenth and twentieth centuries may be immediately traced by any historian of the field. First and second, there came into existence at almost the same time, exactly in the fifty-year period we are concerned with here, two adjacent developments—literary criticism and literary history. Literary criticism, written in English or the regional languages, quite often by writers themselves, but also, more and more, by new professionals in the literary sphere and newspapermen and editors of literary periodicals, took the form of book reviews, extended articles in the periodical press, and stand-alone publications of critical essays or books. From the nineteenth century onward, parallel to the *tazkira* tradition exemplified by the *Āb-e hāyat*,

[12] Blurb description of Sheldon Pollock (ed.), 2003, *Literary Cultures in History: Reconstructions from South Asia*, Berkeley: University of California Press.

there developed the hugely important domain of the creative writer-turned literary critic engaging with the contemporary and traditional production of literature in the varied languages of India.[13] If, in English studies, the writer's or critic's radical reassessment of literary tradition was formative for the field; and if T.S. Eliot's 'Tradition and the Individual Talent' (1917), D.H. Lawrence's *Studies in Classic American Literature* (1923), and F.R. Leavis' *The Great Tradition* (1948), to name three texts at random, were radical reassessments in the formulation of the English literary canon in the twentieth century, quickly becoming essential reading for an understanding of the various positions that defined the literary past—then so too were Bankimchandra Chatterjee's essays on the '*uttar rāmcarit*' or '*gīti kābya*' or Rabindranath Tagore's '*sāhitye svarup*', '*prācīn sāhitya*' or '*chele bhulāno chaṛā*' influential texts for readers of nineteenth-century Bengali literature. Thus, many eminent writer/critics in Bengali have consistently defined the literary culture of their time and of their pasts, though arguably the centrality of the texts mentioned above to English studies is enviable when compared to the utter neglect in the present day of the latter in a culture less and less concerned with its literary heritage and its relationship to history.

At the start, literary criticism in Bengali was often conflated with an attempt at summing up the literary achievements of this particular language, wherein Macherey's distinction in his book, *A Theory of Literary Production*, of literary criticism as an 'art' and literary history as a 'science' had not yet become operational.[14] These brief critical essays-cum-histories were quite often written, in the first instance, in the English language, arguably overtly for the benefit of the colonial British reader, but of no mean significance to the newly educated classes reading them at the same time in the same language. The tradition of writing about Bengali literature in English, for instance, had been inaugurated by a poet in the English language, Kasiprasad Ghosh, in the pages of the *India Gazette* in 1831 in a piece called 'On Bengali Writers'; roughly forty years later, Bankimchandra Chatterjee's

[13] *Āb-e hāyat* [*water of life*] is a hugely popular commentary (or *tazkira*) on Urdu poetry written by Muhammad Husain Azad (1830–1910) in 1880 (2nd edn, 1883).

[14] Pierre Macherey, 2006, *A Theory of Literary Production*, London: Routledge, p. 4.

two influential English essays ('A Popular Literature for Bengal', 1870; 'Bengali Literature', 1871) were landmarks of this particular convention (both started out as review essays).

This was a time when the canon was being invented and put into place side by side with the first important modern works making their way into the public sphere. Thus, in 'Bengali Literature', Bankim starts with medieval poets Mukundaram and Vidyapati, but very quickly comes to 'the present writers in Bengali', reviewing not only the work of immediate predecessors such as Madhusudan or Kaliprasanna Singha, but also, straight-faced, the works of a 'Babu Bankim Chandra Chatarji (*sic*)', the author of works such as '*Kapāl Kundala*', summarizing his own work at great length in this article that was first published anonymously in the *Calcutta Review*. The fluid, excitable, and nebulous nature of the circumstances of the birth of modern Bengali literature becomes apparent from such instances, and although the story of the evolution of the language would not be complete for another fifty years, by which time both a firm conception of a 'high cultural' Bengali and a demarcated space occupied by the academic professional would take over, the importance of our period, 1831–81, lies exactly in the unresolved nature of many of the most important categories of analysis as these evolved over time.

The second and parallel development—of the writing of 'literary history' in the nineteenth century—was one that was spawned by the birth, in this period exactly, of the category of 'Literature' itself since the 1850s. Once such a thing is born, it requires a history, and as we have seen, writers themselves sometimes took the lead in formulating the new spaces and histories of particular literatures for the benefit of contemporary readers. The words '*sāhitya*' (literature) and '*kabi*' (poet) are being reformulated and reinvented in this time to come to mean what they mean to us today, alongside other categories such as '*itihās*'; we are constantly reminded at this time that such words meant something else in the past and signify something quite different now, in the nineteenth century. Side by side, the literariness of the literary is being formulated anew, and the mapping of 'our own' literary heritage is being self-consciously undertaken now in a different way to the traditional commentaries and textual analyses of the past. Many of these issues have been dealt with in this book in individual chapters, especially the discussions on poetry and the modern poet, as issues of aesthetics, of tradition, of authenticity, and of culture are repeatedly brought up and reconfigured to suit modern times.

As these distinct spaces began to carve out a niche for themselves in their respective domains, the responsibility for historicizing their presence in culture fell more and more upon the professional as he succeeded the amateur with the advent of the twentieth century. One of the first histories of Bengali literature in the European model is to be found in Ramgati Nyayaratna's *Bāṅgālā bhāshā o bāṅgālā sāhitya bishayak prastāb* in 1872, succeeding Iswar Gupta's differently ordered, albeit pioneering efforts towards the collection and publication of the lives of poets between 1855 and 1859. Pending further discussion, suffice to say that this genre of the professional history of the literature of Bengal found its greatest exponent in the figure of Dineshchandra Sen, whose nationalist *Baṅga bhāshā o sāhitya* in 1896 was the precursor to a whole field of the histories of Bengali language and literature produced by academics of great distinction and perspicacity. From Sunitikumar Chattopadhyay to Sukumar Sen to Asitkumar Bandyopadhyay, the story of the evolution of the Bengali language and its literature was often told in multi-volume works extending from the twelfth-century *Caryāpad* onward into the present age.

The scene encompassing all of modern India was both different and more complicated because of the multilingual regional strands that constitute 'Indian literary history'. Buddhadeva Bose had remarked that just as there is no such thing as 'Indian food', there is no such thing as 'Indian literature'; would it follow then, for him, that there could be no such thing as 'Indian literary history'?[15] Modern literary history was written with regard to particular languages in India, and each region crafted its own out of their individual literary resources and traditions from the mid-nineteenth century onward. In its older forms, as practised by precolonial litterateurs in the form of literary texts, commentaries, editions of important texts, and 'works on grammar, lexicography, and metrics', it had also, of course, been available in 'two dozen regional and transregional written languages' for centuries.[16] Orientalist selections in the form of anthologies or

[15] Buddhadeva Bose, 1971, 'Bengali Gastronomy', *Ananda Bazar Patrika*, 1–4 January.

[16] Sheldon Pollock, *Literary Cultures in History*, p. 3. Pollock points out that 'such

translations, such as Max Müller's famous *Sacred Books of the East* series or Moriz Winternitz's well-known volumes, *A History of Indian Literature* (1908–22), that dealt with Indian literary history in the Sanskrit, Pali, and Prakrit past, were always dominant in a colonial period where power was invested in such representations. It was from around the 1870s that literary history in the Western style began to be written in the regional languages in India. Narmad's Gujarati-language work, *Kavicaritra* (*Lives of the Poets*) was written in 1865 and Nyayaratna's in Bengali in 1872, while in Tamil, an English compilation by Cavelly Venkataramaswami, *Sketch of the Dekhan Poets* (Calcutta, 1829), foreshadowed Simon Casie Chitty's *The Tamil Plutarch* (1859), although the first 'modern' Tamil literary history in Tamil, *Pavalar Carittiram Tipakam* (*The Galaxy of Tamil Poets*) by J.R. Arnold or A. Catacivam Pillai appeared only in 1886.[17]

The presence of English, unsurprisingly, is ubiquitous in the moment of the writing of modern literary histories in the regional languages; as in Tamil, so too in Bengal and elsewhere, both languages were equally used to address the subject. So from Bankimchandra Chatterjee's seminal English essays on Bengali literature onward (1870 and 1871), through R.C. Dutt, who published several articles on Bengali literature in 1874 as Arcydae in Lal Behari De's *Bengal Magazine*, later collected in his book *The Literature of Bengal* (1877), we have a distinguished tradition of writing about Bengali literature in English continuing into the twentieth century, from Dinesh Chandra Sen's transcreation of his *Baṅga bhāshā o sāhitya* into the *History of Bengali Language and Literature* (1911) to Pramatha Chaudhuri's 'The Story of Bengali Literature' (1917), Sushil Kumar De's *Bengali Literature in the Nineteenth Century* (1919), Priyaranjan Sen's *Western Influence in Bengali Literature* (1932), and J.C. Ghosh's *Bengali Literature* (1948).

Remarkably, there was no significant tradition in English of either writers or critics assessing the entire field of Indian literature, or of

literary study did not of course always proceed uninterruptedly; by the middle of the second millennium much of Tamil *cankam* literature, for example, had fallen into oblivion and Old Kannada literature was hardly read'.

[17] Stuart Blackburn and Vasudha Dalmia, 2004, *Indian Literary History: Essays on the Nineteenth Century*, Delhi: Permanent Black, pp. 2–3.

literary histories enveloping all or most of the Indian languages. Criticism written in English had dealt, as we have seen earlier, either with a particular region, or, indeed, most often with Indian writing in English—from a slightly schematic start made by colonial writers such as E.F. Oaten or T.O.D. Dunn or Latika Basu in the early twentieth century on the subject of Bengalis writing English verse, the field was soon thickly populated by post-Independence academic critics such as K.R. Srinivasa Iyengar, C.D. Narasimhaiah, or M.K. Naik on what was quaintly called 'Indo-Anglian Literature'—but no literary history was written in English which had all of India's languages as its territory. Sisir Kumar Das's two volumes on the nineteenth and twentieth centuries in the projected ten-volume Sahitya Akademi publication, *A History of Indian Literature*, appeared only in 1995, and this has been the only attempt to date to comprehensively sum up the literatures of India in the English language.

Current discourses on the domain of the vernacular in the last decade or so have been dominated by discussions on history-writing in the regional languages. In *History in the Vernacular* (2008), pursuing the question of the emergence of new literary forms in India in the period of early and colonial modernity, a range of texts and genres were explored, from '*vamsavalis*', '*caritras*', and '*bakhars*', to the specifically Assamese '*buranjis*' and the '*tarikh*' of Indo-Persian descent, through to Bengali nineteenth-century poetry and counter-factual history, in order to 'better deal with the problem of pre-colonial vernacular historical traditions and what happens to them under conditions of modernity'.[18] Parallel to, preceding, and following this book, a spate of publications on regional languages and literatures dominated the scene. Working with a notion of the Habermasian public sphere in mind, scholars explored the relationship of language to the politics of the regional or the national, or investigated the histories of print culture and publication (book histories have played a pre-eminent role here). Important titles have made their presence felt in the context of say, Tamil (Sumathi Ramaswamy, A.R. Venkatachalapathy), Marathi (Veena Naregal), Hindi (Vasudha Dalmia, Francesca Orsini), or Bengali (Anindita Ghosh, Tithi Bhattacharya) as scholars have used a

[18] Partha Chatterjee, 2008, 'Introduction', *History in the Vernacular*, Ranikhet: Permanent Black, p. 7.

historical approach to show how specific aspects of the middle class's social history were frequently aligned to social and economic power in the production of the cultural categories of reading and writing in nineteenth- and twentieth-century India.[19]

In his discussion on the vernacular, Partha Chatterjee has underlined what he perceives as the ironical turning point in the nineteenth century whereby

> In a curious twist to the idea of the vernacular, all Indian languages, including hitherto 'classical' languages such as Sanskrit, Arabic, and Persian, were turned, in relation to English, into vernaculars. English became the dominant language of the modern, reducing the worlds inhabited by all Indian languages into vernacular non-modernity.[20]

The nostalgic evocation of such a turn as being one that 'reduced' the vernaculars forever to a second-class status of 'vernacular non-modernity', however, is historically blind to the great alliance between the vernacular and the modern in the colonial period, when the enormous importance of particular regional languages in constituting a variety of the facets of the multivocal Indian modern cannot be emphasized enough. Because it is a fact hardly ever acknowledged that the English language in India was certainly not the only 'dominant language of the modern' at the time, as powerful regional languages

[19] Sumathi Ramaswamy, 1997, *Passions of the Tongue: Language Devotion in Tamil India, 1891–1970*, Berkeley: University of California Press; A.R. Venkatachalapathy, 2011, *The Province of the Book: Scholars, Scribes, and Scribblers in Colonial Tamilnadu*, Ranikhet: Permanent Black; Veena Naregal, 2001, *Language Politics, Elites and the Public Sphere: Western India under Colonialism*, New Delhi: Orient Blackswan; 2002, *Language, Hierarchy, and Identity: Emergence of the Public Sphere in Colonial Western India*, New York, USA: Oxford University Press; Vasudha Dalmia, 1997, *The Nationalization of Hindu Traditions: Bharatendu Harischandra and Nineteenth-Century Benaras*, Delhi: Oxford University Press; Francesca Orsini, 2002, *The Hindi Public Sphere: 1920–1940: Language and Literature in the Age of Nationalism*, New York: Oxford University Press; 2009, *Print and Pleasure: The Genres of Commercial Publishing in Nineteenth-Century North India*, Ranikhet: Permanent Black; Anindita Ghosh, 2006, *Power in Print: Popular Publishing and the Politics of Language and Culture in a Colonial Society*, Delhi: Oxford University Press; Tithi Bhattacharya, 2005, *The Sentinels of Culture: Class, Education, and the Colonial Intellectual in Bengal*, Delhi: Oxford University Press.

[20] Partha Chatterjee, 2008, 'Introduction', *History in the Vernacular*, Ranikhet: Permanent Black, p. 10.

also forged, simultaneously, a vibrant vernacular modern, to which was tied vital productions of modern regional literatures well up to the mid-twentieth century; the apparent decline of the regional languages being, in point of fact, a peculiarly postcolonial, even post-liberalization phenomenon in India.[21]

Why Does Literature Matter?

In a recent book titled *Why Does Literature Matter?* American philosopher Frank B. Farrell has commented on the impoverishment of literary space in the contemporary world. 'To read widely in academic literary criticism of recent decades (that written from 1970 to 2000) is to wonder', he says in the opening sentence, 'why literature matters at all'; subsequently identifying, among the causes, the appearance of the literary text 'as one more site, no more privileged than others, where cultural codes linked with issues of power reveal themselves…'.[22] While such an interrogation cannot return to earlier ways of reading which are 'theoretically unsophisticated about the working of language' or 'politically ignorant of the machineries of social power', with the text having so little integrity of its own, the literary work, he maintains, loses its earlier value.[23]

This phenomenon in the context of literary writing has had its repercussions also on the writing of literary historiography, where the turn toward cultural studies in the late twentieth century in the Western academy resulted in a tectonic shift in the approach to the writing of literary history as well. Earlier, foundational texts of literary history told you exactly why literature mattered; they were concerned not merely with mapping the territory, but also with evaluating the field, staying with the worthwhile, and tracing the evolution of the

[21] Benedict Anderson (2006) writes of a preceding era of European discovery and conquest causing a revolution in the languages of Europe, when 'the old sacred languages—Latin, Greek, and Hebrew—were forced to mingle on equal ontological footing with a motley plebian crowd of vernacular rivals, in a movement which complemented their earlier demotion in the market-place by print-capitalism' (*Imagined Communities*, London: Verso, p. 70).

[22] Frank B. Farrell, 2004, *Why Does Literature Matter?* Ithaca and London: Cornell University Press, p. 1.

[23] Ibid.

literary text; in short, both with qualities that were inherent in the text, as well as the social history in which the text was embedded. Thus, Boris Ford, the editor of the hugely popular ten-volume *The New Pelican Guide to English Literature* (1955), set out his agenda in an instructive sentence in his introduction regarding the formulation of the site of literary history as it was understood in 1955, acknowledging 'a considerable debt to those twentieth-century writers and critics who have made a determined effort to elicit from literature *what is of living value to us today*: to establish a sense of literary tradition and to define the standards that this tradition embodies'.[24]

Literary studies the world over in the postmodern, postcolonial decades of the 1980s and 1990s have moved decisively away from such value-based organizations of the field, turning instead to the methods and language of 'theory' and its manifestation in the new schools of cultural studies and the social sciences in an effort to shrug off the humanistic, Eurocentric, elitist, and patriarchal biases of traditional literary criticism. In India, colonial domination added its own complexities to the repudiation of older ways of reading, with the move away from literature coinciding with an older more fundamental feeling of guilt associated with anything so inconsequential as literature or literary studies in the pre- and post-Independence years of nation-building and civil construction, poverty alleviation and the green revolution, war and peace. That this was, in a sense, a predicament common also to other cultures is testified to by J. Hillis Miller in a timely protest against the state of literary studies in *The Ethics of Reading* (1985), where he suggested that the change in literary studies had been propelled by 'a sense of guilt in occupying oneself with something so trivial, so disconnected from life and reality, as novels and poems, in comparison with the serious business of history, politics, and the class-struggle'.[25] The important role of materialist Marxist critics in this turn was common to most academic literary criticism in these years and hardly needs pointing out in this context.

[24] Boris Ford, General Introduction to *The New Pelican Guide to English Literature*, London: Penguin, 1982 (1955), pp. 8–9. My emphasis.

[25] J. Hillis Miller, 1985, *The Ethics of Reading*, New York: Columbia University Press, p. 5.

The 'cultural-studies model' of Indian literary history, with individual articles on literary texts reading more often like social or political-science treatises replete with the facts and figures of book history, has been marked (apart from the books discussed in the previous section) by two significant publications within a year of one another—Sheldon Pollock's massive *Literary Cultures in History: Reconstructions from South Asia* and Stuart Blackburn and Vasudha Dalmia's *Indian Literary History: Essays on the Nineteenth Century*.[26] The latter book, indeed, opens with a remarkable celebration of this line of study, remarking:

> Ever since Clifford Geertz transformed the drama of Balinese cock-fighting into a text, and new historicism made the complementary gesture of returning culture to the centre of literary studies, students of literature, history and culture have shared a common vocabulary, key concepts, and points of reference.[27]

The effort in both books is pithily summarized in the second as an endeavour 'to understand the place of literature in history, largely through an analysis of the textual production of cultural meanings and the socio-political conditions of creating texts'.[28]

However well-intentioned and rewarding the endeavour, those turning literary criticism and history into a branch of the social sciences might benefit from paying heed to the voice of A.K. Ramanujan, who straddled both spheres with consummate ease:

> Literature may provide facts for social scientists, especially in the absence of other documents. But literature refracts as much as it reflects; one needs to take account of the 'specific density' of the literary medium, its 'refractive index', before we can truly use literary materials as documents. To use them in a literal straightforward fashion is to misuse them... . Unless we enter the realm of symbolic values that writers express through the 'facts' and 'objective entities', the facts themselves would be commonplace or misunderstood.[29]

[26] Sheldon Pollock (ed.), 2003, *Literary Cultures in History*; Stuart Blackburn and Vasudha Dalmia, 2004, *Indian Literary History*.

[27] Blackburn and Dalmia, *Indian Literary History*, p. 1.

[28] Ibid.

[29] A.K. Ramanujan, 1970, 'Toward an Anthology of City Images', in Richard G. Fox (ed.), *Urban India: Society, Space and Image*, New York: Pantheon Books.

It is worth distinguishing here, however, between the problem of using literary works as social documents and the related but different problem of literary studies adopting the vocabulary and methods of the social and political sciences; it is the latter concern that is of greater issue here. This book, in a departure from the current organization of the discourse on literary texts, attempts to restore a point of view that has been obscured for the most part by such sociological, historical, or theoretical approaches to literary studies, to rediscover a lost dimension of literature and literary history not by jettisoning these challenging and important aspects, but by making allowance for a timely change in the perspective with which we view both the field and the text.

In its attempt to return to the regional from within the premises of the English language, this book, therefore, is moving away from both the earlier humanistic twentieth-century model of literary historiography and the later fin de siécle cultural variety of Anglophone Bourdieuian literary studies, from which the literary text itself more or less disappears, and all we are left with is 'the field'. Confronting the central problem with Bourdieu, we are faced with the paradox that while he offers one of the best ways of modelling and understanding how literary cultures are structured and how they work, he still does not—despite, or perhaps because of, his own efforts in *The Rules of Art*—provide a very good basis for reading individual works. How then do we return to the literary work in the new millennium, charting a course in between an assumption of the literary as an essentialist object of determination, and of its role in socio-political contexts of operation and function, so that we may turn in a new way to the pleasures of the individual text and the particularities of the ordering of language?

'The Literary Thing'

What, today, is the category of the literary? Without going into a detailed analysis of answers to this question, with which the French intellectual tradition alone, for instance, has engaged for many years now—from Sartre onward, through Roland Barthes, Maurice Blanchot, or Emmanuel Levinas—it might be possible to articulate an answer via a short piece by Pierre Macherey that usefully summarizes the two contradictory stances taken today in relation to an answer to that question.[30] Moving on from his own pathbreaking overtly Marxian analysis in *A Theory of Literary Production* (1978), where he had applied a cluster of Althusserian concepts to the literary work, homing in on the text's absences, silences, repetitions, and displacements to interrogate the complex relations between text, ideology, and history, Macherey had, in *The Object of Literature* (1995), further deepened his investigation into the force of the literary on rational thought.[31] In 'The Literary Thing', an article published in 2007, Macherey submits the category of the literary to additional interrogation, reflecting upon the fuzzy semantics of the notion of 'the thing' itself in the process.[32]

Transformed from 'an instrument of inculcation into a kind of merchandise', literature today, he says, has 'the status of discounted luxury products'; nonetheless, it is 'an increasingly less consumable thing' intended for a public's common lot in order 'to be educated, raised, disciplined, even to be kept busy or distracted'. Yet Macherey's intent, here, is to expose the dilemma that literature cannot actually be reducible only to the consumable thing, that, as we broach the question of literature, we realize that it is 'in reality two things at once, between which we have not finished going uncertainly back and forth', both 'the "thing": that muddy and potentially nauseous substance we have to wade around in if we want to apprehend it, but also a pure

[30] Jean-Paul Sartre, 1988, 'What is Literature?' in Bernard Frechtman (tr.), '*What is Literature? and Other Essays*, Mass.: Cambridge; Roland Barthes, 1967, *Writing Degree Zero*, translated by Annette Lavers and Colin Smith, New York: Hill and Wang; Maurice Blanchot, 1995, 'Literature and the Right to Death' in *The Work of Fire*, translated by Charlotte Mandell, Stanford, California: Stanford University Press, pp. 300–44; Maurice Blanchot, 1989, *The Space of Literature*, translated by Ann Smock, London: University of Nebraska Press; Emmanuel Levinas, 2004, 'Reality and Its Shadow', in *Unforseen History,* Urbana: University of Illinois Press. The Marxist tradition in the sociology of literature, from George Lukacs to Raymond Williams to Terry Eagleton, also, of course, formed a distinct intervention in the field of literary historiography over these years that is too well known to bear summarization here.

[31] Pierre Macherey, 1978, *A Theory of Literary Production*, London: Routledge; Kegan Paul, 1995, *The Object of Literature*, Cambridge: Cambridge University Press.

[32] Pierre Macherey, 2007, 'The Literary Thing', *Diacritics*, Vol. 37, No. 4, pp. 21–30.

and ethereal reality that eludes every grasp and folds in on itself in impenetrable mystery'.[33]

Negotiating a third path in between either a Bourdieuian conception of a 'literary field', and/or 'a space of literature' as 'envisioned by Blanchot's haunted regard', Macherey submits neither to Bourdieu's determined demystification of the literary thing in his denial of the privileges of exceptionality and autoreferentiality to literature, nor to Blanchot's assignment to the literary thing of 'the space of literature', which restores a pre-eminence to the work itself at the expense of the author.[34] Attempting a reconciliation between the two extremes, he insists on the materiality and immateriality of literature at the same time, joining Bourdieu to Blanchot in an impossible contortionist leap of acrobatic proportions in his suggestion that it would be unfeasible to divide and separate these two aspects in the constitution of the literary, that we must attend to both, that it is imperative to refer to the fact that while it is a production itself, the literary is also what produces an array of effects that one has to work at discovering anew each time. In some sense, perhaps, this desire to bring the materiality of the field of the text into conjunction with the immanent immateriality of the aesthetic impulse of literature belongs to a time 'after theory', when, as Peter D. McDonald has argued in the context of the intensive and divisive debate in literature departments in the period from the mid-1960s to the mid-1990s, it is perhaps now 'more productive, and accurate, to think of the current situation as coming not after theory but after theory's successful bid for hegemony'.[35]

Valorizing that leap of faith which repeatedly joins two irreconcilable positions to each other, negotiating an intermediate space in the cracks of Foucault's contention with Auerbach's, Bourdieu's with Blanchot's, this study of discrete moments in the coming into existence of a literary culture in modern Bengal, then, is a reading that seeks to infer the lesson of historical discontinuity by locating itself outside history writing as it has been conventionally understood. This impulse to

[33] Ibid., p. 23.

[34] Ibid., p. 25.

[35] See, in this regard, Peter D. McDonald, 'After Theory', written prior to Macherey's essay and anticipating presciently its twin thrust in recuperating Bourdieu and Blanchot for a new reading of the category of literature.

bring conflicting positions into dialogue is not new or unprecedented in scholarship and criticism (Dipesh Chakrabarty's intention, in *Provincializing Europe*, he had said, was to bring Marx and Heidegger into conversation with each other).[36] It stems from an unease with the current state of criticism, a discomfort with positions perceived to have become dogmatic, a disinclination to completely accept current intellectual orthodoxies. Such a position attempts to carve out a location juxtaposed with but at a distance from contemporary theoretical premises, attempting thereby in part to clear a space, to mind the gap, to address a felt need. Unlike the Hegelian idea that incompatible opposites were resolvable by means of the dialectic, with a reconciliation of opposites leading up to a grand synthesis at the conclusion, this book, on the contrary, offers no transcendence or unity at the end, keeping the irreconcilables ultimately apart and denying the possibility of closure, thereby leaving the argument perhaps more perplexed and unsettled than before.

Two Ways of Thinking about Criticism

(i) The Distanced

When Eric Auerbach had famously begun *Mimesis in medias res* with the wonderful first chapter, 'Odysseus' Scar', his purpose had been, Aamir Mufti maintains, 'not to analyse the Homeric text as such but rather to contrast two texts and modes of description, the Homeric and the biblical'.[37] In Mufti's reading, which takes its inspiration in turn from Said's reading of the same text, Auerbach's book is seen not so much as a seamless or unitary but a fragmentary work that consists of a series of close readings of fragments of texts. Said contends, in his translation of Auerbach's late 1969 essay, 'Philology and *Weltliteratur*' (1952), that the latter was interested in a philology that treats 'contingent, historical truths'. The project of *Mimesis* becomes possible, according to Said, because of the location of its

[36] Dipesh Chakrabarty, 2001, 'Introduction', *Provincializing Europe*, Delhi: Oxford University Press, p. 18.

[37] Aamir Mufti, 2010, *Auerbach in Istanbul* in Elleke Boehmer and Rosinka Chaudhuri (eds), *The Indian Postcolonial: A Critical Reader*, London: Routledge, pp. 112–13.

composition—written by a German-Jewish refugee in a Muslim city, Istanbul, in exile from Nazism in Turkey, contemplating the missing library of the great works of the West from a haunting distance. Said, himself a practitioner in an exilic mode, shows in this context how this fact of exile becomes the *condition of possibility* for the work to come into existence:

> In other words, the book owed its existence to the very fact of Oriental, non-Occidental exile and homelessness. And if this is so, then *Mimesis* itself is not, as it has so frequently been taken to be, only a massive reaffirmation of the Western cultural tradition, but also a work built upon a critically important alienation from it, a work whose conditions and circumstances of existence are not immediately derived from the culture it describes with such extraordinary insight and brilliance but built rather on an agonizing distance from it.[38]

'Distance', then, is the key word that I will return to (and one that will recur more than once here), that allows for the space for one to step back from the material involved so as to reaffirm it by building, at the same time, a work premised upon a critical alienation from it. Distance allows for perspective, gathers upon a standpoint, and does not entertain a sense of belonging. Many literary critics have been enabled by it; Maurice Blanchot defined the 'space' of literature, *l'espace littéraire*, as the 'distance' of the work, or of literature, with respect, 'not only to "every other object which exists", but with respect to itself. The work is remote from itself, or not quite itself'. He reads the work as 'pure deferral, a void or vacuum', which 'lends itself to be filled up with everything it isn't: with useful meanings, for example, which multiply and change as history progresses'.[39]

If Blanchot was preoccupied with literature's distance from the world, and has spoken of this distance as literature's preserve, he has also dwelt on the thought that literature involves a separation from the world permitting contemplation or critical interpretation of things and events—thus leading us to the critic's distance from 'literature'. In this domain, Said reads Auerbach's as the urtext, but other inspired

[38] Edward Said, 1983, *The World, the Text, and the Critic*, London, pp. 7–8.

[39] Maurice Blanchot, 1989, 'Translator's Introduction', in Ann Smock (tr.), *The Space of Literature*, London: University of Nebraska Press, p. ii.

outsiders, from D.H. Lawrence to Gabriel Josipovici, have produced a perspective upon, in their case, the English literary scene, in a manner not available without an understanding of exile or banishment as a space of literature. As is well known, Lawrence's insistence on the open-ended and the incomplete, on the realization that the 'other' cannot be 'known', reiterated the impossibility of essentializing the other, articulating a politics that was always positioned on the outside in relation to the established view. More recently, Josipovici's book on the fate of Modernism in contemporary England is located in a critical stance that stands outside 'the entire establishment' of reviewers and critics, against whom he addresses his sustained polemic on the provincialization of English literary culture.[40]

The notions of distance dwelt upon here, however, are not in alliance with those ideas of distance that have, from the Russian Formalists onward, also been identified with estrangement, alienation, and the like, where a 'scientific' notion of criticism is advanced that remains unhistorical and aloof from its object. Neither is it in sympathy with the more recent formulation of 'distant reading' formulated by Franco Moretti in a manifesto for 'World Literature'. While agreeing that 'distance', as he says, '*is a condition of knowledge*: it allows you to focus on units that are much smaller or much larger than the text: devices, themes, tropes—or genres and systems', one disagrees with his emphasis on a universal conceptual method of reading (whose metaphor is 'the wave'), which is not overly concerned with the text itself:

> And if, between the very small and the very large, the text itself disappears, well, it is one of those cases when one can justifiably say, Less is more. If we want to understand the system in its entirety, we must accept losing something. We always pay a price for theoretical knowledge: reality is infinitely rich; concepts are abstract, are poor. But it's precisely this 'poverty' that makes it possible to handle them, and therefore to know. This is why less is actually more.[41]

[40] Gabriel Josipovici, 2010, *What Ever Happened to Modernism?* New Haven: Yale University Press, p. xi.

[41] Franco Moretti, 2000, 'Conjectures on World Literature', *New Left Review*, 1, January–February.

The sociological formalism of this interpretative method is not, however, that which informs the notion of distance in this book. Less is not actually more here, and the abstract concept is not privileged over the density of the text itself; here distance is predicated differently, in that it recognizes that no notion of the literary exists which is itself not shot through with historical significance. Distance here is not priced expensively as 'theoretical knowledge', but located in a paradoxically fragile cultural space full of the particularities and finitudes of individual events or particular lines that contain the literary indeterminately. Further, the stances taken by critics such as Lawrence or Josipovici are crucially located in the strange ambiguity of the personal, and clarify a temperamental unease felt within the critic in his relation to the world, to artists, and to art, a dimension remarkably absent from Moretti's approach to literature. Such a route, contrary to Moretti's conceptual stance above and beyond the text itself, zeroes in on the capacity of figurative language to disrupt identification; inhabiting a political stance of disappropriation, it locates literature as a movement toward the outside, a force of uprooting, a restlessness.

(ii) The Organicist

Well-known Bengali critic Bhabatosh Datta, referring to the early-modern productions of eighteenth-century Bengali literature, put the stance of critically important alienation somewhat differently when he said:

> It is not my ambition to judge the autonomous aesthetic merits of Bharatchandra's *maṅgalkābya*, Ramnidhi's *ṭappā* or the kabiwala's *kabigān*; neither is it my intention to give you a detailed description of the literature of the eighteenth century. Following life itself, I have tried to determine the relation of history to the course of literature. That is why I have not gone into extended, autonomous discussions on these subjects ...[42]

[42] My translation. All Bengali translations in this book are my own unless otherwise indicated. Bhabatosh Datta, 1958, 'Introduction', *Īśvarcandra gupter kabijībani* [from now on, simply *Kabijībani*], Calcutta: Calcutta Book House, p. vii.

This movement of stepping back, of 'following life itself' in the course of literature, is rare within Bengali literary studies. More often, the imagery used in the description of the flourishing of modern Bengali literature is organic, pertaining to the soil, seeds, growth, burgeoning, and flowering. The most vivid and unselfconscious instance of this sort of simile in the service of Bengali literary history that I have seen comes from the protestations of Munshi Abdul Karim (1871–1953), famous collector and editor of the manuscripts of medieval Bengal known as *puñthi*:

> I am a son of the soil of East Bengal; I am the adoring reader of that literature which has originated in that selfsame soil, that literature which has provided the inhabitants of that soil with happiness and nourishment, with fuel for the mind over many ages.[43]

Commenting on the passage, Gautam Bhadra remarks, 'It is as if culture was speaking in the voice of nature; creation is here transformed into character'.[44] The preponderance of the image of the soil, the repeated invocation of the land itself, leads to a notion of the seed planted in this soil that then grows into an organic emanation that is the literature of the land.

Sometimes the imagery in Bengali literary histories of modernity is that of foreign seeds planted in native soil and the subsequent strange flowering of the *fleur de mal* of modern Bengali literature. Subsequently, taking the metaphor of organic literature one step further, literature is felt to be in the blood, a matter of authenticity that resides in the nerves and sinew of a poet true to the impulse of his country of origin. Swapan Chakrabarty, writing on the subject of the Bengali cultivation of English literature, has reminded us that those who had objected to English education in India had spoken in the philosophical language of the 'organicist'; he warns that 'in this multi-lingual country, the political implications of an idea of language that is organicist has dangerous implications', quoting from the Sadler Commission Report that was set up to supervise the workings of Calcutta University in 1917 as an example of such ideologies:

[43] Quoted in Gautam Bhadra, 2007 (BE 1414), *Munśī ābdul karīm sāhityabiśārad o ātmashattār rājnīti*, Calcutta: Sangati, p. 36.

[44] Ibid.

> But the mother-tongue is one with the air in which a man is born... A man's native speech is almost like his shadow, inseparable from his personality... For each one of us is a member of a community. We share its energy and its instincts; its memories, however dim, of old far-off things. And it is through our folk-speech, whether actually uttered or harboured in our unspoken thoughts, that most of us attain the characteristic expression of our nature and what our nature allows us to discern.[45]

Eminent poet and critic Bishnu De used very similar terminology, for instance, to describe the talent of Michael Madhusudan Datta, who, according to De, though immersed in Anglophone influences, returned to the call of his blood to write his poetry in his native tongue.[46] Culture is conceived in the voice of nature here too, and that nature not only inheres in the natural world we inhabit, but also within us, in the very constitution of our being. In the concluding passage to the first edition of *Baṅga bhāshā o sāhitya* in 1896, Dineshchandra Sen concluded his dissertation in the introduction by ultimately coming to the issue of the alignment of the old texts to the very shape of what he called 'the Bengali mind':

> In order to read old literature we must have patience and forgiveness; we can say with some conviction that those who go beyond the *payār chanda* and the *gaṇeś bandanā* to analyze old Bengali literature with application will not go unrewarded. At least the Bengali reader will find in it things that he will especially appreciate, for the poetry is constructed with the same materials that shape the stuff of the Bengali mind.[47]

This understanding of the contours of the 'Bengali mind'—whatever that might be—as reflected in Bengali literature leads to an understanding of authenticity as the touchstone of the aesthetic, and from Bankimchandra's famous allusion to Iswar Gupta as the last 'authentic' Bengali poet [*khāṅṭi Bāṅgāli kabi*] to Akshaychandra Sarkar's disapproval of Hemchandra's lack of it, various chapters in this book repeatedly trace the organicist appeal to authenticity in the

[45] Sadler Commission Report, 1917, cited in Swapan Chakrabarty, *Bāṅgālīr ingreji sāhitya carcā*, Calcutta: Anustup, pp. 23–4.

[46] See Chapter 3 (ii).

[47] *Payār chanda* was the most popular metre in poetry and the *gaṇeś bandanā* the most popular prayer to Ganesha. Dineshchandra Sen, 1356 BE/1949 (First edn, 1896), *Baṅga bhāshā o sāhitya*, Calcutta: Dasgupta & Co., p. 12.

creation of a modern literature of Bengal. This appeal for authenticity may be part of a shared understanding among contemporaries of a renaissance or rebirth of culture, but this book attempts to show how conflictual that longing was when premised upon a disruptive cosmopolitanism that was, paradoxically, foundational to that claim.

Kwame Anthony Appiah quotes from Terence, the African writer of Latin comedies in imperial Rome in late second century AD, to provide us with the notion of 'contamination', which was the term by which Roman men of letters referred to Terence's mode of writing. Terence's comedies freely incorporated earlier Greek plays into a single Latin drama—this was known at the time as contamination. One of Terence's observations, 'So many men, so many opinions' is reminiscent for Bengalis almost immediately of the savant Ramakrishna in nineteenth-century Calcutta saying *yata mat tata path* [there are as many paths as there are opinions]. Appiah speaks up for what he calls 'contaminated cosmopolitanism' as a 'counter-ideal' to those who would protect 'their authentic culture', arguing, instead, that 'cultural purity is an oxymoron'; more recently, a related but distinct notion of interculturalism has also suggested that 'cultures are always already intercultural'.[48] The intention of this study in validating a notion of contamination in cosmopolitanism, however, is not to go down the postcolonial route of a valorization of all things hybrid, to celebrate impurity or 'chutnification' merely for its own sake. The critical term to return to in our context, rather, is that of distance or the notion of estrangement, both born of compulsion and situation, but also a choice informed by the personal as political, made from among the many alternative approaches to literature and culture, always with some notion of both affinity as well as alienation as the informing principles in relation to the area of study.

'Western Influence' or the Foreign Hand

Any attempt to study the literature or culture of nineteenth-century Bengal must necessarily deal, right at the start, with the shibboleth of

[48] Kwame Anthony Appiah, 2006, *Cosmopolitanism: Ethics in a World of Strangers*, New York: Norton, pp. 111, 113. See Peter D. McDonald, 'Thinking Interculturally', *Interventions*, Vol. 13, No. 3, pp. 367–85.

'Western influence', a category that needs urgently to be rethought in light of the mutability of history, memory, tradition, and inheritance. Paul Gilroy points out that in the last few pages of *Black Skin, White Masks*, Fanon says that 'the authoritarian nationalist voices in my own political community have to forget certain things in order to instantiate a particular pattern of official memory from which I disengage'. Fanon is not interested in what Gilroy calls the nationalists' 'love affair with their past', but rather in 'embracing an orientation towards the future', for 'to be bound to the past is to become hostage to patterns of political work in our communities which are strongly authoritarian in character'.[49]

The obsession, in Indian literary history or the study of the Indian modern, with reading the Western critical inheritance as a shape-changing foreign import in contestation with the traditional inheritance is an old and time-honoured practice, inextricably bound up with the authoritarian nationalism of the late-nineteenth and early-twentieth centuries. A 'particular pattern of official memory', to use Fanon's words, permeates most discussions on Indian literary history, which are dominated by the 'authoritarian nationalist voices' eager to 'forget certain things', or at least to denigrate and push away certain realities of a dissonant modernity such as was created by the colonial presence in India. Dineshchandra Sen, writing the first 'proper' literary history of the Bengalis in 1896, was emblematic of the authoritarian nationalist voice, repeatedly urging, in his writings, a selective appropriation and shoring up of certain national treasures for reification against the contaminated modernity of colonial Bengal. Time after time, he spoke about the degradation of contemporary India and the need to return to its unsullied past, ironically re-inscribing thereby certain well-known British/Orientalist tropes of Indian history-writing. Suitably operatic in his anguish at the state of affairs in modern Bengal, which he said had forgotten its own writers in its excessive adulation for English works and writers, he concluded his introduction to the first edition of *Baṅga bhāshā o sāhitya* with the following words of lament:

[49] Vikki Bell, 1999, 'Historical Memory, Global Movements and Violence: Paul Gilroy and Arjun Appadurai in Conversation' in *Theory, Culture and Society*, Vol. 16, No. 2, pp. 21–40.

> In conclusion, I wish to say that our educated classes are still, in a sense, indifferent to old Bengali literature. Young men who are in love with the charming Iambic and Trochaic metres become irritated when confronted with the long lines without pause of the *payār chanda*; those who are accustomed to be happy when reading the verses in praise of the imagination in the prefaces to Paradise Lost or The Task cannot keep their patience when confronted with the old Bengali poets' 'tall-and-fat' type of *gaṇeś bandanā.* They are partial to names such as Juliet and Andromache, but toward Behula, Lahana, Kanera and other such old-fashioned names they feel no affection.[50]

This was a repetitive theme in Dineshcandra, repeated sometimes verbatim, with only a change of names to make the same point, as when he later speaks, in the *History of Bengali Language and Literature*, of the admiration of 'the enlightened section of our community' for Cordelia, Haidee or 'even a Donna Julia', but complete ignorance of Behula, Khullana, or Ranjavati.[51] Ironically, of course, every time he emphatically reiterates his distress at the amnesia of the Bengalis (which in itself was a common enough complaint at the time, with Haraprasad Sastri maintaining, memorably, that the Bengalis were a 'self-forgetting race' [*ātma-bismrīta jāti*]), his own extensive knowledge of the English literary canon is on full display, with the invocation of the iambic or trochaic metres and the mention of Andromache (wife of Hector, heroine of Euripedes' eponymous play) or Donna Julia (from Byron's *Don Juan*) or Cordelia (from *King Lear*) bringing a distinctly nineteenth-century English-educated voice to the page.[52]

[50] For an explanation of the *payār chanda*, see Sen, *Bengali Language and Literature*, Second edn, 1954, p. 689. 'Task' refers to Cowper's poem, *The Task*, 1785. 'Advertisement to *The Task*' has an important place in eighteenth-century literary criticism. I am grateful to Swapan Chakrabarty for his help in locating this reference.

[51] Dineshchandra Sen, 1911, *History of Bengali Language and Literature*, Calcutta: Calcutta University Press, p. 346.

[52] Dineshchandra's fascination for English literature is amply evidenced in his autobiography, where he is unrestrained in his recounting of his love for, and knowledge of, English literature. His first impulse in his youth had been to write a literary history of English literature, he says there, if only in order to critique the colonizer's culture from the vantage point of the three thousand year-old literary consciousness of the colonized. Dineshchandra Sen, 2010, *Gharer kathā o yuga sāhitya*, Calcutta: Saraswatkunja, pp. 132–48.

Dineshchandra's monumental work had institutionalized much of the medieval Bengali literature presented in it for the first time. 'We did not know that there was such a vast entity as early Bengali literature', wrote Rabindranath Tagore after the second edition appeared in 1898.[53] Yet it was not as if the nineteenth-century literary sphere was entirely unaware of earlier traditions. Starting from Iswar Gupta's own series of the lives and works of preceding poets published serially in *Saṃbād prabhākar* from 1855–9, through to Harishchandra Mitra (*Kabikalāp*, 1866), Harimohan Mukhopadhyay (*Kabicarit*, 1869), Mahendranath Chattopadhyay (*Baṅgabhāshār itihās*, 1871), Ramgati Nyayaratna (*Bāṅglā bhāshā o bāṅglā sāhitya bishaẏak prastāb*, 1872), Rajnarain Basu (*Bāṅgālā bhāshā o sāhitya bishaẏak baktṛtā*, 1876), Gangacharan Sarkar (*Baṅga sāhitya o baṅga bhāshā*, 1880) and his son Akshaychandra Sarkar, along with Saradacharan and Baradakanta Mitra (*Prācīn kābya saṃgraha*, published serially from 1874–7), many had already begun attempts to collate, preserve, and re-present medieval and early modern texts and poets to the Bengali reading public in a variety of highly lauded publications. It was in the following years, however, that the drive to collect and preserve the old manuscripts of Bengal gathered its greatest impetus under scholars such as Haraprasad Sastri and Rajendralal Mitra and institutions such as the Bangiya Sahitya Parishad; the two greatest icons of this drive, Dineshchandra Sen and Abdul Karim, coming into prominence around the turn of the century.

What was different about the mammoth book Dineshchandra presented the public with in 1896 from most of what had preceded it was its fierce attack on any contamination of the indigenous Bengali tradition with English, or indeed, any 'foreign' literary convention, such as the Persian. That this attack came from within the structures of English-educated discourse itself, rather than, say, from the extreme quarter that contained the revivalist ranting of someone such as Sasadhar Tarkachudamani in late nineteenth-century Bengal, meant that this book came from within those very premises that it now

[53] Rabindranath Tagore, 1902, *Baṅga bhāshā o sāhitya* in *Rabindra rachanabali: ekśapanciśatama rabīndrajanmajaẏantī upalakkhe prakāśita sulabh saṅgskaraṇ*, 18 vols, Vol. 13, Calcutta: Visva-Bharati, 1961, p. 806. [All further references to the *Rabindra rachanabali* in this book are be to this edition.]

assailed, marking a tone and tenor of hostility to outside influences that had not been seen in quite this way until then. Bankimchandra, a prominent exponent of the Anglicist school, had no qualms in remarking on the 'pleasure' with which he turned to the 'Anglicist' school of Bengali writers after having dealt with the Sanskrit school, whose writings, he felt, were full of 'tautology and bombast'. A decade later, Haraprasad Sastri remarked that the astonishing and exponential growth of Bengali literature from Madhusudan's *Tilottamāsambhab* onward was made possible by a situation more exciting than that of the European renaissance, for in Bengal it was not only classical Greek literature that was regained, but 'all of the hidden treasures of the East and West... For in our country today has arrived the literature of England, France, Germany, Italy, that of the ancient Hindus and Buddhists... and none are better equipped than Young Bengal to take advantage of this variety of literatures for new creations'.[54]

Dineshchandra, however, himself an English honors graduate in 1889, had—much like the repetitive and, in the end, risible ascription among post-Independence Indian politicians of all national ills to the 'foreign hand', a euphemism for trouble fomented by India's neighbouring states—repeatedly denounced 'foreign influence' wherever he had found it, whether in the Persian inflections of eighteenth-century literature or even more so in the vile predilection of the newly educated classes of Bengal for English literature at the expense of their own inheritance. Such grumblings were not unique to him alone, but occasionally informed the criticism of writers stretching from Bankimchandra to Rabindranath as they eclectically searched for something they could call their own in their tradition, but Dineshchandra was decrying the 'foreign hand' certainly the most consistently, the most vehemently, and crucially, the most authoritatively, as it was from within the context of the establishment in the academy. Dineshchandra's opinions were given an extended and official lease of life as he held on to his ideological position over a considerable stretch of time with a rigidity eventually bordering on desperation, joining the Bengali department at Calcutta University

[54] Bankimchandra Chatterjee, 'Bengali Literature', in *Bankim rachanabali,* 1998, Calcutta: Sahitya Sansad, p. 109. Haraprasad Sastri, *Baṅgadarśan*, cited in Swapan Chakrabarty, *Bāṅgālīr iṅgreji sāhitya carcā*, p. 35.

as a Reader in 1909 and remaining associated with the University till 1932.

When Dineshchandra rewrote *Baṅga bhāshā o sāhitya* in English as the *History of Bengali Language and Literature* (1911),[55] he held forth, in a remarkable section in the book called 'A New Ideal in the Country', on what he called 'the descent' of Bengali culture from the lofty ideals of Hindu spiritualism to the materialist culture of European civilization. Taking unproblematically for granted some essential category he defined as 'the Bengali race' (perhaps using the word unselfconsciously while translating literally from 'jati', or people), he maintained that 'the literature of the Bengali race' might be comparatively small in scope, 'but within its own narrow limits, it is deeper and purer than one could expect from a literature covering a wider range'. Erratic punctuation and breathless hyphenation attend the long and convoluted passage that followed:

> From the home to the world—it was a descent from the Himalayas to the plains,—from the lofty spiritual idea permeating the Hindu home,—the visions of the beatitude which it was the dream of every great Hindu to attain,—to the matter-of-fact world and to an observation of things that are taking shape and changing all around; from the great example of Bhisma and Rama—cherished in the heart of every Hindu—the loftiest like the loftiest peak of the Himalayas, to the stories of Duval's assiduity in learning, and Sir Philiph (sic) Sydney's offering his cup of water to the dying soldier; from the pursuit and acquisition of *Yoga* to the knowledge of Geographical catechism, to be able to point out Popocatapetl (sic) on a

[55] Although he maintained that the English volume was based on lectures delivered at the University in 1909 and that it had 'very little affinity with my Bengali work on the same subject', he had to concede that it was only the 'arrangement' and the 'latest facts' that were new to the English book (see 'Preface', *History*, p. v). Meanwhile, in his autobiography, he said he began to write the English *Baṅga bhāshā o sāhitya* when he was first appointed Reader at Calcutta University in 1909. Here, he manifested his gratitude to two people for the English volume: Rabindranath, for advice on the writing of literary history, and Sister Nivedita. Nivedita, he said, helped him by critically reading every line of the book and amending it, as he put it, more for the 'feeling (*bhāb*)' than the 'English idiom' (she told him, he mentioned with pride, that 'Your English is good'). She debated several points with him, arguing fiercely against the depiction of Khullana in the *Chaṇḍimaṅgalkābya*, insisting on editorial changes to the content of old texts which showed Hindu society's treatment of women in a poor light (see Dineshchandra Sen, 2010, *Gharer kathā o yugasāhitya*, p. 366).

> map of the globe, from the celestial songs of Radha and Krishna, which, while gratifying all our yearnings for the loftiest of human love, have kept a door constantly open heavenwards,—to the stories of Paul and Virginia or of Aeneas and Dido,—the descent is as great as one from the Himalayas to the plains.[56]

This feeling of degradation was an essential component of the nationalist thought of the time, which consequently strove to carve out an impossible separate sphere of achievement and valour by constituting a domain comprising a past inheritance that was untainted by colonial rule, that would, in Aurobindo Ghosh's words at the time, 'found a new and victorious art, literature, science, and philosophy which will not be European but Indian'.[57] Yet practitioners of culture, however much they strained, like Dineshchandra Sen did, to imagine a 'pure' spiritual past still materially flourished in the cross-breeding engendered by colonial rule in an unavoidable cosmopolitanism of contact.

The Predicament of Modernity

A feeling of loss, of 'modernity' ruining some essence or tradition, is familiar to the nineteenth-century critic of European modernism, when local authenticities were overwhelmingly perceived to have been lost. James Clifford points out that Raymond Williams evoked it as a repetitive pastoral 'structure of feeling' in *The Country and the City* (1973). In the context of Bronislaw Malinowski (1884–1942) and Joseph Conrad's (1857–1924) location in the historical predicament of late Victorian high colonial society, Clifford suggests that 'Victorian social critics discerned a pervasive crisis for which Matthew Arnold's title *Culture and Anarchy* provided the basic diagnosis: against the fragmentation of modern life stood the order and wholeness of culture'.[58] Written as a series of essays in 1867–8, Arnold's response to

[56] Dineshchandra Sen, *History of Bengali Language and Literature*, pp. 741–2.

[57] Aurobindo Ghosh, 1909, 'The Awakening Soul of India', in *On Nationalism*, 2nd edn, Pondicherry, p. 404 . Remarkably, this conception of 'Indian' did not preclude being Indian in English, as Aurobindo wrote and published the longest Indian poem in English, *Savitri*, over many years, published partially in his lifetime and left unfinished at death.

[58] James Clifford, 1988, 'On Ethnographic Self-Fashioning: Conrad and

'the unprecedented technological and ideological transformations at work in the mid-nineteenth century' in *Culture and Anarchy* preceded Dineshchandra's literary history by about three decades, but dealt with substantively the same sorts of changes in society that Dineshchandra is determined to withstand. As Clifford puts it in this context, 'In the culture and anarchy problematic ... personal and collective essences must continuously be *maintained*'.[59] But in opposition to this holistic notion of culture as a meditative balm upon the wounds of modernity, Clifford shows how Conrad and Malinowski see culture as 'a collective fiction', 'the ground for individual identity and freedom'.

In Dineshchandra Sen, however, culture has not yet become visible as a collective fiction, and culture has its essence in roots rather than in the present processes of a heterogeneous reality. The ethnographic standpoint from which culture 'becomes visible as an object and ground, a system of meaning among others' is one in which Dineshchandra is not engaged, for unlike Malinowski or Conrad (contemporaries, both) he affirms, rather, that culture takes root in unmediated identity—in as much as we speak one native language, we belong to a specific cultural world of one self, one culture, one language. It is exactly the power of literature's plurivocity to decentralize meaning, to disenable the closure of certain types of communities that he denies, opting instead for a 'fixed relation of force with *one* group, or *one* state' in surrender to 'the temptation of "Unity-Identity"'.[60]

In this moment around 1900, when in any major world metropolis, ethnographic self-fashioning allowed the self to be culturally constituted as one might choose, as Conrad, for instance, chose to be an English writer, or a century before in Bengal, the Portuguese Antony Firingi had chosen to be a Bengali singer-songwriter, Dineshchandra Sen sees, instead, that the individual is bound up in one culture alone. For him, the Bengali identity, tied to an organicist construction of 'the Bengali race' with its own unique 'Bengali mind', seeks its place in the world through a valorization of tradition that has its roots in an authoritarian

Malinowski', in *The Predicament of Culture*, Harvard: Harvard University Press, p. 106.

[59] Ibid.

[60] Maurice Blanchot, 1993, *The Infinite Conversation*, translated by Susan Hanson, Minneapolis: University of Minnesota Press, pp. 125–6.

nationalism and some sort of inexplicable essence of being. Speaking about the amnesia of the youth as regards Bengali literature, for instance, he concludes: 'Yet it is their own literature which contains elements that they are naturally best fitted to appreciate'.[61] The self here is not a fashioned self, but an inherited one; identity and language are here loyal to and caught up in a tradition, and inhere, somehow, in the very constitution of our beings, for we are 'naturally best fitted to appreciate' our 'own' literature the most. Neither self-reflexive nor ironic, the authorial voice in Dineshchandra is concerned instead with suppression of incoherence and contradiction, endowing meaning to the inscription of cultural authenticity by privileging the pure past over the inchoate present.

Such a reading of culture is inalienably tied up with, of course, a robust invocation of nationalist purpose. In his introduction to the first edition of *Baṅga bhāshā o sāhitya*, Dineshchandra ends (appropriately enough, considering that one of the origins of the powerful link between nation and literature lies in Herder's and his followers' contribution to German nationalist literary historiography) with a quotation from Max Müller:

> Finally, we conclude our introduction with a few words here from Max Müller's invaluable thoughts: 'We have to accept that the country in which its people do not feel pride when they contemplate their own ancient history and ancient literature have been deprived of the most important support to their national culture. When the German nation had fallen into the deepest schism of political decline, then the people of that country had applied themselves to the task of discussing their own country's ancient literature; and from their reading of their ancient literature they inculcated a new hope of future progress'.[62]

A summoning up of nationalist feelings for the future of India enables him, as it did the European literary Orientalists concerned with India at this time, to 'treat literature as a complete (totalized, totalizable)

[61] Dineshchandra Sen, *History of Bengali Language and Literature*, p. 346.

[62] Ibid., p. 12. Rabindranath, in a lecture, '*Sāhitya parishad*', in *Nabaparyāy baṅgadarśan, Caitra* 1313/March–April 1907 had also cited the German philosophers and writers who had created a cultural formation for the country to draw on later in its imperialist ambitions. Also see '*Sāhitya sammelan*'.

expression of the "character", "spirit", or racial and cultural identity of a nation'.[63]

This valiant striving for a 'pure past' to be reflected in a glorious future untouched by any foreign influence, it has to be remembered, was being written a few years after the period dealt with in this book, when Rangalal Bandyopadhyay had ushered in English poetic convention to renovate and reform what he perceived to be corrupt traditional practices in Bengali poetry, Madhusudan Datta had introduced the sonnet and blank verse, the epic poem and tragic drama into Bengali literature to huge acclaim, and after countless writers, from Kaliprasanna Singha to Bankimchandra to Rabindranath, had avowedly appropriated from Charles Dickens or Walter Scott or Irish melody to reconstruct their own traditions. More importantly and more subtly, modern Bengali literature—in contrast to being merely an exercise in inhabiting a particular voice or style from English literary convention, has had, from the outset, literary English intimately imbricated in its fabric in a manner that any unidirectional postcolonial analysis (or indeed, in Dineshchandra's analysis) of the imposition of Shakespeare and Milton in colonized classrooms would fail to do justice to.

This was a period that had, at the time Dineshchandra Sen was writing his books, just begun to be called the Bengal Renaissance. For many writers and thinkers in nineteenth-century Bengal, from Madhusudan to Bankimchandra to Rabindranath, culture and identity are inventive and mobile, reflecting some of the great qualities of modernism the world over. The narrative of entropy and loss that cultural historians such as Dineshchandra represent, it is salutary to remind ourselves, is repeated in other cultures at other times; however, Dineshchandra's narration, even though similarly expressed, is still at some distance from the alienation that gave to Romanticism and Modernism, its nodal defining factors. Speaking of the origins of Modernism, Gabriel Josipovici, in an opening segment, 'The Oracles are Silent', quotes from Hegel's *Phenomenology of Spirit* (1807), where that philosopher wrote of the current age he inhabited as a time when

[63] Vinay Dharwadker, 1994, 'Orientalism and the Study of Indian Literatures', in Carol Breckenridge and Peter Van der Veer (eds), *Orientalism and the Postcolonial Predicament*, Delhi: Oxford University Press, p. 167.

> Trust in the eternal laws of the gods has vanished, and the Oracles, which pronounced on particular questions, are dumb. The statues are now only stones from which the living soul has flown, just as the hymns are words from which belief has gone.[64]

Identifying this feeling of 'having lost for ever something that was once a common possession' as 'a, if not *the*, key Romantic concern', Josipovici relates it to Weber's conception of the 'disenchantment of the world' (the phrase is originally Schiller's) in *The Protestant Ethic and the Spirit of Capitalism* (1904), which he sees as a key ingredient in Modernism.[65] This understanding of the modern condition as 'the disappearance of the older way of looking at things' permeates Dineshchandra's feeling for the irrecoverable nature of the past for the new generation of Bengalis, of whom he said, in tones uncannily reminiscent of Hegel,

> The gods had now become to them mere clay, the temples were unholy and the hallowed precincts of their homes a hole of superstition. Their noble literature was no more than a miserable scribbling and shreds of paper which they should consign to the fire or worms.[66]

The crucial difference between the two quotations above, however, lies in the use of the pronoun. Hegel speaks in the present perfect tense, using the word 'now' repeatedly, and deploying the pronoun 'us' when he elaborates upon the thought by saying of the inaccessibility of the ancient world, 'So fate does not restore their world to us along with the works of antique Art, it gives not the spring and summer of the ethical life in which they blossomed and ripened, but only the veiled recollection of that actual world'.[67]

While Hegel is speaking of the world he himself inhabits, which has no direct access to the past, 'but only the veiled recollection' of it, Dineshchandra is not at one with the alienated soul of Young Bengal; it is not he who speaks at one remove from the ancients, but 'they'—'they' do not recognize 'their' noble literature, 'they' 'exult' in Shakespeare and Milton, 'they' quote from the Elizabethan

[64] Gabriel Josipovici, 2010, *What Ever Happened to Modernism?* p. 13.
[65] Ibid. pp. 13–14.
[66] Dineshchandra Sen, *History of Bengali Language and Literature*, p. 743.
[67] Gabriel Josipovici, *What Ever Happened to Modernism?* p. 13.

dramatists, 'they grew mad after Shelley's Epipsychidion and Keat's (sic) Hyperion'.[68] Nevertheless, Dineshchandra himself is also trapped in the modern world which he is so disgusted with, suffering from the same loss of connection with his past world of oral tales and community life, emblematized for him in the Arcadian beauty of village Bengal and its authentic inhabitants, who are the 'real' people of Bengal. By inclination, then, he is a proto-Romantic, feeling his loss more keenly than is acceptable to many Bengali critics and historians who followed him. However, it is in the political ramifications of his desperate rejection of this loss, when he believes he can be one with his past once again by reliving it in the pages of the *maṅgalkābya*, that the problem lies, for such a return to faith would be reincarnated in right-wing politics in the country a century later, emblematizing a political movement in which structures of belief are given pre-eminence over strictures of law.[69]

Dineshchandra Sen's 'method' has been interrogated by Dipesh Chakrabarty, who reads him and his generation as treating literature as 'quintessentially political'. Against the attacks of a younger generation of critics in Calcutta in the 1930s and 1940s, primarily led by the group around *Śanibārer ciṭhi*, who accused Dineshchandra of sentimentality and of ignoring recent research, Chakrabarty points out that for him 'the past was constituted, ultimately, not merely by historical evidence but also by emotional and experiential recollections of the past. The past in that sense could fuse with the present. It was inhabitable in spirit'.[70] Chakrabarty thus assesses Dineshchandra's sentimentalism and emotionalism as constituting 'a method' of approaching and accessing

[68] *HBLL*.

[69] These lines were written as the Ayodhya case judgements were being published in the Indian newspapers in September 2010, where we read that one of the judges who delivered part of the Ayodhya verdict, Justice Sharma, had insisted on the primacy of faith or belief over any other consideration.

[70] Dipesh Chakrabarty, 'Romantic Archives: Literature and Politics of Identity in Bengal', *Critical Inquiry*, 30 (Spring 2004), pp. 669, 673. While the critics of Dineshchandra were plentiful, his followers too were not few in number, counting amongst their ranks luminaries such as Benoy Sarkar, who praised Dineshchandra's *Baṅga bhāshā o sāhitya* for 'having turned thousands and thousands of "reading-writing" people, from Malda to Chittagong, Jalpaiguri to Medinipur, self-consciously into Bengalis'. See Haridas Mukherjee (ed.), 2003, *Binaẏ sarkārer baiṭhake*, Vol. 1, Calcutta: Dey's, p. 287.

a collective past where sentiments and emotions 'were quite central to Sen's method of constituting the past. The past had to be made palpably present'.[71] This palpable presence of the past, Chakrabarty maintains, is somewhat similar to that of Bengal's presence in the lines written by Jibanananda Das in *Rūpasī bāṅglā*; when Jibanananda writes 'When I return to the banks of the Dhansiri, to this Bengal, / Not as a man, perhaps, but as a *śālik* bird or white hawk', the phrase '*this* Bengal' has 'the same kind of presence as Chandidas has for Dinesh Sen. In fact, the sense of Bengali history that marks these poems is in part the one that Dinesh Sen espoused'.[72] The 'sense of Bengali history' that Chakrabarty talks of here is one that is common to both the poetry and song of twentieth-century Bengal and to the 'workshop of nationalism' in which the 'romantic sentiments' that constitute that history are formed. While Chakrabarty's following suggestion—that 'research and interpretation of the kind pioneered by Sen had a critical role in fostering the imagination embedded in Das's poems' which are 'replete with references to "folk" stories of the kind Dinesh Sen collected', is generally accurate, a crucial distinction needs to be made here between Jibanananda's 'palpable' Bengal and Dineshchandra's.

Jibanananda might owe his awareness of the characters of Chand and Behula or the gods Chandi and Manasa in part to the *maṅgalkābya* collected by Dineshchandra, and these may 'help Das to create' 'a mythical sense of a continuous Bengali history'.[73] But, in spite of all the uses to which Jibanananda puts the folk stories collected in Dineshchandra's research, the space of his poem does not operate on the principle of mythical identification, but rather offers us a mode of poetic speech that ceaselessly interrupts itself, reminding us instead that fulfilment is never attainable. Chakrabarty understands this, warning that 'this was, of course, not a simple return of the spirit of Dineshchandra Sen', but a 'displacement', as 'Das's enunciation of these sentiments had none of the nationalist, programmatic, and optimistic fervour of Dineshchandra Sen's exposition'.[74] In a poet such as Jibanananda, the self's relation to the landscape rouses his deepest

[71] Ibid.
[72] Ibid., p. 678.
[73] Ibid., p. 679.
[74] Ibid.

feelings, but those feelings search for a resolution in art, where syntax, rhythm, and enjambment do most of the work, and which constitutes a separate space beyond the impasses of philosophy and cultural history. Jibanananda's poetry occupies a different place from the strictures that enfold Dineshchandra Sen's work—to compare the palpable presence of Bengal in the lines by the poet to the literary historian's would be to deny that Jibanananda's world is, unlike Dineshchandra's imagined order, one without sure relation to either tradition or authority, where the idealism of poetry (as Dineshchandra envisaged it) is replaced with a troubling realization divorced from the romances of the time, existing in a modern world in which necessity seems too often a form of imprisonment.

Blanchot's rumination that 'Art is primarily the consciousness of unhappiness, not its compensation', can be rewritten to great effect with regard to the distance between the poet and the critic here—for the poet, art remains, over and above all else, 'the consciousness of unhappiness'; literary language here is 'made of uneasiness', it is a language of the outside, 'opaque because it says nothing'.[75] For the critic, art is a 'consolation' against the vicissitudes of the modern world, always safely in the past, it is fused with myth in the way it creates community by providing a narrative of origin and installing the nexus for the political subject's identification with that community—it is the mechanism by which social fusion is created. With the poet, existence is felt to be radically contingent; the poem exists in a moment of disjunction; 'literature becomes the receptacle of existence in all its density and no longer of its meaning alone'. The *Rūpasī bāṅglā* poems are full of what Barthes calls 'the trembling of existence' [*du tremblement de l'existence*] as against the characteristic requirements of realism, of narrative, of causal events that follow each other in some preordained order which he calls the '*récit*', which he says both history and the novel chose as their preferred form in the mid-nineteenth century.[76] As a literary historian, Dineshchandra inhabits the realm

[75] Maurice Blanchot, 'Literature and the Right to Death', in *The Space of Literature*, p. 315.

[76] Roland Barthes, cited in Gabriel Josipovici, *What Ever Happened to Modernism?* p. 81. The quotes from this passage are taken from Josipovici's book as it has been translated to much better effect there than in the Annette Lavers edition.

of the '*récit*', constructing a canon, presenting us with a narrative of events where one follows the other in an endless chain of the 'and then and then and then' of teleological progression. Both Jibanananda and Dineshchandra feel that something is lacking and then feel that lack quite vividly, but unlike the latter, who attempts to translate that lack into a feeling of programmatic action in nationalism, the poet's passion portrays life to us as something ephemeral and passive, which, in the very act of retracing our actions in language, 'reduces them to an illusion, annihilating them in the past without leaving us... with the consolation of activity'.[77]

The Separation of Self from History

The predicament of modernity is that, that which was once unified and whole is now fragmented and dispersed, and can never be put together again. Against this notion of loss is Dineshchandra's particular notion of the retrieval of that past into a palpable present that shall somehow join us all organically into a natural whole once again in a romantic-political movement toward unity–identity–freedom. In this movement, Dineshchandra is also against the very situation of the modernist writer who experiences the pathos of the modern world as one without coherence or reason but instead full of the opacity and solitude of existence. It is no coincidence, therefore, that Dineshchandra's magnum opus, *Baṅga bhāshā o sāhitya*, ends before the advent of modern Bengali literature and the novel. Focusing on the reader of Cervantes, Josipovici points out that he 'is imagined as turning the pages of a printed book in the solitude of his or her own room, simply in order to pass the time', while the author recognizes that he too 'is only a solitary individual, "filled with inconstant thoughts never imagined by anyone else", and therefore with no authority for what he says and no access to the truth…'.[78]

Such a modern viewpoint need not be confined to the precincts of the novel alone, however, and this solitude of reading is most famously rendered in Bengali literature in the lines of a poem by Rabindranath,

[77] Marcel Proust, 1971, 'Journées de lecture', in Pierre Clarac and Yves Sandre (eds), *Contre Saint-Beuve*, Paris: Pléiade, p. 170.

[78] Gabriel Josipovici, 2010, *What Ever Happened to Modernism?* p. 29.

'*Meghadūta*', which is about reading Kalidasa's poem, *Meghadūtam*. The poem, Amit Chaudhuri points out, is 'a tribute to the secular, silent act of reading, which, in that culture, had become a significant activity whereby old texts, and the printed page, were placed in new contexts, and reassessed and reimagined'.[79] In this poem about the experience of reading Kalidasa's poem, Rabindranath speaks of how 'In a gloomy closed room I sit alone / And read the '*Meghadūta*'. Rabindranath's poem is 'pervaded by the sound of thunder (it is raining outside as he reads) and the inward silence of perusal'; as the poet says, 'My mind leaves the room, / Travels on a free-moving cloud, flies far and wide. / There is the Amrakuta mountain, / There is the clear and slender Reva river…'[80] Travelling imaginatively to this ancient past meant, for the nineteenth-century Indian, confronting the question of how he had lost touch with it, according to Chaudhuri, and in an essay on Kalidasa, Rabindranath speaks of this loss, saying: 'Not merely a temporal but an eternal gulf seems to separate us from the great slice of ancient India—stretching from the Ramagiri to the Himalayas—through which life's stream flowed in the form of the *mandākrāntā* metre of the "*Meghadūta*".' Chaudhuri shows how Rabindranath's poem, then, reworks Kalidasa's 'tale of separation from the loved one into a narrative of the separation of self from history'.[81]

'Not merely a temporal but an eternal gulf,' observed Rabindranath, separated him from his past, and in this he is at one with the great Romantics and Modernists of Europe, who inhabit the same feeling of living in a fragmented, liberal, and individualistic world of modernity where one can only long for the ordered world of community, but can never attain it. Buddhadeva Bose, in the introduction to his translation of Kalidasa's *Meghadūtam*, reiterated such a feeling about our 'separation' from the entire tradition of Sanskrit literature that belongs in our past. Struggling against that inimical feeling of separation, he concludes it is due to the lack of inspired literary analysis that we have almost been made to believe that the 'simple trembling life'

[79] Amit Chaudhuri, 2008, 'The Flute of Modernity', in *Clearing a Space: Reflections on India, Literature and Culture*, Ranikhet: Black Kite, p. 71.

[80] Ibid., p. 72. Quoted translation of '*Meghadūta*' by Willliam Radice.

[81] Ibid. Rabindranath wrote extensively about self, history, and discontinuity in essays such as '*Bhāratbarsher itihāser dhārā*' and the subsequent evolution of his thought may be found in essays in *Kālāntar*, *Paricay*, and *Samūha*.

[*sahaj prāṇspandan*] (the phrase is uncannily reminiscent of Barthes' 'trembling of life') that is to be felt in old Greek, Latin, or Chinese literature and in the modern literature of all countries is not to be found in the Sanskrit, that 'in all the world, it is only Sanskrit that has been turned into a vast and venerated corpse which we cannot approach without mastering the technique of dissection'.[82]

In this astonishing essay, he searches for something of value in Kalidasa's poem, praising its metre and its rhythmic tonality above all else, staying for a while with its descriptive prowess and its use of language; but again and again, the poem disappoints him, turns him away, lets him down. Like a paradoxical collector-connoisseur bull in a china shop, he ranges through Kalidasa in line and verse, searching for something of value, and each and every time he holds a Kalidasa quotation up and compares it with Rabindranath, or with his younger contemporaries, Sudhindranath Datta or Jibanananda Das, Kalidasa loses out, and it is the modern-day poet that wins. Buddhadeva Bose points out that the Yaksha in Kalidasa's poem, telling us about the well-being of the beloved, is mere argumentation or reportage, whereas Rabindranath's lines, in the poem '*Svapna*', asking after the welfare of the loved one, are 'the naked utterance of the most deeply felt failure/frustration [*byarthatā*]'.[83] A fascinating parallel may be drawn here with another instance in history where the modern, the local, and the present cannot but jostle out the presence of the past. Much like Buddhadeva struggling to find the meaning of the past in Kalidasa, Rabindranath describes an evening in Shazadpur when he struggled to establish a deeply longed for connection with the same poet, only to concede defeat in the face of the present. As he wrote in a letter to his niece:

> I had written to you that yesterday at *7pm* I would set up an *engagement* with the poet Kalidasa. Just when I had lit the lamps and pulled my armchair up to the table and was quite ready, in the place of the poet Kalidasa, the postmaster of this place turned up. A living postmaster has far greater claim than a dead poet—I couldn't say to him, 'why don't you leave now, I have some urgent work with Kalidasa'—even if I had said so,

[82] Buddhadeva Bose, 1957, '*Saṃskṛta kabitā o "meghadūta"*' in *Kālidāser meghadūta*, First edn, Calcutta: M.C. Sarkar and Sons, p. 7.

[83] Ibid., p. 54.

> he would not have understood what I meant. Consequently Kalidasa had to vacate his chair for the postmaster and slowly take his leave.[84]

Whether we agree with Buddhadeva Bose or not in his assessment that Kalidasa's Sanskrit is irretrievable (and very few of us today are as qualified as he was in Sanskrit *and* Bengali *and* English to be able to hold an informed opinion), his relentless exposition of the failure of this Sanskrit poetry to function meaningfully in the modern world is in itself a magnificent, heroic attempt to cope with the disconnect between his past and the modernity he inhabits, an attempt that was always doomed, in this 'disenchanted world', to breakdown.

Schiller's expression of the feeling of loss that characterizes the modern era was contained in writings that grappled with the issue of the disappearance of a golden age of the Greeks, and was emblematic of the German Romantics' 'unhappy consciousness' (the phrase is Hegel's). These German practitioners were conscious of being embedded in the phenomenon they strove to understand, whereas Dineshchandra is similarly placed, but refuses to see himself as part of the fabric of change, although he is, of course, inescapably so. The authority which he claims for himself is impossible to attain in the modern age in which the transcendental is inaccessible, for this age has lost access to authority, and, as moderns, we know deep down, as Dineshchandra too must have done, that we have none. But is he wilfully blind to his own position in the modern, or is he fully aware of it, but in profound reaction against it, just as Matthew Arnold saw a return to classical poetic forms as a stay against the anarchy of the modern? Choosing to locate himself rather as one removed from the fragmented modern world that can never be whole again (and this position must indisputably have some relation to the violation of colonial rule), Dineshchandra chose to go back to the world of tradition, authority, and the folk as a resource to hold on to against the tide of change he sees all around him, imposing a shape upon the world of the text in an attempt to give it a meaning which the world around him does not have.

The other difference in the situation as regards the Indian modern, importantly, was that, while in Europe the passage from an era of

[84] Italicized words originally in English. Rabindranath Tagore to Indira Devi, Shazadpur, 29 June 1892, Letter 62, *Chinnapatrābalī*, 2004, Visva-Bharati, p. 99.

superstition into a modern age of rationality and common sense and science is located in a teleological narrative of transition from the dark Middle Ages to the light of Enlightenment, which is generally in the English-speaking world celebrated as an emancipation by Protestant historians, in India, the passage into modernity is complicated by an awareness of dislocation that is rooted in the violence of colonial rule. As a result, what is lost is perceived as that which was inalienably 'our own', while the modern present has been thrust upon us by a 'foreign' source. That this imposition of the foreign element was an old and cyclical occurrence in the context of Indian history is conveniently forgotten by a historian such as Dineshchandra, who is unremitting in his condemnation of any 'foreign influence'. Bharatchandra's *Bidyāsundar* has failed because it follows a foreign ideal (*bijātīya ādarśa*); Sen mentions, 'This is a composition recited by god-fearing Persian-loving poets who are deceived by the sound of the Chandi mantras into thinking it a poem to be sung in temples', whereas in reality 'the shadow of a foreign literature falls heavily upon it'.[85]

In relation to modern Western assumptions (which sound remarkably similar to those made by the writers in colonial Calcutta since the 1850s onward) that identities no longer presuppose continuous cultures or traditions, with individuals everywhere improvising individual performances from recollected pasts, drawing on foreign materials, symbols, and languages, Dineshchandra Sen perceives this existence among fragments as a process of ruin and cultural decay. Dineshchandra's vision of the tears of Kabi Kankan and Vidyapati falling upon the unheeding ears of Young Bengal, therefore, embodies the inescapable truth of the disintegration of old Bengali culture as it disappears into an expansive cosmopolitan culture that belongs as much to the world as to the home. In his introduction to his last book, *Bṛhat baṅga* [Great Bengal] he spoke of his own retreat from the cosmopolitan Calcutta of the late nineteenth century; 'I am not a lover of the world', he maintained in his defence, 'I remain hopelessly provincial'.[86] So too did Abdul Karim, his contemporary and his peer, say of himself in mocking self-deprecation: 'I am a village person of East Bengal, a country bumpkin [*geñyo mānush*], what in

[85] Dineshchandra Sen, 1902, *Baṅga bhāshā o sāhitya*, pp. 318, 325.

[86] Dineshchandra Sen, 1935, *Bṛhat baṅga*, Calcutta: Dey's Publication, p. 33.

Chattagram's language is called *gāñyiā*. My West Bengali brothers may also call me a *bāṅgāl*... The attractive gleam of modern literature is missing from both my unfashionable life and my materials'.[87] Such self-deprecation functions here, of course, as an ironical device for the celebration of the authentic rural people's literature and the world that both men feel they are proud to belong to.[88]

Dineshchandra's work presented a narrative of a progressive monoculture that was, eventually, too neat, too sure of its self-regarding position at the 'end' of a unified human history, his inward-looking position seeking to gather up and memorialize a culture and history in its authentic wholeness. In seeking to do so, it is against any reinvention of tradition, against the experience of culture as a process of translation or cultural eclecticism. That is why, perhaps, he fails to take his literary history beyond the mid-nineteenth century—'Our review of the Bengali Literature (*sic*), however, ends with 1850', he says in the penultimate line of his *History*. Although the last chapter is titled 'The Modern Age', it stops short at a subsection headed 'The writers that followed Raja Ram Mohan Roy—Devendra Nath Tagore—Aksay Kumar Dutta and others'.[89] The last line of the book gives some indication of the problem he faces: 'The historian of a later epoch of this literature will have to acknowledge with gratitude

[87] Abdul Karim, Lecture delivered on 21–22 January 1950 in East Pakistan, extracted in Azharuddin Khan, 1986, *Magh nishither kokil*, Calcutta, pp. 122–3. See Gautam Bhadra, 2007, *Munśī ābdul karim sāhityabiśārad o ātmasattvār rājnitī*, Dhaka: Sanghati, p. 35.

[88] 'My unfashionable life and materials', Abdul Karim says of his life's work; those materials, in the context of both his and Dineshchandra's world, lie in the category of folklore that he remained a dedicated collector of, as together they retrieved some of the vanished manuscripts of village Bengal for storage in the treasure house of a newly constructed category called old Bengali literature. The stories of the pain withstood and fortitude displayed by these two men, trudging the remote paths of dangerous countryside in inclement weather, through driving rain and overcoming the fear of wild beasts, to find, preserve, and collect the *puṅthi* literature of old Bengal are legendary. In these narratives of struggle and indomitable perseverance, work is privileged as a site upon which the self is grounded, a self that is essential, and which is the foundation of an ethics based on character; ultimately, personality and ethics are indistinguishable and relentlessly achieved through work, and the narrative shares with the Protestant work ethic some remarkable similarities of representation.

[89] Dineshchandra Sen, *History of Bengali Language and Literature*, p. 840.

the deep debt which our tongue has owed to England and her people in comparatively recent times'.[90] Here, in this last line, it is almost as if reading culture as a project of creative cross-contamination, as he would inevitably have had to in dealing with the writers of the late nineteenth century, is too much for him. For Dineshchandra failed to realize that his vision of Bengali literature and culture taking root and flourishing in ancestral plots was actually a constructed picture; that he himself, in his enterprise of collecting and then presenting this old literature of Bengal to its people, was engaged in an activity that enabled him in cutting and retying those roots of tradition in new configurations.

Importantly, therefore, what must be kept in mind in relation to Dineshchandra's cultural nationalism at the turn of the century is that it was as much a product of the conflicted modernity of the foreign influences he so maligned in his impassioned, if occasionally ungrammatical, English prose. The manner in which Dineshchandra reconstitutes his tradition is a modern activity; his presentation of the old and medieval literature of Bengal as a unified corpus of unbelievable beauty and rusticity was at its base very similar to the activity of cutting and retying the roots of tradition that a 'tremendous literary rebel' such as Madhusudan Datta too was engaged in when he imported the sonnet and blank verse into the language, though both would have, no doubt, abhorred the comparison. His objection to Bharatchandra, for instance, for being 'not-national' or *bijātīya* was a modern revivalist objection, grounded in a sensibility engendered by imperial domination, and one that would have left the Bengali audiences who received Bharatchandra with such enthusiasm in the late eighteenth and early nineteenth century puzzled and confused.

The self division of Dineshchandra Sen was perhaps inherent in his very upbringing, in the divided inheritance he imbibed from his culturally conflicted parents. He describes his mother as an 'orthodox Hindu' who was opinionated and impassioned about her traditional gods and ritual worship, always up in arms against his mild-mannered father, a monotheist and Brahmo-influenced English-educated teacher and lawyer. The argument between these two ways of living was never resolved in his home or his heart, sometimes coming out into open

[90] Ibid.

confrontation, and he recalls how his mother one day entered a room where his father was lecturing him on the oneness of the godhead, telling him that the Hindu idols were like so many clay dolls made to represent the one god, and physically dragged him away from his father, attacking him for turning her only son into an irreligious person [*bidharmi*]. In his books he had chastised Young Bengal for knowing English literature too well, but in his memoirs he mentions with admiration how well his father knew 'Edison's Spectator, Johnson's Rambler and Rasselas, Life of Emperor Charles the Fifth, Alexander Pope, Goldsmith and Dryden's poetry', describing how he saw these books, with their carefully made notes in his father's hand, in his library when he was a child.[91] This tremendous split within the premises of his childhood is retold by him as exactly that—an enormous divide that was not to be brought into any tame resolution. As he put it, 'On the one side, I experienced the burning faith of the Hindu dharma up close, on the other, I saw my father [*pitridevata*], a picture of dignity, an image of calm meditation—like a still lamp of knowledge. His influence was no less than that of the worship [*arati*] in the temple.'[92]

His response to Rabindranath Tagore was marked by the same self-division. It is well-known that he privately described Rabindranath to Edward Thompson as a European writer of Bengali, complaining in a letter that it was only those Bengalis who were thoroughly immersed in European traditions who enjoyed his work.[93] Equally infamous is the (perhaps apocryphal) story of Calcutta University in his time to including a passage of Rabindranath's in an examination paper, asking students to re-write the passage in chaste Bengali. Yet this was the man who publicly said Rabindranath's writing heralded a new era in Bengali literature, describing how he had not read the novels *Noukadubi*, *Chokher bali*, or *Gora*, but had heard them read out by the author himself, and that he had never heard any other books before with so much eagerness. Rabindranath's writing here, he said, was not song, it was not music, yet what came to his mind as he listened was

[91] Dineshchandra Sen, 2010, *Gharer kathā o yugasāhitya*, p. 49.

[92] Ibid. p. 89.

[93] E.P. Thompson, 1993, 'Alien Homage', in *Edward Thompson and Rabindranath Tagore*, New Delhi: Oxford University Press, p. 53.

the sound of the *veena*—'it was as if the words of these three books were dancing to a rhythm such as that of the anklets of the goddess of the *veena* as she stepped by.' Even more telling is his pinpointing of the sort of detail that these books were made up of; he is of the opinion that Rabindranath describes love with a nuance that even the extraordinary Vaishnav poets had not had for the description of beauty. He compares such attention to detail to the fine craftsmanship of the goldsmiths of Dhaka, famed for their intricate designs with gold wire—similarly, Rabindranath has drawn love with such finely wrought lines that they blind the vision. What are these details? He mentions two—the smell of a lover's hair, and the fragrant oil-stain upon a much-read book—these are like 'soft, fine psychological traces, things of dreams, like the red designs [*alaktaker alpana*] of the unsaid that show us women in a new light'.[94]

Culture and identity are being reinvented by him here just as much as by any other literary practitioner in Bengal at the time. Here, in his close reading of Rabindranath, he is open to the detail, to the concreteness of the image that was so much an aspiration of the Imagists, and to the ambiguities of interpretation that informed the New Critics who followed, yet in his self-imaging, in his critical stance in his literary histories, he was not happy to belong to the modern world, always looking back to a more perfect time and place. Through and within the history he was living, he was engaged in a collective re-imagining of symbols, seeking to restore the meaning of language, culture, and identity so that they could lose their uncertain open-endedness in the predicament of modernity through his 'backward-looking idealism'. That phrase was used to describe the mindset that characterized Cesaire's friend, Leopold Senghor's project of 'a falsely naturalized, consistent African mentality that tends to reinscribe the categories of a romantic, sometimes racialist European ethnography', but it applies to Dineshchandra Sen equally well.[95]

*

The birth of the modern in India has been a contested site, with generations of Indian commentators succeeding Dineshchandra Sen

[94] Ibid, p. 346.

[95] James Clifford, *The Predicament of Culture*, p. 178.

displaying some unease at the colonial provenance of its inception and birth, calling the Indian modern a 'weak' or 'mistaken' modernity, always already flawed by the shamed circumstances of its origin under colonial subjugation. Yet these critiques themselves, of course, are enabled by the very conditions of the modernity they deride, and are peculiarly dated by the conditions of their production. While acknowledging the real anxieties of this generation of commentators and without wishing to mitigate even fractionally the oppressions suffered under colonial rule, it is time now, perhaps, to celebrate without triumphalism the astonishing achievements and the heterogeneous contexts of the many modernities produced in India, one of the most neglected of which has been that of the literary, within which poetry was the most contested site in the context of the nineteenth century.

The following series of studies of moments from the making of a modern literary culture in Bengal begins its work from the perception of disjunction and conjunction in the literary sphere of the nineteenth century in Bengal. The first chapter uses the reception of Bharatchandra Ray (pre-eminent poet of the preceding century) in the nineteenth-century literary sphere to investigate issues of bilingualism and multilingualism and the gradual evolution of 'high' and 'low' cultural constructions in relation to the Bengali literary sphere. The second examines the work of Iswar Gupta, exploring the materiality of his modern urban poetry centred on the physical, the transitory, and the felt experience, in order to show how a language is yet to be put in place regarding the place of his poetry in Bengali literary criticism. Rangalal Bandyopadhyay's determined espousal of English poetic convention and his revolutionary manifesto toward the institution of a modern poetry for Bengal is then examined closely, followed by an attempt at arriving at an understanding of the Marxist reception of Madhusudan Datta and the manner in which the event has metamorphosed into metaphor in the public's memory of an iconic poet of his age. The construction of a Hindu nationalist imagery in the poetry of Hemchandra Bandyopadhyay is looked at through the lens of a single image in the following chapter, leading to a related development in tropes of authenticity in the reading of his poetry by his chief critic, Akshaychandra Sarkar. Nabinchandra Sen's *Palāśīr yuddha* of 1875 is explored from two different contexts—that of the politics of its exclusion from the school textbook syllabus and the subsequent changes to the text to satisfy damaging communal and sectarian demands, and that of the confusion about the historicity of the poem itself and of the debates it generated regarding the wider nature of history and poetry as distinct genres. The book concludes with a chapter on Rabindranath in his teenage years, at first writing a political poetry that attempted to synchronize with the nationalist demands of the period, ending with the writing of '*Nirjharer svapnabhaṅga*', within whose premises he felt he attained his true poetic vocation.

This roughly fifty-year period was a period in flux, with several developments and changes being implemented within a short space of time. It was a heterogeneous space, full of odd impulses and conflicting movements, in which the old coexisted with the new, while the experience of the modern shot through and permeated every offshoot of the literary enterprise. It was also a time that changed the manner of being Indian irrevocably, putting in place certain parameters of identity and experience that may have been integral to the Bengali experience but was also informative for the shaping of a larger Indian cultural sphere coming into being at this time. As a literary critic once pointed out, there was a time when the word *itihās* had implied tradition, not history, necessarily reminding his modern reader thereby that *itihās* had meant something else in another time.[96] This book attempts to distil, through the particularity of certain arguments and readings, some of those situations in the nineteenth century which ultimately led to *itihās* irremediably transforming itself (alongside the concept of '*sāhitya*' in relation to 'literature', '*darśan*' apropos 'philosophy', or the '*kabi*' in lieu of 'poet') into something that was understood as history, not tradition, although that sense of it as tradition stubbornly refused, as it still refuses, to die away entirely in our memory and linguistic practice.

[96] '*Saṃskṛte itihās balite History bojhāẏ nā, tradition bojhāẏ.*' Tripurashankar Senshastri, 1975, '*Kabi īśvarcandra gupta o bāṅglā sāhitya*', in Santikumar Dasgupta and Haribandhu Mukhati (eds), *Īśvar gupta rachanābalī*, Vol. 2, Calcutta: Dattachowdhury and Sons, p. 19.

1 Disjunctions, Conjunctions

The Common Politics of Literary Reading

In an article in the *New York Times* in 2008, art critic Holand Cotter had an insight he wanted to share with the Western world. Reviewing a show called 'Rhythms of India: The Art of Nandalal Bose (1882–1966)' at the Philadelphia Museum of Art, he wrote of how modernity is conceived of as having happened exclusively in the West and then distributed like food aid to the rest:

> Along with detailed information about one artist's life and times, the show delivers a significant piece of news, or what is still probably news to many people: that modernism wasn't a purely Western product sent out like so many CARE packages to a hungry and waiting world. It was a phenomenon that unfolded everywhere, in different forms, at different speeds, for different reasons, under different pressures, but always under pressure. As cool and above-it-all as modern may sound, it was a response to emergency. In India the emergency was a bruising colonialism that had become as intolerable to artists as to everyone else.[1]

The message Cotter wishes to convey to the readership he is writing for in America announces what should long ago have been a commonplace fact; the astounding thing is Cotter's understanding that the majority of those who read the *New York Times* have no knowledge yet of India's multiple modernities. At the end of his retrospection on the modern art of Nandalal Bose, and on the bed of modern Indian culture from which it sprang, Cotter concludes with a sentiment the rest of the world might

[1] Holand Cotter, 2008, 'Indian Modernism via an Eclectic and Elusive Artist', *New York Times*, 19 August.

want to wholeheartedly endorse, 'that every Museum of Modern Art in the United States and Europe should be required, in the spirit of truth in advertising, to change its name to Museum of Western Modernism until it has earned the right to do otherwise'.[2]

The preceding year, art historian Partha Mitter had mentioned in his book on modern Indian art, *The Triumph of Modernism*—somewhat sweepingly perhaps—that 'the rise of modernist art in India' can be located in the ambitious exhibition of the Bauhaus artists Paul Klee, Wassily Kandinsky, and others in Calcutta in 1922, which 'marks the beginning of the avant-garde in India'.[3] The poet Rabindranath Tagore was instrumental in initiating the effort to bring the works of these artists to Calcutta after his own visit to the Bauhaus in Weimar in 1921, where the teaching methods, he felt, had great affinities with his own experiments at Santiniketan.[4] It remains, however, that Rabindranath's own understanding of art, as well those of his contemporaries, had sprung from sensibilities that were deeply imbued with the modern, and that one of the primary forms through which that modern had come to them was that of literature—of the newly inaugurated novel and the proscenium theatre, of the short story and the essay, of literary criticism, and of course, of poetry.

I would like to suggest that to uncover the construction of cultural production—whereby the dominant group constructs its reality and its history—it is essential to interrogate the key notion of derivation; not the old question of a derivative discourse, but another equally old question about transition and complex historical transaction. This is best highlighted by placing the notion of 'the derived' within the old rhetoric of the 'influence' of the English presence in India, and by mapping the tradition/modernity debate (that has structured so much of the speculative, interventionist or didactic practice of language, form and style) in order to come up with an alternative reading. To come to terms with our cultural modernity, particularly the literary modern, one is making an attempt here to specifically work in an analysis of

[2] Ibid.

[3] Partha Mitter, 2007, *The Triumph of Modernism: India's Artists and the Avant-garde 1922–1947*, Delhi: Oxford University Press, p. 10.

[4] Ibid., p. 17.

the complex paths of the colonial past that have 'impure' beginnings and heterogeneous articulations, so that, taken together, these modes can enter and complicate the prevalent discourse, constituted of the common politics of literary reading to do with ideas of imitation and the place of tradition that has been the staple so far.

The nineteenth-century literary sphere contributed toward the creation of some aspects of the Indian modern through, as well as in opposition to, the colonial presence, mediated, among other things, by critical notions of language and literature. Two contiguous traditions, often perceived in oppositional terms, need to be re-examined in the light of the formation of a modern literary practice in Bengal in the nineteenth century. One of these is the often-discussed contribution made by the English language to Bengali literary modernity, emblematized in the works of Bankimchandra or Madhusudan, while the other consists of the indigenous inheritances of traditional poetic practices, some of which, such as the legacy of the poet Bharatchandra, came to be stigmatized by charges of immorality and licentiousness made chiefly in Bengal's Victorian age, which categorized him as unworthy of inclusion in the national project of a modern literature for Bengal. (This tradition includes also the nouveau-urban adaptations of the *kabiẏāls* of Calcutta—the compositions of Bhola-maẏrā, Ram Basu, Haru Thakur, or the songs of the vicariously named Keshta-*muci*, Lalu Nandalal, Gojla Guin, or Antony Firingi; but it was Bharatchandra's that was the most contested legacy in literary critical terms.) Bharatchandra Ray (1712–1760) was the court poet of Raja Krishnachandra of Nadia in an age when the English were already a troublesome presence in Bengal; his best known work, the *Annadāmaṅgal*, was written five years before the fateful Battle at Palashi that Sirajuddaula lost to Clive in 1757. Bharatchandra's *Annadāmaṅgal* was published in an illustrated edition for the first time in 1816, and the early literary scene in Bengal is dominated by the success, popularity and reach of this work, and by the struggle to either disinherit or recuperate him. This alternate inheritance in Bengali literature—that of the older traditions of *kabi gān*, *ākhyān*, *upākhyān*, and sections of *maṅgalkābya*—remains a distant presence in its literary histories, valorized for its roots in the authenticity of tradition, but in practice often derided and criticized by nineteenth-century practitioners such as Rangalal and Madhusudan, pushed aside deliberately in the cause of the high-minded literary/ethical formation of a national culture in the nineteenth century.

The 'modern' conventions that attempted to supplant the 'low' traditions in the nineteenth century existed at the opposite end of the popular immoral indigenous inheritance, resembling, in form, an overarching architecture of many lofty columns and sublime archways constituted by a partial recuperation of Sanskritic legacy and an overwhelming interaction with English literary language, with its forms, its style, and its conventions. (The fact that much of the literary criticism addressed to this edifice has been preoccupied with how to pull it down, or has usually dealt with it with derision, is another matter altogether, and one that I will continuously address.) The standard terminology that characterizes this particular interaction has included words like 'influence' and 'impact' at one end, and 'response' or 'reaction' at the other; even so distinguished a commentator as Sisir Kumar Das typically titled the second volume of his *A History of Indian Literature*, consisting of eight hundred and fifteen pages documenting the literary achievements of every Indian language in this age: '1800–1910: Western Impact: Indian Response'.[5]

The attempt here, rather, will be to move away from such conceptual frameworks whose underlying assumption, 'first in the West and then elsewhere', frames the argument in a linear, teleological, and developmental perspective, where modernity is conceived of as having been an emanation from Europe that gradually filtered through to the rest of the world in successive stages, bringing progress and light in its wake. These two traditions within Bengali literature coexist and compete for space at various junctures, although, when we look at histories of Bengali literature, we see that critics and practitioners tend to emphasize the rupture with the past by focusing on the new 'Englishness' of many of the initiatives in the literary sphere. That focus on the break with the old and the foreignness of the new is, of course, every modern project's foundational moment; what complicates the picture in a colonized situation is that the new is then both celebrated and questioned—celebrated for its obvious achievements, but questioned

[5] Sisir Kumar Das, 1991, *A History of Indian Literature 1800–1910: Western Impact, Indian Response*, New Delhi: Sahitya Akademi.

for its provenance and its spirit, which is perceived to be emanating from the colonizer's camp. Yet, indisputably, the Bengali language and its literature, in their modern trajectory, needed the English language as a facilitator as well as a necessary, perhaps indispensable, 'Other'.

The literary sphere of early nineteenth-century Calcutta was dominated in part by the polemical tracts of Rammohun Roy, as is well known. With regard to his location in relation to the emergence of the Bengali literary sphere, however, few will recall Kishorichand Mitra's shrewd observation in the *Calcutta Review*, 'The truth is Rammohun Roy was exceedingly ambitious of literary fame'.[6] About his involvement with Bengali, of which he is considered a pioneer in prose, a writer in the *Gyānanveshaṇ* had remarked:

> We remember a conversation with him in which he mentioned his endeavours at the first commencement of his literary career to become a poet, 'but failing' he said 'to excel Bharut Caunder Roy, the author of Unnadah Mongul, in his poetical diction, in which I could only equal him[,] I turned my attention to prose writings and never ceased practising … [until] I effected that polish in my style to which I have arrived, though I had not a single writer before me to be guided by his example'.[7]

What is remarkable about the sentiment expressed above is that such a validation of Bharatchandra's 'poetical diction' would not be heard again in the course of the century among the new literary men of Bengal. Madhusudan Datta had commented, regarding the forthcoming publication of 'Tilottama' in 1860, 'I see that I have actually done something that ought to give our national poetry a good lift, at any rate, that will teach the future poets of Bengal to write in a strain very different from that of the man of Krishnanagar—the father of a very vile school of poetry, though himself a man of elegant genius'.[8] The passage from Rammohun's desire to emulate Bharatchandra to Madhusudan's dismissal of his legacy (although he attributed to the poet an 'elegant genius') is completed in a space of about twenty-five

[6] Bruce Robertson, 2003, 'The English Writings of Raja Rammohan Ray', in Arvind Krishna Mehrotra (ed.), *An Illustrated History of English Literature*, New Delhi: Permanent Black, p. 34.

[7] *Bengal Hurkaru*, 12 February 1834.

[8] Michael Madhusudan Datta, letter to Raj Narain Bose, in K. Gupta (ed.), 1993, *Madhusudan rachanabali*, Calcutta: Sahitya Sansad, p. 545.

years, by which time the project of nationalism and high cultural literary form seem to have come together in an apparently happy conjugality.

The Long March to Progress

Employing the sort of Puranic description that seems to be the staple of the Bengali literary historian, distinguished commentator Brajendranath Bandyopadhyay wrote in praise of Iswarchandra Gupta's attempts to rescue the already forgotten poetry of Bharatchandra for mid-nineteenth-century readers:

> It is because he [Iswarchandra] rent his own breast, like the Gangotri, so that the nameless, featureless streams of remote mountainous regions could be directed into the kingdom of air and light, that Madhusudan-Biharilal-Rabindranath's achievements have been possible; and on the other side, when Bengali poetry was in the process of dying an untimely death at the ignoble and rustic window-ledge of the poet and artist Bharatchandra's *kabi-ṭappā, pāñcāli, hāph-ākhṛāi*, it was Iswarchandra's efforts that imparted to these very things the grandeur of wealth, uplifting them so that it was possible for them to be ushered in at the front door to attain freedom and new life.[9]

Iswar Gupta's attempt to 'usher in at the front door' the traditions kept at bay at 'the ignoble and rustic window-ledge' of Bharatchandra, however, went against the temper of the morality police of the following age. Iswarchandra's endorsement of Bharatchandra, in the biography of the poet he published in 1855, had been unambiguous: 'This book contains many poems that have not been seen or heard by anybody, including many wonderful Sanskrit, Bengali, Hindi and Persian language poems. Readers who study these poems carefully will be wonderstruck by the extraordinary gift and scholarship of Bharatchandra'.[10] But the succeeding generations in Bengal belonged to a time in which the structural binary of high and 'low' culture was first formulated, which showcased to Bengalis how modern poetry was to be written according to 'pure' English literary convention, leading

[9] Brajendranath Bandyopadhyay (ed.), 1987, *Sāhitya sādhak caritmālā* (1st edn, 1949). Vol. 1, Calcutta: Bangiya Sahitya Parishad, p. 5.

[10] Cited in Ibid, p. 13.

to the perceived marginalization of indigenous literary culture for being both immodest and mean. Those words were used by Rangalal Bandyopadhyay in the manifesto of his pioneering volume of modern Bengali poetry, *Padminī upākhyān*, written self-consciously to suit 'Westernized' tastes: 'the greater the number of poems composed in the Bengali language along the purer system of English poetic conventions, the more we shall witness the exit of the immodest, mean body of poetry that currently exists...'.[11]

A cursory glance at the history of Bengali poetry will reveal a narrative that includes the accomplishment of Rangalal Bandopadhyay in *Padminī upākhyān* in 1858 at a crucial juncture in the formulation of a national modernity, after Iswar Gupta and before Michael Madhusudan Datta and Hemchandra Bandopadhyay, who followed. This evolutionary model of progress, like the charts that show the Neanderthal man, half-man, half-ape, gradually straighten into erect homo sapiens, is also followed in Brajendranath Bandyopadhyay and Sajanikanta Das's introduction to the Bangiya Sahitya Parishad edition of Rangalal's *Padminī upākhyān*:

> At the end of the eighteenth century, Ramprasad Sen and Bharatchandra Ray had propagated the erotic narrative of *Bidyāsundar*; weak imitations then flooded the countryside of Bengal. The *kabi*-groups also inundated the fallen Bengali race with songs of *biraha* or *kheuṛ*. Not long after this appeared Ramnidhi Gupta and Dasharathi Ray. Their tuneful poetry too undulated like the creeper; firm footsteps trodden on solid foundations were yet to be sighted. Iswar Chandra Gupta then embarked upon a mission to give Bengali poetry novelty as well as solidity in individual short poems. To Rangalal Bandyopadhyay belongs the honour of signifying the turn by composing poetry that was extensive. *Padminī Upākhyān* was published in 1858. After this arose Madhusudan.[12]

Emblematic of the standard interpretation of the coming of the modern age to literary endeavour in Bengal, as well as reflective of the rhetoric, in colonial histories of British India, of decline/decay in

[11] Rangalal Bandyopadhyay, 1951, *Padminī upākhyān, Rājasthānīya itihāsā biśes* [*The Story of Padmini, Selections from Rajasthani History*] edited by Brajendranath Bandyopadhyay and Sajanikanta Sen [3rd edn printed in February 1872; first published in 1858], Calcutta: Bangiya Sahitya Parishad, p. 14.

[12] Ibid.

the Muslim era followed by regeneration in the British period, this standard history of the teleological development of Bengali literature was written in 1951. To understand the solemn resonance of the last sentence, 'After this arose Madhusudan', we need to return to another of Bankimchandra's famous pronouncements which also marked the moment, albeit with a different compass: '1859 and 1860 are the years that will remain forever imprinted upon Bengali literature—they are the watershed between the old and the new. The last of the old party, Iswar Chandra's sun had set, and the first poet of the new, Madhusudan's, had just risen. Iswar Chandra was an authentic Bengali, Madhusudan a die-hard Englishman (*ḍāhā Iṅgrej*)!'

After this, the story goes, began the march of the high cultural creative accomplishment of the nineteenth-century Bengali literary scene—the glorious turn of Madhusudan and Bankimchandra from their first compositions in the English language (*Captive Ladie* in 1849 and *Rajmohan's Wife* in 1854) to create some of the brightest gems of Bengali literature. Iswarchandra Gupta had famously written in his poem '*Svadeś*', 'Throw away those foreign gods / Worship instead the native dog'; such resistance to the story of the inexorable march of progress was not slow to come—there were the not so occasional grumblings from Bankimchandra himself (the phrase '*ḍāhā Iṅgrej*', quoted in the preceding passage, is itself pejorative), and keen-eyed literary critics such as Akshaychandra Sarkar complained, apropos the anglicized nature of Hemchandra Bandyopadhyay's poetry: 'The Bengali's authentic Bengali poetry has taken shelter in the margins. English fragrance, English rhythm … a sort of foreign poetry has occupied centrestage and does business. Do you not feel sad? Maybe you do not. But we do'.[13]

Eminent Bengali literary historian, Sukumar Sen, while acknowledging the heterogeneity of the literary arena in early nineteenth-century Bengal, was still conventionally disapproving of the legacy of Bharatchandra's *Bidyāsundar*. In a chapter titled, 'The Rise of New Poetry', he starts: 'At the start of the nineteenth century, poetry was in a very bad way… Bharatchandra's *Bidyāsundar* had such an all-encompassing reach that almost all poetical composition was being

[13] Akshaychandra Sarkar, 1912, *Kabi hemcandra*, Calcutta: Bangiya Sahitya Parishad, pp. 21–2. See Chapter 5 (ii).

conducted in imitation of aunt Malini's adulterous assignations...', invoking a particularly scandalous character in the story, popular and immoral in equal measure.[14] The imagery employed here of cheap contemporary poetry being like 'aunt Malini's adulterous liaisons' is taken from no less a predecessor than Akshaychandra Sarkar, who had made the same comparison. Writing in the *Baṅgadarśan*, Akshaychandra had mentioned, to quote one indicative sentence, 'Malini's talents made her popular among the lumpen youth; Bharat's talents are exactly like hers, they have helped him reign over the uneducated classes'. The level of satire and contempt in Akshaychandra's opinion of Bharatchandra was indicative of the nineteenth-century response generally, throughout which Bankimchandra, Bharatchandra was indicted by leading critics such as Kishorichand Mittra, Harchandra Datta, Bankimchandra Chatterjee, and Akshaychandra Sarkar, amongst others, while writers and scholars such as Rameshchandra Datta and Dineshchandra Sen too attacked him precisely for his indecency, indelicacy, his low character, and his excessive use of alliteration. This quarrel between the 'high' and the 'low' is of fundamental importance to modern literary formation and self-awareness. Moral and ethical coarseness, on the one hand (as in Bharatchandra), and literary and aesthetic refinement (paradoxically in Bharatchandra again, as well as predominantly in the high Sanskritic and Western literary conventions) on the other, were inextricable from formulations of Bengali identity at this time. Both these cultural perceptions were enmeshed, confusingly, but also creatively, with notions of the authentic or the local and the foreign or the imported, the quarrel constituting a source of creative and critical friction in the modern.

Writing against the grain of this conventional framing of the indigenous traditions as belonging to 'low' culture, Gautam Bhadra, in an article in *Ababhās*, has questioned the received wisdom of nineteenth-century Bengali critics as well as contemporary academics (such as Sumanta Banerjee), objecting to the latter's division of the scene into the 'upper-class *bhadralok*' and the 'lower-class common

[14] Sukumar Sen, 1970, '*Nabīn kabitār abhyuday*', in *Bāṅgla sāhityer itihās*, First edn 1943, Vol. 2, Calcutta: Eastern Publishers, p. 120.

people' (*itar-santān*) or into the parlour and the street.[15] Analysing the literary criticism of three nineteenth-century literary critics on the art of the novel, Bhadra shows, in this essay, how mixed languages and mixed forms were created, for instance in Bankimchandra, in order to establish a connection with a readership with tastes that spanned both the old and the new. Bankimchandra's writings, thus, 'are shown to contain, according to context, Iswar Gupta and Pearychand; in their profoundly unconscious depths, however, Bharatchandra, Vidyapati, and Ramprasad are like so many submerged mountains (*magna-maināk*)'.[16] Bhadra shows here how Bankimchandra, in his depictions of the radiant beauty of Bimala, Tilottama or Ayesha, took recourse to the conventions of the *ākhyān*, describing these women in language wrested from the conventions of the popular and the folk. Always a self-conscious artist, Bankim, Bhadra maintains, is well aware of indigenous tradition and uses it to make the impossible sound plausible; he knows that he must fight for space in the minds of the popular readership with Bharatchandra and Dasharathi Ray, and he is not willing to concede an inch to them in this respect. In describing Asmani in his very first novel, *Durgeśnandinī*, he is entering, it seems, into a contest to wean the reader away from the discourse of the *ākhyān*, and to do so, he is willing to fight it with its own weapons:

> Oh *Baṭ-talā*, provider of oil to the lamp of knowledge! Come once and light the lamp of my intellect brightly. Ma! You exist in two forms; one is the form in which you granted your boon to Kalidasa, from the nature of which was born the *Raghubaṃśa, Kumārsambhab, Meghdūt, Sakuntalā*; meditating on which Valmiki composed the Ramayana, Bhavabhuti the *Uttar Rāmcarit*, Bharavi the *Kirātārjunīa*. Do not come in that form and descend upon my shoulders and oppress me; instead, come to me in the form in which Sri Harsha wrote *Naishādh*, in which incarnation Bharatchandra wrote of Bidya's astonishing beauty and charmed the hearts of Bengal, in the form of the mansion in which Dasharathi Ray was born—in the way in which you illuminate the *Baṭ-talā* to this day—in that shape come to me on the shoulders of hope, and let me try to describe the beauty of Asmani.[17]

[15] Sumanta Banerjee, 1998, *The Parlour and the Streets: Elite and Popular Culture in Nineteenth-century Calcutta*, Calcutta: Seagull.

[16] Gautam Bhadra, 2006, '*Naeda bat-talay jay kabar*?', *Ababhās*, Vol. 3, p. 28.

[17] Ibid.

The traditions are incarnate in two different forms in this invocation, the high-Sanskritic, which sits upon his shoulder and oppresses him, and the seductive charms of the *baṭ-talā* which he wishes to access in this instant when he has to describe the charms of Asmani (although the relegation of the Muslim Asmani to the realm of the *baṭ-talā*, however charming a space that might conceivably be, may be a little more predictable a consignment than Bhadra allows for). In this manner, Bankimchandra will return again and again, Bhadra says, to the *baṭ-talā* and the *ākhyān*, treating these elements, not whimsically, but with due respect, dividing the literary inheritance of the Bengali into two streams, *both* of which are incarnations of the divine.

To arrive at such a reading, which is self-aware of the manner in which the *baṭ-talā* and the *ākhyān-upākhyān* penetrated the literary scene at many levels, many branches and in many locations, it is necessary, Bhadra reiterates, to abandon the vertical, lengthwise or linear '*khāṛā-khāṛi*' judgemental mode, or we will miss the '*āṛā-āṛi*' cross-section of exchange and interchange that characterized the literary field in the nineteenth century. The discourse of literary writing in the nineteenth century is thus shown not as seamless and internally consistent, but rather as suffering from various tensions, disjunctions, and contradictions that opened creative possibilities to fashion new syntheses from constituent elements of this discourse. This type of epistemological 'bricolage' is certainly not revolutionary, but it is a method that, in the context of nineteenth-century Bengal, has not been attempted very often in the past either. This book will attempt to address that lack, and in doing so, will be as much about literary criticism and the construction of certain dominant tropes of modernity through literary practice as about the practice of literature itself, aiming to highlight and understand the suppressed lineages and traditions within the central discourse of nineteenth-century poetics and nationalism.

Constituting 'the Public'

In Bengal in the 1850s and 1860s, writers such as Rangalal Bandyopadhyay and Madhusudan Datta were quite categorical about who they were writing for, and why. Trying to push through certain formal and schematic changes in the writing of Bengali poetry,

Madhusudan Datta in 1859 had reminded a friend impatiently, 'Besides, remember I am writing for that portion of my countrymen who think as I think, whose minds have been more or less imbued with western ideas and *modes of thinking* (original emphasis)'.[18] This held true for Rangalal as well, who, a year before this, in 1858, had written in his preface to *Padminī upākhyān* that he was writing the book for his friends and well-wishers who had urged him to embark upon this project of the reformation of Bengali poetry, among whom were mentioned the zamindar Kalichandra Ray Chowdhury, Raja Satyacharan Ghoshal, the Rev. W. O'Brien Smith, Rajendralal Mitra, and the members of the Vernacular Literature Society or the Bethune Samaj. Both writers conceived of a wider public which was constituted of a very small highly educated minority, who taught in the same schools and colleges, held the same sorts of positions in administrative work and in society, and, crucially, read the same sorts of books.

This narrow involvement with writing for friends and other like-minded people was to slowly broaden out, as time went on, into a larger slice of civil society than had been originally thought of in the conceptual stages of the project to bring a modern literature for Bengal into being. Speaking of his first work, the long poem 'Tilottama', as he called it while writing his letters, all of which were written in English, Madhusudan quoted from the opinion of 'a Banian's assistant in a mercantile firm' who had written to him admiring his poem in a letter he wrote to Rajnarain Basu.[19] In a few days, he writes to his friend again in the context of the introduction of blank verse to the Bengali reader unaccustomed to its cadence, relating an incident well known in the annals of the modern history of Bengali literature:

> Talking about Blank-Verse, you must allow me to give you a jolly little anecdote. Some days ago I had occasion to go to the Chinabazar. I saw a man seated in a shop and deeply pouring (*sic*) over Meghnad. I stepped in and asked him what he was reading. He said in very good English; 'I am reading a new poem, Sir!' 'A poem!' I said, 'I thought there was no poetry in your language.' He replied—'Why, sir, here is poetry that would make my nation proud.' I said, 'Well, read and let me know.' My literary shopkeeper looked hard at me and said, 'Sir, I am afraid, you wouldn't

[18] Letters, *Madhusudan rachanabali*, p. 545.

[19] Ibid.

understand this author.' I replied, 'Let me try my chance.' He read out of Book II that part wherein Kam returns to Rati, standing at the ivory gate of the palace of Siva, and Rati says to him,

bāñcāle dāsīre
āśu āsi tār pāśe he ratiranjan

How beautifully the young fellow read. I thought of the men who pretend to be scholars and Pandits. I took the poem from him and read out a few passages to the infinite astonishment of my new friend. How eagerly he asked where I lived? I gave him an evasive reply, for I hate to be bothered with visitors. I shook hands with him, and on parting asked him if he thought Blank Verse would do in Bengali. His reply was, 'Certainly, Sir, it is the noblest measure in the language.'[20]

This extraordinary exchange in the Chinabazar area of Central Calcutta stands as testament to the fact that this shopkeeper's assistant, found in a chance encounter by Madhusudan in 1861, was the living image of the audience Bankimchandra would want to address his work to ten years later in his essays about the future of Bengali literature. Bankim's famous English essays advocating a Bengali literature for Bengalis—*A Popular Literature for Bengal* (1870) and *Bengali Literature* (1871)—were, typically of the time, written in English, the very language deemed to be the source of all the trouble:

By a popular literature for Bengal I mean a Bengali literature. Bengali literature must for a long time to come be nothing more than merely the popular literature of Bengal. As long as the higher education continues to have English for its medium, as long as English literature and English science continue to maintain their present immeasurable superiority, these will form *the* sources of intellectual cultivation to the more educated classes. To Bengali literature must continue to be assigned the subordinate function of being the literature for the *people* of Bengal, and it is as yet hardly capable of occupying even that subordinate, but extremely important, position. (original emphasis)[21]

Who exactly, for Bankim, are the 'people'? By the 'people of Bengal' he meant, he clarified, 'the artizan and the shopkeeper who keep

[20] Ibid., p. 561.

[21] Bankimchandra Chatterjee, 1998, 'A Popular Literature for Bengal', in Jogesh Chandra Bagal (ed.), *Bankim rachanavali*, Vol. 3, Calcutta, Sahitya Samsad, p. 97.

their own accounts, the village zemindar and the mofussil lawyer, the humble official employé whose English carries him no further than the duties of his office, and the small proprietor who has as little to do with English as with office, all these classes read Bengali and Bengali only; all in fact between the ignorant peasant and the really well-educated classes.[22] This is the middle class before the term has become commonplace; the 'shopkeeper' or 'small proprietor' envisaged by Bankimchandra here was, as we have seen, already in place by the time Madhusudan Datta was publishing his work, evidence of a reading public that was already out there, waiting for the works to come into being. This literature, yet to be created for these people, he then famously declared, 'is just blundering into existence'. Since the 'popular literature of a nation and the national character act and react upon each other', he feels it incumbent upon him to regulate the taste of the public, and in order to do so, he presents, in this essay, a brief description of past achievements and current trends. Within a couple of years, he would go on to found the epochal *Baṅgadarśan* journal in 1872, which led in its magnificent wake a flotilla of various other Bengali periodical publications of substantive worth and value, apart from continuing with his corpus of novels, essays, satire and criticism over a career spanning several decades.

Bankimchandra's understanding of the public sphere and of the making of a modern national literature for it has much in common with Madhusudan's own preceding obsession with producing a 'national literature' for Bengal. In the English essays he wrote, Bankim reiterated what Michael had repeatedly said in private correspondence: that his first poem 'ought to give our national Poetry a good lift', that we have 'not yet established a National Theatre', and again about the need for 'founding a real National Theatre'. Both men abandoned their own early writing in English to turn to their mother tongue; Madhusudan feelingly wrote from France that 'European scholarship is good in as much as it renders us masters of the intellectual resources of the most civilized quarters of the globe; but when we speak to the world, let us speak in our own language'.[23] Both men thus share a common concern about founding and establishing a modern national literature for their

[22] Ibid. Original spellings.

[23] Letters, *Madhusudan rachanabali*, pp. 547, 599.

age, and both imagine as well as encounter the reading public that this modern literature would speak to. This understanding of the Bengali public sphere, still a common consensus in these two behemoths straddling the foundational period of literature in Bengali, would then proceed to change with time.

Other correspondences may be found in the language used by both writers to speak of the current state of the people of Bengal. Writing about the need for a popular literature for Bengal, Bankim said that the poetical literature of the generations preceding his was an 'effeminate poetical literature', produced by 'indolent habits and a feeble moral organization', and of the need for the rejuvenation of the 'spiritless' Bengali producing this literature. In phrases that were very reminiscent of Madhusudan's English essay of 1854, 'The Anglo-Saxon and the Hindu', Bankim spoke of a 'new light' upon the Bengali, as he stood, 'crushed', which 'dawned on him, to rouse him, if that were possible from his state of lethargy'.[24] Madhusudan too had spoken of the Hindu, 'as he stands before you', as 'a fallen being—once—a green, a beautiful, a tall, a majestical, a flowering tree; now—blasted by lightning! Who can recall him to life?' His answer had been unequivocal: 'it is the glorious mission of the Anglo-Saxon to regenerate, to renovate the Hindu race!'[25] Although Bankim would not directly invoke the English presence in India as the saving grace of the Hindu as Michael had done, he used similar imagery to speak, rather, of the coming of modernity: 'And with this new dawn of life came into the country one of the mightiest instruments of civilization, the printing-press'.[26]

The time period covered in this book is still a moment, then, when the material and the spiritual are not separated into conclaves at odds with one another in the nationalist theatre of late nineteenth-century Bengal, and Bankim here is certainly not the champion of the Hindu as he has been made out to be in his later writings. That separation of the sanctified inner domain of Hindu spirituality may be seen, rather, in the manner in which Dineshchandra, another

[24] 'A Popular Literature For Bengal', in *Bankim rachabnabali*, p. 99.

[25] Essays, 'The Anglo-Saxon and the Hindu', *Madhusudan rachanabali*, pp. 630, 635.

[26] Ibid.

couple of decades later, had also spoken of how the Bengalis 'forgot their wonderful success in metaphysical learning, and their great spirituality, and felt that they were dwarfed in the presence of that great materialistic civilisation which, armed with thunder and lightning and with the tremendous power of steam, stood knocking at their door—demanding audience'.[27] He too invoked the material power of the modern, but identified it entirely with the violence of colonial rule rather than as an instrument to be gladly appropriated, as Bankim had done. In the intervening years between the use of the two metaphors—of the power of the printing press and the power of steam—something had changed irrevocably, resulting in a separation of domains unprecedented in colonial experience. With the century drawing to a close, a change can be traced even within the work of the earlier and later Bankim himself, as the revivalist years led inexorably toward the Swadeshi era, drawing in even Rabindranath in its political ambit before he eventually withdrew from the idea of nationalism and its extremist phase with some recoil.

As I have shown in the chapter on Akshaychandra Sarkar's criticism of Hemchandra Bandyopadhyay's mode of writing in this book, Hindu revivalists like Akshaychandra began to develop what became a common complaint amongst critics of a modernity deemed unacceptable because it did not penetrate into the heart of the villages to the common people of Bengal. Apropos Hemchandra, Akshaychandra wrote:

> ... despite of the feeling of hostility (*jāti-baira*) in courts, colleges, and civilized society that it had been our good fortune for Hemchandra's talent to have induced, his influence is still limited to those areas alone. The word has not reached the bazaars, the fields, the riverside or the road; the man in the market does not know who Hembabu is, the farmer in his field has never heard or caught a whiff of his name. The young village girl who bathes in the river does not comprehend that 'Bharat is still sunk in slumber'.[28]

This extension of the Bengali public sphere by the turn of the century to the 'young village girl who bathes in the river' was unlooked for in

[27] Dineshchandra Sen, 1922 (2010), *Gharer kathā o yugasāhitya*, p. 743.

[28] Akshaychandra Sarkar, 1911, *Kabi hemcandra*. See Chapter 4(ii).

the 1870s in the imagination of Madhusudan or Bankim; the idealism of the thought, however, is valid only in the rhetorical mode of a critical oppositional stance. The desire to have works by Hemchandra Bandyopadhyay read in 'the bazaars, the fields, the riverside or the road', by the 'man in the market' or the 'farmer in his field', is an impossible objective, whether the writer concerned is Hemchandra or Akshaychandra's idol and guru, Bankimchandra; it is doubtful, indeed, that Akshaychandra's desired objective is attainable in the real world at any time.

In extension, this argument is the same as that which has been commonly used for the flagellation of writers who use the English language to this day, the questions most commonly asked being—for whom do they write, who reads them, and what does that say about their endeavour? The hostility stems 'in large measure from the animosity toward the social class English has come to be identified with: a narrow well-entrenched, metropolitan-based ruling elite', exactly the sort of class that the lawyers, barristers, and civilian poets dealt with in this book belong to.[29] Yet, as Arvind Krishna Mehrotra proceeds to point out, while it is true that many (although increasingly, and crucially, certainly not all) writers of English in India belong to the metropolitan elite, 'it is also true that many who write at all, irrespective of language, belong to a privileged stratum'.[30] The utilitarianism of the greatest good for the greatest number that Akshaychandra articulated still seems to find a resonance in a postcolonial nation unsure of its relation with authenticity. For this is the language of politics, not the space of literature, and this is the language in which literature will continue to be most frequently spoken of in India in the long twentieth century.

In the meanwhile, when Bankimchandra died in 1894, the whole question of the constitution of the 'public' took a decisively public turn in a controversy over the memorial meeting or *śoksabhā* organized on the occasion; Partha Chatterjee has written persuasively of that incident in relation to the public and the private in the context of

[29] Arvind Krishna Mehrotra, 2011, *Parial Recall: Essays on Literature and Literary History*, Ranikhet: Permanent Black, p. 225.

[30] Ibid.

political modernity in a formative period for Indian civil society.[31] Nabinchandra Sen had refused Rabindranath's invitation to preside at a condolence meeting for Bankimchandra, criticizing the very idea as 'un-Hindu'; the latter then wrote a defence in which he spoke of something new called '*the public*', 'an untranslatable word', the notion of which, he said, 'had recently transformed our family oriented society like new flood-water'.[32] From here on, the discussion turns political, although the initial occasion for the reflections on the nature of the Bengali public was the death of a literary man. Wearied of this intense and aggravated concern with all that was public among the Marxist-materialist younger critics of the time who were his fiercest detractors, Rabindranath then asserted angrily, in the last year of his life in an article on 'Historicality in Literature' (referring to himself in the generalized third person), that 'in his own field of creativity Rabindranath has been entirely alone and tied to no public by history. Where history was public, he was there merely as a British subject but not as Rabindranath himself'.[33] But this was the last gasp of a lone voice in the twentieth-century Bengali literary sphere, which, regardless of whether one was formally affiliated to Left politics or not, typically spoke of the achievements of the nineteenth century in a tone of disavowal. Thus Asitkumar Bandyopadhyay, in his 1973 introduction to the fourth volume of his *Bāṅglā sāhityer itibṛtta*, put across a commonly held view apropos the 'Bengal Renaissance', saying:

[31] Partha Chatterjee, 2000, 'Two Poets and Death: On Civil Society in the Non-Christian World', in Timothy Mitchell (ed.), *Questions of Modernity*, Minneapolis: University of Minnesota Press; 'On Civil and Political Society in Post-colonial Democracies', in Sudipta Kaviraj and Sunil Khilnani (eds), 2001, *Civil Society: History and Possibilities*, Cambridge University Press, pp. 165–79.

[32] Rabindranath Tagore, *Śoksabhā,* first published in *Sādhanā, Jyaishṭha* 1301. Appendix to *Ādhunik Sāhitya, Rabindra rachanabali.* The *śoksabhā* has also been discussed in Sourin Bhattacharya, 2007, '*Alpabayaska Public*' [A Young Public] in *Kena āmrā rabīndranāthke cai ebaṃ ki bhābe* [Why We Want Rabindranath and in What Way], Calcutta: Anustup, pp.70–76.

[33] Rabindranath Tagore, *Sāhitye Aitihāsikatā*, 1941. Translated in Ranajit Guha, 2002, *History at the Limit of World-History*, New York: Columbia University Press. For a further discussion, see Rosinka Chaudhuri, 2004, '*The Flute, Gerontion*, and Subalternist Misreadings of Tagore', *Social Text,* 78, Vol. 22, No. 1, Spring.

> When we speak of a renaissance or reawakening we must first of all try to understand the Chaitanya culture of the middle ages. The modern, i.e. the nineteenth-century reawakening is primarily a matter of the middle-class urban Bengali. The education and culture of the last century was centred on Calcutta's 'babu' society. It is impossible to understand this culture without recourse to the English language. Therefore, however rich this English language oriented nineteenth-century literature and culture might have been, its limits were fixed—outside of gentle society, it remained an unknown identity.[34]

Here, the resonance of the 'fixed limits' of the middle-class Bengali is of course crucially mediated by Marxist discourse and the Naxalite movement's valorization of the peasant over the bourgeoisie that had peaked in the years 1968–71 in Calcutta, relegating the achievements of the nineteenth-century literary sphere—itself an astonishing efflorescence in comparison to any other world literature—to the domain of 'babu' society or the sphere of the hollow man.

Fundamental Bi- and Multi-lingualism

If we look at modern Bengali literature as commentators have traditionally done, that is, as arising indisputably in part from Western literary convention, as an offshoot or by-product, it is not surprising that this attribution would have traditionally been denigrated by nationalist writers. However, a more productive route to mapping the occurrences in a period of literary ferment for Bengal has been gestured at by the same literary historian who spoke of the 'fixed limits' of 'the nineteenth-century reawakening', Asitkumar Bandyopadhyay, who began his discussion on the Western inheritance by conceding that 'modern Bengali literature was, at its root, fundamentally bilingual', and went on to use an epic simile in support of his essentially cosmopolitan insight:

> A literature that was formed in the culture of a foreign language should have had only death written in its destiny; yet like the Puranic story of Shiva, who swallowed poison and stored it in his death-blue throat so

[34] Asitkumar Bandyopadhyay, 1985, Introduction to *Bāṅglā Sāhityer Itibṛtta* [1st edn, 1973; from now on *BSI*], Calcutta: Modern Book Agency, p. 5.

the world could celebrate life; nineteenth-century Bengali literature too scorned death, and instead, was invigorated with life.[35]

The 'foreign language' evoked here is, of course, the English language, which should have worked like an insidious poison on modern Bengali literature, killing it at birth, but, as in the story of the poison stored in Shiva's throat, turning it blue, it became instead a life-giving force. This book argues that the 'Western' in the discourse of modern Indian literature be freed from its typically negative association with the 'foreign' or the 'poisonous' in the context of Indian languages, especially in view of the fact that all extant Indian literatures had been permeated, at different times, by 'foreign' impressions in an unavoidable and incorrigible manner.

The new and the changing idioms of literary production, rather than located in colonial coercion and the 'impact' of Western forms, should be found instead within certain newly evolving contemporary literary practices of reading and writing that were readily available to Indians in the early nineteenth century through the printing press, the publishing industry, and the public space of the newspaper, journal, or periodical, providing readers with an immediate instructive arena from which to fashion the implements of their own modernity in an insistently original form. Reading against the grain of conventional literary critical approaches, it should be possible to acknowledge the enabling element in certain aspects of both English and Bengali literary conventions in the formulation of a modern literature, and here I shall place the common inheritance of the various languages as they came together to formulate the idea of the literary in the nineteenth century side by side.

The career of English in the early literary modernity of Bengal provides material for an exploration of the new notion of the individual as it emerged, not in the European sense of post-Enlightenment rationality being replicated in various provincial outposts, but as evidence of the new symbolic and ideological constructs that made up distinct evolving modernities in the Western and non-Western world. While on the one hand, writers such as Toru Dutt and Bankimchandra, writing side by side in the same city, are never read together, separated

[35] Ibid., p. 34.

on to two ends of the sharpest of binaries by language, on the other, generations of literary scholars have expended innumerable pages upon the 'impact' or 'influence' of English literature upon the Bengali. Yet the influences are always canonical and at a great distance—Shakespeare, Milton, Wordsworth, Byron, Shelley; the local productions of a Derozio or D.L. Richardson and the detailed reviews to which their work was subject, available contemporaneously in readily obtainable newspapers and journals, have been completely neglected. It is my argument that contentions between the major literary languages of India, including the classical and folk languages, nouveau urban and mixed languages, colonial and 'native' languages, played an instrumental role in the many negotiations between modernity and literary craft in nineteenth-century Bengal.

The milieu of modernity in which Rammohun Roy became one of the earliest to use the English and Bengali languages to the instrumental advantage of himself and his putative nation was an increasingly complex and cosmopolitan Calcutta, which, as the centre of British administration, trade and commerce, was already burgeoning with a populace of 'Chinese and Frenchmen, Persians and Germans, Arabs and Spaniards, Armenians and Portuguese, Jews and Dutchmen, in addition to the Indians and the British'.[36] The literary sphere of early nineteenth-century Calcutta was populated, apart from the commissioned academic and evangelical publications at Fort William and Serampore, by the religious and political writings of Rammohun Roy—in English, Bengali, Sanskrit and Persian/Arabic—as well as the first English poems of Derozio and Kasiprasad Ghosh, apart from the plethora of magazine, periodical, and newspaper publications that dominated the literary productions of this era.

As was to be the case with the majority of India's literary practitioners in the nineteenth and twentieth centuries, Rammohun Roy oscillated between the uses of several languages to several ends, serving as a salutary reminder thereby that the practice of multilingualism in India had its antecedents in normative pre-colonial conditions. The first of Rammohun's published tracts that has survived was the *Tuhfatu'l-Muwāhhidin*, written in Persian with an introduction in Arabic in

[36] Ajit Kumar Ray, 1976, *The Religious Ideas of Rammohun Roy*, Calcutta: Kanak Publications, pp. 3–4.

1803. Persian was a language of literary prestige in the early nineteenth century, and apart from Rammohun Roy, other practitioners in Calcutta at the turn of the century included William Jones, whose Persian translations and grammar of Persian, written while at Oxford, were said 'to have been read by almost everyone in the West who was literate in the nineteenth century'.[37] Derozio, for instance, published four translations of odes from Hafiz in all between 1826 and 1828. Did Derozio know Persian? There is no definite answer to that, but, certainly, these translations testify not only to the popularity of Hafiz among the newly emergent Indian intelligentsia trained in the older conventions—Rammohun's *Tuhfat* ends with a quotation from Hafiz, and Hafiz is also repeatedly quoted by Debendranath Tagore in his autobiography—but also to the currency of Persian among the Orientalists and the newly English-educated, inaugurating what was to remain an enduring fascination among the Bengali educated classes.[38]

Bilingualism, or a further mixture of languages in literary composition, was not a condition that was unique to the imposition of British rule in India; Bharatchandra Ray, as had already been noticed, had written poetry in Hindi as well as in Bengali and Persian. An incomplete play he left behind at the time of his death, '*Caṇḍi nāṭak*', was composed in a Bengali that consisted of a mixture of Sanskrit and Hindi, while in one particular poem collected by Iswar Gupta in his life of the poet, he used four different languages—Sanskrit, Bengali, Persian, and Hindi—in the same poem:

Śyām hit prāṇeśvar, *bāydke goẏed ruba*
Kātar dekhe ādar kar, *kāhe mar, ro royke*
Baktṛaṃ bedaṃ candramā, *chuñ lālā, ce remā,*
Krodhit par deo kshamā, *mettime kāhe śoẏ ke.*[39]

Equally amazing is a short poem by Bharatchandra in Bengali that was written around the same time, presumably in the mid-eighteenth century, that was called '*Kardrāphtha barṇan*' [*Kardrāphtha*

[37] A.J. Arberry, 1960, *Oriental Essays: Portraits of Seven Scholars*, London: George Allen, p. 82.

[38] See Rosinka Chaudhuri, 2008, Introduction to *Derozio, Poet of India*, New Delhi: Oxford University Press.

[39] See *Kabijībanī*, p. 25.

Described].[40] Iswar Gupta added a note preceding the poem, saying, '*Kardrāphtha*—this word is a Persian word, which means one who has done something and who, after having done it, has left the place' ['*Kardrāphtha.—Ei śabdaṭi parāsya śabda, ihār artha kāhār dvārā ekarmma haiẏacāhe ebaṃ ke ekarmma kariẏā prasthān karila*], adding after the poem his own comment, 'The amazing skill and knowledge this poem displays will be appreciated only by the knowledgeable'. The six line poem is as follows:

Pancapadī

Kāminī jāminī mukhe, nidrāgatā śuye sukhe
Dhīr śaṭh tār mukhe, cumbite cumban sukhe,
Dhīre dhīre kārddoraphth.
[The night on her beautiful face, she sleeps in peace
The placid cheat on her face, pleasurably plants a kiss
Very slow, very slow, *kārddoraphth*.]

Nidrā hate uṭhe nārī, alase abaś bhārī,
Āarśite mukh heri, cumba cinha drisṭi kari,
Bhābe bhāl kārdoraphth.
[When she wakes from sleep, she is languid, inert, heavy,
On her face in the mirror, she sees the mark of the kiss
Thinks of her fate: *kārddoraphth*.][41]

These poems would have been written towards the middle of the eighteenth century, in a Bengal dominated by Persian and Sanskrit as the classical languages, and Bengali and Hindi as the people's lingua franca. Bharatchandra, born in 1712, learnt Sanskrit from the pandits at the age of fourteen, and was then so stung by the criticism that he had wasted his time in learning that would be useless to him, that he proceeded to master Persian under the tutelage of a munshi named Ramchandra, subsequently composing his best works in the court of Raja Krishnachandra of Nadia. Never seeming to feel the pressure of adhering to any one language, he used, in one of his earliest works, Persian words in the composition of a devotional poem celebrating the deity Satyanarayan, to the extent that even his admirer and anthologist, Iswar Gupta, was constrained to comment, a century later, 'Some

[40] The Persian word '*Kardraft*' may ostensibly be translated in Hindi as '*Kar do raft*' meaning to do and then to disappear, such as in '*kiya aur gaya*'.

[41] *Kabijībanī*, '*Bhāratcandra*', pp. 23–4.

Persian, some Bengali and some Sanskrit—"seven different imitations spoil the original" ["*sāt nakale āsal khāsta*"]'.[42] Bharatchandra himself, however, was unapologetic about such usage, commenting that a great deal of pure Sanskrit inflicted as much suffering upon the Bengali language as an excessive use of Arabic/Persian words. As a result, 'clarity would be lost, and it would cease to be entertaining', which is why he preferred to use a mixed language of different ingredients, saying, 'therefore I speak a language *yabanī miśāl*' [*atayeb kahi bhāshā yabanī miśāl*].[43]

Arguably, then, both modern and early modern Bengali literature and culture is premised on a condition of multilingualism or bilingualism—some fields, such as the literary, showing more evidence of that divided inheritance from a variety of languages than perhaps others. In the debate on a written language for Bengal, Bankimchandra had beautifully documented, in an essay called '*Bāṅgālā bhāshā*' [The Bengali Language] published in the *Baṅgadarśan* in the summer of 1878, the linguistic requirements for literary composition, almost echoing Bharatchandra in his demand for clarity:

> The first requirement and most important quality of any writing is simplicity and clarity... . The things that need to be said should be said clearly—whatever little needs to be said should be said fully—to achieve this end, words from whichever language are necessary should be used—English, Persian, Arabic, Sanskrit, rural, wild—apart from the vulgar, everything else should be permissible.[44]

Here, the only category beyond the pale for Bankimchandra is that of the immoral, rude, or low; a newly constructed banishment that would attempt to ensure the expulsion of Bharatchandra from the canon on the grounds of licentiousness. In this essay, he is arraigning himself against Vidyasagar and Ramgati Nyayratna on the one hand, and allying himself to the proponents of popular language led by Tekchand Thakur, coming down firmly and unequivocally on the side of the

[42] Ibid., p. 10.

[43] Quoted in Haraprasad Mitra, n.d., *Bāṅglā kābye prāk-rabīndra*, Calcutta: The Book Emporium, p. 20. *Yabanī miśāl* may be translated as 'mixture of the Yavanas', where the word 'jaban' might be interchangeably read as meaning 'foreign' or 'Muslim'.

[44] Bankimchandra Chattopadhyay, [1878] 1998, '*Bāṅgālā bhāshā*', in J. Bagal (ed.), *Bankim rachanavali*, Vol. 2, Calcutta: Sahitya Sansad, p. 321.

latter. Regarding the mixture of all sorts of words into the language, he sounds almost identical to his popular predecessor, Bharatchandra, unapologetic about the mixture of several linguistic registers in a piece of writing as long as 'simplicity and clarity' are achieved. It is, in fact, a late nineteenth-century cultural imposition to suppose that a language should be 'pure', purged of all foreign contamination, unmixed and authentic, a desire built upon the nationalist impulse to forge a homogeneous template of cultural achievement, to create a language that was 'one's own', and had the strength to stand on its own.

Setting aside that wholly understandable urge under colonial rule to discard words, concepts, and conventions that have their origins in other languages, it is possible to see now that one of the promising signs to emerge from a cross-sectional view of Bengali literary modernity is the realization that bilingualism or multilingualism was germane to the quest for modernity in the secular literary space of Bengal.[45] Such a cross-sectional reading creates a changed signification in the already available practices of reading, creating, instead of a binary understanding of good and bad, moral and immoral, foreign and traditional, or a linear development of a narrative of progress from darkness into light, a realization that the production of India's many modernities involved various members of a historical situation acting together and upon each other in unexpected ways. Such a polyvalent approach can free us from the insistence that modernity is an import to be associated with British imperialism, showing us concretely how India's distinctive modernities were sourced from foreign as well as regional indigenous materials. If we are to find, in the constitutive arenas of the Indian modern, some notion of creativity and specificity

[45] The realization, for instance, that not only were the first translations of Bharatchandra and the first article on him written in English by Kasiprasad Ghosh in 1830, but that the best interpretative essays on Bharatchandra in that century too were in English rather than Bengali, adds a third dimension to the literary scene not many critics have been perceptive to. The list of Bharatchandra's admirers who wrote of him in English language begins with Reverend Wenger, who wrote on him in the *Calcutta Review* of 1850, and continues with Harchandra Datta, Rameshchandra Datta, Gourdas Bairagi, Pramatha Chaudhuri, Nirad Chaudhuri, and J.C. Ghosh. Of all of these, it is Pramatha Chaudhuri's essay, 'The Story of Bengali Literature', written in 1917 at the request of Rabindranath, which is remarkable for its perception of the early elements of modernity in Bharatchandra.

independently of the argument of 'Western influence', then this sort of transverse reading becomes significant for the self-created identity of India's multiple modernities.

2 (i) Reading Iswarchandra Gupta (1812–1859)

The Domain of the Vernacular

[*Haṭāt* house-light *jvale oṭhe. Bismita dr̥shti-te Kr̥pārām tākiye thāke darśak-der dike. Tārpar mr̥du ektā hāñsi phote tār mukhe.*]

Kr̥pā: Namaskār bābumuśāirā! (haṭāṯ theme tikkhna dr̥shtite darśakder dekhte thāke) Bābbāh, camaṯkār! Namaskār bibigan babugan! Āpnārā esechen tāhale ei hatabhāgya br̥dhher nimantraṅ rakkhā karte. Āmār śesh āsarer śrotā āpnārā; śata śata praṅam āpnāder. Śuru kari tāhale? Ektu sabur karun. (Koṅe table-er dike yay! thāla theke ektā mishti tule ney.) Nikhuṅt! Bāgbājārer madan mayrār dokān theke ānā. (Mukhe deẏ) Bāgbājāre ārek maẏrār-o dokān āche—Bholā, Haru ṭhakurer celā chila. Tār mishti māchi-teo choṅẏ nā.

[Suddenly the *house-lights* are switched on. Amazed, Kriparam stares at the audience for a while. Slowly, a faint smile appears on his face.]

Kripa: Greetings gentlemen! (Stops suddenly and looks hard at the audience) Oh, oh, wonderful! Greetings ladies and gentlemen! So you have come after all, you have honoured the invitation sent out by this wretched old man. You are the audience of my last show; many many felicitations to you. Shall I start then? Just hold on for a moment. (Goes towards the corner *table*! Picks up a sweet from the plate.) Perfect! Brought from Madan *maẏrā*'s shop at Bagbazaar. (Puts it in his mouth) There is another *maẏrā*'s shop [confectioner] at Bagbazaar—Bhola—Haru Thakur's disciple. Not even a fly would want to touch his sweets.[1]

[1] Partha Chatterjee's play, *Rāmnidhi*. First performed in 1991. Published in *Ekhhan*, 1985, *Śāradiyā saṃkhya*, p. 70.

The lines above are spoken by Kriparam Shure, the protagonist of a play called *Rāmnidhi*, on the life of the famous Bengali poet and composer Ramnidhi Gupta (1741–1839). The playwright (normally the historian) Partha Chatterjee, in a note on the title page, mentions that the play is *not* an adaptation of *Amadeus*—handing us thereby in a single sentence the thematic concern of the work before us, where the lesser Kriparam's Salieri will be played against the greater Ramnidhi's Mozart. Peter Shaffer's play was made into a film in 1984 by Milos Forman, names that are perhaps better known to us today than the names from the ranks of the *kabiẏāls* that are to be found in this passage itself—Haru Thakur, Bhola-maẏrā, and Kriparam Shure—of whom the last named was an invention of the playwright. Meanwhile, the eponymous hero of the play—Ramnidhi—was the most respected and famous composer of that age, also popularly known as Nidhu babu; *Nidhu bābur ṭappā* is a form of song, Hindustani semi-classical in form but Bengali in language, that most Bengalis even today would have some idea of.

Ramnidhi Gupta's impress upon the culture of his time was much greater than that of the other *kabiẏāls*, singer-songwriters of whom there was a whole disparate bunch who flourished in Calcutta in an age of transition, in between what has of late come to be designated as the early modern and the colonial modern period in Indian historiography. The distinction made in the context of history writing between the early modern and the colonial modern is a political one, and Partha Chatterjee, following upon the work of Shulman, Subrahmanyam, and Rao, draws a clear line at 1830 between the two periods.[2] Economically, politically, and institutionally, the period after 1830, he maintains, consolidated into a recognizable shape many of the impulses and fluctuations of the preceding century, with the establishment of British power acquiring a governmentality, reach, and efficacy not possible in the earlier period. While that might be, it remains, however, that in the field of creative endeavour, especially in the theatre of the literary, it would be untenable to draw such a line with any degree of firmness, as a quick glance at the accomplishments of Derozio, who died in 1831, and the nebulous nature of those of

[2] Partha Chatterjee, 2008, *History in the Vernacular*, Delhi: Permanent Black, Introduction, p. 8.

Iswar Gupta, whose career had only just begun in the same year, will immediately show. Early modern themes were being transformed at this time under the pressure of colonial modernity in unexpected ways in the work of Iswar Gupta, while the parameters of Western aesthetics were firmly in place in the literary output of the man writing in English who preceded him—thus within the arena of the Indian modern, which must perforce include both contributions, the chronology of development from the early to the colonial modern is confused and interchangeable here, and does not flow in a linear progression of development from one to the other. Ramnidhi belonged to a period with a character distinctively its own, which should not be read in the light of developments in the later nineteenth century, but should be explored, rather, for possibilities 'not teleologically predetermined by the ascendancy of the colonial modern'.[3]

Significant markers of an age of transition, Nidhu babu's songs might be read as lyric poetry in their earliest incarnation in modern Bengal, love songs that sound a note of interiority uncommon till then in poetic composition. Bhabatosh Datta called Ramnidhi 'the first English-educated middle-class poet in Bengali literature', remarking, 'If the fundamental sign of the Renaissance is the discovery of self, then do we not find the first faint notice of it in Nidhu babu's songs? A particular feeling resonated in Nidhu babu's love songs, a feeling that was permeated with the mystery of the inner self. He set love free from the ties of *dharma* or *śāstra*'.[4] Ramnidhi produced his best work spanning the end of the eighteenth century and continuing well into the next as the pre-eminent poet and songwriter of his time. His childhood was spent in the Kumartuli area of Calcutta, where he picked up an adequate enough education to be able to spend the final invalid years of his long life (he was ninety-seven when he died) reading books in Awadhi and Sanskrit and Bengali and English, according to the testimony of Iswar Gupta.[5] English he is said to have learnt from a missionary as a child; this knowledge of English led to his service as a clerk with the East India Company, working in the collector, Mr

[3] Ibid., p. 9.

[4] Iswar Gupta in Bhabatosh Datta (ed.), 1998, '*Rāmnidhi gupter jīban carit*,' in *Kabijībanī*, pp. 8, 27.

[5] Ibid., p. 115.

Montgomery's office at Chhapra in present-day Bihar. Here he first learnt the Hindustani *ṭappā* mode, subsequently composing his own Bengali lyrics in this style.

Very famous in his lifetime, Nidhu babu was the only one of the songwriters of that age who published his songs in book form a couple of years before he died, apparently out of concern at the manner in which the songs were being changed or corrupted by their very popularity. *Gītratna* was published in 1837–8 and is the first compilation of Bengali *ṭappā* songs of their kind. In contrast, of the legions of *kabiyāls* dotting the map at this time there are barely any records. Both, however, followed the *kabi-gān*, roughly translatable as 'poet's songs', which had been organized in rural and urban Bengal for about roughly two centuries, the eighteenth and nineteenth, peaking in the period from the end of the eighteenth to the mid-nineteenth century in Calcutta, where it metamorphosed into an urban phenomenon known first as the *ākhṛāi* and then the 'half-*ākhṛāi*'. The *kabi-gān* as it existed before was chiefly concerned with the Radha–Krishna love story, and borrowed heavily from the *Baishṅab padābalī*; the first printed compilation of *kabi-gān*, the *Karuṇānidhanbilās*, was published in the name of Joynarain Ghoshal in 1813–15. Yet later, sung as it was in the urban contexts of the *ākhṛāi* and half-*ākhṛāi*, replete with satire, witticism, and ribaldry, its reputation came to incorporate debasement and corruption in contrast to the earlier transcendent impulse of devotion. In the newspapers of the time, these were referred to as '*śakher kabitā*' or '*kabitā-saṅgītsaṃgrām*', and *The Englishman* of 13 January 1837, referred to this type of poet as 'cobbetta wallah'. Apparently, it was only after Iswar Gupta's publications of the songs sung by these composers in 1853–5 in the *Saṃbād prabhākar*, which was the first effort made in that direction, that the performance began to be referred to as '*kabi-gān*', and the performer as '*kabi-wālā*'; the further compression into the term '*kabiyāl*' seems to be have been a later occurrence.[6]

Sung to the accompaniment of music and movement, these songs, originally composed for festivals and ceremonies in the countryside, turned into a sort of extempore performance in the houses of the nouveau riche where the element of competition between two opposing parties became the main attraction, along with the wit and linguistic

[6] Asitkumar Bandyopadhyay, *BSI*, Vol. 4, p. 49.

dexterity displayed by the songwriters. From the end of the eighteenth century onward, the *ākhṛāi* (which was also, after the coinage of its successor as the half-*ākhṛāi*, later referred to as the full-*ākhṛāi*) was sung by ten or twelve people together in two groups that rehearsed for a year before a public performance, settling on a consensual date for their performance/competition; on the day, whichever side's composition and singing was better won. The *ākhṛāi* was popularized at this time by Nidhu babu, who, along with his uncle Kuluichandra Sen, was responsible for reconstituting it in the mould of Hindustani classical vocal compositions. The leading families of Calcutta such as the Pathuriaghata Tagores, the Singha family of Jorasanko, the Basaks of Goranhata and the Shobhabazaar Ghosh's then all established their own groups of *ākhṛāi* singers, and Raja Nabakrishna Deb became one of its chief patrons.[7]

In 1832, Ramnidhi Gupta's principal disciple, Mohanchand Basu, invented the half-*ākhṛāi*, which established a question-answer form and reduced the complexity of its classical content, increasing its popularity, but in the opinion of the critics, degrading its character. These songs subsequently began to be perceived as 'low' by later literary historians, who spoke of the 'debasement' in their character due to the degeneration in the nature of both audience and patron, who belonged to a 'capricious and half-educated' new class created by the British presence in Bengal.[8] A footnote written by Sushil Kumar De, who used these adjectives in his well-known English treatise on the subject, *Bengali Literature in the Nineteenth Century*, however, painstakingly contradicts the conflation of the 'low' character of the verse with the 'low' origins of the audience:

> The suggestion [in Dinesh Chandra Sen's *History*, p. 697] that the low caste of the songsters shows that the institution was essentially for the amusement of the illiterate rustics who formed its chief audience, is hardly borne out by the facts. This form of entertainment obtained specifically in urban centres like Chandannagar, Chinsurah and Calcutta and most of the Kabiwalas were not rural rustics but men bred up in the cities.

[7] Arun Nag (ed.), 1991, *Satīk hutom pyañcār nakśā*, Calcutta: Subarnarekha, pp. 81–2, fn. 209.

[8] Sushil Kumar De, 1962, *Bengali Literature in the Nineteenth Century*, Calcutta: K.L. Mukhopadhyay, p. 278.

> Ram Basu, Haru Thakur, Nitai Bairagi and indeed a whole host of them lived in Calcutta or in the neighbouring cities. Kabi-poetry itself, if not completely urban, is, however, devoid of all stamps of rusticity.[9]

De had noted, in yet another footnote following the one quoted above: 'Kabi-poetry counted its votary amongst the lowest classes. Except Haru Thakur, Rasu and Narsimha, Ram Basu and a few others, the *kabi-wālās* belonged to the lowest social grades of a '*muci*' (shoemaker), a '*mayrā*' (sweetmeat-vendor), a '*chutar*' (carpenter), a '*feringi*' (half-bred Eurasian), a '*svarnakār*' (goldsmith), a '*tanti*' (weaver), etc. In this catholicity it resembles earlier Baisnabism itself'.[10] Yet in keeping with the conflicted character of this period, the exceptions mentioned by De could be multiplied until the statement itself is rendered meaningless. For apart from the four and a few others mentioned as exceptions in the above list, another well-known part-time *kabiyāl* in that period was Iswar Gupta, writing the lyrics for the group located at Bagbazaar, in an occupation known as that of the '*bañdhandār*' or wordsmith.[11] In this occupation he was joined also by Rangalal Bandyopadhyay, who was part of Chatu-babu and Latu-babu's group, this being someone who worked as an apprentice writer with him in the *Saṃbād prabhākar* and whose working life was spent in the British administrative services, while also being author of the first historical narrative verse tale explicitly fashioned in an 'English style' in 1858, the *Padminī upākhyān*.

Poetry of the People

While Rangalal's background was more conventionally '*bhadralok*' in the sense that the word came to embody in the nineteenth century,

[9] Ibid., p. 279.

[10] Ibid.

[11] 'When Iswar Gupta became the *bañdhandār* of the *dāñṛākabi* and Manmohan Basu accepted him as his guru and joined in the performances [*saṅgītsaṃgrām*] of the *dāñṛākabi* and the half-*ākhṛāi*, then Mohanchand Basu had grown old. We see that in the November of 1854, Iswar Gupta is writing songs for the half-*ākhṛāi* and an old and infirm Mohanchand is setting those in tune.' Asitkumar Bandyopadhyay, *BIS*, Vol. 4, p. 269. The term '*dāñṛākabi*' refers to the *kabiyāl* in the half-*ākhṛāi* performance who stands while singing.

Iswar Gupta lived a life that was far more fluidly contradictory in its politics. Traditionally a member of the intermediate upper castes, Iswar Gupta belonged to a class of administrators and professionals created in Calcutta by the exigencies of colonialism, whose life story could only have been thrown up by the paradoxical modernities which themselves also generated the unprecedented spaces occupied by the various *kabiyāls* of the time. Typically, it was Kaliprasanna Singha who captured the turmoil unforgettably in a passage worth quoting entirely:

> Reader! The *nabābī* era set like the sun in winter. Like the light appearing from behind the clouds, the might of the English began to grow greater. The tallest bamboos were uprooted from the root. In their stems, new bamboo dynasties began to take birth, nouveau-*munsī* [*Nabomunsī*], mister-merchant [*chire bene*], and small-fry oil-seller [*puṅte teli*] became kings. Sepoy guards, thick staffs and titled rajas began to go rolling down the roads, garbage dumps, and wastelands like *India rubber* shoes and *Śāntipur* striped scarves. Krishnachandra, Rajballabh, Mansingha, Nandakumar, Jagatseth and other big families began to get wasted; seeing this, the Hindu dharma, the pride of poets, the enthusiasm of knowledge, charity and dramatic performances began to run away from the country. Half-*ākhṛāi,* full-*ākhṛāi, pāñcali*s and *yātrā* groups began to come into existence. The youth of the city were divided up in groups given to drug addiction and inexcusable follies. Money flooded out the pride of ancestry. Raama Muddafarash, Keshta Bagdi, Pencho Mallik and Chuncho Sheel became the gang leaders of Calcutta's Kayasthas and Brahmins and the chief personages of the city. It was at this time that the half-*ākhṛāi* and full-*ākhṛāi* were created, and ever since, the city's biggest people took up the amusement of half-*ākhṛāi*. The most important unemployed babus of Shyambazaar, Rambazaar, Chak and Shanko became the gang leaders of individual half-*ākhṛāi* groups. Toadies [*mosāheb*], job-seekers [*umedār*], and the most wretched indigent groups in localities and households joined refined choir groups. Many obtained jobs thanks to the half-*ākhṛāi*. From the poorest grand daddy of *pūjārī* Brahmins onward, many became positively rich—acquiring two storied house, garden, livery and carriage in a matter of days.[12]

[12] Arun Nag (ed.) 1991, *Satīk hutom pyañcār nakśa*, p. 75. The word used here was '*Nabomunsī*' which means both 'new' *munsī* and refers also to Nabakrishna Deb, the munsī (teacher of Arabic and Persian) to Warren Hastings who became a raja. Two people who belonged to the '*bene*' and '*teli*' communities respectively and who were

The poor *pūjārī* Brahmin referred to here was Haru Thakur, who came from an impoverished background, acquiring substance and property later under the patronage of Nabakrishna Deb. Meanwhile, Rambazaar and Shyambazaar are still identifiable Calcutta localities, and Chak, according to Arun Nag's footnotes, refers to Bagbazaar or Shobhabazaar, while Shanko pertains to Jorasanko, where the famous half-*ākhṛāi* groups were based.

Jorasanko in Calcutta was also where Iswar Gupta came as a child; born in 1811, he moved to Calcutta after his father died, and standard biographies take care to mention that he was never formally educated, emphasizing instead his natural abilities in versification and song-writing, his keen memory, and sharp intellect. He was known to have composed poems and songs even as a child (Bankim says, in this context, quoting Pope: 'He lisped in numbers, for the numbers came'.) The next noteworthy biographical fact that follows is about his friendship with the Pathuriaghata Tagores, specifically Jogendramohan Tagore, who helped him to establish the *Saṃbād prabhākar* in 1831 when he was only nineteen. From this date till his death in 1859 at the untimely age of forty-seven, Iswar Gupta flourished as the pre-eminent poet and editor of Calcutta, publishing poetry regularly in the columns of his newspaper, composing songs for a *kabiyāl* group of Bagbazaar, collecting the songs and poems of the preceding era to create an unprecedented archive of literary gleanings, as well as commenting, in verse and prose, on most aspects of the new life of the Bengali people in the mid-nineteenth century.

Iswarchandra Gupta first began to collect and publish the songs and lives of the *kabiyāls* in 1853, bringing them out in the pages of the *Saṃbād prabhākar* in a series that continued till the year of his death. Whether he knew of Johnson's influential work, *Lives of the Poets*, or not, will remain a matter of conjecture, but a closer look at the full title of Johnson's 1781 work—*Prefaces, Biographical and Critical, to the Works of the English Poets*—shows that the underlying motivation in his own untiring work at collecting material on the lives of the poets

---

made 'rajas' by the British at this time were Naku Dhar and Kanta Nandy. See *Satik hutom*, pp. 77–9, fn. 204.

of Bengal was essentially similar.[13] The other source for such a project could well have been the Indo-Persian poetic *tazkiras*, which can be roughly described as collections of biographical sketches of writers and specimens of their verse. These were a type of heterogeneous, open group of texts in Mughal society that would have been widely available and therefore accessible to Iswar Gupta in the mid-nineteenth century, but once again, as with Johnson's work, it is unclear whether he had the requisite knowledge of Persian in order to have read any of these works—he certainly used both Persian and English in his poetry criticism with a knowledgeable air, but how far his actual reading went remains unclear.

In their publication in the pages of his newspaper, Iswar Gupta made no distinction whatsoever between the 'major' and 'minor' poets, publishing them serially in the newspaper he edited from 1853 onward. Although he had plans to print these in book form eventually, he was able to publish only one of these, on the poet Bharatchandra Ray, as a separate book in 1855.[14] It is Bhabatosh Datta, the twentieth-century editor who brought together the disparate materials on the *kabiyāls* published by Iswar Gupta in his newspaper in a collected edition in 1958, who makes the distinction between the *kabis* or poets and *kabi-wālās* or poetasters in the contents page of the book he called *Īśvarcandra gupta racita kabijībanī* [Lives of Poets Composed by Iswarchandra Gupta].[15] Datta makes a value judgment by placing Ramnidhi not among the *kabi-wālās*, but among the three poets who make it to the first list of *kabi*, after Bharatchandra Ray (1712–60) and Ramprasad Sen (1720–81). But it is only in the latter list of *kabi-wālās* that Haru Thakur appears, alongside Rasu Nrisingha, Nityananda Das Bairagi, Ram Basu, and Lakkhikanta Biswas. Apart

[13] Johnson's *Prefaces, Biographical and Critical, to the Works of the English Poets* (familiarly known as the *Lives of the Poets*), originally appeared between 1779 and 1781 in the format their title suggests: as prefatory material to a large collection of the works of around fifty poets. They were first collected together in 1781.

[14] Iswar Gupta (ed.), 1855, *Kabibar bhāratcandra rāy guṇākarer jīban-bṛttānta*, Calcutta: Prabhakar Press. Iswar Gupta had earlier published an anthology called *Kālikirtan* in 1833 that was a collection of Kali kirtans by Ramprasad Sen and others. A notice in the *Saṃbād prabhākar* in 1855 had declared his intention of a '*jīban carit*' on Ramprasad Sen, with songs and notes, but this project remained unfulfilled.

[15] Bhabatosh Datta (ed.), *Kabijībanī*, Contents page.

from these five *kabiyāls* included in Bhabatosh Datta's edition, Iswar Gupta also published in the *Saṃbād prabhākar* the songs of five more *kabiyāls*, Keshta Muci, Gojla Guin, Ramsundar Ray, Lalu Nandalal, and Balaidas Bairagi, thus taking the total list to ten. Bhola Maẏrā does not make the cut even in this extended list, though perhaps due to practical exigencies—Iswar Gupta's project was an ambitious and extended one, but it was cut short by his untimely death at the age of forty-seven in 1859.

Kabi-wālā, rather than *kabiyāl*, was the common term used for these men in the nineteenth century; *wala* is a common Hindi suffix used after the commodity dealt in by a man to denote his occupation—thus, just as the *dudh-wālā* sells milk, so the *kabi-wālā* sells poetry. It is both quality and commerce, then, that distinguishes between the two categories of poet and seller of poetry, *kabi* and *kabi-wālā*. The songs of the *kabi-wālās* were urban and city-based, dying out by the 1870s, when the nationalist high modern in the shape of a new race of educated men attempted to stamp out the last vestiges of these popular, 'vulgar' entertainments. There is confusion in the literary historical accounts about whether the change in form of the *ākhṛāi* of Nidhu babu to the half-*ākhṛāi* invented by his pupil Mohanchand Basu around 1832, seven years before his death, was welcomed or disdained by the older poet; while some accounts speak of the purist's disappointment and anger, others maintain he gave his consent to the new form.[16] The *ākhṛāi* had necessitated great craft and skill in the display of command over *rāga* and *tāla*; some of that intricacy remained in its successor, but the question-answer format now introduced added to its popularity to such an extent that *Hutom* commented, 'Whether the *yār* type of schoolboy or the seventy-two year old *invalid*, everybody was mad about the half-*ākhṛāi*'.[17] However, the idea that their populism had resulted in their degeneration was one that was also constructed by literary historians from the end of the nineteenth century onward till the age of Bhabatosh Datta; Iswar Gupta himself had, for instance, while valuing the poetry of Bharatchandra very highly indeed, nevertheless *not* made any such distinction explicit in his treatment of the works of the rest of the poets that he published in his newspaper.

[16] Asitkumar Bandyopadhyay, 1985, *BSI*, Vol. 4, p. 258.

[17] Arun Nag (ed.), 1991, *Satīk hutom*, p. 87.

Collecting the works of these 'illiterate' songwriters was a mission that involved hardwork and tireless effort—many of these people had very little status in society generally, coming as they did from the subaltern classes, as indicated by their names, and any verifiable information on their life or work would have been acquired with difficulty. The trouble also was that by the mid-nineteenth century, the middle and upper classes were undergoing a rapid gentrification; educated in the English style, if not always in English, they were moving away from the tastes and knowledge of their predecessors, so much so that Iswar Gupta wrote that a mere fifteen or sixteen years after Nidhu babu's death, society had moved on at such an alarming rate that 'Many say Nidhu, Nidhu, but what is that word Nidhu; that is, this Nidhu, is it the name of a song, of a tune, of a *rāga*, of a man, or of what? That remains unknown'.[18]

The new generation educated at the Hindu College from the second decade of the century onward was not inclined to patronize these old entertainments. In an article called 'Bengali Games and Amusements' written for the *Calcutta Review* of 1851 in what can only be termed today as in an anthropological spirit, an anonymous member of this class fulminated:

> Our enumeration of the amusements of the Bengalis would be incomplete, if we made no mention of the *Kabis*, which deserves a place on this list, not because of their intrinsic importance, but because of the vast influence they exert, and the great attractions they possess for nine-tenths of the people of Bengal. 'Kavi', in the original Sanskrit, means a poet: but how this honourable appellation came to be applied to a crew of half-witted poetasters and songsters, it is difficult to say. A band of *Kavis* or *Kavi-walas*, as they are oftener called, is composed of a number of songsters of different castes, leagued together under a leader, who gives his name to the association. The leader may be a Brahmin, a confectioner, or of any caste. The *animus* of the *kavis* is rivalry. Two bands under different leaders vie with each other in winning the applause of the audience. Their songs in the first instance celebrate the loves of Krishnā and Rādhā, or the praises of the bloody goddess, Kāli; but, these over, they indulge in songs of the most wanton licentiousness, and crown the whole with calling each

[18] Iswar Gupta, *Kabijībanī*, p. 115. However, Asitkumar Bandyopadhyay, in a footnote, credits this quotation to Ramnidhi's son Joygopal Gupta in the second edition of Ramnidhi Gupta's *Gītratna*, p. 14; see Bandyopadhyay, *BSI*, Vol. 4, p. 283.

> other bad names. So far for the matter; the manner of singing is one of which Young Bengal may well be ashamed. '*Kavis*' must be seen, heard, and tested in order to be known and appreciated. The houses of some of the rich Babus of Calcutta are annually the scenes of these disgraceful exhibitions. Others have got heartily tired of them, and have substituted the less barbarous, but not the less immoral *nātches*. But the *Kavis* are in high repute in the Moffusil; and women, from behind the screens, may be observed greedily devouring their licentious effusions.[19]

In this passage, the '*kavi-walas*' are listed under the 'amusements' of Bengal and the fall from the Sanskrit understanding of the term *kavi* is emphasized. (Remarkably, but perhaps expectedly, the use of the term *kavi* to mean 'poet' is not problematized here as it would be later in Bankimchandra's introduction to Iswar Gupta's poetry.) The class rather than caste of the leaders of these groups is jeered at; thus Bhola-maẏrā—who was referred to in Partha Chatterjee's play as the confectioner whose sweets the fly would not touch—would have been the confectioner referred to in the passage, while the Brahmin is equally a target of contempt alongside the confectioner. Given the well-known predilections of the class of reformist commentators (named as Young Bengal in the passage itself) to which the writer of this article—called Horatio Smith—seems to belong, it is the 'disgraceful exhibitions' and licentious content of the songs—rather than caste—which are the sore points with the writer.

It was this educated strata that Iswar Gupta was aiming his anthology at; unable to give up his deep love of and appreciation for the older style of song-writing and composition, he had obviously felt an urgent need to historically archive this material for the modern world that was already upon him. In his capacity as an anthologist of the *kabi-wālā* who occupies a subaltern space, however, Iswar Gupta himself is not subaltern but citizen—sufficiently close to the everyday world of the subaltern to incorporate their themes into his poetry, but in his capacity as historian, anthologist, editor, and journalist, very much a citizen poet, self-aware in his chosen modes of self-expression. In this incarnation, he was also the member of many different societies in Calcutta and its suburbs—the *Tattvabodhinī Sabhā*, the *Nīti*

[19] Horatio Smith, 'Bengali Games and Amusements', *The Calcutta Review*, January–June 1851, pp. 349–50.

Taraṅginī Sabhā of Taki, the *Nīti Sabhā* of Darjipara—as well as a member of school committees and literary societies.

This delineation of Iswar Gupta's place in history is closely allied to the citizenry—just as the *kabi-gān* of eighteenth-century Bengal belonged to the people in contradistinction to the *maṅgalkābya* that dominated courtly culture, Iswar Gupta's poetry too is well known today as a poetry of the people, their everyday habits and peculiarities, their food, manners, dress, and carriage. These, however, were not the vast majority of the people who belonged to the villages of Bengal for whom the *kabi-gān* had been composed, for this was, very specifically, a poetry of the city in a new category such as had not existed before. In this Iswar Gupta had no predecessors. The self as subject might have first attained lyric form in Ramnidhi Gupta, and had certainly been manifested before him in the devotional songs of Ramprasad, or even in the shorter poems of Bharatchandra, in all of which the older manuscript or *pāñcāli* format were partly being abandoned in lieu of metaphors and images taken from daily life, imparting a new materiality to these compositions.

The city, and the city's various localities, had been crucial to the composition of the half-*ākhṛāi* songs too, and the city was sometimes the subject matter of those songs, as it pervasively was in the satire of the urban performative skits known as *saṅg*. Nonetheless, it was in Iswar Gupta's verse that the city, for the first time, occupies centrestage in a manner that survived the test of time, often enduring epigrammatically as encapsulations of urban experience ('*Rete mośā, dine māchi, ei tāṛiye Kolketāy āchi*').[20] This poetry, or *khaṇḍa kabitā* (by which was meant fragments of poems, or shorter poems, to distinguish them from the longer narrative poems of the *maṅgalkābya*), was a new form with new content. It was given life, literally, by the modern exigencies of the spaces of its publication, which were frequently the blank columns or half columns in newspapers and journals that needed fillers, and it filled them up with material that related directly to the city that gave it birth.

[20] This couplet is attributed not to a poem but a saying by Iswar Gupta in Bankimchandra's introduction to the poet in 1885. Bankimchandra Chatterjee (ed.), 1995 (1885), *Īśvarcandra gupta-r kabitā saṃgraha*, Calcutta: De Book Store, College Street Publication Pvt Ltd, p. 7.

The Authenticity Argument or '*Kelā kā phul*'

Engaged, in 1885, in the task of editing a selection of Iswar Gupta's poems, Bankimchandra Chatterjee sought, right at the outset, to explain why he had embarked upon such a mission. In a deadpan tone, he announced, in the first sentence of his introduction to the volume, 'Whatever else Bengali literature lacks, it does not lack poetry. Nor is there any dearth of excellent poems—from Vidyapati to Rabindranath, many good poets have been born in Bengal and they have written many outstanding poems; in fact, if one must say anything, it has to be said that Bengali literature is somewhat afflicted by the excessive weight of sheaves of poetry. Then why increase that load by collecting the poetry of Iswar Gupta? Let me explain.' He continues,

> *Prabād āche ye, garib bāṅgālīr chele sāheb haiyā, mocār ghante atisaẏ bismita haiyāchilen. Sāmagrītā ki e? Bahu kashte pisīmā tāhāke sāmagrītā bujhāiyā dile, tini sthir karilen je, e 'kelā kā phul'. Rāge sarbāṅga jvaliyā yāy ye, ekhan āmrā sakalei mocā bhuliyā kelā kā phul bolite śikhiyāchi. Tāi āj Īśvargupter kabitā saṃgraha karite basiyāchi. Ār yei kelā kā phul baluk, Īśvargupta mocā balen.*

> [I have heard it said, that the son of a poor Bengali became a sahib and was utterly astonished at the sight of *mocār ghanta* [preparation made from chopped banana flower]—What is this thing here? When his aunt then took a great deal of trouble to explain what it was, he came to the conclusion that this was the '*kelā kā phul*' ['flower of the banana']. It suffuses me with rage that today we have all forgotten *mocā* and have learnt to say '*kelā kā phul*' instead. That is why I have started today to collect the poetry of Iswar Gupta. Whoever else might say '*kelā kā phul*,' Iswar Gupta says '*mocā*'.] [21]

This is, of course, inimitably Bankim. This apocryphal anecdote sets the tone of the discussion in an essay that became, subsequently, a benchmark in Bengali literary criticism, coining both a terminology

[21] Bankimchandra Chattopadhyay, *Īśvarcandra gupta-r kabitā saṃgraha*, p. 3. The Hindustani term, '*kelā kā phul*', is used here by Bankim as a sign of double deracination, signifying that Bengali man is twice removed from his culture—first not recognizing the substance itself, *mocār ghanta*, and then in not knowing the Bengali word for its ingredient.

and certain parameters of authenticity by which contemporary literature would be measured for some time to come. (Ironically, of all the poets of modern Bengal, if there was anyone who used a mixed language in his poetry, using words belonging to other languages rather than the original Bengali term, then that was Iswar Gupta, but that is an issue we will come to later.) In this essay, Bankimchandra used, for the first time in Bengali literary criticism, the yardstick of the '*khāñṭi Bāṅgālī*' [authentically Bengali/ pure Bengali] poet or work as a parameter of valuation and validation. Also of note is the fact that the paradigms set by Bankim in this essay remained the only ones by which Iswar Gupta has been assessed by every successive critic in the coming ages. Very rarely is any other yardstick other than that of the '*khāñṭi Bāṅgālī*' poet ever applied to Iswar Gupta by literary critics; how dependant they are on this formulation can be measured by the extreme instance of Brajendranath Bandyopadhyay, who quotes long passages from this essay no less than exactly *nine* times in the course of his short overview of the poet, or in Asitkumar Bandyopadhay's assertion (twice in the space of a single paragraph) that 'Fundamentally, Bankimchandra's criticism is the best analysis of Iswar Gupta's talent'.[22] More recently, Sudipta Kaviraj, in an article on 'The Self-Ironical Tradition in Bengali Literature', has also conformed to tradition by unhesitatingly endorsing Bankim's introduction as 'an excellently well judged criticism of Ishwarchadra (*sic*) Gupta's poetic works'.[23] The other indication of the axiomatic status of this essay is that it is used almost ubiquitously as an introduction to various editions of Iswar Gupta's poems, from the Manindrakrishna Gupta edition, to the *Basumati* edition, to the Kamalkumar edition, sometimes without any acknowledgement of the fact that the selection of poems presented is different from the original Bankim edition.[24]

[22] Brajendranath Bandyopadhyay, 'Iswar Gupta', SSC, pp. 5–64; Asitkumar Bandyopadhyay, *BSI*, Vol. 7, pp. 133–4.

[23] Brajendranath Bandyopadhyay, '*Īśvar guptā*', pp. 5–64. Sudipta Kaviraj, 2000, 'Laughter and Subjectivity: The Self-Ironical Tradition in Bengali Literature', *Modern Asian Studies*, Vol. 34, No. 2, May, p. 386.

[24] See *Īśvarcandra gupter granthābalī*, Calcutta, Basumati Sahitya Mandir, 1900). This edition included the poem '*Mānbhanjan*' when Bankim's introduction specifically says it has been excluded; thus the selection of poems here seems to follow Manindrakrishna, while the introduction remains Bankim's.

In a long essay that dealt with many different aspects of Iswar Gupta's writings, the core issue, as Bankim presented it, was that Iswar Gupta was a *khā̃ṇṭi Bāṅgālī* poet, and that is why he must be respected. Subsequently, eight years later, Akshaychandra Sarkar wrote a second piece, 'Hemchandra O Iswar Gupta' in the journal he edited, *Nabajīban*, which was then turned into a chapter in the book on the poet Hemchandra Bandyopadhyay that followed.[25] Suffice to say that, here, Akshaychandra used the same coinage—*khā̃ṇṭi*—repeatedly in the context of a construction of '*nijasva*' and '*parasva*' [ours and others'] elements in the literary aesthetic in order to valorize the authenticity of Iswar Gupta's verse in comparison with the later poet. The argument was premised on the category of something called 'Western' or, simply, 'English' literary convention that was perceived to be changing the way in which Bengalis were both reading and writing—a poet such as Iswar Gupta was held up in contrast to later poets formed by these 'foreign' paradigms as a standard bearer of the original, the old, the pure, all that was 'our own'. Chafing under colonial rule, the colonized subject composed a rhetoric of authenticity that belonged to no one but himself; no shadow of the British presence in India would be allowed to contaminate its aesthetic appreciation. The Indian modern was self-divided into the Western foreign inheritance brought in by the colonial modern, and the indigenous, personal traditions that were constituted in time immemorial—very strangely, Iswar Gupta is placed squarely in the latter category by both Bankim and Akshay Sarkar, who thus jointly initiate a move whereby he continued to be read as a byword of authenticity even by twentieth-century critics, who had no hesitation in endorsing Bankim's claim.

Brajendranath Bandyopadhyay had merely echoed Bankim in his summary, 'Iswarchandra is a genuine poet of Bengal (*khā̃ṇṭi Bāṅglā deser kabi*), that is why he is memorable for us', but Bishnu De brought his characteristic passion into the argument in his own terms, urging the Bengali reader, 'if we are to rediscover our ancestors today, a special importance needs to be accorded to Iswarchandra Gupta among those whose works we shall have to judge. And in

[25] I have dealt with that discussion in detail in Chapter 5.

that discovery, Bankimchandra will be our guide.[26] He then quotes Bankim's appellation, '*khāñṭi Bāṅgālī kabi*' and proceeds to dissect how individualism had destroyed the community-based social life of pre-colonial Bengal. Why was Iswar Gupta chosen especially to carry the burden of the authentic or *khāñṭi*? If it was because he incorporated everyday life and practice into his poems, then certainly his contemporaries such as Kaliprasanna Singha or predecessor such as Bhabanicharan Bandyopadhyay too would have qualified for consideration. From Akshaychandra onward, Iswar Gupta was also thought of as *khāñṭi* in some measure because of his love for his country, his passion for the indigenous. Yet none of these qualities are exclusive to him in his era, leaving us to conclude that the only reason Iswar Gupta was (and still is) considered a *khāñṭi Bāṅgālī* poet was because Bankimchandra said so. If we look closely at Bankimchandra's argument, however, we will see that the argument of authenticity was in fact premised upon a misreading, revealing more about his own project in the creation of a national literature for Bengal than illuminating us about the actual nature of Iswar Gupta's poetry.

The potency of this category of criticism in the conflicted arena of the Bengali cultural sphere can be understood when we see, in an essay written in 2005, the same term, *khāñṭi Bāṅgālī*, being used in proximity to the name of Iswar Gupta to certify the twentieth-century work of maverick cult figure and writer Kamalkumar Majumdar. In a discussion of Kamalkumar's place in Bengali literature, Raghab Bandyopadhyay quotes, in order to refute it, a comment by Sandipan Chattopadhyay, then a young *Krittibās* writer and an admirer of Kamalkumar, who had asked once, 'Can't an ultra-modern [*ati-ādhunik*] literature also have been born of the Western tradition in Bengal?' In consternation, Raghab Bandyopadhyay writes, apropos this suggestion:

> Kamalkumar, the absorbed reader of western literature, was overwhelmed by the literary music of Bharatchandra-Iswar Gupta-Ramprasad and the prose of Bankim-Krishnakamal-Sibnath Sastri-Keshabchandra. His plan was for a *khāñṭi bāṅglā* literature in a *khāñṭi bangla* language. In this scheme, western literature may play in some places like light and shade,

[26] Brajendranath Bandyopadhyay, 'Iswar Gupta', pp. 6–7. Bishnu De, 1997, *Bishñu de prabanda saṃgraha*, Vol.1, Calcutta: Dey's Publishing, p. 21.

> but not more than that. The guru is almost murdered by the disciple here. Sandipan has put us into a lot of trouble.[27]

The trouble, of course, both here and always, is caused by the problem of the Western inheritance in our modernity—a creative artist perceived to be immersed in Western traditions is a hollow man, for a modern idiom fashioned out of English reading can only result in a false renaissance, as Bishnu De notably maintained in the context of Madhusudan Datta.[28] On Iswar Gupta, De hawked the same line, privileging authenticity over and above all else, urging the modern Bengali poet to rediscover Iswar Gupta as an ancestor-saviour. Iswarchandra's 'indigenous way of constructing language' and his 'object-oriented ordinary healthy mind' were held up as 'tradition', against which the contemporary English-educated middle-class tastes of Bengalis shown to be as a 'corruption' into which 'we' have degenerated.[29] Raghab Bandyopadhyay is only articulating for the contemporary reader a felt emotion first put in place in the nineteenth century, that there is an indigenous inheritance that is 'native' to us and a colonial imposition that has forcibly made a place for itself in our literature. In 1912, the President of the Bangiya Sahitya Parishad said, in a speech to condole the death of Manmohan Basu, a literary figure of some importance in his time:

> One can see the unmistakable shadow of European influence in the tone, articulation and method of composition of the great Madhusudan, Dinabandhu, Hemchandra, Nabinchandra etc.; they have lit up our literature by their fusion of western and occidental embellishments, meanings, moods and characters in their compositions. Manmohan was an authentic Bengali [*khāṅṭi Bāṅgālī*]; he was a successor to Bharatchandra, Madanmohan and Iswarchandra's way of writing.[30]

[27] Raghab Bandyopadhyay, 2005, *Kamalkumār, kalkātā: pichutāner itihās*, Kolkata: Ananda Publishers, p. 18.

[28] This reading by Bishnu De is discussed in detail in the chapter 4(ii): 'Michael Madhusudan Datta and the Marxist Understanding of the Real Renaissance in Bengal'.

[29] Bishnu De, 1997, '*Sāhityer bhabishyāt*', *Bishñu de prabanda saṃgraha*, Vol. 1, Calcutta: Dey's Publishing, p. 21.

[30] Saradacharan Mitra, *Sāhitya parishad patrikā*, No. 2: 1319, pp. 66–7. Manmohan Basu (1831–1912) was a writer, journalist, novelist, song-writer, poet,

Such a reading—of a *khāṅṭi Bāṅgālī* literary tradition in opposition to a Western-influenced modernity brought in by colonial rule—is commonplace in the field of Bengali literary history, and these parameters were first put in place with relevance to the poetry of Iswar Gupta.

The irony of such a construction, however, is that it would have been quite meaningless to the practice of the very poet it was meant to endorse, as well as in the context of many who *preceded* him, among whom the most stellar example is that of Bharatchandra. Iswar Gupta's endorsement of this aspect of Bharatchandra, in the biography of the poet he published in 1855, had been unambiguous: 'This book contains many poems that have not been seen or heard by anybody, including many wonderful Sanskrit, Bengali, Hindi and Persian language poems. Readers who study these poems carefully will be wonderstruck by the extraordinary gift and scholarship of Bharatchandra.'[31] Bharatchandra self-consciously used Hindi, Persian, and Sanskrit indiscriminately as and when he needed to, sometimes even within a single poem, as we have seen. Iswar Gupta too, at his most unselfconscious moments, had a voracious appetite for words from different languages, using the most appropriate word in contemporary usage in his verse. Unselfconscious because, unlike Bharatchandra, Iswar Gupta did not coin a term such as '*yabanīmiśāl*' to justify his hybrid practice, and could even, as we have seen, be critical of his admired predecessor for its excessive use. Nevertheless, he seems to have shared Bharatchandra's belief '*ye hauk se hauk bhāshā kābya ras lāye*' [let language be what it will be taking the *rasa* of poetry], proceeding, like a magpie, to bring to his verse's nest many disparate usages from different languages in order to construct a homely and earthy poetry of the everyday.[32] Homely is a term advisedly used, for Akshaychandra had said that Iswar Gupta's poetry was like fish curry, an everyday but indispensable item in a Bengali meal, unlike the English-inspired cutlet, an analogy that seemed to draw upon Bankim's initial remark, in his essay on Iswar Gupta, that

---

and playwright, but above all, well known as a nationalist. He was one of the main organizers of the Hindu Mela.

[31] Cited in Brajendranth Bandyopadhyay (ed.), *SSC*, Vol. 1, p. 13.

[32] Quoted in Alok Ray (ed.) 2009, *Īśvarcandra gupter śreshṭha kabitā* [*Best Poems of Iswarchandra Gupta*; from now on, *IGSK*], Calcutta: Bharabi, p. 8.

it would not do to forget our native selves and for 'people countrywide to be turned into the third edition of the Jones's and the Gomes's', that is why we must read Iswar Gupta.[33] This irritation with an abject mimicry of the white man, it is worth remarking here, is a most potent and oft-repeated trope in Iswar Gupta's own satirical poetry, such as most famously, of course, in the lines '*katarūp sneha kari, deśer kukur dhari/ bideśer ṭhākur pheliyā*' [throwing away the foreign god, I make the object of my affection the country dog] or again in the poem '*Iṅgrājī nababarsha*': '*Dhanya re botolbasi dhanya lāl jal /dhanya dhanya bilāter sabhyatār bal*' [Bless those who live by the bottle, bless the red water / Bless most of all England's civilizing power].[34]

The irony of Bankimchandra's reading of Iswar Gupta as a hallmark of the 'pure Bengali' poet, of course, is inherent even in the quotation where '*mocā*' is being replaced by its Hindi equivalent, '*kelā kā phul*', to show the distance travelled, the fall from one's own traditions. For Iswar Gupta himself, unaware of how Bengali literary criticism would organize itself in the years following him, had no such qualms, and would, one suspects, have happily called '*mocā*' '*kelā kā phul*' if it answered his need for a witticism or a pun, writing poems called '*Eṇḍāoyālā tapsya māch*' or '*Sab hyā phāk*' or '*Duel yuddha*' without apology or explanation. It was not only the title of a poem that signified the use of a mixed language; poems on war such as 'Victory at Kanpur' had lines such as '*Yata pāo, kheye sherry,/ yata pāo kheye sherry, hoye merry,/ pātra hāte dhore / nece nece mukhe bala, "hip hip hurre"*' ['Have as much sherry as you can/ and be merry with glass in hand / Dance about and sing and shout, "Hip hip hurray"']. One interesting instance a few lines later sees him using the English phrase 'keeping rank' in a Bengali line that even follows English syntax, saying, '*Rakhilen rank God, thank Lord, Colin Campbell / Sādhu sādhu shadhu tumi, bipaksher śel*' ['God has kept rank, the Lord we thank, for

[33] Bankimchandra Chatterjee, *Īśvarcandra gupta-r kabitā saṃgraha*, p. 4. (A further irony needs to be noted here—what the Indian understands as the cutlet bears no resemblance at all to the English use of the word, to denote a neck-chop of mutton or lamb. Bankim means, instead, the flat, fried, fish or meat fillet preparation made from minced meat that it means in India to this day.

[34] '*Ingreji Nababarsha*', 1900, in *Īśvarcandra gupter granthabali*, Calcutta: Basumati Sahitya Mandir; henceforth *Basumati* edition, p. 144.

Colin Campbell / Good, good, you are good, the enemy's hell'],[35] or a Hindustani word such as '*joru*' is used with virulent prejudice: '*Garu joru labe keṛe cāñpdeṛe yata neṛe / ei belā sāmāl sāmāl*' ['Cows, wives, will be taken by those bearded Muslims / This is the time to take care, take care'].[36] In the *Hitprabhākar*, a character depends entirely upon Hindi to give vent to his rage, saying angrily to the doorman (by profession usually Hindustani-speaking):

Ko-hyāy, ko-hyāy, ābi, hiñyā āo, śālo
Nekālo nekālo, esko, juti-se nekālo
Gedhaṛ hārāmjād, kāhāko bajjāṯ
Hāmārā sāmne āke, kahe aysā bāṯ.

[Who's there, who's there, now come here *sala*
Throw him out, kick him out, and beat him with your shoe
Bastard's a jackal, rascal from some place
How dare he say such things in my presence?][37]

After this, therefore, when Bankim returns, at the end of his long introduction, to the same motif, and reiterates, 'Iswar Gupta articulates the country's thoughts in the country's language. There is no *kelā kā phul* in his poems', Bankim seems completely off the mark, at least in the fact of usage of Hindi words in Iswar Gupta's Bengali poetry, and, perhaps more crucially, as regards the perceived 'authenticity' of his verse as well.

What is a Poet?

It was only in the third and last section of his introduction to Iswar Gupta's poetry, however, that Bankimchandra finally came to the core issue of the poetic. 'Iswar Gupta is a poet (*kabi*). But what sort of poet?' was the question asked directly, right at the start. The answer was unambiguous. Iswar Gupta was not a *kabi* in the modern sense of the term, that is—and here Bankim uses the English word—Iswar Gupta was not a '*poet*'. A very interesting split is created here between the high literary canon and the popular and low usage current at

35 '*Kānpurer yuddhe jaỳ*', *Basumati* edition, p. 226.
36 '*Kābuler yuddha*', ibid., p. 228.
37 Quoted in Asitkumar Bandyopadhyay, *BSI*, Vol. 7, p. 125.

the time. Discussing the disjunction between the old and the new sense of the word *kabi*, Bankim says that in ancient times, in the *shastras*, any man of knowledge was referred to as *kabi*, whether he was a writer of theosophy or astrology. The meaning of the term has changed over time, and at the start of the century it also referred to performers in singer-songwriter teams, confronting each other in the contest known as *kabir loṛāi*; now, however, it is used in the sense of what the English call a *poet*. Interestingly, he uses a colloquial Sanskrit expression to explain this sense of the usage: '*Kābyeshu Māghaḥ kabiḥ Kālidāsaḥ*' ('among poets, [the greatest are] Magha and the poet Kalidasa'). The distinction Bankim makes, therefore, is between the great poetry of India, epitomized by Magha and Kalidasa at the apex of Indian literary accomplishment, where the word is used in the English sense of the term, of 'pure poetry' so to speak, as opposed to the ancient pre-modern sense of writing or to the current debased sense of song. But nowadays, he continues, '*kabi* means poet, although there is a great deal of confusion about "the poetic" [*kabitva*]. Now, the poetic is that which in English is called *Poetry*. This is the common usage, so we are compelled to judge whether or not Iswar Gupta is poet in this sense.'[38]

Why was Iswar Gupta not a poet in the sense that Kalidasa was a poet? Because, Bankim said, 'he did not have the ability to give form to the indistinct, soft, serious and high aspects of the human soul; he could not articulate the inarticulate; he was not skilled in the creation of beauty'. This conception of poetry, of course, was indisputably derivative of the Romantic notion of poetry, echoing as it does Wordsworth's idea of the poet in the preface to the *Lyrical Ballads* of 1815, or Keats's equally well-known pronouncement that 'Beauty is Truth and Truth Beauty...'. Bankimchandra then creates a canon of 'true poets' for the Bengali reader, in which Madhusudan, Hemchandra, Nabinchandra, and Rabindranath are mentioned among those following Iswar Gupta; preceding him far into antiquity was a list that ran backwards in time, from Bharatchandra (who created Hiramalini), Kasiram (who described the abduction of Subhadra), Krittibas (who wrote of the slaying of Taranisen), and Mukundaram (who made Phullora), to the resonant tones of the Baishnab poets.

[38] *Īśvarcandra gupta-r kabitā saṃgraha*, p. 22.

Iswar Gupta himself, however, had been quite clear in his own mind about what poetry was, writing a poem about it called 'Poetry' [*Kabitā*]. Reputed to have translated Cowper and Campbell's poetry for his paper, Iswar Gupta's notion of poetry was not tied to the Romantic notion as Bankim's was; rather, in this poem, he envisioned the form of poetry literally, personified as the female form of the Goddess of Wealth. Personification here, however, does not work in the idealized manner of Romantic poetry, but is closely allied in spirit to the traditional North-Indian devotional song, invoking the form, raiment, and ornamentation of the gods in loving detail. Just as a traditional Hindustani classical *bandish* in the *rāga Kedār* may picture a youthful Krishna with the women of Vrindavan around him as pearls strung around the neck—'*Kanha re nanda nandana, karama niranjana, he dukhbhanjana / kantha bani motiyan ki mala, payrita modita bhai braja bala re...*'; or other lyrics might describe the yellow or *pitambar* garments of the god or of the attributes of the god and his mercy pictured in the aspect of the god, similarly, in this poem, Poetry is shown in the orange-yellow (*kamalā*) robes associated with Lakshmi, bedecked in the jewels that evoke *rasa*, descending upon the tender heart (*kamal-hṛde*) of the poet, the thirty-six *rāginis* and six *rāgas* as her attendants in tow. Alliteration, *alankār* or ornamentation, similes and comparisons are her ornaments, while her body is swathed in the bluest of blue (*nīlāmbarī*) that is the appearance of feeling. The last quartet ends with a plea from the poet for her to come into his heart and dance awhile so he can forsake all unhappiness at her manifestation.

Immediately following his assertion that at least Iswar Gupta could be relied upon to say '*mocā*' and not '*kelā kā phul*', Bankim had recounted a memory that is instructive about his project of the evaluation of Iswarchandra's poetry. Sitting in a house by the Bhagirathi River on a rainy moonlit night, watching the starlight play upon the waves, he had once felt like reading some poetry to enjoy the moment. English poetry would not do the job—the Bhagirathi River had no equivalence in the English tradition. Kalidasa and Bhavabhuti too felt very distant to him at that moment. Madhusudan, Hemchandra, Nabinchandra, he says, were not satisfying. At that moment, a fisherman on the river sang out, and hearing that song, his heart was satiated; the mind was in tune with the moment, and suddenly all aspects of that moment seemed to become one's own.[39] This memory leads then to a reflection upon the element of distance, of the 'otherness' of modern Bengali literature, which 'today is ceremonially and solemnly installed upon the beauteous road of progress and novelty'. However, there is a problem—this literature might be beautiful, but it does not feel as if it is one's own. And that is why, he says, he has embarked upon the collection of Iswar Gupta's poems. For in them, 'everything is genuinely Bengali [*khāṅṭi bāṅgla*]', and Iswar Gupta is the poet of Bengal [*bāṅglār kabi*]. Through Iswar Gupta one leaves the high classical epic simile behind and partakes of the pleasure of '*paush-pārbaṇ*' and '*piṭhā-puli*'. These poems are 'the *prasād* at the altar of the mother deity herself'.[40]

A number of displacements occur here in this argument. The folk song of the fisherman, whose lines he quotes as '*sādho āche mā mane / Durgā bale prāṇ tyajiba / Jāhnabī-jībane*' [My heart's desire, mother / Is to die uttering the name of Durga / On this river (of life)], belongs specifically to an oral tradition of boatmen's songs known as the *Bhātiyāli*. Without going into the history and etymology of such folk songs, it should be obvious that its idiom is certainly not that which is to be found in the poetry of Iswar Gupta. Even a cursory glance at the short poems Iswar Gupta wrote in a modern age of transition under the enormous pressure of rapidly changing urban metamorphoses will show how his poetry belongs completely to the opposite milieu of the boatman, how his individual poems of satire and sharpness, mocking the pretensions of an ambitious commercial imperialist ethos in the city, exist as the obverse of the time immemorial frozen in the boatman's song floating out to Bankim from the middle of the eternal river. The primary emotion animating Bankim here is nostalgia for a lost arcadia symbolized by a village boatman; ironically, in Iswar Gupta's own poetry, which deals with the material everyday world of the present, there is no simlar nostalgia for the irretrievable mood of the past.

[39] Bankimchandra Chatterjee, *Īśvarcandra gupta-r kabitā saṃgraha*, p. 34.

[40] Ibid.; '*poush-pārbaṇ*' refers to both a poem by Iswar Gupta and the winter month of Poush and the festivities associated with it, and '*piṭhā-puli*' are the traditional Bengali sweets made at the time.

The further irony of Bankimchandra's essay on Iswar Gupta also resides in the fact, as many commentators have noted, that Bankim was actually not advocating this poetry as something to be emulated, even desired, in the modern age. Modern Bengali poetry, Bankim had concluded, with its progress, its novelty, its Arcadian beauty, often feels as if it is not one's own. In contradistinction, Iswar Gupta is a 'real' Bengali poet. Such poets, he crucially goes on to say, are not born anymore; further, '*janmiyā kāj nāi*'—there is no use for such poets anymore. 'Unless Bengal turns again towards decline, such *khāṅṭi Bāṅgālī* poets cannot be born. We do not want to reject *Bṛttasaṃhār* [an epic poem by Hemchandra Bandyopadhyay] for '*Poush-pārban*'. But still, there is a pleasure a Bengali gets from *Poushparban* that is not there in *Bṛttasaṃhār*. It will not do for us to leave that behind entirely.'[41] There is no doubt in his mind that the world of Iswar Gupta is dead. Not only is it dead, but that, unless we want to regress ('*abanati*' is the Bengali word used) into that condition again, it should remain dead. However, there are elements of pleasure in that world which Iswar Gupta encapsulated in his poems that we must not let go of—they reach out to us in places untouched by the edifice of modern Bengali literature.

Most of Iswar Gupta's poetry, in fact, he says later in the introduction, 'was in the nature of ribbing, or "*iyārki*", although this was not the joking around of the monkeys inhabiting modern society, but a hugely talented great soul's *iyārki* or teasing; thus God himself is not spared in the lines '*Kahite nā pāra kathā—ki rākhiba nām / tumi he āmār bābā hābā ātmārām*' (You cannot speak in words—what shall I call you / You are my Father, Idiot Soul of mine). This sort of ribbing, Bankim maintains, 'is not something we want to let go of, it is a rare commodity in Bengali literature. Having found such a gem, we do not want to lose it; our only disappointment is that so much talent ended up merely in this'.[42] This identification of a special quality in a gem of a line such as the one quoted, however, seems to have been a later discovery that somewhat alleviated the severity of the opinion presented in his English essay, 'Bengali Literature', written when he was younger. There Bankim had, in fact, been even more categorical in his

41 *IGKS*, p. 4. For the poem '*Poush-pārban*', see Ibid., p. 82.

42 Ibid., p. 8.

dismissal of the older poet on the premises of a disqualification of the 'rude' from the literary, calling him a 'poetaster', saying, 'Of the higher qualities of a poet he possessed none, and his work was extremely rude and uncultivated. His writings were generally disfigured by the grossest obscenity. His popularity was chiefly owing to his perpetual alliteration and play upon words'.[43]

The argument against Iswar Chandra qualifying as a real 'poet', then, was fundamentally based upon the premise of being unable to allow the proliferation of low taste. This was made clear when Bankimchandra lamented the two things most lacking in Iswar Gupta's compositions—good taste and high aims. Bankimchandra had admitted that 'by leaving out the indecency which was the chief fault of Iswar Gupta's poetry, I have Bowdlerized his poetry and weakened it, but there is no choice in the matter .... At the state in which the Bengali reader and writer was at the time, it was impossible that the poems could be allowed to retain any element of indecency'.[44] Here, Bankim devoted around six long paragraphs to the question of obscenity (*aślīlatā*) in Iswar Gupta's poetry, apart from returning to the issue time and again in other places in the introduction as well. Relying frequently on notions of the impermissible in good writing that were Victorian in tone but which could also have come to him from Sanskrit poetic convention, he explained anew that obscenity was to be judged in the context of place, time, and subject (*sthān kāl pātra*), minutely analysing the nature of impropriety in Iswar Gupta's verse, absolving it in some places and indicting it in others.[45]

[43] Bankimchandra Chatterjee, 1998, 'Bengali Literature', J.C. Bagal (ed.), *Bankim rachanavali*, Vol. 3, Calcutta: Sahitya Samsad, p. 106.

[44] IGKS, p. 26.

[45] Sibaji Bandyopadhyay points out: 'Bankimchandra's understanding of the conceptual category of blemish or *dosh* in good writing may have been inherited from taxonomic orders proposed centuries before. Bharat's *Natyashastra*, written before the commencement of the Christian era, marks the deployment of '*asabhyam*' or '*grāmyam*' words as a primary fault, while the early 9th century AD rhetorician Baman conflated *grāmyam* with *ashleel*. Thus the modern critical approach to works produced in the colonial period is often in keeping with a 'grammar of appreciation' which predates the modern.' Comments on my paper titled 'Poet of the Present: (Mis) Reading Iswarchandra Gupta (1812–1859) and the Nature of the Bengali Modern,' Conference on New Cultural Histories, CSSSC, 6 January 2010.

Not every explanation, however, is above board and to be taken at face value. Criticizing Iswar Gupta's attitude towards women, who were always objects of satire, Bankim maintained that he edited out only those poems—conceding that this meant almost all the poems that referred to women—which used unacceptable, ugly terms of abuse and slang in the context of women, such as in the poem '*Mānbhanjan*'.[46] However, a close study of the poem itself reveals that Bankim is being disingenuous, and should not be taken at his word. A careful reading of the poem reveals no such lewd usage; rather, the situation in the overly long poem, where a man woos his wife by a river on a moonlit night, has much imaginary disrobing and viewing of bodily parts such as breasts and thighs, her ultimate capitulation, their union and return home at dawn, and it seems self-evident that Bankim's famous intolerance of impropriety would have kicked in, and he must have taken exception to the explicit detail rather than the stated reason of disallowing any linguistic insult to womanhood. It also remains to be noted that Iswar Gupta himself was no stranger to 'Bowdlerization', omitting sections from the songs of Haru Thakur when he published them in the *Prabhākar* because he felt they were 'filled with such dreadful (*jaghanya*), contemptible (*ghṛṇita*), obscene (*aśrābya*) and unutterable (*abācya*) words that it is unadvisable to print them under any circumstance.'[47] He goes on to criticize the old times when 'very important and well respected personages such as Maharaja Krishnachandra Ray Bahadur and Nabakrishna Bahadur' would be 'extremely pleased' and 'greatly delighted' to hear this sort of vocabulary in front of relatives, friends, and the general public, finding such behaviour both reprehensible and puzzling.[48]

Svabhāb-kabi Iswar Gupta

If cultural authenticity was one of the most important premises underpinning any appreciation of Iswar Gupta's poetry in the nationalist

[46] Bankimchandra, *IGKS*, p. 10.

[47] Iswar Gupta, 'Haru Thakur', in Santikumar Dasgupta and Haribandhu Mukhati (ed.), 1974, *Iswar gupta rachanabali*, Vol. 1, (Calcutta: Dattachowdhury and Sons), p. 190. This was first published in the *Saṃbād prabhākar*, 15 December 1854.

[48] Ibid.

generations, then the other term that was repeatedly invoked in relation to him was that of the *svabhāb-kabi*. Iswar Gupta was called *svabhāb-kabi* or 'natural poet' because of his status as a self-taught autodidact whose natural talent for song composition saw him associated with the amateur *kabyiāl* groups, while an equally self-acquired way with words resulted in his publishing his own short poems on a variety of topics in the paper he edited for almost all of his adult life, the *Saṃbād prabhākar*. These latter were emblems of a new cultural form, the *khaṇḍa-kabitā* or individual short poem, through the medium of which Iswar Gupta is credited with having captured the *zeitgeist* of the new Bengali urban culture of the first half of the nineteenth century. The subject matter of the poems ranged over a variety of subjects, among which the most popular and best remembered are those that parodied Calcutta society and its foibles, poking fun at subjects as diverse as Queen Victoria and her loyal Bengali subjects on the one hand, and Vidyasagar's campaign for widow remarriage on the other. Although a contemporary writer such as Bhabanicharan Bandyopadhyay had short poems in the form of *khaṇḍa-kabitā* inserted in the text of *Nababābubilās* (1823), and Bharatchandra too had written short poems which Iswar Gupta himself had included in his life of that poet, Iswar Gupta was certainly the first to publish short poems on a diversity of political, social, and religious issues in a sustained manner over a long period of time in the pages of his newspaper, thus making him the first modern poet of the city in the Bengali language.

The category of the *svabhāb-kabi* is an important one in any understanding of the poet Iswar Gupta, for it explains not only his minor status in the canon but also provides an insight into the secondary scaffolding upon which critics have based their treatment of this poet. A *svabhāb-kabi* is a poet of the moment, perceived to compose songs or poems spontaneously and ephemerally—while the dexterity of the performance is much appreciated by a contemporary audience, nothing long lasting is thought to have been achieved for posterity. Iswar Gupta was a poet who was very quickly put aside by his contemporaries after his death, as they did not share his sensibility or his style. In a famous sonnet written a few years after his death, Madhusudan Datta (ironically the man who put in place the poetic conventions that swept away the space for poets such as Iswar Gupta) wrote lamenting this forgetfulness, where he said, 'Just as the short-lived stream runs its path in the rains—briefly, and with a violent resonance—to the lake; by the mockery of the gods, have you too suffered a similar fate in all of this good Bengal, learned *Baidya*?'[49]

It is not surprising, then, that when Buddhadeva Bose, writing an essay called '*Rabīndranāth o uttarsādhak*' [Rabindranath and his Successors] in 1952, begins with a gloss on the word *svabhāb-kabi*, he has forgotten about Iswar Gupta entirely, beginning his article with the sentence: 'In Bengali, the word *svabhāb-kabi* was probably first used in the context of Gobindachandra Das', followed by description of the entity itself:

> In this sense, 'natural poet' [*svabhāb-kabi*] means not just this, that he is naturally a poet—you do not, after all, need to actually say that of any poet; it means that sort of poet who is essentially heartfelt, who has faith in enthusiasm, that is, someone who writes whenever and whatever he feels like writing, but never reflects on what he writes, someone in whose mind the heart and the head are divorced. It is, of course, true that without the heat of enthusiasm, poetry is nothing, but if that enthusiasm is to be reached to the mind of the reader, one cannot be its slave, it has to be overtaken and disciplined. Where this power to discipline or to organise is missing, that is the place which can be labelled, in a special sense, as 'poetic naturalness' [*svabhāb kabitva*].[50]

This description of Gobinda Das as *svabhāb-kabi* encapsulates exactly the feeling behind the nomenclature, and is useful in understanding the analysis of Iswar Gupta as a *svabhāb-kabi*, for it emphasizes the spontaneous element in his work for which he is remembered. Sushilkumar De, the sternest of his critics, said, 'The chief confirmation of Iswar Gupta's poetry came from the ordinary people of that time—the ordinary Bengali of this multi-hued Bengal (*raṅgabharā baṅgadeśer sādhāraṇ bāṅgālī*). Consequently, the poet's mind too was the mind of the ordinary Bengali person.'[51] Ironically, yet perhaps intentionally, De is here paraphrasing Iswar Gupta himself when he uses the phrase '*raṅgabharā baṅgadeś*'. Iswar Gupta's famous line, '*Eto bhaṅga baṅgadeś tabu raṅgabharā*', familiar to most Bengalis to this day, is also quoted

[49] Michael Madhusudan Datta, 1993, 'Iswarchandra Gupta', *Madhusudan rachanabali*, Calcutta: Sahitya Sansad, p. 176.

[50] Buddhadeva Bose, 2007, '*Rabīndranāth o uttarsādhak*', *Sāhityacarca*, Calcutta: Dey's Publishing, p. 102.

[51] Sushilkumar De, Preface to *Kabijībanī*, p. iii.

to great effect by the thin bespectacled playwright character in Ritwick Ghatak's 1961 film, *Komal Gāndhār*.

Poets who are immensely popular among ordinary readers of their time, as well as poets whose phrases survive epigrammatically in common speech, are not usually those valued highly by future readers or by other poets. Kipling is the example, of course, that comes immediately to mind, and Kipling's reception by Eliot was much like Bankim with Iswar Gupta in nineteenth-century Calcutta. The formidable T.S. Eliot wrote an introduction to a selection of the verse of Rudyard Kipling in 1941; and as Bankim did, Eliot too asked, right at the start, 'whether Kipling's verse really is poetry; and, if not, what it is'. His summation of the problem with reading Kipling is instructive if read with Iswar Gupta in mind:

> The starting point for Kipling's verse is the motive of the ballad-maker; and the modern ballad is a type of verse for the appreciation of which we are not provided with the proper critical tools. We are therefore inclined to dismiss the poems, by reference to poetic criteria which do not apply. It must therefore be our task to understand the type to which they belong, before attempting to value them: we must consider what Kipling was trying to do and what he was not trying to do. The task is the opposite of that with which we are ordinarily faced when attempting to defend contemporary verse. We expect to have to defend a poet against the charge of obscurity: we have to defend Kipling against the charge of excessive lucidity. We expect a poet to be reproached for lack of respect for the intelligence of the common man, or even for deliberately flouting the intelligence of the common man: we have to defend Kipling against the charge of being a 'journalist' appealing only to the commonest collective emotions. We expect a poet to be ridiculed because his verse does not appear to scan: we must defend Kipling against the charge of writing jingles. In short, people are exasperated by poetry which they do not understand, and contemptuous of poetry which they understand without effort....[52]

The problem of evaluation in both cases, we see then, is very similar, and Eliot, like Bankim, even while attempting to salvage something of value from the corpus of the earlier poet's works, confessed to

[52] T.S. Eliot (ed.), 1941, *A Choice of Kipling's Verse*, London: Faber and Faber, p. 6.

failure, concluding, 'I confess therefore that the critical tools which we are accustomed to use in analysing and criticising poetry do not seem to work; I confess furthermore that introspection into my own processes affords no assistance…'.[53] The commonality in the failure of Bankim and Eliot here lies, it seems, in the domain of the high modern; both are traditionalists, intent upon retrieving the authentic voice of an age preceding their own, yet both are frustrated in that attempt by the very constitution of their selves as representatives of a colonial and imperial high modernity that was fundamental to their temperaments. The interesting parallel between these two high priests of two flourishing high cultural spheres, surprisingly similarly situated within their place in their own literary worlds, lies—despite Eliot's self-reflexive modernism—in the commonality of their agreement, their confluence of tone and temper, their essential agreement on the value of literature and the literary.

In his English book, *Bengali Literature in the Nineteenth Century*, De had summed up Iswarchandra as a 'fluent and facile versifier' who 'wrote too copiously to write well, but [whose] journalistic diction was adequate for his pedestrian verses'.[54] In this general opinion De was not alone. His thoughts acquired a further lease of life when they were reiterated by Sukumar Sen, the pre-eminent literary historian of his time, a few decades later:

> At the start of the nineteenth century, periodical publications opened up a window into the Bengali literary field through which fresh breezes blew in. Bengali prose learnt to stand on its own feet with the help of periodicals. Bengali poetry too found a sign of a new path. The person in whose work this sign first found a response was Iswarchandra Gupta (1812–1859). This sign was a sign of the times. But Iswarchandra Gupta was not ready to follow this sign, so he was unable to show the way for this new poetry. However, he understood at least this much, that a repetition of the older poetic forms might colour the new poetry, but it could not awaken feeling (*ras jāgite pāre nā*).[55]

[53] Ibid.

[54] Sushilkumar De, 1962, *Bengali Literature in the Nineteenth Century*, Calcutta: K.L. Mukhopadhyay, pp. 572–3.

[55] Sukumar Sen, 1970 (1943), 'Nineteenth Century', *Bāṅglā Sāhityer Itihās*, vol. 2, Calcutta: Eastern Publishers, p. 121.

Sen then goes on to point out that it is as an anthologist that Iswarchandra is to be the most praised, and that 'the modern aspect of his literary cultivation is best expressed in his historical sense .... It is this historical sense that impelled him toward the collection of the lives and works of the poets Bharatchandra and Ramprasad and the *kabi-wālās* Lalu Nandalal and others'.[56] This historical sense, then, was understood by both Iswar Gupta in 1855 and his commentator Sukumar Sen in 1943 as history in the sense of historical archiving, not in the sense of literary tradition. The modern understanding that history meant the creation of an archive available for public consumption had been a new awareness at the time Iswar Gupta was compiling his lives of the poets, but already he was an energetic proponent of this new understanding. His achievement in chronicling the lives and works of the early modern poets of Bengal was necessarily an imperfect achievement, as the subject matter was not only scattered but already almost forgotten; nonetheless, what he attempted in this work has been compared by Bhabatosh Datta to Dineshchandra Sen's seminal project, *Baṅgabhāshā o sahitya* (1896)—because both Dineshchandra and Iswar Gupta had used original manuscript material in the form of *puñthi*s as primary sources in pursuance of their objectives.[57] In this capacity, therefore, like Sen, Iswar Gupta was working as a historian, actively involved in the construction of an archive that would be constitutive to modern public life, a citizen poet compiling information of value to all citizens of a putative nation that had not yet been imagined into political being.

[56] Ibid., p. 123.

[57] Bhabatosh Datta, '*Dineścandra o itihās-carcār pratham yug*' in *Viśvā-bhāratī Patrikā*, Year 23: No. 2, *Kartik-Poush* 1373 [Nov–Dec 1966], pp. 128–9.

(ii) Poet of the Present: The Material Object in the World of Iswar Gupta

By 'modernity' I mean the ephemeral, the fugitive, the contingent, the half of art whose other half is the eternal and the immutable.

—Charles Baudelaire, 1863[58]

At the very moment when the withdrawal of functions obscures the relations existing in the world, the object in discourse assumes an exalted place: modern poetry is a poetry of the object.

—Roland Barthes, 1953[59]

Historical Memory and Its Politics

An appreciation of the achievements of Iswar Gupta is something that has receded with time—the further Bengal travelled the road of the nationalist high modern, the further away it went from any understanding of, or sympathy for, the works of Iswarchandra. This is glaringly evident in most of the commentaries that accompanied the various editions of Iswarchandra's works as well as in the meagre attention spent upon him in standard literary histories; a small detail should suffice here to illustrate this descent into condescension. Iswar Gupta had had an informal education, in that he is said to have had no formal knowledge of English and very little of formal Bengali. In 1904 Sibnath Sastri wrote, 'Iswarchandra, so to speak, had not received anything that can be called an education. English education he never had, and whatever he learnt of Bengali from his own reading became his only resource'.[60] In the very next sentence,

[58] Charles Baudelaire, 2008, 'The Painter of Modern Life', in Jonathan Mayne (tr. and ed.), *The Painter of Modern Life and Other Essays*, London: Phaidon Press p. 12.

[59] Roland Barthes, 1953, 'Is There Any Poetic Writing?' in Annette Lavers and Colin Smith (trs), *Writing Degree Zero*; New York: Hill and Wang, 1967, p. 50.

[60] Sibnath Sastri, 2003 (1904), *Rāmtanu lāhirī o tatkālīn baṅga-samāj*, Calcutta: New Age Publishers, p. 223. It still remains, however, that this 'uneducated' man had,

however, he added: 'Nevertheless, even with these meagre resources, in a very short time he came to be known as a good poet (*sukabi*) and good writer (*sulekhak*) of Bengal'. This comment by Sibnath Sastri, of Iswarchandra being more or less uneducated, was repeated in 1958 by Sushilkumar De in his forward to Bhabatosh Datta's edition of the *Kabijībanī* verbatim; De's intention seemed to be to highlight the 'naturalness' of Iswar Gupta's attainments in order to praise the extent of his 'astonishing uneducated skill' (*apūrba aśiksita-patutva*). De then goes on to declare (although Iswarchandra was the first to publish an edition of Bharatchandra) that,

> it is to be doubted whether he actually understood the real meaning of Bharatchandra's poetry. He and his contemporary song-writers did not have the education, understanding, or imagination to have taken in Bharatchandra's refined and dense language, educated sensibility, easily-learned wit, and condensed presentation style. That is why Bharatchandra's flawless classical language did not endure in the following era. All we see in the half a century following the start of the nineteenth century are incompetent and disgusting imitations of *Bidyāsundar*.
>
> Iswar Gupta's own poetry too did not reach a very high standard.[61]

How could it? De is convinced that this rustic, uneducated, and unrefined natural poet was out of place in the educated world of new Bengali poetry, and he approvingly (and selectively) quotes from Bankimchandra, prophet of the new age, who had said, in his introduction to Iswar Gupta, that there is no room for such a poet as this in the modern world. How far we have come, in De, from the time of Sibnath Sastri may be measured by the fact that Sastri's concluding sentence in praise of Iswar Gupta as a good poet and a good writer (*sukabi, sulekhak*) is not similarly endorsed in De's text, for De has already concluded that the new age had no time for the old poets, and in this he is partly following the high priest of the Bengali modern, Bankimchandra, who had held up Iswar Gupta's case as a dire warning to the youth of his time. 'If there is one great truth that we imbibe from an analysis of Iswarchandra's life', Bankim had said, 'then it is this—

---

in 1832, translated a part of Tom Paine's *Age of Reason* into Bengali and published it in the *Saṃbād prabhākar*, challenging the missionaries, chiefly Alexander Duff, to reply to its charges. See Bhabatosh Datta, *Kabijībanī*, p. 46.

[61] *Kabijībanī*, p. ii.

talent cannot reach its fullest apotheosis without good education'. He had also said, 'It is a very sad thing that he [Iswar Gupta] did not complete his education. If he had, then with the talent he had, if he had used it well, he would have had a much greater command over his poetry, work and society… . Bengal's progress would have moved further ahead by almost thirty years'.[62] Bankim, however, was nothing if not conflicted in his opinions, and a classic instance of this conflict of opinion is present in the 1885 introduction, which veers from high praise to open censure, from delight to condescension, from respect to rejection to appreciation in a regular pendulum-like motion in the space of the few pages of the essay. In his earlier English essay of 1871, 'Bengali Literature', he is more categorical in his opinion, saying, 'He [Iswar Gupta] was a very remarkable man. He was ignorant and uneducated. He knew no language but his own, and was singularly narrow and un-enlightened in his views; yet for more than twenty years he was the most popular author among the Bengalis'.[63]

Remarkably, this opinion, repeated ever after Bankimchandra right up to the time of Sushilkumar De, has persisted even among critics writing in the twenty-first century, who have been unable to step outside of the humanist, universalist, and fundamentally bourgeois preoccupations of the preceding eras. Typically, therefore, Sudipta Kaviraj, perhaps both unwilling as well as unable to dispel with the enormous shadow of the revolutionary accomplishments of Bankimchandra upon the modern Bengali man, has no hesitation in marking the difference between Iswar Gupta and Bankimchandra as essentially the difference between the high and the low, the pre-modern and the modern:

> From *a vehicle of frivolous enjoyment of insignificant objects* in the world, exploitation of the infinite resources of punning and *slesha* on things like the *tapse* fish or babus who for altogether contingent reasons incurred the hostility of Iswar Gupta, irony came in Bankim to have a serious object, indeed an object beyond which nothing could be more serious to the modern consciousness. Instead of *trivial things* in a world which *is not fixed in a historically serious gaze*, it now reflected on three objects entirely

[62] *IGKS*, p. 8.

[63] Bankimchandra Chatterjee, 1969, 'Bengali Literature', *Bankim rachanavali*, Vol. 3, Calcutta: Sahitya Sansad, p. 106.

> distinct from each other, all implicated in the historical world. These are the self, the collective of which the self was a part, and the civilization of colonial India which formed the theatre in which this darkly comic spectacle of the search for the self unfolds.[64] (My emphases)

From Bankimchandra onward, irony achieves 'a new dignity' it had never had before, Kaviraj states; thus, with Bankim, a new tradition of Bengali self-irony is born. Iswar Gupta's poetry is about the 'frivolous enjoyment of insignificant objects in the world'; he writes about 'trivial things' such as the *topse* fish or the babu, and if Bankim too made the babu the special object of his satire, then Bankim is different because he did so as a babu himself, which presumably Iswar Gupta was not. Here, Kaviraj finds that 'irony came in Bankim to have a serious object', unlike in Iswar Gupta's poems, which exist 'in a world which is not fixed in a historically serious gaze'.

The argument assumes that selfhood came to the Bengali only with the advent of Bankimchandra, for the 'frivolous' was not 'serious', and the 'contingent' reason was somehow not an adequate one. Kaviraj sees Iswar Gupta through the lens of Bankimchandra, as someone who is, in Bankim's words, 'singularly narrow and un-enlightened in his views', for essentially the concern here is with progress and evolution (Bengal would have moved forward thirty years, Bankim had claimed, if Iswar Gupta had had an education). For Kaviraj, Bengali subjectivity appears to have been absent until a certain date, which is why he reads Kaliprasanna Singha too as inadequate, for Kaliprasanna 'did not realise *yet* the gravity, and the tragic taste of turning banter towards the self. (my emphasis)'.[65] The use of the 'yet' in this sentence gestures towards a notion of arrival, of deferral—modern subjectivity is yet to be realized in the gravity of selfhood by the writer of *Hutom*. Bankim, then, is shown to have attained a self-ironical mode denied to Iswar Gupta and Kaliprasanna, both of whose choice of subject matter lacked dignity, and who personify the unreconstructed self of the Indian that we have (hopefully) left behind in our serious and progressive march on the road to the attainment, and the critiquing, of self-hood.

[64] Sudipta Kaviraj, 2000, 'Laughter and Subjectivity', p. 388.

[65] Ibid., p. 384.

A simple juxtaposition of two passages from either writer, however, confounds the basic assumptions of Kaviraj's enquiry, for when we read the passage Kaviraj quotes from Bankim's *Kamalākānta* on the babu ('I shall do whatever you consider proper. I shall wear boots and trousers; put spectacles on my nose, eat with knife and fork, dine at a table…')[66], what comes immediately to mind are Iswar Gupta's already extant lines on the spectacle of the bibi who shall eat with knife and fork [*sab kāñṭa cāmce dharbe śeshe*] and the uncaring babu who will say 'hoot', wear 'boots', smoke 'cheroots' and go to heaven [*bujhi 'hut' bole, 'but' pāye diye, / 'cherut' phuñke svarge yābe*] in the vastly dire scenario of scarcity of food among the common people in the country, in a poem/song named 'Famine' [*durbhiksha*].[67] The long shadow of Iswar Gupta's trenchant lines fall upon Bankimchandra's depiction unmistakably; only the satire is less pungent in the later writer, depoliticized of its horrible context of starvation in the countryside, made safer and sounder and altogether more harmless and containable as a vehicle for laughter.

Kaviraj is not alone in having been unable to find any new insight into the textured world of Iswar Gupta's poetry. A long line of distinguished Bengali literary critics have been left bewildered by the chaotic confusion of Iswar Gupta's poems, their apparent formal conventionality hiding from sight the modern urban language of material pleasure they encapsulate with so much energy and verve. The commonest metaphor that has been used in the context of his poetry, then, has been that of the conjunction—in him and his poetry—of the old and the new. It was Bankimchandra, once again, who put these terms in place in his essay on Dinabandhu Mitra when he said, of the years 1859–60, that they were 'the meeting point [*sandhisthal*] between the old and the new', because 'The last of the old party, Iswar Chandra's sun had set, and the first poet of the new, Madhusudan's, had just risen'.[68] But Bankimchandra had used these terms of the years, not of the poet; unfortunately, the metaphor came to be displaced subsequently to the poet and his poetry rather than to the

[66] Ibid., p. 389.

[67] Iswar Gupta, *Durbhiksha*, *IGKS*, p. 111.

[68] Bankimchandra Chattopadhyay, '*Kabitva*' [1886] in J. Bagal (ed.), *Bankim rachanavali*, Vol. II, p. 758.

era in question. Brajendranath Bandyopadhyay, in his introduction to the poet in the *Sāhitya sādhak caritmālā* written in 1941 could only emphasize: 'In the conflict between the old and the new, just at the spot where there is an upheaval on the road, exactly at that spot, he presides like a *milestone* planted in the bowels of the earth…', using the English word milestone in this description.[69] Sukumar Sen falls back upon the same metaphor: 'I do not say that Iswar Gupta bade farewell to the old poetry and welcomed the new, and I do not claim that his works proclaim the conjunction of two worlds. But he had wanted to grasp the old and the new world together at the same time—in this lay his uniqueness. Yet he was not the prophet of an age'.[70] Mired firmly as they were in the progressive, modern, and nationalist prejudices of their time, every commentator, from Sushilkumar De to Bishnu De, had much the same to say in his evaluation of the significance of the poetry of Iswar Gupta. The crucial point, however, is that neither the old nor the new are configured here in terms of calendar time—instead, both the temporal markers refer to the *same* moment of modernity.[71]

Readers, Publics

Almost every established zamindar in Bengal and all the wealthy families of Calcutta were subscribers to Iswar Gupta's *Saṃbād prabhākar*. Further, Iswar Gupta gave a free copy of the paper to many persons who were unable to pay the subscription—at least three or four hundred in number. Out-of-station Bengalis living in the western and northern provinces were also grouped together as subscribers, sending local news of importance to the paper—these contributions became especially valuable to the paper at the time of the rebellion in 1857, when it became established as the pre-eminent Bengali newspaper of its time.[72] Since Iswar Gupta's poetry appeared regularly in the columns of his newspaper, his poetry reached a wide

[69] Brajendranath Bandyopadhyay, 'Īśvarcandra Gupta', *SSC*, Vol. 1, p. 6.

[70] Sukumar Sen, 1970, *BSI*, Vol. 2, Calcutta: Eastern Publishers, pp. 122–3.

[71] I am grateful to Sibaji Bandyopadhyay for pointing this out in his comments on the paper.

[72] *IGKS*, p. 15.

audience of receptive readers, unparalleled in his time or the following ages for the manner in which a newspaper and a poet each benefited from proximity to the other. This bond between paper and poet was reflected in a popular refrain, which, typically, punned upon several words ('īśvar' referred to both the poet and god himself, and 'gupta' means hidden, but is also the poet's surname, while 'prabhākar', of course, indicated both the sun and the newspaper): '*Ke bale īśvar gupta byapta carācar / jāhār prabhāy prabhā pāy prabhākar*'. [Who says Iswar Gupta is absent, he is present all over the world / In his radiating influence glows the Prabhakar.]

The *Saṃbād prabhākar* was the first daily newspaper in Bengali, starting as a weekly in 1831, developing into a thrice-weekly publication from August 1836, and finally morphing into a daily from 14 June 1839. A notice at the end of the last column in the newspaper of 5 April 1849, proclaimed: '*Ei prabhākar patra rabibār byatireke prati dibas kalikātār simuliyā heduyā puskariṇīr daksin pārśastha prakāśya rāstār daksin digastha galir madhye 44/3 nambar bhabane prakāś hay. Barshik agrim mūlya koṭh 10 tākā.*' [This *Prabhakar* newspaper is published every day excepting Sundays from house No. 44/3, situated in the lane on the southern end of the open road appearing on the south side of Calcutta's Simuliya Hendua pond. Yearly advance is valued at Rs 10.] After Iswar Gupta's death in 1859, it continued to be edited by his brother, Ramchandra Gupta, circulating till the 1880s, after which it became irregular, and finally ceased operations.

In Walter Benjamin's reading of Baudelaire's poetry of the same era in Paris, he shows how art throws up new strategies of survival to adapt to the changed conditions imposed by industrial society in an era of high capitalism. One of the great motifs of this age, for Iswar Gupta no less than for Baudelaire, was the newspaper, and Benjamin remarks upon the manner in which at this time the newspaper signified 'the replacement of the older narration by information, and of information by sensation, reflect[ing] the increasing atrophy of experience'.[73] Keeping in mind the essentially urban character of Iswar Gupta's poetry, it should be possible to see, in Benjamin's foregrounding in Baudelaire of the metropolitan masses that inhabit 'giant cities', the public as

[73] Walter Benjamin, 1973, *Charles Baudelaire: A Lyric Poet in the Era of High Capitalism*, translated by Harry Zohn, London: Verso, p. 113.

it was taking shape in mid-nineteenth century Calcutta. The verse of Iswar Gupta, so different in form from his French contemporary, was similarly inhabited by the pressure of a public made up of 'the people in the street'—this crowd, he feels, is unique in this period in the nineteenth century, when 'it was getting ready to take shape as a public in broad strata who had acquired facility in reading'.[74]

For Iswar Gupta, these are the readers of a poetry which, both in its physical incarnation and in its content, was essentially poetry that was fundamentally designed to be sold in the streets. Sibnath Sastri describes the scene upon which the theatre of Iswar Gupta's poetry was enacted before the public readership in the city of the time in an unforgettable vignette:

> When the *Prabhākar* was published, newspaper-sellers would stand at the cross-roads and read aloud from the poetry in it and in no time at all a huge number of papers would be sold. Slowly, a group of Iswarchandra-type poets began to grow and a new age was inaugurated in Bengali literature. Just as nowadays every person—young or old, male or female—who composes poetry does so in the mould of Rabindranath, in those days whenever anybody desired to compose poetry he did so, consciously or unconsciously, in the mould of Iswarchandra. As time went on, Iswarchandra's imitators and followers, his students and students' students all branched out in many directions and gave birth to a school of poetry. Among these followers, the composer of *Sudhīranjan* Dwarakanath Adhikari, Bankimchandra Chattopadhyay, Dinabandhu Mitra, Harimohan Sen, Rangalal Bandyopadhyay and Manmohan Basu achieved fame and status in later life.[75]

This list of followers makes its way into almost every biography and notice of the poet Iswar Gupta, almost as if the list of names that it boasts as his followers were of more importance historically than the poems that he wrote. Whereas a Bengali reader would be inclined to remember Madhusudan because of the *Meghnādbadh kābya* and Rabindranath perhaps for *Sonār tari* or *Mānasī*, Iswar Gupta, it seems, is liable to be remembered not for his works, but for his men—the stalwarts of Bengali modernity that he forged, like Prometheus, in the workshop of the *Prabhākar*.

[74] Ibid., p. 120.

[75] Sibnath Sastri, 1909, *Rāmtanu lāhirī o tatkālīn baṅga-samāj*, p. 231.

The poetry in the *Prabhākar* had appeared in narrow newspaper columns, filling up the back sheets with its effervescent content, sometimes with a small heading on top that proclaimed, simply, '*padya*' [Poetry]. When it was not printing his own poetry, on occasion the poems were contributions sent in to the editor, who presumably published them at his discretion, and here a short prefatory line would include the address to the editor. One such insertion in the last page of the paper on 26 *Caitra* [April–May] 1849 proclaimed, at the head of the verse, with each word following the other in separate lines: '*Rūpak / Praṇaẏ / Padya*' [Rupak *tāl* / Love / Poetry], and at the bottom, it carried the poet's nom de plume: '*premānurakta janashya*' [love-smitten one]. In another, the poem, '*Sīkh pārājāẏ*' [Sikh Defeat], was preceded by the line 'Submitted with respect to the esteemed editor of the *Prabhakar*', the *tāl* given as *tripadī* and the poet's identity given as '*kasyacidraṇraṅga bilāsin*', which might tentatively be translated as 'one whose heart delights in pleasure'.[76] In this it was following quite closely upon the conventions followed, for instance, in the pages of the *India Gazette* when Derozio was contributing regularly to that paper between 1825 and 1831.

The *Saṃbād prabhākar* was perhaps the first Indian regional language newspaper to carry a literary supplement—from the Bengali New Year of 1853 it published a monthly supplement that provided a much more substantial space than the daily newspaper for the publication of a variety of occasional verse, as well as an eclectic range of prose and imaginative writing, providing Iswar Gupta with more space in which to indulge his creative output than was available in the news-oriented daily newspaper.[77] Through the newspaper and then the literary supplement, a poet such as Iswar Gupta first seems to enter the marketplace in the 'style of the *flaneur* who goes botanizing on the asphalt', and poetry becomes a commodity that helps fashion the phantasmagoria of city life in its own way.[78]

[76] *Saṃbād prabhākar*, 11 April 1849. 'rūpak' is a particular *tāl* or rhythmic pattern on the *tabla* to the accompaniment of which a song may be sung. Many of the poems of this time were prefaced with an indication of the *tāl* in which it should be sung.

[77] *IGKS*, p. 18.

[78] Benjamin, *Charles Baudelaire*, p. 36.

Although critics have been unwilling to identify Iswar Gupta as a member of civil society in the sense of the Bengali *bhadralok* or babu as these categories evolved over the course of the century, the society he belonged to was undeniably one in which the markers of a modern urban culture of the city such as literary societies and clubs, debating societies and philosophical associations were already very much in place, as indeed they had been since the time of Derozio. The first literary society in Calcutta that I have found evidence of participation in by Indians was the Oriental Literary Society of 1825, which had members primarily from both the East Indian and Indian communities of the professional class.[79] From 1851 onward, Iswar Gupta began to organize a literary festival in Calcutta on the day of the Bengali New Year on the 15 of April at his printing press. Almost every person with any pretension to an education was to be found there, from the wealthy zamindar to the impoverished pundit, as they travelled to attend this gathering from the city and its outskirts, as well as from the mofussils. Bankimchandra writes of the presence of Calcutta's most respected and established families—the Mallicks, the Dattas, and Shobhabazaar's Debs—as well as of some of Calcutta's most important men, such as Debendranath Tagore, at the festival. Iswar Gupta would read and recite from his prose and poetry, followed by his best students, who were then awarded prizes in order of merit for their compositions by the wealthy men of the city and districts. At the end of the proceedings, Iswarchandra would organize a feast for about four to five hundred people.[80]

Crucially, Iswar Gupta's ambit was not confined to the precincts of the city of Calcutta alone. Publishing profusely in the *Saṃbād prabhākar*, he reached a wide and eager audience in the towns and villages of Bengal; in the annals of Bengali literary history, no less significant than Rabindranath's description of the eagerness with which every issue of Bankimchandra's *Baṅgadarśan* was awaited, is Nabinchandra's account of the reception of Iswar Gupta's poems by

[79] See Rosinka Chaudhuri, 2012, 'The Politics of Naming: India's First Modern Literary Society, Calcutta, 1825', in *Freedom and Beef Steaks: Colonial Calcutta Culture*, Delhi: Orient Blackswan, pp. 68–92.

[80] Bankimchandra Chatterjee (ed.), *IGKS*, pp. 17–18. Bankim mentions that Iswar Gupta was 'a Brahmo at one time', and belonged to the Adi Brahmo Samaj, and that Debendranath Tagore was a close friend. Ibid., p. 36.

his father's circle in his childhood and youth in Chittagong in the 1850s:

> In those days, Bengal's *Sarasvatī debī's* pale and poor image was to be found installed at the *Baṭ-tāla*. There, whatever rubbish was birthed by the mother on the poorest paper in illegible print—I read it all. Gradually, Iswarchandra Gupta and the god-like (*debpratim*) Iswarchandra Vidyasagar began to dawn upon the sky of Bengali literature. That both of them are the gods (*īśvar*) of Bengali verse and prose is a universally acknowledged fact today. In those days Bengal was blinded by the light of Gupta-ja's 'Prabhākar'...
>
> '*Ke bale īśvar gupta byaptā carācar*
> *Jāhār prabhāy prabhā pāy prabhākar.*'
>
> [Who says god / *iswar* is absent / *gupta*, he is present all over the world
> In whose lustre glows the radiant Prabhakar.]
>
> This proud and cutting remark was known to everybody and accepted as if it were the word of the Vedas....
>
> My father was a great follower of Gupta-ja. Gupta-ja had once come to Chattagram on his travels and had charmed everybody with his talents. My father used to read the *Prabhākar* with his friends all the time—he used to love to read poetry. So much so, that there were days spent reading poetry when he would forget to sleep or eat.[81]

This description of the birth of Bengali literature in poor circumstances achieves one memorable connection—it perspicaciously links the *Bat-tala* to *Sarasvatī debī*, a historically wholly accurate conjunction. From those mean surroundings, Nabinchandra seems to imply, rose the powerful Bengali literature that was in its adolescence in his own heyday in the 1870s and achieved manhood in Bankim; but of the two gods he mentions who take that infant literature forward towards glory, it is Vidyasagar who is described as god-like, '*debpratim*'. For undeniably Iswar Gupta, whose paper, like the sun's light, 'had blinded them all', remained very much a man of this world, not a god, or even one who was made in his image, but a material man who, his poems made abundantly clear, liked his meat and drink, his alliances firmly rooted in the newspaper he edited and published his poems in, as well

[81] Nabinchandra Sen, 1959, *Āmār Jīban*, Vol. 1, *Nabinchandra rachanabali*, Calcutta: Bangiya Sahitya Parishad, pp. 91–2.

as in the *baṭ-talā* that existed in close proximity to the half-*ākhṛāi* he composed songs for.

The self-division of Bengali modernity, at odds between the *baṭ-talā* and *Sarasvatī debī*, found a fusion of form and figure in the personality of Iswar Gupta in mid nineteenth-century Bengal. In that battle, it seemed to be the newly incarnate form of the goddess of learning that won the field in the coming years, as a new generation of men was created far exceeding the pattern of Iswar Gupta's performance, of whose initial overwhelming influence nothing seems to have survived except a few perfunctory pages mandatory in the telling of literary histories. Yet the fuzzy intermediate space of fusion between the two that Iswar Gupta carved out as his own domain was not to be wiped out by all the zeal of reforming Young Bengal, persisting in the interstices with tenacity to outlive many other trends and schools that developed at this time in the battlefield of Bengali literature, whether Sanskritic or Anglicist, orthodox or reformist, country or western.

Popular Poems

It might be instructive, at this point, to pause for a moment and consider the total corpus of Iswar Gupta's poetic production. Iswar Gupta had published more poems than any other Bengali poet up to the time of Bankimchandra; the latter remarks that Gopalchandra Mukhopadhyay, the man who did the actual work in compiling the material for the anthology edited by Bankimchandra, estimated that Iswar Gupta 'wrote almost fifty thousand lines of verse', of which only a fraction was presented in their edition of 1885.[82] All of this poetry, it is worth emphasizing, was published in the pages of the newspaper he edited, the *Saṃbād prabhākar*, as none of it was collected and published in book form in his life time. Yet the editions of Iswar Gupta's poetry, that first began to appear from the year 1861, have continued to appear unabated in some form or the other through the

[82] *IGKS*, p. 36. The first book of Iswar Gupta's poetry was Bankimchandra Chattopadhyay (ed.), 1885-6, *Īśvarcandra gupta-r kabitā saṃgraha*, Calcutta, with a life of the poet and appreciation. This was followed by Kaliprasanna Vidyaratna (ed.), 1900, *Īśvarcandra gupter granthābalī*, Basumati Press; Manindra Krishna Gupta (ed.), 1901, *Īśvarcandra gupta praṇīta granthābalī*, Gurudas Chatterjee.

course of the century and a half that has followed. Eight slim editions of his poetry were published after Iswarchandra's death by his brother Ramchandra Gupta, the first three appearing in 1861, the fourth in 1869, the fifth, sixth, and seventh in 1873, and the eighth in 1874. After Bankim's famous 1885 edition, two subsequent editions, one from the Basumati Press in 1900 edited by Kaliprasanna Vidyaratna and the other by his grand nephew, Manindrakrishna Gupta, in 1901 followed in quick succession. Both these editions presented a more complete selection than had been available so far to readers, in so far as they include poems left out by Bankim in 1885 for immoral content.[83] Testifying to the fact that this poet, who was not deemed to be a proper poet at all, is still read up to the current day is the fact that the latest edition of his work, titled *Īśvarcandra gupter śreshṭha kabitā* [*Best Poems of Iswarchandra Gupta*], edited by Alok Ray, was published in 2002 and reprinted in 2009, while the Bankimchandra edition is still in print, reprinted in 1995, as is the Kamalkumar Majumdar selection, reprinted in 2007.

It is very important to note that in keeping with the priorities of an age when religion and worship were the primary priorities of all men of intellect, from Rammohun Roy and Debendranath Tagore to Akshay Datta and Bhudev Mukhopadhyay, the first section in the 1901 edition, of near about a hundred poems, is called 'Moral and Spiritual' [*Naitik ebaṃ pāramārthik*]. This section contains poems with titles like 'God's Mercy' [*Īśvarer karuṇā*], 'Prayer' [*Prārthanā*] and 'Who is a Man' [*Mānush ke*]. This was followed by sections called 'Society and Satire' [*Sāmājik o byaṅga*], 'Of War' [*Yuddha bishayak*], 'Description of the Seasons' [*Ṛtu barṇan*], 'Love' [*Prem*], and finally, 'Various' [*Bibidha*].[84] In the third section on war, apart from a few general poems called simply 'War' (*Yuddha*) or 'Victory in War' [*Yuddher jay*], all the poems are about contemporary wars in India, and so we have 'Sikh Conflict', 'Nana Saheb', 'Victory in Kanpur', and eponymous poems on the Delhi, Kanpur, Allahabad, Kabul, and Agra battles. Iswar Gupta's loyalties were firmly with the British every

[83] The Manindrakrishna edition and Basumati edition are essentially similar with only a slight difference in section headings.

[84] The section called 'Love' in the *Basumati* edition is renamed 'Poems of Pleasure' [*Rasatmabodhak kabita*] in the Manindrakrishna edition.

time, and in this he was no different from the poets of the *Dutt Family Album* (1870) who wrote in English and were looked at askance for writing eulogies to Lord Canning after 1857.[85] The difference lay, in fact, in the treatment, for Iswar Gupta is contemptuous of leaders such as Nana Saheb ('even though he is Hindu, he is an ocean of evil') and the Rani of Jhansi (using debased slang to call her 'cut-lip aunt' [*thoṅṭkāṭā kākī*] and 'she-fox' [*māgī kheṅkī*]), sneering at them for, as he saw it, their impudence and idiocy in language far more vitriolic than the 'well-educated' Dutts would have used. It is the language he uses against the Muslims that is the most offensive, however, and they are described as 'worse than the most fallen' (*narādham nīc nāi, neṛeder mata*), 'filled with badness like the chilly that is burnt whole' (*yena jhāl lankā poṛā, āgā goṛā, nashtamte bharā*), whose throne the British should seize and whose blood they should suck. Such sentiments, expressed with an appalling coarseness of language in the context of Muslims, are repeatedly present in poems such as 'Delhi's War', where he asks the Hindu community, who are Bharat's favourite children, to freely say: Victory to the British (*Bhārater priyaputra hindu samuday / muktamukhe bala sabe britiśer jaẏ*), or 'Kabul's War' which has an image of the British shaking the Muslim by his beard, or 'Peace after War' which celebrates the British destruction of Delhi, ending with the lines 'Say Victory to the British, say Victory, brothers all / Come let us sing and dance and praise the Lord'.[86]

Iswar Gupta's hostility towards women, reformed babus and Anglicized Indians in his poetry (rather than his prose, which was altogether more tempered, liberal, and generous) marks it out as representative of the most common prejudices of his time, aligning it in spirit with the bazaar painters of the Kalighat *paṭ* or the performances of *saṅg*, who mercilessly satirized the pretension and hollowness of a society rapidly on the make. Thus whereas in a poem he might denounce educated women, saying '*āge meẏegulo chila bhālo, bratadharma karto sabe / ekā bethune ese śesh kareche, ār ki tāder teman pābe*?' [The girls were better before, they performed all the religious

[85] See Rosinka Chaudhuri, 2002, *Gentlemen Poets in Colonial Bengal*, Calcutta: Seagull.

[86] '*Yuddha sānti*', Basumati edition, p. 231. '*britiś-er jay jay bala sabe bhāi re/ eso sabe nece kuṅde bibhuguṇ gāi re*'.

rites / Bethune alone has put an end to all that, will you ever find them like before anymore?], in an opinion piece in his paper, he could express exactly the opposite view:

> Alas, it is impossible to describe the worry caused to us by the fact that women are unable to access routes towards an education. If we ever look into the reasons for the falling apart of families, of brothers, or of other unpleasant incidents, we will have to admit that at its root lies the ignorance of women. Therefore, if they are educated then all these illnesses may easily be overcome and society will be happier and pleasanter than before.[87]

This dichotomy between poetry and prose might well have been premised upon an understanding of poetry as a performative genre, prone to the hyperbolic gesture or the rhetorical flourish, and to always keeping its sensation-seeking audience in mind.

The sectioning of the poems by Manindrakrishna in 1901 is interesting for the fact that the poems on nation, for which Iswar Gupta was praised by critics such as Akshaychandra Sarkar, are lumped together into the last section, which therefore contains '*Mātṛibhāsha*', '*Svadeś*', '*Bhārater abasthā*', and '*Bhārater bhāgya bilāp*', as well as '*Duel yuddha*' and '*Bābājān buṛo śiber stotra*'. The sections on love and the seasons may automatically remind one of Rabindranath's famous sections of the *Gītabitān*, but the love poems here belong to an entirely different sensibility. Poems such as 'The Proud Woman Appeased' [*Māninīr mānbhaṅga*] were very far from the Tagorean definition of '*Prem*' and did not find a place in Bankim's anthology, while neither did those such as 'Meeting after Separation' [*Biccheder par milan*] or 'Unrequited Love' [*Prem nairāsya*] that harked back to an earlier pre-colonial idiom of separation and longing with roots in either the Hindustani *khayal* or Bengali *baishnab* poetic traditions.

If Bankim left out the poems that according to him contained obscenity, then later modernist/nationalist generations simply ignored or forgot about the poems on the wars, on ethics and morality and on the seasons. As a result, the modern reader has little idea of what an astonishing range of poems are to be found in the complete volumes of his works. Some of these were retrieved and reprinted by Kamalkumar

87 Quoted in Asitkumar Bandyopadhyay, 2009, *BSI*, Vol. 7, p. 133.

Majumdar for his famous selection of 1954, where the poems were accompanied by his own woodcuts to accompany the text.[88] The only poems to have merited sustained discussion over the years, apart from the odd occasion when a poem such as '*Nirguṇ īśvar*' [God Without Attributes] was praised by the modern critic, were those satirical poems that commented scathingly on contemporary manners, and those that contained aphorisms that have survived as one or two liners in colloquial speech. Both the satiric poems and the poems about 'things' were immensely popular, and survived the passage of time; their accent on the ordinary and on lived life led later critics to emphasize these above his other works, for the acerbic humour they contained continued to be celebrated by one and all. Here we have reflections on 'The English New Year' [*Iṅgrājī nababarsa*], 'Widow Remarriage Law' [*Bidhabā bibāha āin*], 'Babu Chandicharan Singha's Love for the Christian Religion' [*Bābu caṇdicaransiṃhar khrishṭhadharmānurakti*], 'Status' [*Koulīnya*], 'The Topshe Fish with Eggs' [*Eṇḍāwālā tapsyā māch*] and 'Pineapple' [*ānāras*]. Many of these made it into Kamalkumar Majumdar's selection, which also included the famous eulogy to the goat, '*Pāñṭha*', on the disguised missionary, '*chadmabeśī miśanari*', and on Christmas Day, '*Baṛadin*'. While the satirical pointedness of many of these poems mocked the colonial dilemma with a topicality that lingers on in the neo-colonial world order, and while 'laughter and subjectivity' might remain one of the commoner tropes towards a reading of Iswar Gupta's poems, it might be profitable to explore further the conflicted reasons behind the enduring validity of this body of work.[89]

Objects in the World: *yāhā āche* [Whatever is There]

The reason why poets such as Madhusudan were considered great, and Iswar Gupta low class (*nimnaśreṇī*), Bankimchandra had said in his evaluation of the poet, was because those poets had articulated the

[88] Kamalkumar Majumdar (ed.), 1954, *Īśvar gupta: chaṛā o chabi*, first published 9 Aswin, 1361 BE, Mahalaya.

[89] Sudipta Kaviraj, 2000, 'Laughter and Subjectivity', pp. 379–406; Milinda Banerjee, 2009, *A History of Laughter: Iswar Gupta and Early Modern Bengal*, Calcutta: Dasgupta and Company.

highest ideals of man. However, Bankim went on to say, that was not the last word to be said on the subject. Iswar Gupta had 'an ability that was unmatched by others—what he had, none other had, he was king in his own domain'.[90] This domain Bankim named as the domain of the present, of the real—'Whatever is there, Iswar Gupta is its poet' (*yāhā āche, Īśvar Gupta tāhār kabi*).[91] Among the reasons Eliot enumerated when he spoke of the peculiar problem in the evaluation of Rudyard Kipling's poetry, was a 'further obstacle'—'their topicality, their occasional character, and their political associations'.[92] Yet Bankimchandra, in his appreciation of Iswar Gupta, had pointed to exactly this lack of transcendence of the contextual as the very reason for the survival of the poems. Iswar Gupta brought something into the Bengal language, he said, that was not there before him, which had given the Bengali language strength. Iswar Gupta's poems in the *Prabhākar* showed for the first time how 'everyday business, political events, and social events—all this can become the subject matter of poetry'. Thus 'today the Sikh war, tomorrow the festival of *poush*, today the missionary, tomorrow soliciting for a job, that all this is under literature, is the stuff of literature [*sāhityer adhīn, sāhityer sāmagrī*], was shown by the *Prabhākar*'.[93]

In a short introduction to the most recent edition of Iswar Gupta's poems available to a Bengali-reading public—*Īśvar Gupta: Chaṛā o Chabi* [*Iswar Gupta: Rhymes and Pictures*]—republished in January 2007 after its initial appearance in 1954 as the Kamalkumar edition, the current editor, Aniruddha Lahiri, tries to put his finger on the pulse of the matter: what constitutes Iswar Gupta's enduring appeal to modern Bengal? The question is asked in the context of the illustrations around which the book is constituted—the *chabi* of the title—which are a series of woodcuts by the writer Kamalkumar Majumdar, who created these in conjunction with his own selection of Iswar Gupta's poems here. *Chaṛā*, the word used for 'poem', is a word that in Bengali primarily indicates 'nursery rhymes', although here it seems to have been used in the context of alliterative word use and prosody, for these

[90] *IGKS*, p. 23.

[91] Ibid.

[92] T.S. Eliot (ed.), 1941, *A Choice of Kipling's Verse*, p. 6.

[93] *IGKS*, p. 13.

are hardly children's poems, ranging as they do in subject matter from war and ethics to the seasons and satire.

The historical force of these poems, Aniruddha Lahiri suggests in introducing Kamalkumar's selection, lies in the fact that

> as time went on, the pressure behind the spread of Gupta *kabi*'s poetry shifted from the circle of tradition to that which is accidental, suddenly put together and therefore *topical*, and thereby historical. In the *Historical Novel* Lukács had noticed at one point that the inclination towards historicality became strong in all of Europe after the French revolution. Even if not expressed as forcefully, could not a similar inclination have accelerated in British India's centre of power, at the nerve centre of the flow of events, Calcutta? Even if unknown to himself, Iswar Gupta gave a shape to that historicality—in that sense probably is he not India's first modern poet?... From the point of view of this spurt in the awareness of history, his claim will not be either easy or wise to destroy.[94]

Taking the argument further, one might suggest that the shape that Iswar Gupta gave to the historicality of events in Calcutta resided in his emphasis, in the poems, on the materiality of things-as-they-are. Here, in poems on contemporary urban life, on manners and the lack of them, on politics and the hypocrisy of status, in short addresses on food, dress, and speech, Iswar Gupta was *sui generis*, writing in a genre peculiar to himself in that age, managing to baffle the later historian of literature and the literary critic, who remained at a loss about whether to read these as 'literature' or not. More often than not, these poems were cutting edge in their subject matter, but in their style and form, they were in 'tradition' or the older styles of Bengali literary composition. Falling uneasily in the cracks of modern Bengali literature, this corpus of poetry confounded the subsequent literary historian, who could only manage, therefore, to reiterate old clichés rather than find a new language with which to read these poems.

The materialism, almost commercialism, in the subject matter of the poems points toward a modern sensibility that captures an element of historicity in the evocation of concrete presence—*yāhā āche*. Bankimchandra identifies the elements of the poetic in Iswar Gupta as 'that which is real, that which is experienced, that which is

[94] Aniruddha Lahiri, 2007, 'Introduction', *Īśvar gupta: chaṛā o chabi*, Calcutta: Kahini, *ga*.

found' (*yāhā prakṛta, yāhā pratyakkha, yāhā prāpta*). In identifying the rasa that soaks the poetry of Iswar Gupta with such plenitude, Bankim lists the spaces that *are* Iswar Gupta's poetry:

> Iswar Gupta's poetry is in the thorn in the rice, in the smoke in the kitchen, in the push of the boatman's oar in Natore, in the indigo loan, in *hotel* food, in the corporeal being of goat-mutton. In the pineapple, he finds not only the juice of sweetness but that of poetry, in the *tapse* fish he finds not just the fishiness of the fish, but its ascetic look, in goat meat he finds not only the smell of meat but that of the body of the sage Dadhichi.[95]

In this sense, then, Iswar Gupta's poetry is that of the found object, 'readymades' like Duchamp's that are neither attractive nor beautiful but exist by virtue of their selection by the poet or artist. André Breton and Paul Éluard's *Dictionnaire abrégé du Surréalisme* defined a readymade as 'an ordinary object elevated to the dignity of a work of art by the mere choice of an artist', a definition applicable to the best of Iswar Gupta's poems on things of ordinary everyday materiality, particularly in their slightly surreal quality that Bankimchandra has tried to capture in his passage without recourse to the vocabulary of the surrealist manifesto. With the self-consciousness of the surrealist artist, where the displaced bottle rack or the inverted porcelain urinal were the exhibited objects, Iswar Gupta's pineapple or goat inhabits a similar surrealism; as in Duchamp's famous addition of the moustache and goatee on the Mona Lisa print titled L.H.O.O.Q., he writes a poetry of irreverence, satire, and mockery in an unmistakable statement of intent.

The element of materiality in Iswar Gupta's poetry is factored in two ways: it is tangible and it exists in the image. The subject matter of the Kalighat *paṭ* is almost exactly the subject matter of Iswar Gupta's poems—the cat with the fish in its mouth in one instance, and the *tapse* fish with eggs in the other, the babu being beaten by a woman with a *jhāṛu* in one, and the babu in the boot and hat, scooting off with some urgency ('"*Huṭ*" *bale uṭhi* "*Buṭ*" *pāye chuṭi / Keman āmār bhāb*'[96]) in the other. Sometimes, the image in the poetry springs up with such immediacy that one can almost picture the painting

[95] *IGKS*, p. 24.

[96] '*Īśvarer karuṇā*', *Charā o chabi*, p. 8.

the Kalighat artist should have arrived at—thus when the disguised missionary is described as 'the corpulent tiger in the Hendo woods, the one with the red face' ('*Hedo bane keñdo bāgh rāṅgāmukh yār*'), 'the missionary child-eater who eats up kids' ('*Miśanari cheledhara chele dhare khāẏ*') one can just see the big traditional striped tiger painted in black and yellow with a small figure of a boy babu in its mouth.[97]

This pictorial element in Iswar Gupta's poetry and its resemblance to the traditional work of the *paṭuā* or artist (*chitrakar*—literally one who paints pictures) was picked up on by Iswar Gupta himself; crucially however, he felt that the poet was dealing in an immateriality that had no equivalent in the world of the painter. Thus about the *citrakar* he said, '*Citrakare citra kare, kare tuli tuli / kabisaha tāhār tulanā, kise tuli? / Citrakar dekhe yata, bāhya abayab / tulite tulite raṅga, lekhe sei sab / phale se bicitra citra, citra aparūp / Kintu tāhe nāhi dekhi prakṛitir rūp*' [The painter paints by picking up his brush / How do I hold up a comparison with the poet? / The painter looks at the material body / With his brush, he writes of it all / Thus making a variety of pictures, beautiful depictions / But in them you do not see the beauty of nature].[98] Without a doubt, he is talking here of the *paṭuā*—whom he names as such in the poem itself—the traditional rural artist of mythological themes, whose bold lines and stylized forms had by his time entered the Calcutta bazaar in the incarnation of the Kalighat *paṭ*, who had no truck with naturalism or perspective, and therefore could not show you 'the beauty of nature' as it was. On the other hand, the poet or *kabi* was one who made both the unreal and the real visible, ('*kibā dṛśya ki adṛśya, sakali prakaṭ*'), who expressed feeling and love ('*bhāb-cintā, prem-ras, ādi bahutar*'), and in whose descriptions we see the play of God ('*kabir barṇane dekhi, īśvarīyā līlā*'). The painter, he says, 'writes a plenitude of hands, faces, feet' (*Paṭuẏāẏ lekhe kata, hāt mukh pad*), while the poet-painter writes only in lines (*kabi citrakar lekhe, śudhu mātra pad*), punning incessantly on words such as *pad* which can mean both feet and a line of verse, or *tuli*, which can mean both brush and to hold up or pick up, repeating words in

[97] '*Chadmabeśi Miśanari*', ibid, p. 15. The '*Hendo*' woods refer to the water tank and area called Hendua in north Calcutta where Duff set up what became Scottish Church College and Bethune established the Bethune Collegiate School.

[98] Alok Ray (ed.), 2009, *Īśvarcandra gupter śreshṭhā kabita*, p. 11.

an excess of alliterative zeal, designing a decorative verse to exhibit his showmanship in language and his expertise in its traditional poetic usage.

Alok Ray, who notices these lines in his introduction to the latest edition of Iswar Gupta's poetry, feels that although he had wanted to speak, as a poet, of the ineffable, he had managed only to achieve in his works a display of the skills of a *paṭuā*—there lay the contradiction of the poet's vision of himself and all he had managed to achieve. The assumption here continues from Bankimchandra's criticism, which is then quoted to corroborate the judgement; Bankim had said, 'He did not know how to express the unsaid. He was not skilled in the creation of beauty. In fact, he did not create very much.'[99] The fundamental premise here on the function of poetry is expressed in the verb 'create'—the modern poet from the Romantic period onward 'creates', he expresses the unsaid, his individual vision transforms the felt experience into essence—this Iswar Gupta failed to do, therefore he was not a 'poet' in the sense that Kalidasa, Bankim said, was a poet, in the sense that we understand *poetry* (and he uses the English word) today. The English word is used because there is no equivalent to the word *poetry* in the Indian languages, because *kavya* and *kavi* in Sanskrit poetic convention had different connotations from that of the English *poet*.

The modern poet, Barthes shows us in 'Is There Any Poetic Writing?', uses words with 'a violent and unexpected abruptness', reproducing 'the depth and singularity of individual experience' in the 'power or beauty' of poetry. 'In modern poetics', he observes, 'words produce a kind of formal continuum from which there gradually emanates an intellectual or emotional density... speech is then the solidified time of a more spiritual gestation, during with the "thought" is prepared, installed little by little by the contingency of words'. In contrast, classical poetry depends entirely on 'techniquc'; it is 'merely an ornamental variation of prose, the fruit of an *art* (that is, a technique), never a different language, or the product of a particular sensibility'. An older traditional poet like Iswar Gupta was in some senses analogous to the European classical poet Barthes invokes, in that he embodies no particular depth of feeling, he does not project

[99] Ibid.

out an inner thought, he uses ornamental variation in accordance with 'a whole ritual of expression' laid down already for him by social convention. This is poetry, then, that is rooted in the *social*, recognized by the 'conspicuousness of its conventions', by its display of verbal skill, its *relational* ties with language. Its aim is 'to bring a thought exactly within the compass of a metre', and here language is not in-depth but on the surface, spread out according to 'the exigencies of an elegant or decorative purpose'. Here, 'poetic vocabulary itself is one of usage, not of invention', 'they are due to long custom, not to individual creation'.[100] That is why the poetic practice of Iswar Gupta fails to meet Bankim's or Alok Ray's standard, because individual *creation* is not the criterion that governs its existence at all.

Yet the division Barthes makes between the classical poet and the modern poet in Europe establishes a dichotomy that does not stand up to scrutiny in the conflicted present of the poetry of Iswar Gupta. For Barthes holds up modern poetry as being, on the contrary, about reducing 'discourse to words as static things', where the primacy of the word is absolute. 'Modern poetry is a poetry of the object', he mentions, but the unexpected object here is 'each poetic word'; this 'Hunger of the Word, common to the whole of modern poetry, makes poetic speech terrible and inhuman', 'full of gaps and full of lights', 'filled with absences', and 'without stability of intention'. 'The bursting upon us of the poetic word then institutes an absolute object' and here, the object cannot have any 'resort to the content of the discourse', it is not about the subject matter, because it 'turns its back' on both 'History' and 'social life'. But in Iswar Gupta's poetry, the object remains an object, it is material, it has a body and attributes, it is physical and tangible in the image. In this it does not aspire to the interiority of the modern individual poet, it has not turned its back on History and social life. Nevertheless, its unmistakable modernity of the urban and the spatial finds a manifestation in all that is anonymous (all of his poetry appeared unsigned in his lifetime), that is of the crowd, the city, the newspaper, and of the lived materiality of things. In this it also has 'something good, solid and delightful to offer' as Baudelaire noticed in the minor poets, for it is permeated by a '*particular* beauty, the

[100] Roland Barthes, 'Is there Any Poetic Writings?' in *Writing Degree Zero*, pp. 41–52.

beauty of circumstance and the sketch of manners'. As such, then, like Constantin Guys, the obscure painter Baudelaire is concerned with in this essay, Iswar Gupta too is 'the painter of the passing moment and of all the suggestions of eternity that it contains'. 'Every country, to its pleasure and glory,' Baudelaire continues, 'has possessed a few men of this stamp', and here in Calcutta in the 1850s it is unmistakably Iswar Gupta who occupies that space.[101]

Such an artist is a *flaneur*, a traveller, a cosmopolitan, but he has a loftier aim. Baudelaire observes, 'He is looking for that quality which you must allow me to call "modernity" for I know of no better word to express the idea I have in mind. He makes it his business to extract from fashion whatever element it may contain of poetry within history, to distil the eternal from the transitory'.[102] The task of such a poet is to separate out, from the garb of an age, the 'mysterious element of beauty that it may contain', and if, for Iswar Gupta, that transitory beauty was to be found in the celebration of the English New Year's Day or succulent goat meat, then that was the deportment of the age, the special nature of beauty in his day. While the modern painter in Baudelaire's time captures the gesture and bearing of the woman of his day in the cut of skirt and bodice, the crinoline and the starched muslin petticoats, for 'every age has its own gait, glance and gesture', in Iswar Gupta's descriptions, something like that glance and gesture is present, for instance, in the depiction of the freshened-up Englishwoman in her polka-dotted dress in *Iṅgrājī nababarsa.*[103] Iswar Gupta is urban in his location and contemporary in his subject matter, writing a performative poetry for his audience in traditional metre and style. The city and its society—with its hypocrisy and sham, its love of pomp and ceremony, its manners and customs, dress, and deportment—is pitilessly reflected in his poetic productions in different forms. This immersion in the city and its ways was something the nationalist modern in the late nineteenth century would decisively turn its back upon, and the material world of urban life as subject matter for poetry would only return to Bengal in the avant-garde 1930s.

[101] Charles Baudelaire, 'The Painter of Modern Life', pp. 1, 5.

[102] Ibid., p. 12.

[103] Ibid., pp. 12–13.

Between Sound and Image: The Sound-image

If the visual element of the language used allows a graphic pictorial imagery to spring up in the reader's mind, then the other dimension that is indispensable to the success of the best of Iswar Gupta's poetry is that of sound. Alliteration, punning, and a clever jugglery with words was taken to such an extreme in Bengali poetry in line with Bharatchandra in the nineteenth century that it was specifically identified as a fault by later literary critics. However, what is remarkable in such usage in Iswar Gupta is how an astonishing onomatopoeia of correspondence created between sound and image in the poem results in something that can only be called, uniquely, a 'sound image'. Take, for instance, the celebrated satirical poem *Iṅgrājī nababarsa* [English New Year]. This extraordinary poem was written to commemorate the arrival of the English year 1852, and records, in minute detail, the sights and sounds of the celebrations in the city. Beginning with a reference to the Bengali lunar year that is losing its relevance with the coming of the English Gregorian calendar, the poem initially describes the white man on this occasion—well-dressed, joyous, and indulgent—in his carriage on the way to church and then in his well-decorated home. At his side, his wife looks 'fresh' in a 'polka-dotted dress' (*mānmade bibi sab hailen phres / pheadarer (feather-er) pholoris phuṭikāṭā ḍres*').[104] A detailed description of her appearance follows. However, typically of Iswar Gupta, there is a sting in the tail, for, after describing the slippers (*śilipar*) on her white feet and the scarf around her neck, the decorative comb in her hair and the spray of flowers that descend to her cheek, he concludes in a notorious line, '*biṛālākhhī bidhumukhī, mukhe gandha chuṭe*' [cat-eyed, moon-faced, she has bad breath]. Another famous line, '*bibijān cale yān labejān kare*', follows two lines that use the sound effect of fluttering and flowing in the service of an image:

Ribiṇ uṛiche kata, phar phar kari
ḍhal ḍhal ḍhal ḍhal, bāṅkā bhāb dhare
bibijān cale yān, labejān kare

[So many ribbons fly fluttering away
Leaning, flowing, reclining at an angle
The beloved bibi goes her way, and one feels like dying].

[104] Alok Ray (ed.), 2009, *Īśvarcandra gupter śreshṭhā kabita,*, p. 83.

This repeated use of words such as '*phar phar*' for the sound of the ribbon flying in the wind or '*ḍhāl ḍhāl*', which is actually repeated four times, to indicate the delicious ease of attitude in the posturing *bibi*, is impossible to translate effectively. This repetition, as well as the use of such sounding words for description is, in a subsequent section of the poem, taken to its logical extreme. After a hugely subversive and mischievous section where the poet imagines himself to be a fly buzzing around the couple in their carriage to church, and then accompanying them home to sit at their table—sometimes licking her glass of sherry, sometimes sitting on her gown or her face and happily rubbing its wings, there follows a section on the consumption of '*aparūp khānā*' [amazing food] in the sahib's house. Here, the scene is evoked entirely and only through sound, framed by the preceding and following couplets, as follows:

Berybest, seritest merirest yāte
Āge bhāge den giyā śrīmatīr hāte

Kaṭ kaṭ kaṭākaṭ ṭak ṭak ṭak
Ṭhuno ṭhuno ṭhun ṭhun, ḍhak ḍhak ḍhak

Cupa cupa cup cup, cop cop cop
Sup supu sup sup, sap sap sap

Ṭhakās ṭhakās ṭhak, phas phas phas
Kas kas ṭas ṭas, ghas ghas ghas

Hip hip hurre, dāke hol klās
Diyār myadām iu tek dis glās.

This does not need translating, except for the framing couplets, of which the preceding one says that the very best sherry that makes the rest merry is given to the missus before anybody else, while the one at this end is almost entirely in English except for the word '*dāke*' which means 'calls'. Compare the dissociation and alienation in the description of the scene to a letter written in 1893, where the inherent feeling of repulsion toward the *sound* of English culture in India is brought out into the open by the letter-writer:

> When I went and sat in one corner of that drawing room, it all appeared like a shadow to my eyes... Yet in front of me were *memsahibs* in *evening dress* and in my ear was the murmur of English conversation and laughter—

> all in all such discordance! How true was my eternal *Bhāratbarsha* to me, and this dinner table, with its sugary English smiles and polite English conversation, how empty, how false, how deeply untrue! When the *mems* were talking in their low sweet cultivated voices then I was thinking of you, oh wealth of my country. After all, you are of this *Bhāratbarsha.*[105]

Rabindranath's letter to Indiradebi is sensitive where Iswar Gupta is acerbic, but the impulse to portray the foreignness of the English dinner table remains. Iswar Gupta is fascinated by the sounds the English make and records their difference in objective detail, following up the lines ending '... take this glass' with a rendition of the sounds of the music and dance that follows, all so completely foreign to the Indian ear:

> *Sukher sakher khāna, hale samādhān*
> *Tārā rārā rārā rārā, sumadhur gān*
>
> [When the pleasurable and exotic food was finished
> Tara rara rara rara [went the] tuneful songs]
>
> *Guḍu guḍu gum gum, lāphe lāphe tāl*
> *Tārā rārā rārā rārā lālā lālā lāl*
>
> [Guru guru gum gum goes the leaping rhythm
> Tara rara rara rara lala lala lal]

This emphasis on sound had its roots in a conception of poetry that was closely allied to the performative aspect of the lyrics he also wrote as a songwriter for the *kabi-wālā*s of Bagbazaar; fundamentally, his conception of poetry was that of lines that were meant to be recited rather than read on the page, as indeed they were, from the street-seller newspaper vendor in Calcutta to the assembled friends of Nabin Sen's father at Chittagong, as we have seen. He himself described his idea of poetry in a poem called '*Kabitā*' as that which 'expresses one's feeling or opinion as it is *spoken* by the people, bringing cheer to the public' [*manobhāb byakta hay̆, lokete kabitā kay̆, ānanda bitare janagaṇe*].[106] '*Lakete kabitā kay̆*', he says here, 'people speak poetry', and in the lines of the poem above we see exactly the function then of

[105] Rabindranath Tagore, letter to Indira Devi, Cuttack, 10 February 1893. See *Chinnapatrābalī*, Calcutta: Visva-Bharati Press, 2004, p. 122.

[106] Alok Ray (ed.), 2009, *Īśvarcandra gupter śreshṭhā kabita*, p. 9.

the onomatopoeia of sound and image as it is recited rather than read in front of a public or *janagaṇ*, to bring them good cheer.

The poem goes on to describe the shops and hotels, cakes, and 'chops' of Anglo India, and ends, eventually, with a scathing indictment of the anglicized Indian woman, or as he calls her, the 'black native lady' (which appellation is followed by the words 'shame shame shame') and the half-acculturated Indian toady who is neither here nor there, determined to eat at a table, but scared of getting cut by the fork and knife, and therefore using both his hands as paws to lift up heaps of rice. This is a poem often quoted for its sarcasm at the expense of the half-anglicized upstarts who dominate Calcutta society, for it is at the fountainhead of an honourable literary tradition that continued right into the Bengali high modern through Bankim and Tagore to D.L. Roy and Sukumar Ray. The physicality of the sound images it so uniquely contains, however, has never been held up to scrutiny, nor has the effect of these onomatopoeic syllables upon the page. What they bring to life with some vitality, however, is the materiality of cultural difference, the sheer obdurate strength of certain sounds to convey a tonality, mood, or atmosphere as nothing else may do. In their sheer presence of being, they are a live playback record of the changing shape of the everyday on New Year's Day, 1852, bringing to the contemporary reader a sense of lived experience as no other imagery can. This is history in the process of being made, history happening without notice all around the colonial city, history as noise.

In Iswar Gupta's poems, then, literature approaches historicality along a path of everydayness, an everydayness that is necessarily informed by a sense of the past. Heidegger's notion that 'Everydayness is a way *to be*—to which, of course, that which is publicly manifest belongs', if applied to Iswar Gupta's poems on the topical, the everyday, and the historical, reveal that all of these poems belong to the realm of the 'publicly manifest'.[107] There is, here, no interiority in the sense of the endlessly interiorized self of bourgeois subjectivity; rather, time and literature work together in the poems to recuperate the living history of the banal. The focus, in these poems on the pineapple or the English New Year, is on the detail, detail which is

[107] Martin Heidegger, 1987, *Being and Time*, translated by John Macquarrie and Edward Robinson, Oxford: Basil Blackwell, p. 422.

configured in terms of description (sound or image) and the everyday which is rooted in the domestic sphere of local social life. This focus belongs, conversely, to a politicized account of the traditional, the ordinary, and the domestic as sites of knowledge which are outside of the normative Western expectations of subjectivity and interiority on the one hand and the drama of nation and history on the other. Iswar Gupta's poems belong, thus, to a culture of irony that is located in the local and the ordinary—not in the grand mission of a nationalist high modern or in the sombre tones of a fraught modernity as they are perceived in his inheritors from Michael and Bankim onward. He is not preoccupied with the polar conflicts of the colonizer versus the colonized, or the state versus the people, but with textures of life that circumvent those epic battles to concentrate insouciantly in the cracks of the edifices that will proceed to build Bengali modernity.

The historicist imperative is conspicuous in its absence in Iswar Gupta's poems, which are based on a total involvement with the overwhelming rush of the present contained in a miscellany of items. In a sense, then, Iswar Gupta's ouevre is like the gossip in Hutom's Calcutta, which is constituted, as Ranajit Guha describes it, by an 'immediacy of presence' that 'as a phenomenon', 'lives only for the day, literally as an ephemoros or *adyatana*, in a state of utter transience'.[108] Like the gossip of Hutom's city, the poems of Iswar Gupta too 'create a sense of shared time out of the sum of short-lived sensations', helping thereby, 'together with other factors, to form the worldhood of a colonial public'. Further, as Guha notes, 'this incessantly unsettled contemporaneity' contains 'fragments of the past' that 'show up in it from time to time as tradition, genealogy or plain nostalgia, but are burnt up at once'. Guha is right to contrast this 'perpetual restlessness' of being in the city with the Wordsworthian mode in 'Westminster Bridge', or the Dickensian in *Sketches of Boz*, both of which subscribe to a historicizing tendency, 'adding depth to the ongoing historicization of the great metropolitan city in English literature'.[109] Their particular schematic lies within the Western aesthetic and epistemological traditions, where the masculine suspicion of the quotidian, of

[108] Ranajit Guha, 2008, 'A Colonial City and Its Time(s)', *Indian Economic and Social History Review*, Vol. 45, pp. 341, 342.

[109] Ibid., pp. 340, 342.

the ordinary, of minute detail, has been inherited in part from the organicist aesthetics of G.W.F. Hegel, and the 'contempt he flaunts for "the little stories of everyday domestic existence" and "the multiform particularities of everyday life"—in short, for all he lumps under the dismissive heading "the prose of the world"'.[110]

Irony, the local, and the ordinary inhabit Iswar Gupta's poems outside of the grand narrative of a developmental history inaugurated in his wake in the epic poetry of Madhusudan or the historical novels of Bankimchandra. The subjectivity in these poems cannot, however, be denied self-reflexivity—if the colonial everyday was 'irreparably split in the middle, with one part assimilated to official time and [the other] alienated from the civil society', and the question Guha asked is 'How, then could everyday life and everyday people be inscribed in the discourse of the colonial city?', then the answer must lie not only in parody, as Guha finds with Kaliprasanna's *Naksā*, but in a divided self-reflexivity that was both despairing and hopeful in turn.[111] Once we acknowledge Iswar Gupta's treatment of the ordinary and trivial detail of life as a site of critical knowledge production, it might be possible to read in the details an indication of a self-reflexive worldview that refuses to take part in the valorized and self-important anti-colonial modernity that was beginning to take shape in Bengal, providing in its place an overlooked alternative of self inscription in the unacclaimed, the unnoticed, the comic—in whatever was there.

[110] Naomi Schor, 1989, *Reading in Detail: Aesthetics and the Feminine*, New York: Routledge, p. 7.

[111] Ranajit Guha, 2008, 'A Colonial City and Its Time(s)', p. 344.

3 'Another Wonder of the Nineteenth Century': Rangalal Bandyopadhyay (1827–1887)

Babu Ranga Lal Banerji is a poet with a high reputation among his countrymen, but we must say he has done very little to deserve it.

—Bankimchandra Chatterjee[1]

For a century now, every mode of writing has thus been an exercise in reconciliation with, or aversion from, that objectified Form inevitably met by the writer on his way, and which he must scrutinize, challenge and accept with all its consequences.... Form hovers before his gaze like an object; whatever he does, it is a scandal: if it stands resplendent, it appears outmoded; if it is a law unto itself, it is asocial; in so far as it is particular in relation to time or mankind, it cannot but mean solitude.

—Roland Barthes[2]

One Immortal Line

Attempting a summation of the achievements of Rangalal Bandyopadhyay in his literary history, Asitkumar Bandyopadhyay observes, 'Editor, journalist and the torchbearer of modern Bengali poetry, especially beloved of Iswar Gupta, famous for both prose and verse and

[1] Bankimchandra Chatterjee, 1998, 'Bengali Literature', *Bankim rachanavali*, Calcutta: Sahitya Samsad, p. 11.

[2] Roland Barthes, 1968, *Writing Degree Zero*, p. 4.

extremely skilful in English composition, Rangalal Bandyopadhyay was another wonder of the nineteenth century'.[3] 'Another wonder' he certainly was; prior to the publication of the *Padminī upākhyān* in 1858, Rangalal Bandyopadhyay had already published a verse translation of the *Ṛtusaṃhār* from the Sanskrit in 1851, a long polemical essay, *Bāṅgālā kabitābishayak prabandha* in 1852, and *Bhek-Mūshiker Yuddha*, a translation from the Greek of the *Batracomiomachia*, in 1848, apart from several prose articles, poems, and translations of poetry that appeared regularly in Iswar Gupta's *Saṃbād prabhākar*, the *Education Gazette*, and the *Saṃbād sāgar*. Periodicals and newspapers were undoubtedly the most popular disseminators not only of news but of literary expression at this time—Iswar Gupta, the predominant and most famous poet of his day, had brought out his verse regularly in the columns of his own newspaper rather than in any published collection. A vibrant and responsive civil society was already in place, Derozio had published both his books of English verse in 1827 and 1828, and Kasiprasad Ghosh had written *The Shair and Other Poems* in 1830—both poets also published prolifically in the *India Gazette*, the *Calcutta Literary Gazette*, and a variety of other periodicals.

In keeping with the bilingual nature of modern Indian literary endeavour, Kasiprasad had also written many Bengali songs in the *ṭappā* mode. The Bengali literary sphere was so closely entwined with the English language press at this time that it would be a mistake to try and separate the strands; yet that is what most standard histories of Bengali literature have traditionally attempted to do. So while Kasiprasad is celebrated as the first Bengali poet to write English poetry, it is generally not mentioned in conjunction with that achievement that this was also a person who studied Sanskrit, Persian, and Hindi after completing his studies at the Hindu College in English in 1829, translating portions of the omnipotent Bharatchandra into English, while at the same time, amending the excessively Sanskritized Bengali of the Bible produced by the Serampore missionaries. Kasiprasad was also the first Indian to review Mill's *History of British India* for

[3] Asitkumar Bandyopadhyay, 2009, *BSI*, Vol. 7, Calcutta: Modern Book Agency, p. 181.

the Indian press, and the first Bengali to write an English article on Bengali writers.[4]

Rangalal, after completing the writing of *Padminī Upākhyān*, submitted his manuscript to various friends and supporters in Calcutta, pre-eminent among whom was the Reverend W. O'Brien Smith, whose was the first name in a list that also contained other 'friends of refined tastes' such as 'Babu Rajendralal Mitra', 'Raja Satyacharán Ghoshal' and those who headed the 'famous Vernacular Literature Society', who had expressed their enthusiasm and requested him to publish his verse.[5] Any attempt to separate out the civil society of the time into the English mode of assemblies, meetings and societies and the Bengali inheritance of performance rituals or religious festivities would necessarily have to deal with a conflation of the two spaces in one aspect of habitation. Similarly, the polyglot practitioners of poetry in the nineteenth century occupied a space that was informed by not only both the English and the Bengali, but equally by the classical languages of Sanskrit and Persian, as well as, in the case of Rangalal specifically, the regional language, Oriya.

Ironically, Rangalal Bandyopadhyay, who wrote, in his lifetime, at least four full-fledged books of narrative poetry, several essays, songs, plays, and translations from the Sanskrit, the Hindi *dohas*, Oriya, and Greek, is best remembered by the educated Bengali today for exactly one immortal line that is recited to this day by those of the old school (the new having forgotten him entirely): *svādhīnatā hīnatāẏ ke bāñcite cāẏ he, ke bāñcite cāẏ?* ['From life without freedom, say, who would not fly?']. Further, the line itself is a translation from Thomas Moore's popular ballad of the time, 'From Life Without Freedom', put here into the mouth of the king of Chittor, Rana Bhimsingh, as he defends his kingdom against the lustful Muslim emperor covetous of his wife Padmini, heroine of Rangalal's eponymous tale, *Padminī Upākhyān* (1858), in which the line occurs. Equal, at one time, to the venerated chant of Bankimchandra's *Bande Mātaram* in fame

[4] See Rosinka Chaudhuri, 2002, *Gentlemen Poets in Colonial Bengal: Emergent Nationalism and the Orientalist Project*, Calcutta: Seagull.

[5] Rangalal Bandyopadhyay, Preface to *Padminī upākhyān* [1858] edited by Brajendranath Banerjee and Sajanikanta Das, Calcutta: Bangiya Sahitya Parishad, 1951, p. 12.

and popularity, this line by Rangalal was the enduring bequest of this polymath and poet to the Bengali generations which succeeded him, featuring not only in every critical appreciation of his work that followed but in every ordinary Bengali reader's repertoire of quotable poetry in the service of an inflamed nationalism. Thus, the publisher of the last edition of his collected works to date, published in Calcutta in 1974, Sanjib Dattachowdhury, began his 'Publisher's Note' by mentioning, 'The composer of *svādhīnatā hīnatāy ke bāñcite cāy he, ke bāñcite cāy*, Rangalal Bandyopadhyay's works are now collected in this publication'.[6] The editor of the volume, Tripurashankar Senshastri, then began his discussion in the Introduction with a section titled: 'Iswar Gupta and Rangalal: Love of One's Country and Awareness of Bharat' [*svadeś-prem o bhārat cetanā*].[7] Nationalism and patriotism, then, were the prime markers of distinction with regard to Rangalal, and he has usually been read by Bengali literary critics from the nineteenth century onward with these flags firmly in place, as any and every commentary on his work has focused first of all upon his devotion to his country, sometimes to the exclusion of any other aspect of his considerable output.

The book in which this one most frequently quoted line occurs, *Padminī upākhyān*, was published in 1858 with an English translation of the title printed on the title page alongside the Bengali: *Padmini, A Tale of Rajasthan*. The proximity of the English subtitle is important, as it signals the twin thrust of his thinking on matters of poetry, acquiring importance in the context of the preface to the work which followed. While the title page of Iswar Gupta's *Hitprabhākar* was printed in both English and Bengali in 1860, and *Padmini* in 1858 and *Hutom* in 1861 had English subtitles, the practice died out, despite epigraphs from Horace or Milton cropping up on title pages for some years to come. To have an English subtitle or English epigraphs on the title page of a Bengali publication was a common enough convention at the time,

[6] Santikumar Dasgupta and Haribandhu Mukhati (eds), 1974, *Rangalal rachanabali*, Complete in One Volume, Calcutta: Dattachowdhury and Sons.

[7] Tripurashankar Senshastri, 'Introduction', Ibid., p. 1.

but in Rangalal, it signalled a programme of cross-fertilization that was particularly schematic and deliberate in intent.[8]

Rangalal Bandyopadhyay's *Padminī upākhyān* contained an Introduction that declared his objective and purposes behind his composition—this document, without exaggeration, could be said to be the first literary manifesto for a modern and national literature for India. Certainly, nothing preceding this had contained such a programmatic announcement of an imagined future literature for the country, laying out the paths that should be taken and the pitfalls to be avoided, mentioning both that the past should be forsaken and that the present should be enacted. Although the roadmap thus sketched pertained to Bengali language and literature, the rhetoric was always addressed to an imagined and putative Indian nation. Far from being an obvious instance of Bengali chauvinism, this conflation of the idea of India and the particularity of the situation in Bengal was premised upon a multilingual and multidisciplinary groundwork of travel through vast stretches of the country on administrative work and familiarity with many different Indian and European languages in the course of a lifetime. There is thus no easy equation to be made between the fact that, while many Bengali intellectuals of this time were, certainly, supercilious and self-contained about the supremacy of Bengali culture, there were, at the same time, many writers self-aware of the territorial differences that made up the nation, and self-taught in a myriad different languages and literatures, both of the country and without.

This category of the culturally syncretic protagonist of nineteenth-century Indian modernity was peopled not by one or two isolated poets, but by a whole generation of novelists and playwrights, essayists and activists, who spanned a distinctive space of cultural creativity. In this space, the experiences of 'other' places of location come home to roost, creating thereby, in cross-fertilization with the trans-imperial cosmopolitanism of the history of ideas available to the colonial reader

[8] Iswar Gupta's title page read: 'Hit Probhakur / By the Late / Baboo Issurchunder Goopto' followed by the Bengali title and publisher's details. Kaliprasanna Singha's *Hutom pyañcār nakśa* had an English translation of the title on the title page that echoed Dickens' *Sketches of Boz*, 'Sketches By Hootum Illustrative of Every Day Life and Every Day People'.

of English, a literary modernity informed by the aegis of travel, multilingual registers of thought, temporary diasporic experience, and metropolitan thinking. Apart from Michael Madhusudan Datta and Rangalal Bandyopadhyay, there was Bhudev Mukhopadhyay, leading editor, essayist, and prose writer, Dinabandhu Mitra, Calcutta's most famous playwright, Nabinchandra Sen, famous poet and vice-president of the Bangiya Sahitya Parishad, as well as, most eminently, Bankimchandra Chattopadhyay, novelist, nationalist, literary editor, and pre-eminent intellectual of nineteenth-century Calcutta.

These Europeanized intellectuals knew their Greek and Latin, their Persian and Sanskrit, and above all, their English literature quite intimately, but it should equally be noted that they were also conversant with not only the lived cultures but the languages and literatures in Tamil or Oriya, Telegu or Hindi equally. Madras was as formative for Michael as Orissa was for Rangalal, and Bhudev was famous in Bihar for promoting the cause of the Hindi language among its people in an organized and institutional way. The degree of Europeanization, of course, differed according to education, and if Michael and Bhudev were formed by a Hindu College education, supplemented in the case of Michael by an Oxford-style curriculum in Latin, Greek, and Hebrew at the Bishop's College, then Dinabandhu, who came to Calcutta aged sixteen, was village-educated until he joined Reverend Long's school in 1846, and subsequently, the Hindu College in 1850, although he never took his final exams in 1855, joining as Postmaster at Patna in that same year. The Indian Postal Service sent him from Orissa to Nadia to Dhaka, and from Kachhar to Birbhum to Darjeeling to Bihar. Rangalal, similarly, worked for the colonial government all his life, starting as income tax assessor and deputy collector at Nadia, and then travelling from Balasore to Hoogly to Cuttack and Habra as deputy magistrate and deputy collector. Educated, unlike the others, at Hoogly College, he was well read in English literature (though Michael is disparaging of his reading in one of his letters, as he does not appreciate Milton), and acquired Latin and Greek from O'Brien Smith (to whom he was assistant editor at the Education Gazette) well enough to translate the *Batracomiomachia* from the original Greek into the Bengali *Bhek mūshiker yuddha* (1848).

These, then, were scholar administrators in the mould of Benedict Anderson's Latin American functionaries of the first Creole nationalisms in the world, their journeys through the provinces creating and giving shape to an imagined community through the lived particularity of their lives.[9] The remarkable difference, however, from the Latin American situation, was that while there the language of the Creole pioneers—Spanish or Portuguese—was the same as that of their imperial metropole, in India a variety of regional languages developed at this time in contestation with the English language into modern, national literatures, mutating from spoken dialects or written languages into literatures of great distinction and power. Largely through the efforts of exactly this class of men and women, functioning through colonial categories but exceeding them in linguistic imagination and play in a manner inconceivable in many other equally nationalist communities, such as the Irish, new literatures came into being at different times and in different aspects in the provinces of the Indian subcontinent. The local and the national were here in interplay with the global currents of empire in a complex equation of reading and writing habits, but the inter-regional, trans-national movements and flows within the country's own languages, from Bengali to Oriya and Oriya to Bengali in the case of Rangalal, for instance, are not to be underestimated.

Thus, when Rangalal speaks of the reform of the country's poetry, to be shaped into something modern and elevated for its people, he is addressing the Bengali situation but also has the 'country' as a diverse whole, one that he has traversed and experienced at first hand, incipiently in mind. This class of men were active as functionaries of the British administration and as creative intellectuals engaged in the self-conscious task of forging a modern literature for their country. After the generation of Michael, Rangalal, Dinabandhu, and Bhudev, who were friends and acquaintances of one another, this mantle was inherited by the likes of Nabinchandra Sen, who also travelled the length and breadth of the Presidency while engaged in the creation of his literary corpus. Bankimchandra, too, worked and travelled for the government, though both were less involved with other languages and cultures than their predecessors. With Hemchandra Bandyopadhyay, Akshaychandra Sarkar, Chandranath Basu, and then with the advent

[9] Benedict Anderson, 2006, Chapter One: 'Creole Pioneers', *Imagined Communities*, London: Verso.

of Biharilal and Rabindranath, this distinctive type was to slowly die out as the literary enterprise took on a different shape and other preoccupations with the passage of time.

'Pure Poetry'

The long literary manifesto that forms the Preface to *Padminī upākhyān* follows upon the themes already elaborated upon in Rangalal's 1852 polemic and is in many respects more revolutionary than the poem itself which followed it. Its radical advice, to break decisively with the past towards a future that was at the same time more Indian and more English, was to be found better implemented in the essay of intent rather than in the poem, which was unable to completely break the shackles that he himself advocated breaking. Its objection to the vulgarity of the Bengali indigenous inheritance, which was perceived to characterize even the greatest of Bengal's eighteenth-century poets, Bharatchandra, was a common complaint among the literate sections of society by the mid-nineteenth century. Speaking of the preceding era, the leading dramatist and theatre personality of the nineteenth century, Girishchandra Ghosh, described the ambiance of those earlier performative spheres:

> Before the spread of theatre, the *kabi, half-ākhṛāi, pāñcāli* and *yātrā* were predominant. The *half-ākhṛāi, kabi and pāñcāli* traded abuse and obscenities freely, and society was especially happy with all of that. The *yātrā* did not have much dialogue—after one or two lines, they said, 'Will you elucidate what you mean?' and the songs would begin. These songs were popular, but even more popular were the *saṅg*. The *saṅg* sang lighter tunes, therefore in comparison with the heavier and more involved *pālā*, they were popular among a greater number of people. The *saṅg* would abuse. People enjoyed this. People were so fond of abuse that editors of newspapers would swear at each other in the most unspeakable language, and the newspaper with the most subscribers would be the one that was better at abuse, and it would also be the most popular.[10]

[10] Girishchandra Ghosh, 1333, *Sacitra śiśir*, Vol. 1, No. 4, 18th *Agrahāyaṇ*, p. 58. The word *saṅg* is used to refer both to the performance itself and to the performer of the *saṅg*.

Local newspapers at the time reported often on the obscenity and indecency of the performances on offer; Bireshwar Bandyopadhyay, writing on the *sang*, mentions that the songs were so full of indecency that 'anybody hearing these now would shudder with revulsion', quoting from the Baptist missionary William Ward, who wrote that 'The Songs of the Hindoos, sung at religious festivals, and even by individuals on boats and in the streets are intolerably offensive to a modest person'.[11] Bankimchandra Chatterjee described the performances of the *kabi*, 'of which the wealthy Hindus of the last generation were so passionately fond, and on which they lavished immense sums of money' as that of

> a series of songs not often much connected with each other, sung by two opposite bands of performers. Each sought to abuse the other, and the more pungent the abuse, the greater was the triumph of the abuser and the pleasure of the listeners. The singing was generally the most execrable to which human folly has ever given the name of music…[12]

Roland Barthes, in *Writing Degree Zero*, begins his Introduction to the book by mentioning that 'Hébert, the revolutionary, never began a number of his news-sheet *Le Père Duchêne* without introducing a sprinkling of obscenities. These improprieties', he goes on to say, 'had no real meaning, but they had significance. In what way?'

> In that they expressed a whole revolutionary situation. Now here is an example of a mode of writing whose function is no longer only communication or expression, but the imposition of something beyond language, which is both History and the stand we take in it.[13]

Jacques René Hébert (1757–1794) was editor of the extreme radical newspaper *Le Père Duchêne* during the French Revolution. Hébert's influence was mainly due to his articles, written between 1790–94; these were polemical articles written with wit, but were also violent and abusive, and deliberately couched in foul language in order to

[11] Bireshwar Bandyopadhyay, 1972, *Bāṅglādeśer saṅg prasaṅge* [*About the saṅgs of Bangladesh*], Calcutta: Manisha, pp. 4–5.

[12] Bankimchandra Chatterjee, 'Bengali Literature', *Bankim rachanavali*, Vol. 3, p. 105.

[13] Roland Barthes, 1968, *Writing Degree Zero*, p. 1.

appeal to the *sans culottes*; the correspondences with the nature of the abusive and the witty within the nineteenth-century public sphere in Calcutta in the context of print culture, public space, and performativity in the cusp of historical change are remarkable. No doubt the intentionality in the usage of foul language and wit by the participants in the performative sphere of early nineteenth-century Calcutta was similarly premised on its appeal to the vaster majority of the common audiences, notwithstanding the presence of the elite or the nouveau riche who organized some of these affairs.

Rangalal Bandopadhyay pursued the eradication of this ribald public culture with a missionary zeal belied by his own participation as a songwriter in one of the *kabiyāl* groups. Writing in the preface to *Padminī upākhyān* in the mid-1850s, he supported his own opinions with those expressed by the renowned zamindar, the late Kalichandra Raychowdhury of Rangpur, who had written a letter to him expressing his regret on the matter of the current state of Bengali poetry in the following verse:

ādhunik yubājane svadeśīya kabigaṇe
ghṛṇā kare nāhi sahe prāṇe
bāṅgālīr manaḥ-padma, kabitā-sudhār sadma,
ei mātra rākha he pramāṇe.

[The modern youths detest their country's poets
And cannot take them to heart
The Bengali's mind is the home of poetry's nectar
Mark only this in your evidence][14]

The zamindar did not stop at mere observances in verse made in private correspondence; he also urged Rangalal repeatedly to write an 'untainted' [*nirabadya*] book of verse. Rangalal then mentions yet another patron, the late Raja Satyacharan Ghoshal, who subsequently requested him 'again and again' [*bhūyo bhūyo anurodh karen*] to compose poetry in a 'pure form' [*biśuddha praṇālīte*], because of his disgust at the manner in which people from every station of life, including the youth, the elderly, and women, were so deeply enamoured of the enjoyment derived from the obscenity and indecency prevalent in most poetry collections in this country. 'It was at the insistence of this

[14] 'Preface', *Padminī upākhyān*, p. 11.

great soul,' Rangalal continues, 'that I turned to Colonel Tod's stories describing Rajasthan, selecting one from which I began to compose this tale.'[15]

Rangalal therefore addresses two different constituencies here—ostensibly first to the landowning zamindars and rich babus who were the patrons and financiers of the *half-ākhṛāi*, asking them to reform their tastes and remould their preferences, but also, incipiently, the arena in which the *saṅg*, with its carnivalesque aspects, or the *kabigān*, with its competitive, frequently low-level exchanges of aspersions and insults, was performed and appreciated, constituted of the general and lay audience who formed the crowds around the performers in these spaces. Popular culture in Bengal at this time is premised upon a multitude of registers with competing and coexisting publics; if the revelry of this performative sphere belonged to one aspect, then certainly the devotional songs of Ramprasad or the popular saga of Bharatchandra's *Bidyāsundar* was constitutive of still others. Crucially, this was also the public sphere that adulated Iswar Gupta, pre-eminent editor of the *Saṃbād prabhākar* till his sudden and untimely death in 1859, and mentor to Rangalal, whom he employed to write in his newspaper with some regularity, a fact that serves to remind us of the inextricability of each of these contrasting strands of modernity and urban culture in mid nineteenth-century Bengal.

Establishment of a Modern 'Literature'

Speaking of the establishment of 'Literature' in the French context, Barthes writes of the manner in which 'History' 'underlies the fortunes of modes of writing'. After the demise of the classical and romantic periods came the moment of the birth of 'Literature':

> ...as soon as the writer ceased to be a witness to the universal, to become the incarnation of a tragic awareness (around 1850), his first gesture was to choose the commitment of his form, either by adopting or rejecting the writing of his past. Classical writing therefore disintegrated, and the whole of Literature, from Flaubert to the present day, became the problematics of language.

[15] Ibid., pp. 11–12.

> This was precisely the time when Literature (the word having come into being shortly before) was finally established as an object.[16]

The resonance here with the situation in Bengal is intriguing, all the more so because the process of 'adopting or rejecting the writing of his past' has been contaminated, in the context of the Indian writer, by the advent of colonialism. Nevertheless, classical writing did disintegrate, and 'the whole of Literature', from Vidyasagar through Bankimchandra to Rabindranath to the modern poets, turned to 'the probematics of language'.

Madhusudan and his erstwhile neighbour, Rangalal, are the two practicing poets who embody this exercise in reconciliation with, or aversion to, objectified Form; what Barthes says in relation to Chateaubriand and Flaubert may be read profitably—though not in the Orientalist mode—in connection with Rangalal and Madhusudan:

> The whole nineteenth century witnessed the progress of this dramatic phenomenon of concretion. In Chateaubriand it is still only a trace, a light pressure of linguistic euphoria, a kind of narcissism in which the manner of writing is scarcely separable from its instrumental function and merely mirrors itself. Flaubert—to take only the typical stages of this process—finally established Literature as an object, through promoting literary labour to the status of a value; form became the end-product of craftsmanship, like a piece of pottery or a jewel (one must understand that craftsmanship was here made manifest, that is, it was for the first time imposed on the reader as a spectacle).[17]

This analogy is only useful in so far as it introduces the issue at the heart of many of the debates and developments in the preface to *Padminī upākhyān* specifically (and more generally, in this period, in Madhusudan's plays and poems, which followed in a couple of years time)—the issue of Form. Form, in the case of Madhusudan, achieved the status of a scandal (as Barthes calls it)—he was the singular architect of its refashioning in the project to build a literature for Bengal that was commensurate with the desires of a modern world. Reshaping the literary language he inherited with violence, Madhusudan's whole effort was exerted towards destruction, and in that effort Form was

[16] Roland Barthes, 1968, *Writing Degree Zero*, p. 3.

[17] Ibid., pp. 4–5.

his resplendent tool of creative action, transmuting the texture of the literary into something that had no antecedents. Whether it was in the introduction of blank verse, in the creation of the Bengali sonnet, in the use of punctuation, or in the grand idea itself of a national poetry for Bengal, Madhusudan stood unaided in this period in the loneliness of style. For it was the great failure of Rangalal's vision—pioneer of change in the reformation of modern Bengali literature though he was—that it was confined to what was until recently called 'content', believing that a change in subject matter was the keystone to a new literature for Bengal. Rangalal himself is not unaware of the pioneering status of his project; repeatedly, he asserts in different ways the thought contained in the modest statement in the preface to *Padminī upākhyān*: 'How far I have been successful in my good intention of becoming the title-holder of the first to try to compose poetry in the Bengali language in a new way, only the future will tell'.[18] The future, however, has not been kind, and part of the reason for that is the manner in which that thought, with all its prophetic overtones, then dovetails immediately into a lengthy discussion on the revolutionary new subject matter of the poetic narrative that follows the preface.

Sukumar Sen, writing the definitive literary history of his time in 1943, is not far removed from Rangalal in his summation of the situation in the Bengali literary sphere. Beginning a chapter called 'The Rise of a New Poetry' [*Nabīn kabitār abhyuday*], he says:

> Towards the start of the nineteenth century, poetry was in a very bad way. Even if you put aside the old Ramayan-Mahabharat-Gaurimangal etc., the overwhelming influence of Bharatchandra's *Bidyāsundar* devoured almost every poetic composition of the time, all of which were then conducted along the lines of the indecent affair of aunt Malini. The one or two Persian/Arabic love stories that were composed via media of English translations too were almost invariably of the same sort. The *kabigān* and *half-ākhṛāi* were full of the cacophony of musical instruments and the torture of vocal techniques...
>
> Rangalal Bandyopadhyay turned the face of Bengali literature towards the new age by providing it with source materials in English narrative verse tales and romances and by replacing the unreal imaginary world

[18] 'Preface', *Padminī upākhyān*, p. 12.

of gross love-play with an acceptance of the love of one's country in a historical scenario as fit subject matter for poetry.[19]

Two elements in this evaluation—standard in tone and texture in comparison to many other literary histories that both preceded and followed it—stand out. These are, respectively, the disowning of the traditions grounded in indigenous inheritances, coupled with a welcoming of the English 'influence' on Bengali compositions, and a marking of the moral uplift inherent in patriotic sentiment expressed in literary form. The welcoming of English narrative forms into Bengali is an impulse that is in danger of being forgotten today. In post-Independence period, as well as at the peak of the anti-colonial movements, it was the nationalist urge to move away from any conjunction with the English language that was theoretically at its strongest, if a bit weak in implementation, as poets from Bishnu Dey to Sarat Mukhopadhyay continued to be shaped by English and European forms of poetry well into the 1960s.

Rhetorically, however, it became politically unacceptable to put down one's allegiances to English poetic convention quite so baldly as Rangalal had once done in the 1858 preface, when he had unequivocally stated that 'Those persons today who are not well-educated in English studies [*Iṃlaṇḍīo bidyāỳ*] are incapable of enjoying the happiness that accompanies mental organization and strength as they spend their leisure in the most lowly and trivial of pursuits'.[20] Holding forth on the impact of English reading upon his own development, he had further maintained:

> Moreover, I have loved poetry deeply ever since I was a child, and therefore I have spent a lot of time reading or listening to poetry in many languages. But above all I have spent time studying the poetry of England [*Iṃlaṇḍīo kabitā*] and composing Bengali poetry along its purer methods [*biśuddha praṇālīte*] is something I have practiced for a very long time. I have published poetry of this sort in Bengali newspapers and periodicals since I was fourteen or fifteen; this was praised by many people, no doubt out of their own goodness rather than because of my ability. The significance of mentioning this here lies in the fact that my

[19] Sukumar Sen, 1970 (1943), *Bangla sahityer itihās*, Vol. 2, Nineteenth Century, Calcutta: Eastern Publishers, p. 120.

[20] *Padminī upākhyān*, p. 17.

> poem is, in many places, substantially in the mould of English poetry, seeing which lovers of English poetry may deem me a plagiarist; however, I have, in fact, deliberately tried to express many charming expressions in my own language, hoping thereby to achieve two results. Firstly, many of my esteemed countrymen who are inexperienced in the English language think that there is no superior poetry in that language; secondly, the more Bengali poetry is composed along the lines of the purer English methods [*imlandio biśuddha praṇālīte*], the sooner will the immodest, ugly poetic compositions continue to disappear, and the number of groups who love that sort of poetry will also begin to become fewer in number.[21]

Rangalal is careful, however, to qualify his allegiances; immediately following the above statement, he is quick to assert that it is not true that in every instance he has followed the great English poets alone, for on this occasion he should also make it clear that there are many feelings that come spontaneously to many minds in the same form, and when those are published before or after each other, it is our duty not to call those poets plagiarists. So saying, he then quotes 'an English poet' to support his claim, not naming the poet, but putting his statement within quotation marks.

The document is full of such quotations. Rangalal is quoting here extensively from English, Bengali, and Sanskrit, putting the quoted material within quotation marks, but usually not providing the author quoted from. Remarkably, these quotations are not only from poems, but also from works of literary criticism and analysis, of which he has already displayed a remarkable breadth of knowledge in his preceding essay of 1852. In a section on one of the virtues of poetry, he adds a footnote to mention: 'A part of this section of the essay has been written according to the opinions of a famous European gentleman who desires the welfare of our countrymen'. This formal arrangement of footnotes and quotations in a Bengali literary text was, of course, unprecedented, and closely followed English or European literary convention—Rangalal was, certainly, one of the earliest essayists in the Bengali language to compose a disquisition on the merits of an elevated national poetry for Bengal along these lines. Evidence of a cosmopolitanism engendered by empire—the presence of the quotations and footnotes, both here and in the 1852

[21] Ibid., pp. 13–14.

essay, are testament to an emerging modernity premised on a distinct set of ideas and sensibilities that engaged equally with civilizational qualities perceived to belong to a traditional high culture as well as with techniques from European or Western traditions adapted and transformed for local and relevant use.

The Narrative Impulse: 'In the Likeness of History'

The *Padminī upākhyān* is specifically informed by two twin intertwined strands or preoccupations: of, on the one hand, English poetic conventions and the reform of the Bengali indigenous inheritance, as we have just seen, but on the other, also equally importantly, of the need to discard the older mythical content of traditional tales in favour of modern, historical material as subject matter. Subsequent literary historians have identified these twin impulses by issuing magisterial pronouncements of the following kind: 'His [Rangalal's] fundamental importance lies in the fact that he rescued Bengali literature from the low and temporary triviality of Gupta-kabi's fun and satire [*raṅga-byaṅga*] by composing a narrative verse-tale [*ākhyānkābya*] in the likeness of History'.[22] Rangalal himself put forward his motivations quite clearly in his Preface:

> Here I may also be asked why I have taken my story from the modern history of Rajasthan rather than from our land's ancient *Purāṇ-itihās*—what is the reason for that?—In reply, my statement is this, that most of the populace of India are well acquainted with the various stories narrated in the *Purāṇ-itihās*, especially those in which there are plenty of supernatural events, which are therefore not suitable material for the perusal of well-educated, modern young men; also, it is the opinion of several friends and well-wishers who feel deeply for this country's people and society that it is not right to flood the hearts of Indian youths with those sorts of poetic conventions that are full of the strange and the wonderful [*adbhūt rasāśrita*].[23]

Rather, 'what is necessary', Rangalal then goes on to say, is to 'make available *a serialized real history of India* [*dhārābāhik prakṛta purābṛtta*] from the loss of her independence to the present day' (my italics).

[22] Asitkumar Bandyopadhay, 2009, *BSI*, Vol. 7, p. 181.

[23] *Padminī upākhyān*, p. 13.

Teleology and history, then, are the desired replacements of myth and fable as the required accompaniments for a modern age. Deciding that Rajasthan is appropriate because of the valour of her warriors and the purity of her women, whose stories might then inspire readers to emulation, Rangalal decides then to write the verse tale from the history of Rajasthan that follows: *Padminī upākhyān*.

No other poet in Bengal prior to Rangalal had envisioned the writing of 'a serialized real history of India' in verse form—not Derozio, whose longest poem, 'The Fakeer of Jungheera', was a fanciful story of thwarted love, nor Kasiprasad, whose composition, 'The Shair', told of a Persian-style minstrel, and certainly not Rangalal's mentor, Iswarchandra Gupta, whose short poems covered a diversity of everyday topics from God to the goat in his own irrepressible style. Iswarchandra had written poems on contemporary history, on the wars in Kabul and the Punjab, on the Mutiny and its brutal repression, which he celebrated, but these were in the manner almost of reportage or commentary, not ambitious of representing, in successive episodes, the 'real history' of the country from the moment of her subjugation to foreign powers to the present day. Almost half a century later, it was R.C. Dutt who had subsequently articulated something like a similar desire when he had said:

> I remember the solitary evenings when I was encamped in the midst of the rice fields of Dakhin Shahbazpur, a sea-washed island in the mouth of the Ganges, when I read Grant Duff's inspiring work on the history of the Mahrattas, and spent my nights dreaming over a story of Sivaji. I remember the days when I travelled over Tippera, and occasionally crossed over to Hill Tippera, with Tod's spirited 'History of Rajasthan' in my knapsack, and when I ventured to compose a story of Pratap Sinha. I remember how ... I sought recreation and rest amidst the countless volumes of European and Indian scholars who have written on Indian antiquities, and I conceived the idea of writing a connected history of civilisation in ancient India.[24]

The end result of this desire to write 'a connected history' of ancient India in Dutt had resulted in a history book on ancient Indian civilization and history that were not dissimilar to Rangalal's depiction

[24] Cited in J.N. Gupta (ed.), 1911, *The Life and Work of Romesh Chunder Dutt*, London: J.M. Dent & Sons, p. 53.

of a story from the legends of Rajasthan. Rangalal's impulse, therefore, belongs to the realm of narrative which is structured on an idea of history, as he attempts to present one segment from what he conceives of as 'a serialized real history of India', one episode of the 'connected history' that Dutt envisaged. His effort belonged, however, more to the domain of Derozio's characterization of his own endeavour in 'The Enchantress of the Cave: A Tale', about which he had said in the introductory verse: 'And though but poor in "legendary lore" / I strive to sing in legendary strain'.[25] The words 'legendary lore', used within quotation marks in the poem by Derozio, echo in intention the Orientalist's local rejuvenation of Indian mythology, folklore, and history in concurrence with the overwhelmingly metropolitan literary drive to embody such subject matter in ballads and lays after Walter Scott. These were areas of India that were currently being rediscovered, studied, and transformed by British and Indian scholars in Calcutta in conjunction with a worldwide renewal of interest in such themes. Derozio's poem, no less than Rangalal's, is therefore very contemporary in its concerns, and their common use of the subtitle 'A Tale', appended to the title of their poems, points toward the currency of an idea popular at the time. Rangalal's desire to inscribe the nation within narrative, then, apart from its stated objective of inspiring his countrymen, also obviously had its roots within the world-historical contexts of publishing and reading prevalent at the time.

Speaking of the 'serial story' of those 'long recitatives', the novel and history, Barthes called them 'plane projections of a curved and organic world of which the serial story… presents, through its involved complications, a degraded image'.[26] In this conceptualization of these closely related forms, narration is necessarily conceived as 'a law of the form' of a particular historical moment, i.e., the nineteenth century, for it was perfectly possible for other historical eras to conceive the novel, for instance, in the form of letters. The function of the nineteenth-century narrator, therefore, is to reduce 'exploded reality to a slim and pure logos, without density, without volume, without spread, and

[25] Derozio, 1827, 'The Enchantress of the Cave: A Tale'. See Rosinka Chaudhuri (ed.), 2008, *Derozio, Poet of India: The Definitive Edition*, Delhi: Oxford University Press, p. 128.

[26] Roland Barthes, 1968, *Writing Degree Zero*, p. 29.

whose sole function is to unite as rapidly as possible a cause and an end'.[27] If narrativity, then, is conceived of as that which purges the past of uncertainty, giving it stability and outline, Rangalal's mission to bring it to the Bengali world of letters is synchronic with the desire of all the great storytellers of the nineteenth century, who had aspired to the order of narrative so as to bring coherence and a structure of relations to reality; thanks to it, Barthes points out, 'reality is neither mysterious nor absurd' any more, 'it is clear, almost familiar, repeatedly gathered up and contained in the hands of a creator'.[28] The mysterious and the absurd: the use of these words brings to mind in this context of Rangalal the preceding creations of Ramprasad Sen and Iswar Gupta, respectively; Ramprasad's evocation of the mystery and the terror of Kali in the green expanses of a changing Bengal landscape, followed by Iswar Gupta's keen sense of the absurd in the urban contexts of rapid transformation and renewal in the colonial city. Modern poetry too disassociates itself from the order of narrative in as much as it is a poetry of the object, of fragmented space, of the solitary. It is only the nineteenth-century poet who subscribes, then, to the rationale of the narrative and, in doing so, subscribes also to a pedagogical imperative of connecting the world to history, and thereby of imparting to it the second-order appearance of a reality.

What is Poetry?

If the 1850s was the period when Literature was finally established as an object, in Bengal no less than in France, then the proof of it lay not only in the obsession with Form in the practice of writing, but also in the obsession with the subject, 'Literature', itself.[29] Repeatedly, the question was framed—by Madhusudan, Rangalal, Pearychand Mittra, Bankimchandra—around the issue of what constitutes literature, with

[27] Ibid.

[28] Ibid., p. 31.

[29] 1848 was also the year in which the Union Bank in Bengal failed, and the economy moved irrevocably from indigenous capital invested in foreign trade and industry to become fixed in *zamindari* and the internal agricultural market, with Calcutta's flourishing trade and commerce being taken over entirely by foreign firms. See Partha Chatterjee, 2009, 'The Universal History of Bengali Culture', *Bāromās* (*śāradīya*), pp.56–7.

a special emphasis on the subject of poetry. Considering that in the mid-nineteenth century poetry was almost a synonym for literature, this obsession with the question of poetry was not surprising. Bankimchandra was to address the issue in some detail in his preface to the poems of Iswar Gupta in 1885, as we have seen, and preceding him, Madhusudan had wrangled and argued with his peers on the constitution of a literary language; but it was Rangalal who first put the question to the Bengali literary sphere with some force. 'Now, at this moment, what is poetry?—and what is the result of analyzing it?' he asks towards the end of his Preface to *Padminī upākhyān*, saying thereafter that he was going to write now about the solution to these two difficult questions, as many of his countrymen had mistaken notions about this subject. The importance of the sub-clause in this question is beyond dispute—'at this moment' is surely the most significant part of the question, for undoubtedly, it is the moment that makes the question relevant, gives it its urgency and importance, and ultimately provides the answer. Subsequently, Rangalal writes five to six lengthy paragraphs on the theme, enumerating his reasons one by one as he proceeds.

Poetry, Rangalal is very clear, is not just anything—any arrangement in verse that is rhythmical and well composed, with pauses in the right places, and 'adorned with alliterative jewellery' is not poetry. He then quotes from 'that famous book', the *Sāhitya darpaṇ*, which said, quite rightly, that '*kābyam rasātmakam bākyam*' or 'poetry is that expression that is replete with *rasa*'.[30] This short sentence, he says, illuminates the poetic techniques elucidated in many voluminous books, holding forth then with a brief disquisition on *rasa*, that ancient Indian theoretical trope of literary expression generally designating emotional essence, often described as 'rhetorical sentiment', always roughly translated because it is so difficult to capture its complexity with any exactitude.[31] The 'extraordinary power of poetry', then, lies in its ability to excite emotion, to arouse fear, pity or laughter when

[30] *Padminī upākhyān*, p. 15. He is referring here to the fifteenth-century Sanskrit text by Vishwanath Kabiraj that was the ur-text for aesthetics for the literate classes across India from the medieval period up to the modern.

[31] See the chapter on Bharatamuni, 'On *Natya* and *Rasa*: Aesthetics of Dramatic Experience', 2002, in G.N. Devy (ed.), *Indian Literary Criticism*, Delhi: Orient Longman.

there is no 'real' reason for such feelings outside of the text. Another distinction that poetry possesses is, Rangalal maintains, its capacity to arouse humanity in man. In this way, then, point follows point, and various other achievements are attributed to the power of poetry—the ability to feel the finer feelings—pity, mercy, tenderness, the ability to raise people above their daily cares and concerns to finer spiritual freedom. Poetry, then, 'is a form of religion'.[32] It brings one closer to God, and away from the low, the corrupt and the selfish. Poetry is greater than science, because science alone will not enable man to achieve a complete education, and develop his inner self to its fullest possibility. In conclusion, therefore, Rangalal is of the opinion that 'In order to understand in what sorts of ways God has flooded this earth with the nectar of beauty, our countrymen need to read the poetry of the great poets in Sanskrit and English. Those who have studied these have been blessed, for their inner happiness is unlimited'.[33]

As further disquisition on the subject might provide 'enough material for an entire book', Rangalal then concludes his Preface with a final appeal addressed to his fellow citizens in a rhetorical epistolary style, ending by signing off in the manner of an open letter: 'Let me conclude by saying at least this much—dear countrymen, I would ask you to forsake your love for contemptible, naked, erotic poetry [*ghṛṇita ulaṅga ādiraser kabitā*] in favour of the unsullied, joy-giving poetry [such as has been discussed above]. Yours [*iti*]'.[34] Picking up exactly this phrase ('*ulaṅga ādiraser kabitā*'), one of the editors of the *Rangalal rachanabali* writes that

> Rangalal realised, due to his own hard-won far-sightedness, that a class of readers of refined tastes was coming about. That is why his intention was to rescue the country from the clutches of naked erotic poetry ('*ulaṅga ādiraser kabitā*') and exhibit the glories of womanhood... . Rangalal brought the outer forms of his poetry from England. Its inner soul he arranged according to the best selection of its dreams. In every way, the distinct footsteps of a new age sounded clearly in his poetry.[35]

[32] *Padminī upākhyān*, p. 16.

[33] Ibid., p. 18.

[34] Ibid.

[35] Santikumar Dasgupta and H. Mukhati (eds), 1974, *Rangalal rachanabali*, Calcutta: Dattachowdhury and Sons, p. 3.

Those footstep as they sounded in his writing, however, became fainter and fainter with the passage of time, as the legacy of Rangalal became shackled to the one memorable phrase by which he is remembered today, if at all, '*Svādhinatā hīnatāy...*'. The variety of essays he wrote, such as *Baṅgabidyār ādya bibaraṇ* in the Education Gazette in 1859 on the origins and evolution of Bengali language and literature, or the more forceful *Essay on Bengali Poetry* that preceded it in 1852, a spirited defence of a canon yet to be imagined into being, have been entirely forgotten, not even discussed in the literary history of this period. The various books of poetry that followed *Padminī upākhyān*, such as *Karmadebī* or *Śurasundarī*, remained textbook exercises, unread and unloved, mute and forgotten testaments to the intra-national networks of colonial British India at most.[36] *Padminī* itself gathered considerable renown, but was more heard of than read, gaining long-term fame from the one line that was quoted endlessly from it, uprooted from its unremarkable surrounding text to glow in the pantheon of Bengali nationalist slogans with a fiercer light than anything else ever written by the poet.

Distinctly, however, Rangalal's essays and Preface had announced the coming of a new age, inserting themselves into history by dint of sheer application and force of intent. In this, interestingly, Rangalal was not alone, but emblematic of the age. The year 1858, that saw the publication of *Padminī upākhyān* with its revolutionary Preface, was also the year that the Gujarati poet Narmad published an essay, '*Kavi āni kavitā*' or *The Poet and Poetry*. Described by Sisir Kumar Das in his monumental *History of Indian Literature* as a parallel phenomenon to Rangalal, Narmad was equally another 'wonder of the nineteenth century', revolutionizing Gujarati writing in a variety of genres with his self-aggrandizing brand of stormy reformism. In *The Poet and Poetry*, he wrote a manifesto for a new poetry, attempting here almost exactly what Rangalal was endeavouring in Calcutta at the same time—to sweep away the older forms in favour of the new. Like Rangalal, strongly rooted in his own traditions while at the same time

[36] It might be worth mentioning that Rangalal published another essay as a pamphlet ten years later, '*Śarīr-sādhanī bidyār guṇotkīrttan*' or 'Celebratory Song on the Care of the Body', typical of a particular Bengali obsession with body-building in the colonial period.

thoroughly impressed with the need to reform them in order to usher in a modern poetry for the people, Narmad described the concept of *rasa* in this article as '*andarni majā*' or inner delight, using both Aristotle and Wordsworth in his attempt to redefine poetry not as representations of events but as a work of the imagination, and as he put it, as 'the spontaneous expression of feelings'.[37]

Deeply committed to English poetic theory and practice, both poets felt the need to declare that they were the prophets of a new age, with Narmad pronouncing, like Madhusudan, that great poetry in Gujarati was yet to be written. Issuing a clarion call for the ushering in of a new poetry for Bengal and Gujarat respectively, Rangalal and Narmad were unequivocal in their announcement of change; yet as Das rightly points out, change had already arrived in the work of poets such as Iswar Gupta, Dalpatram, and Nazir Akbarabadi, though none of them had much English education.[38] To that list may be added Ramnidhi Gupta in Bengal, as perhaps many others, who wrote at the turn of a century that saw the departure of the old regime and the establishment of the new British hegemony in varying degrees across India. If individualization and the lyric impulse were the predominant insignia of the new poetry, then strangely enough Rangalal was a poet in whose work none of these signs appeared with any force, leading to the overwhelming perception of his failure as a creative artist among the following generations of literary practitioners evaluating him.

Bāṅgālā kabitā bishayak prabandha

The literary manifesto that is to be found in the 1858 Introduction to *Padminī upākhyān* had been preceded by the publication of a pamphlet in 1852 called *Bāṅgālā kabitā bishayak prabandha* [An Essay on the Subject of Bengali Poetry], which had first set down the premises of much of the argumentation that Rangalal re-rehearsed in the pages of the Introduction to *Padminī upākhyān* six years later. One of the first instances of Bengali literary criticism in Bengali prose, this essay, its advertisement maintained, had been delivered as a lecture at the Bethune Society, and it was styled, therefore, as a lecture rather

37 Sisir Kumar Das, 1991, *A History of Indian Literature*, p. 145.

38 Ibid., p. 146.

than an essay. The brief, two-line advertisement, headed Khidirpur, 2 *Jaishṭha*, 1259 BE, then declared that the lecture had been composed in response to certain unnecessary and false remarks made about Bengali poetry by some members of the society, and that the author had the intention of publishing a proper defence of Bengali poetry in book form in the future. The booklet, it said further, would be available free of cost to all subscribers to the *Saṃbād sāgar*.[39]

The Society mentioned in the advertisment was the Bethune Society, which was established on 11 December 1851 to commemorate the services of John Drinkwater Bethune—promoter of women's education as founder member of the 'Native Female School' and the man who advised Michael Madhusudan Datta to turn to Bengali literature—who had died on 12 August 1851. The story told here of argument and dispute at the Bethune Society meeting is central to the narrative of both the essay and the Introduction, and bears repetition. In the essay, Rangalal first spends some time in establishing the character of English and Indian poetry, which he does by personifying each one's appearance in turn. To him, 'Pure European poetry [*kabitāsatī*] is clad in white, clothed, and full of modesty, while her face is solemn, Aryan, and mature', whereas 'in our own country' she is 'eternally a young girl, always smiling, reigning like a queen in her manner, her ways, her play [*līlā*] and the various other charms of a demure beauty [*rasaśālinī sundarīrūpe*]'. However, 'let no one conclude therefore, that he is, contemptuous of the European muse while venerating the Asian', for 'the good and modest woman can never be made fun of, although we will always love our own poetry with a deep adoration'.[40]

This essay, as might not be evident from the quotations above, is mostly composed in a Bengali that is so old-style that its variety of sub-clauses and conjunctural constructions are difficult to read for the modern reader, the sentences running into one another without much pause or punctuation. Sometimes, a colloquial expression finds its way in, as when he exclaims, in the next paragraph, 'As if we could have poetry, and then that we could even talk of it!' [*Āmārdiger*

[39] Rangalal Bandyopadhyay, Advertisement, *Bāṅgālā kabitā bishayak prabandha*, *Rangalal rachanabali*, p. 69. Rangalal edited and published the *Saṃbād ras-sāgar* from 1850–3.

[40] *Rangalal rachanabali*, p. 71.

ābār kabitā—tāhār ābār kathā] 'But,' he continues, 'I am absolutely indomitable [*durddharsha*], and that is why I am stating, in the meeting of this civilized society, that although the English-educated young Babus may laugh at me to hear it, pure poetry [*kabitāsatī*] is present in Bengal.' After a couple of pages spent in establishing that Bengalis had both a poetry and poets of whom one might profitably speak, even if languishing undiscovered and unknown (and here he quotes from Gray's 'Elegy in a Country Churchyard'), Rangalal comes to the issue at hand:

> At the previous meeting of this society, my friend Babu Kailashchandra Basu had said that, not being free, there can be no possibility of mental well-being among us, and so it follows that an unhappy race cannot in any event produce a proper poet. As the Bengalis have been a subject race for many ages, the result is that a true poet has not been born here, and it doesn't seem as if such a poet will ever be born.[41]

The list of poets that Kailash-babu provides (Rangalal then goes on to say) contradicts his own logic, for Kailashchandra has mentioned Valmiki, Vyasa, Kalidas and Jayadeva as poets who lived in a free India, but, Rangalal goes on to say, this logic contradicts itself, for 'if it was so, then the poet Jayadeva would not have been born in Agradeep at the time of the Mughal empire'.[42] Extending the analogy, Rangalal then furnishes an enormous list, mentioning the straitened circumstances of poets who in his estimation had functioned under adverse conditions, belying the thesis that the 'flower of poetry did not bloom unless the circumstances were happy'. So 'Surdas and Tulsidas had lived under Muslim kings, while among the Europeans, Homer had been tempted by a fistful of food, while Ovid was a political exile, and Bhartrahari and Silhan and Lord Byron had all wearied of and been alienated from household life'. He concludes: 'Kailashbabu must not be unaware of the fact that "the dying swan sings the sweetest",

[41] Ibid., p. 73.

[42] Ibid. In this statement he is historically inaccurate, as Jayadeva was a twelfth-century poet and could not have been born in the Mughal empire; perhaps Rangalal meant Muslim rather than Mughal.

like the king of Ayodhya, Uzir Ali, who composed his sweetest verses from the jail in Calcutta?'[43]

Rangalal's defence of Bengali poetry then proceeds to establish a genealogy of poets and works—if it is argued, he says, that the *Gītagobinda* or *Haṃsadūt* are Sanskrit works, then he can establish that Bengali poetry, 'if not older than the European, is certainly the same age, born only a few years after Petrarch and Chaucer', and the instance he has in mind is that of 'the poet Kabikankan, whom Harachandra Datta has only recently established as the first Bengali poet'.[44] The achievements of Krittibas, Kasidas, and Kabikankan are then extolled, and Bharatchandra is defended from the charge of not being a true poet. Here, a lengthy defence against the charge of obscenity in Bharatchandra is presented, running on to some pages in length, a large part of which consists of quotations from classical and canonical English verse studied by English students which are, strikingly, furnished as examples of low taste. Here we find a surfeit of extracts from English literary criticism—of quotations within quotations—ranging from Bishop Hall's satires by Warton as they were quoted in Samuel Johnson, to lines from John Davies of Hereford in 1611 as quoted by Nathaniel Drake in *Shakespeare and His Times* (1838). Shakespeare's *Venus and Adonis* is then cited, and passage after passage from the poem is compared to particular verses from the *Bidyāsundar*.

'The English are always very proud that they are related to Shakespeare, but in comparison with that very Shakespeare's *Venus and Adonis* can *Bidyāsundar* be said to contain greater lewdness?' Rangalal asks memorably; then, after dismissing 'low-class poets such as Lock and Hudson, Marlow and Marsden, in whose case the argument is already won', he concludes that Shakespeare is no better

[43] *Rangalal rachanabali*, p. 73. Rangalal means Wajid Ali, the Nawab of Oudh, who was exiled to Calcutta after being defeated by the British in 1856.

[44] Ibid. There is some confusion, in many later accounts, including Sukumar Sen, about the name of the friend who made the first provocative assumption that Bengalis do not have any good poets. This is often given as Harachandra Datta. In fact, here Datta is mentioned in the context of Kabikankan, while the original remark, that the Bengalis had no genuine poets as they were a subject race, was made by Kailashchandra Basu.

in the matter of shamelessness. A wonderful comparison ends this section:

> All this while, I have kept before you a box of Ribble London Baked Sweetmeat and one spoonful of Krishnanagar's original *sarbhājā* [a Bengali sweet made of clotted cream]; according to your taste each one of you may take whichever pleases him, but remember that in order to digest English sweets [*Bilātī meṭhāi*] you need good Castillian red wine [*lāl jal*], while a glass of clear water from the Kharia river is enough for the *sarbhājā*.[45]

A major portion of the remaining part of the essay is then spent on defending Bharatchandra, not unsurprising for an era that was obsessed with 'the man of Krishnanagar'.[46]

Quoting extensively from Bharatchandra in full verses, lines, or single similes or metaphors, Rangalal is determined to show how cultural contexts determine beauty ('The European pundits often speak of the poetry of Biblical language and its true human feeling. But the similes in that book seem quite abominable to most of us'), and contends that if Bharatchandra is accused of borrowing from other poets, despite being a sophisticated poet who was deliberately alluding to Sanskrit and Persian traditions, then what about Virgil and Milton? Much of the rest of the essay is spent in praising Bharatchandra's qualities, sometimes using English quotation to buttress a point, as when he praises Bharatchandra's just descriptions, which are like felt sensations, or like 'Thoughts that breathe and words that burn', quoting from Thomas Gray's 'The Progress of Poesy' without naming Gray. 'If only the babus of Young Bengal would discard their foreign English habit of hostility and read *Ratibilāp* or the description of first love in *Bidyāsundar*, they would see that these descriptive passages are as sharp as Lord Byron's range of expressions of emotions', Rangalal maintains. Towards the end, Rangalal compiles a directory of contemporary writers in Bengali, naming Ramprasad, Durgaprasad,

[45] *Rangalal Rachanabali*, p. 82.

[46] Commenting on the forthcoming publication of 'Tilottama', Michael wrote to his friend Raj Narain in 1860, 'I see that I have actually done something that ought to give our national poetry a good lift, at any rate, that will teach the future poets of Bengal to write in a strain very different from that of the man of Krishnanagar—the father of a very vile school of poetry, though himself a man of elegant genius'. See *Madhusudan rachanabali*,1993, Calcutta: Sahitya Sansad, p. 545.

Ramchandra, Rameswar, Dewan Raghunath Rai, Raja Rammohun Roy, Nidhu babu, Ram Basu, Radhamohan Sen, and Bhabanicharan Bandyopadhyay as 'those who are loved', providing brief descriptions of their work and accomplishments.

The essay ends with a rousing ovation to the strength and beauty of the Bengali language, and of the propitious moment of its arrival 'on the road to civilization and freedom'. These are the times, after all, when 'the children of Hindus and Christians can sit down together in a hall such as this and contemplate the welfare of the country—what joy! Who would have thought that such a time would come when the educated class of Calcutta's natives and foreigners would sit down together and listen to a lecture on Bengali poetry?' Rangalal has reached full oratorial flow here, and his prose is a series of sentences comprising exclamations and questions that lead inexorably to the only conclusion reachable—that a glorious future awaits Bengali poetry, if only people such as Kasiprasad Ghosh, Govin Chunder Dutt, and Rajnarain Dutt would devote as much effort to its cultivation as they do to the writing of English verse! Presaging Bankimchandra's famous exhortation to Romeshchandra Datta (1848–1909) to turn to writing in the Bengali language for the advancement of Bengali literature, Rangalal here is confident as well that these writers, if they had only cultivated Bengali, would have been great poets in the Bengali language, and then 'what a greatly daring thing that would have been!'

An Essay on the Subject of Bengali Poetry is an astonishing document for its time—written in 1852, before the publication of any of the major foundational works of Bengali literature, when the first modern novel, play, and narrative poem in the language still awaited birth by another six years. The first piece of Bengali literary criticism to apply English literary theory to its premises and conclusions, this essay deftly employs a vast array of reading in English, Bengali, Sanskrit, Greek, and Latin to defend the premises of Bengali literature, an entity yet to be properly born in modernity. Bankimchandra was still to put forward his proposals for 'a popular literature for Bengal' (1871), and his flagship *Baṅgadarśan* (1872) was still to see the light of day. The pioneering polemical works of Rammohun Roy behind it, the modern Bengali language had then just begun to take shape in the hands of Vidyasagar and Akshay Datta, in the ideology-driven newspaper journalese of Iswar Gupta or in the rarefied premises of the *Tattvabodhinī patrikā*, but as a literature it was still in its fledgling state, yet to find its modern voice and vocation. Into that breach of becoming stepped Rangalal, minor poet of historical tales, and in a moment of energy and enterprise, took the daring step of making a public proclamation on the nature of modern Bengali poetry.

In this essay, Rangalal is forming a canon for us even as he speaks—Bengali literature, he has hastened to tell us, is coeval with the English or European in antiquity, for Chaucer and Petrarch began to write their modern literatures at the same time as Kabikankan, who has only just been declared the first Bengali poet, as he says, by Harachandra Datta. This exercise in canon formation, however, is not a new or imported practice, but an old and venerated tradition in Sanskrit poetics, where such lists of the great writers abound in commentaries and analyses over the ages; what is new, rather, is the impulse to compare and contrast 'our' list with the English canon, and to declare that both, in fact, are equal to each other in merit. Once the genealogy is drawn, and the lineage well established, he is quick to turn to morality and beauty, and using his extensive knowledge of the Western canon, quoting from Shakespeare, Gray, and Johnson, he then shows how Bengali poetry can compare with the best of the colonizer's works.

Kasiprasad Ghosh, writing in English of Bengali writers and their works in the *India Gazette* in 1831, was certainly the first Bengali to write literary criticism about the works of modern Bengali writers, but that particular piece, 'On Bengali Writers', was an article for a newspaper, and accordingly much more constrained in scope and ambition.[47] It was Rangalal who was the first to publish a lecture in the Bengali language in the form of an essay on Bengali literature—on its form and content, its style and accomplishment, quoting extensive passages for aesthetic appreciation in comparison with the English—as a stand-alone publication available for distribution and dissemination. This is literary criticism as practiced from the time of Samuel Johnson to William Hazlitt; if it bears any resemblance to Sanskrit commentary and poetics, which it well might have taken from, not as many readers of his time would have been aware of it. If we compare Rangalal's writing here, in this 1852 essay, to anything written at this time by Vidyasagar or Ramgati Nyayratna, the extraordinary nature of his

[47] Kasiprasad Ghosh, 1831, 'On Bengali Writers', *India Gazette*.

accomplishment becomes apparent. It is difficult to think of too many works of Bengali prose at this time that have endured in the popular imagination—or even in literary histories—as works worth reading on their own merit, and in this context, to read a document such as Rangalal's *Essay*, fully formed and wholly confident in its assumptions and prescriptions, its contestations and its presumptions, is to marvel at the conjunction of the man and the moment in this document of unrivalled perspicacity and foresight on the shape of the future to come.

4 (i) Event, Anecdote, Iconicity: The Legend of Michael Madhusudan Datta

I am anxious that the work should be finished by the end of the year, and I am anxious to know how far I have succeeded in getting into the true heroic style. Besides, my position, as a tremendous literary rebel, demands the consolation and the encouraging sympathy of friendship. I have thrown down the gauntlet, and proudly denounced those, whom our countrymen have worshipped for years, as imposters, and unworthy of the honours heaped upon them!

—Michael Madhusudan Datta[1]

An inadequation, a gap between the act of transmission and the thing to be transmitted, and a valuing of the latter independently of the former appear only when tradition loses its vital force, and constitute the foundation of a characteristic phenomenon of non-traditional societies: the accumulation of culture. For, contrary to what one might think at first sight, the breaking of tradition does not mean the loss or devaluation of the past: it is, rather, likely that only now can the past reveal itself with a weight and an influence it never had before.

—Giorgio Agamben[2]

Remembrance of Things Past

In an amazing coincidence, not widely celebrated by the Bengali reading public, modern Bengali literature in all three of its main genres—poetry, drama, and fiction—could be said to have been self-consciously 'born again'

[1] Letter to Rajnarain, dated 14-7-60, in 1993, Kshetra Gupta (ed.), *Madhusudan rachanabali*, Calcutta: Sahitya Sansad, p. 550.

[2] Giorgio Agamben, 1999, 'The Melancholy Angel', in *The Man Without Content*, Stanford: Stanford University Press, p. 108.

in the same year, 1858. Rangalal Bandyopadhyay published his long verse narrative with a modern literary manifesto preceding it, *Padminīr upākhyān*, in 1858; Pearychand Mittra published the first Bengali novel in book form, *Ālāler ghare dulāl*, in 1858; and Madhusudan Datta inaugurated his career in Bengali by writing a modern Bengali play, *Śarmiṣṭhā nāṭak*, in 1858—this was subsequently published in January 1859. Equally telling is the fact that all three enterprises were born out of argument and perceived insult or challenge, in a tension between native enterprise and colonial denigration, and in a context when older forms were beginning to be discarded or refashioned for being inadequate to the requirements of the modern age.

In the biographies of Madhusudan Datta, in the plays and stories based on his life, as well as in the literary criticism of his work, among the many anecdotes told and retold for their significance and import for the future of modern Bengali language and literature, most are about literary arguments. One of these tells of how, in the suburban country house (*bāgān bāṛi*) of Kishorichand Mittra, an argument ensued one day in 1856 between Madhusudan and Kishorichand's brother, Pearychand Mittra. This was a time when Bengali was still in the process of being self-consciously fashioned into a modern and usable thing, and Pearychand, whose novel, *Ālāler ghare dulāl*, was being serially published under the name of Tekchand Thakur, had embarked on a mission to initiate the practice of using spoken Bengali for literary composition. Here, in an argument between Madhusudan and Pearychand, the passion and disputation the fledgling issue aroused is available to us only in anecdotal form, repeatedly recounted in literary criticism in the following years. Nagendranath Som, one of Madhusudan's biographers, writes:

> Referring to his [Pearychand's] efforts, Madhusudan suddenly exclaimed, 'What on earth are you trying to write?—People wear everyday clothes at home and mingle with their close relatives; but you cannot go outside in that apparel. For that you need formal wear. It appears that you seem to be advocating the disuse of formal clothes and the use of informal attire in the house and outside it, in society and at functions, in short, everywhere. How can that be possible?' Although Madhusudan was a skilled practitioner of English, and well versed in some other languages, nobody present thought that he had any truck with Bengali. Thinking the remark unwarranted, Pearychand retorted, 'What do you know about

> the Bengali language? But mark my words, it is my style of composition that the Bengali language will adopt and this will become permanent.' In reply, Madhusudan, in his usual easy humorous way remarked: '*It is the language of Fishermen, unless you import largely from Sanskrit.* You call that a language! You will see it is the language I create that will be permanent.' Hearing this mysterious statement, everyone present began to laugh loudly; some said, contemptuously, 'You will write Bengali, and that Bengali will be permanent! *Not till the Greek Calends*!'[3]

The Greek Calends, however, arrived sooner than anybody present had bargained for, since Madhusudan's first play in Bengali appeared within two years of this argument. (It is worth remarking here, though, that when he spoke of importing largely from the Sanskrit in order to create a language fit for literary activity, Madhusudan was not speaking literally, as the language in his historical plays and epic poems was sonorous, resonant, and in places, archaic, but never subordinate in all aspects to the Sanskrit; as he himself stated contrarily in a letter to Gaurdas Basak, 'it is my intention to throw off the fetters forged for us by a servile admiration of everything Sanskrit'.[4])

The discussion about what an authentic literary Bengali would or should be continued in the latter half of the century in a more polemical and vigorous manner through the works of Vidyasagar and the contestations between Rabindranath and Bankimchandra; it is an argument whose vestigial traces are to be found even up until the mid-twentieth century. Thus, in a review of cult figure Kamalkumar Majumdar's essays, the writer Sunil Gangopadhyay wrote in *Deś* that the famous (or notorious) difficulty of Kamalkumar's prose was located in a wilful obscurity of form that had its origins in the tussle between the '*sādhu*' and '*calit*' *bhāshā* [formal and informal language]:

> Everybody knows about the transformation, in the Bengali language, from formal Bengali [*shādhu*] to colloquial Bengali [*calit*]. Rabindranath himself and even the *Kallol* group of writers left the formal Bengali

[3] Italicized portions are originally in English. Nagendranath Som, 1989 (1921), *Madhu-smṛti* [Memories of Madhu], Calcutta: Vidyodaya, pp. 97–8. 'Not till the Greek calends' means something that will never happen, as the Greeks had no calends, which was the first day of every Roman month. Greek months began with the new moon and were calculated according to lunar and solar cycles.

[4] Jogindranath Basu, 2004 (1893), *Māikel madhusūdan datter jībancarit* [The Life of Michael Madhusudan Datta], Calcutta: Dey's Publishing, p. 163.

> prose [*sādhu bāṅglā gadya*] behind to come to colloquial Bengali [*calit bhāshā*]. Kamalkumar is the only writer in Bengali literature who went in the opposite direction, beginning in colloquial Bengali and coming later to formal Bengali. Not only the use of verbs, the construction of the sentences themselves became more and more tangled and complex. Yet he spoke in a manner not unlike Sri Ramkrishna, in the language of humorous folk idiom. Many of us had asked him why his written language was so difficult to understand. The reply was different at different times. Once he had said, literature is the offering made to the *debī* [goddess] Saraswati, one has to create a special language for that. I'm not sure what *debī* Saraswati's spoken language is, perhaps this too was one of his jokes.[5]

The eternal alternation, in the Bengali literary sphere, between the *baṭtalā* and Saraswati that we first saw in Nabinchandra's understanding of the place of Iswar Gupta in relation to Vidyasagar, and that Michael too is struggling with in his understanding of formal wear in contrast to informal apparel, continues, it can be seen, into the self-construction of a writer such as Kamalkumar Majumdar, whose writings bear upon the 1960s and 1970s (he died in 1979) with their own unique force.

Madhusudan's life story abounds with such stories of challenges, disputations, arguments, and sudden turns; a similar tale is recounted in a letter written entirely in English by Jatindramohan Tagore regarding Madhusudan's introduction of blank verse into Bengali, which, too, was apparently undertaken in response to a challenge thrown out by Jatindramohan, who thought it was impossible to write blank verse in Bengali. The raconteur relates: 'It was a fine evening, and we were sitting in the lower hall of the Belgatchia Villa where the stage had been set up for the performance of the "Ratnavali" .... [when] Michael said that "no real improvement in the Bengali Drama could be expected until blank verse was introduced into it."' In response, Jatindramohan had reminded Madhusudan that Iswar Gupta, Bengal's most well-known poet at the time, had 'made a caricature of blank verse in Bengali, beginning with the lines "*kabitā kamalā kalā pākā yena kāñdi / ichhā hay yata pāi peṭ bhare khāi*"'. In reply, Madhusudan, typically, said to his interlocutor, 'Oh!... it is no reason because old Issur Chunder Gupta made a caricature of blank

[5] Sunil Gangopadhyay, 2011, '*Durbodhyo, tabu romānchakar*', ['Difficult, but still exciting'], *Deś*, 2 January, p. 52.

verse in Bengali that nobody else will be able to write it.' After some further exchanges, Madhusudan takes up the challenge: '"Write me down an ass," said he laughingly, "if I am not able to convince you of your error within a short time."' The conversation ended with a promise that Jatindramohan would pay all the expenses of printing and publishing any poem Madhusudan wrote in blank verse, and within three or four days, the first canto of the *Tilottamāsambhab* turned up on his desk.[6]

Another story (once again written in English), recounted by Madhusudan's childhood best friend, Gourdas Basak, tells the story about how he was provoked into writing *Śarmisṭhā Nāṭak*:

> After his admission to the first rehearsal, and before he had entered upon his task of the English translation of the Ratnavali, Modhu, with his partiality for English taste exclaimed to me (aside), 'What a pity the Rajas should have spent such a lot of money on such a miserable play. I wish I had known it before, as I could have given you a piece worthy of your Theatre.' I laughed at the idea of his offering to write a Bengali play, and chaffingly asked if it was his wish to see us introduce a wretched Vidya Sundar on our stage. Conscious of the dearth of really good plays in our language, he could not but feel the sting of my remark as a home-thrust and simply muttered, 'We shall see, we shall see.'
>
> The next morning he called on me at the rooms of the Asiatic Society for the loan of a few Vernacular and Sanskrit books, dramas specially, and in the course of a week or two read to me the first few scenes of his Sarmishtha which struck me as having the ring of true metal. I wished to take the MS with me to Belgatchia, but he said I must wait till he had finished the First Act.[7]

The Pathuriaghata Tagores had instituted a theatre at Belgatchia in which Bengali plays of decency could be performed (note the reference to the inadmissibility of staging what was a popular choice among the Bengali public at the time—the 'wretched Vidya Sundar'); to this end they had staged *Ratnavali*, a Sanskrit play translated into Bengali by a well-known scholar and Bengali writer, Ramnarayan Tarkaratna.

[6] Brajendranath Bandyopadhyay (ed.), 2001 (1942), *Madhusudan Datta* in *Sāhitya sadhak charitmala*, Vol. 2, Calcutta: Bangiya Sahitya Parishad, p. 48.

[7] Ibid., p. 37.

For those in the audience who could not follow Bengali, a substantial section of important Englishmen in the city, Madhusudan had been commissioned in 1858 to translate the play into English, which he did. The English-language *Ratnavali* had then been performed in the Belgatchia Theatre on 31 July 1858, and Madhusudan was paid five hundred rupees for his services. It was at this time, then, and in these circumstances, that Madhusudan first thought of writing a Bengali play, the *Śarmiṣṭhā nāṭak*, which he completed in a few months time.

Such accounts, repeatedly told and retold, are not confined to Madhusudan's life alone, though, certainly, the legends surrounding him and the mythology that later enshrined these stories of his life seem to reflect the same excess that appeared to be so much a characteristic of his personality. In form they resemble Vidyasagar's life story, which is similarly recounted within particular episodic frames: of swimming the river to set out on his journey from his village, of learning the English numbers from the milestones in his path, of putting his feet up on the table to receive an arrogant Englishman who had treated him similarly, and so on. These stories, like those about Ramakrishna or Vivekananda, are to do with the national life, emblematized in illustrative boxes of the kind in *Amar Chitra Katha* or Bengali comic book illustrations, where each frame holds within its box a symptomatic moment in the attainment of selfhood under colonial subjugation. The literary life seems less amenable to such narrative treatment, and has rarely been the source material for popular national identity formation. Instead, as we see with Madhusudan, the literary anecdote is constituted within the structure of literary criticism, although the relation with the national is always of some significance.

This repetition of certain stories around Madhusudan Datta perceived to be seminal to the construction of Bengali literary modernity is a kind of remembering that consists of a recall of the original event as a recurring, ceremonial date in the life of the nation. As Shahid Amin has remarked in a different context, 'The master saga of nationalist struggles is built around the reading of certain well-known and memorable events. There is often an exasperating and chronicle-like quality about such celebratory accounts, but the significance of nationalist narratives lies in their elaborate and heroic setting down, or "figurating", the triumph of good over evil (or of the native over the colonial).[8] The politics of remembering these stories related to the foundational moments of a new Bengali literature belongs to the realm of 'memorializing', which constitutes the politics of representation. Rescuing, from the depths of time, certain anecdotal material related to the lives of our iconic figures, these memory-practices, celebratory and almost triumphalist in tone, wherein the same stories are repeated and recycled, support historical representation by establishing just the sort of source material that the historian routinely looks for. Here, this representation that exists at the primary level forms a base or foundation for the 'second or third-order representation that we usually call history', which then gives rise to 'the politics of memorializing and memorizing of the event'.[9] Functioning as a persistent, official rite in the narrative of the nation that is produced whenever there is a requirement, these anecdotes embody the desire for the creation of memorials that is inherent in national life, performing the function of a collective ritual of remembering that is so integral to nation building. Nation building, or a preoccupation with the enhancement of national feeling, was not just incipiently present in the stated intentions of Madhusudan, but was a declared objective.

National Poet, Secular Canon

Bankimchandra, writing after Madhusudan's death in 1874, famously asked:

> If some modern, rich and proud European asks us, what hope do people like you have? Who has been born a man yet in Bengal? We will say, among religious leaders, we have Sri Chaitanyadeb, among philosophers, Raghunath, among poets, Sri Joydeb and Sri Madhusudan…
>
> Different countries have different steps leading towards national progress. Knowledge made ancient India great—follow the same road, and you will again be great. The times are positive, Europe is ready to

[8] Shahid Amin, 1995, *Event, Metaphor, Memory: Chauri Chaura 1922–1992*, Berkeley: University of California Press, p. 2.

[9] Dipesh Chakrabarty, 2007, 'Remembering 1857: An Introductory Note', *Economic and Political Weekly*, 12 May, p. 1693.

> help, seeing that a favourable wind is blowing, unfurl your national flag—on it, write the name—'Sri Madhusudan'.[10]

This passage is printed on the back cover of the standard edition of Madhusudan's collected works, the Sahitya Sansad edition of the *Madhusudan rachanabali*, highlighting the publisher's feeling of its great importance in advertising Madhusudan for the contemporary reader. In the essay from which the quotation is extracted, preceding this conclusion, Bankimchandra had repeatedly made an equation between Madhusudan's fame as a poet and the achievement of national glory, saying:

> That country is fortunate in which a good poet is born. That country is even more fortunate in which a good poet achieves fame… That country whose best poet achieves fame before he dies has truly joined the road to progress. Michael Madhusudan Datta has died famous; from this we may realise that Bengal has joined the path of progress.[11]

The deft elision here of any serious examination of literary achievement is not accidental. Bankim's views on Madhusudan had been clearly stated in his English essay for the *Calcutta Review*, 'Bengali Literature', written in 1871, just a couple of years before Michael died in 1873, where he had said of Madhusudan, that 'while admitting his considerable merits, we are not prepared to rank him among great poets'. Praising certain qualities as displaying a 'high order of art', he complained nonetheless, 'Mr. Datta, however, is not faultless. He wants repose. The winds rage their loudest when there is no necessity for the lightest puff. Clouds gather and pour down a deluge, when they need do nothing of the kind; and the sea grows terrible in its wrath, when everybody feels inclined to resent its interference. All this bombast is unworthy of Mr. Datta's genius and cultivated taste'.[12]

Madhusudan himself, perhaps unsure of his status based on the literary or aesthetic parameters of Bengali, had repeatedly asserted his credentials in the domain of the national. The point is also perhaps

[10] Bankimchandra Chattopadhyay, 1998, '*Mṛta māikel madhusūdan datta*' [The Late Michael Madhusudan Datta] *Bankim rachanavali*, Vol. 2, Calcutta: Sahitya Sansad, p. 808.

[11] Ibid.

[12] Bankimchandra Chatterjee, 1998, 'Bengali Literature', *Bankim rachanavali*, Vol. 3, p. 115.

worth making that the decades of the 1860s and 1870s in Bengal were subsumed under the excitement of the 'national'; it was not only Madhusudan who ventured to place all his works under the rubric of the nation, but others too, such as the Tagore family and the group around the organization of the Hindu Mela. Its chief organizer Nabagopal Mitra's enthusiasm in using the prefix 'national' was caricatured by Manmohan Basu at the time:

> In those days, he had ended up being labelled '*national* Nabagopal'. Somebody said that he had a '*national* habit'. He spoke always of the '*national, national, national*'. All his work was '*national, national, national*'. The newspaper he published was called 'National'; the sabha he set up with such care was called '*national*'; the school he established was named '*national*'; the yoga centre was '*national*'; the Mela was '*national*'... when he slept, his dreams were '*national*'. He was the living embodiment of '*national*'.[13]

In this passage, the word in recurrent use was the English 'national', spelt in Bengali script, rather than any Bengali equivalent, and it is remarkable that almost whenever the nation was invoked in this way, it was the English-language word that was used. When Derozio and Kasiprasad Ghosh had written nationalist sonnets or poems, they had done so in the English language, and in the 1870s, Bankimchandra, Hemchandra, Nabinchandra, Akshaychandra, and many others would begin to translate the term into Bengali in various ways, but at this moment, still, at the time of Madhusudan, in 1860/61, the word used was still the English one. (It might be instructive to keep in mind, here, that Rabindranath refused to translate the English word 'nation' in his Bengali essay written in 1901, 'Nation *ki?*' ['What is the Nation?'], where he advocated instead that the English word be incorporated into the Bengali language to avoid confusion.)

The forging of a new 'national' poetry and drama are among Madhusudan's prime concerns at this time. He wrote to Rajnarain Basu, regretting his brilliant farces—'You know that as yet we have not established a National Theatre. I mean we have not as yet got a body of sound, classical Dramas to regulate the national taste, and therefore

[13] From Manmohan Basu's journal, cited in Gita Chattopadhyay, 1983, *Bāṅglā svadeśī gān*, Delhi: Delhi University, p. 8.

we ought not to have Farces.'[14] Using the word 'national' again and again in his letters, all of which were written in English, on another occasion he proclaims: '... you may rest assured, I shall not allow myself to be bound by the dicta of Mr.Vishwanath of the Sahitya-Darpan. I shall look to the great dramatists of Europe for models. That would be founding a real National Theatre.'[15] (Typically, 'Mr Vishwanath' is Vishwanath Kabiraj, author of the fifteenth-century Sanskrit text on aesthetics, the *Sāhitya darpaṇ.*)

This foundation of a national literature, as Madhusudan articulated it into being, was also, necessarily and newly, the inauguration of a completely secular literature. Almost every Bengali literary historian has remarked on the shift, in the nineteenth century, toward Western forms and conventions, marking the moment as one that resulted in the creation of a secular domain of culture. Dinanath Sanyal, one of the best-known among the commentators on *Meghnādbadh*, remarked in 1906:

> Before this, all of the literature extant in Bengal was devotional. In fact, Bharatchandra's *Bidyāsundar* too was merely a part of the *Annadāmaṅgal* [paean to the goddess Annada]. The purely literary work (*Pure Literature*) did not exist in Bengali literature. There is no dearth of it in the Sanskrit, nor in Western literature, but not in Bengali. It is Madhusudan who is its progenitor in Bengali literature. So the *Meghnādbadh* needs to be read from the point of view of a purely literary work. Just as Bhavabhuti's *Uttar Rāmcarit* is about the life of Ram but not devotional literature, so too, the *Meghnādbadh* is about events in the *Rāmāyan*, but cannot be discussed in the light of devotional literature; it is, rather, the first and most important victory flag of the establishment of the purely literary in a new Bengal.[16]

The motif of the flag recurs here, and whether knowingly or not, Dinanath has resurrected it alongside Bankimchandra, in whose passage the flag, fluttering with Madhusudan's name on it, was first and foremost about national pride. Here, however, its character is represented as unabashedly literary, though of course in the nineteenth century the role of literary culture in constituting the national was

[14] *Madhusudan rachanabali*, p. 545.

[15] Ibid.

[16] Dinanath Sanyal (ed.), 1324, *Meghnādbadh kābya*, Calcutta, Introduction, p. 16.

taken for granted. 'Pure Literature' is the term in English that he put in parenthesis after the statement '*biśuddha sāhitya bāṅglā sāhitye chila nā*', which I have preferred to render as 'the purely literary work did not exist in Bengali literature'. In order to bring this 'purely literary work' into being, Dinanath had correctly suggested that the conception of literature needed to be secularized, moved away from the domain of religion.

Following Iswar Gupta and Rangalal, Madhusudan became the most important landmark in the inauguration of a new modern and secular space of culture, a turning point in the construction of the secular self in Indian cultural history. About his recovery and use of Hindu religious narratives for the purpose of literary construction, especially in the *Meghnādbadh kābya,*, and on the significance of this moment for the emergence of a secular domain of culture, Amit Chaudhuri has commented:

> The composition of the *Meghnādbadh kābya* might be said to constitute an important moment, a moment when a poem with an overtly religious subject was transplanted from the domain of religion into the domain of culture; in looking back at the space in which that poem was written and read, we become witness to the outline of a secular, modern space that is also 'spiritual' and mythopoeic.[17]

In this conflation of the secular with the 'mythopoeic', Madhusudan had no immediate predecessors in the modern literary sphere, for neither Iswar Gupta nor Rangalal had created their oeuvre from religious mythology; indeed, the latter was emphatic in his self-conscious disavowal of such subject matter. The transplantation of such material from the 'domain of religion' to the 'domain of culture', then, was first inaugurated in the Bengali literary sphere by Madhusudan, who faced much indignant criticism for his treatment of the protagonist Ram (including from the young Rabindranath), whom he professed to hating ('I despise Ram and his rabble; but the idea of Ravan elevates and kindles my imagination; he was a grand fellow'.[18]) thereby establishing the foundation for a modern secular literary tradition that continues right up to A.K. Ramanujan's famous

[17] Amit Chaudhuri, 2008, 'This is Not Music: The Emergence of a Domain of Culture', *Clearing a Space*, London: Peter Lang, p. 111.

[18] *Madhusudan rachanabali*, p. 562.

essay, 'Three Hundred Ramayanas', that has aroused the fury of conservative right wingers in the present day.[19]

The Great Silence of Poetry

Sudipta Kaviraj has remarked, in an essay exploring the history of Bengali literary culture, on the inception, in the time of Madhusudan, of 'a more introspective literary culture, marking a fundamental shift in the nature of the literary itself'. 'Above all', he remarks, 'the culture of reading was fundamentally transformed. The presupposition of the silent reader introduced a series of interesting changes in poetry's technical structure, the most significant of which was the slow decline of the aural in favour of semantic delectation... Poetry now came to be enshrouded in a great silence of refinement'.[20] Kaviraj, however, fails to develop on the significance of this shift in any literary detail, preferring, as most commentators from the sphere of the social sciences have done, to dwell on the relation of literary modernity in Bengal to the political and the social.[21]

Arguably, however, at the same time as the silent reader was coming into being, poetry in Bengali continued to retain an element of what Kaviraj calls the 'aural' well into the twentieth century. There was certainly a change in 'the culture of reading'; this much is indisputable, but whether from the time of Madhusudan onward, 'Poetry now came to be enshrouded in a great silence of refinement' is entirely debatable. Kaviraj's further claims that from now on, literary culture was transformed into 'an impersonal "audience" of readers sitting and perusing texts in private', and that literature was henceforth 'turned into a primarily lonely pleasure' does not take cognizance of the specificity of Bengali culture, where the onset of modernity was surely

[19] In October 2011, the Delhi University Academic Council removed A.K. Ramanujan's essay, 'Three Hundred Ramayanas: Five Examples and Three Thoughts on Translation' from the syllabus, a move celebrated by right-wing ABVP supporters. This resulted in nationwide outrage in the English language press but no remedial action on the part of the University; the book has not been reinstated to date.

[20] Sudipta Kaviraj, 2007, 'The Two Histories of Literary Culture in Bengal', in Sheldon Pollock (ed.), *Literary Cultures in History Reconstruction from South Asia*, Delhi: Oxford University Press, pp. 503–66.

[21] Ibid.

distinct from the course of its development in the West. The lines quoted above, of readers sitting and reading in private silence, might have been apposite for the British reader of Keats or Wordsworth in his or her library or boudoir, and might certainly be applicable to certain scenes of reading in modern Bengal (the outstanding beauty of the passage in *Pather pāñcāli* of Apu sitting alone by the village pond as the light fades, immersed in his reading, comes immediately to mind), but it ignores the different private and public contexts of literary culture in Bengal.[22]

Certainly it is true that the 1860s and 1870s were a time when the recitation of poetry was changing in a context that was both 'public' and 'literary' in a new way. The literary public sphere that formed in the early nineteenth century conducted itself primarily in English and revolved around debating societies and academic associations such as the Society for the Acquisition of General Knowledge in the 1830s or memorial lectures such as the one set up in memory of David Hare in the 1850s; indeed, the skills of oratory, as required in public lectures and speeches in the English language to large audiences, were an invaluable repository of prestige and fame for individuals such as Ram Gopal Ghosh, and were constitutive of the literary sphere of Bengal in the first part of the nineteenth century.

Coming specifically to Bengali poetry, however, we see it being recited aloud in literary gatherings such as those annually organized by Iswar Gupta with much fanfare from 1851 onward, and also being discussed in venues such as the Bethune Society, as Rangalal has recorded so memorably. But apart from these public venues, which were, after all, structured according to a new space of Western institutional practices in public culture, the importance of recitation and declamation in the Bengali private sphere too needs acknowledgement. While Madhusudan's sonnets gave full reign to the introspective character of modern Bengali sensibility, the resonance of his words and the high dramatic form of the themes resulted in poetry that was, for the first time in the history of modern Bengali literature, uniquely inflected with the personal anguish, hopes, and meditations of an individual. Yet these intensely individual and almost private sonnets attained, in

[22] Bibhutibhusan Bandyopadhyay, 1928, *Pather pāñcāli*, Calcutta.

their reception by Bengali readers, an inevitably declamatory nature—recited aloud in performative poses by generations of Bengali readers.

Madhusudan, in fact, more than any other modern Bengali poet, lends himself to this treatment, and his extraordinary *caturddaśpadī* poems, some of the action-packed scenes of the *Meghnādbadh kābya*, and even, perhaps most popularly of all, his self-composed epitaph (*Dāṅṛāo pathikbar, jamma yadi taba baṅge…*) are still recited line for line by countless Bengali readers of a certain generation.[23] Bengalis have incorporated into their appreciation of poetry a tendency to recite from it in a manner that disappeared from the West a long time ago, tearing a considerable hole in that great shroud of refined silence that Kaviraj has evoked. One could hazard that almost every Bengali middle-class family, even a generation ago, had characters who would burst into lines of poetry in an entirely uncalled for manner, from Michael or Rabindranath to Nazrul or D.L. Roy as the occasion demanded, adding to the enjoyment of the moment in unforgettable ways.

This habit of recitation, which confers upon poetry an aural and public element that exists alongside the private space of the individual reader, was perhaps a continuation of earlier practices of recitation and song as modes of recreation that continues in all parts of South Asia, for instance, in the Urdu *shairi* or the Hindi *kavi sammelan*. Writing of the 1860s, Nabinchandra Sen proudly recorded being profoundly influenced by the older modes of poetic practice he had inherited from relations and neighbours in his native Chittagong, where poetry and song are mentioned in the same breath. He writes of the poetic accomplishments of his father, his father's brothers, and family friend Shyamacharan Khastgir, who established Chittagong's first professional theatre company. Praising his father's recitation of *Bidyāsundar* and Kabikankan, he mentions how the audience would

[23] I was once accosted by a man at the Calcutta Book Fair in the *maydān* in the 1990s who, for some unknown reason, made me stop and listen to an entire passage from the *Meghnād* as he recited it from memory. The example is not exceptional, though the incident might be—Gautam Bhadra is living proof of someone who will recite entire passages from Madhusudan to illustrate an argument or merely for the pleasure in the beauty of the flow of words to this day. Partha Chatterjee points out that there is a full two-hour stage production of the *Meghnādbadh* where Gautam Haldar recites the entire poem for the audience.

be reduced to tears by the sweetness of the rendition. Poetry, in this traditional incarnation, is almost always conflated with song and with performance, and he quotes from particular songs and *yātrā* composed by his family. Not only family, all of Chattagram's residents were poetry lovers, he claims, going on to describe a scene indelibly etched in his memory.

> Midnight, winter. Shyamacharan was sitting in Harachandra Ray's second house on the hilltop and singing his self-composed songs of the *Caṇḍi-yātrā* to my father and him. Our exams were near, we left to go and study. He was playing the *ḍholok* and singing alone. His sweet-as-nectar full-throated voice flooded the mountains and silent night sky, rising and falling melodiously. We left our open books and, enchanted, ran to that two-storey house. We saw that the place was crowded with people. As far as Shaymacharan's voice could be heard, no one had been able to sleep. They had all, like us, been drawn as in a magic spell and stood there in silence.... In this manner, so many people's songs, so many poems, *bāromās* [songs of everyday joy and sorrow], *sārigān* [boat-song] were then prevalent in the country.[24]

Nabinchandra's own deployment of stanza and metre were traditionally mellifluous. Recitation is important for him, and numerous passages in his autobiography record instances of him declaiming verses from his own poetry aloud, and he himself repeatedly asserts the importance of 'rasa', or enjoyment of the 'beauty' of poetry. So older practices of declamation or recitation continued in altered contexts and situations, divorced from their everyday aspect as part of religious or community practices, and transplanted instead into the halls of literary societies, gatherings of literary practitioners, in drawing-room conversations and *āddā*s, and even, as Nabinchandra testified, in railway carriages and steamers amongst the newly met.[25]

'A Variety of Pause': Punctuation and the Anxiety of Influence

Intriguingly, while the advent of the silent reader needs to be qualified with some discussion on the altered declamatory aspects of modern

[24] Nabinchandra Sen, 1999, *Āmār Jīban*, *Nabinchandra rachanabali*, Vol. 1, Calcutta: Bangiya Sahitya Parishad, pp. 91-91.

[25] See Nabinchandra Sen, *Āmār jīban*, Vols 1–3.

Bengali poetry, as I have attempted in the preceding paragraphs, little attention seems to have been paid to some of the other fundamental developments in Bengali poetry from the old to the new in which Madhusudan played an important role, such as the growth of literary criticism or the aspect of punctuation. He had himself, perspicaciously, been well aware of the watershed moment he occupied in the field of Bengali literature, commenting excitedly,

> What a vast field does our country now present for literary enterprise! I wish to God, I had time. Poetry, the Drama, Criticism, Romance—a man would leave a name behind him, 'above all Greek, above all Roman fame'.[26]

This was said in the context of asking his friend Rajnarain to review his book: 'When you get your copy of Tilottoma you must send me a regular Aristotelian letter about the fable, the characters, the sentiments and the language. You must also review it in such a way (publicly) so as to initiate our countrymen into the mysteries of a just and enlightened criticism.' Perhaps Rajnarain himself should take up the subject of criticism, he then offers, advising him to follow, in this regard, 'Aristotle, Longinus, Quintilian, the Sahitya-Darpan, Burke, Kames, Alison, Addison, Dryden and a host of others, not forgetting old Blair's lectures or the German Schlegel'.[27]

While the 'mysteries of a just and enlightened criticism' still seem to be eluding the English-educated in India, the regional languages such as Bengali or Marathi or Malayalam seem to have an altogether more robust and informed point of view on the literary-critical. It is worth pointing out in this context that Madhusudan's works played a crucial role in the rise of literary criticism in the Bengali language. Later practitioners like Bankimchandra (who had also memorably lamented 'the absence of a sound and intelligent criticism' as 'a thing unknown to the Native Press'[28]) or Rabindranath went on to write a substantial amount of literary criticism themselves, but to Madhusudan belongs

[26] Letter to Rajnarain, 15 May 1860. *Madhusudan rachanabali*, pp. 547–8. The quotation is from Alexander Pope, 'Imitations of Horace', (1733-8), Epistle 1, Book 2, line 26.

[27] Ibid.

[28] Bankimchandra Chattopadhyay, 1998, 'A Popular Literature for Bengal', *Bankim rachanavali*, Vol. 3, Calcutta: Sahitya Sansad, p. 100.

the singular honour of spawning an entire industry of interpretation, analysis, and literary criticism around his few but all-important books of poetry. For Madhusudan's works went on to bring into being the most exhaustive close reading and the most voluminous commentary that had been occasioned by any single Bengali writer till then, or after. Line by line, and sometimes word for word, in an effort that has almost Eliotesque or Joycean overtones, reminding us of the books of notes to 'The Wasteland' or *Ulysses*, Madhusudan's allusions and use of language in his various publications, especially in the *Meghnādbadh kābya*, were annotated and explained for Bengali readers over the years in notebooks by Dinanath Sanyal, Gyanendramohan Das, or Jahnabikumar Chakrabarti, teaching how to interpret allusion, metaphor, image, and language in an intensive lesson all at once.

It was also undoubtedly Madhusudan who introduced to the Bengali language, not only the sonnet form and blank verse, but punctuation, so vital to the modern reader, for whom the line breaks and the punctuation marks were of utmost significance. Even in the self-consciously 'modern' poetry of Rangalal, who preceded him, the verse patterns were traditional, and the metre used was always traditional Bengali metre. Thus Rangalal's most famous nationalist lines in *Padminīr upākhyān*, '*svādhīnatā hīnatāy̆ ke bañcite cāy̆ he, ke bañcite cāy̆*', although allegedly borrowed from Moore's Irish Melodies ('From life without freedom oh who would not fly?'), were set to a distinctively Bengali rhythmic pattern in the traditional *pay̆ār* scheme. The entire poem was composed in *pay̆ār*, which employed a metre or *chanda* called *miśrakalābṛtta*, which admitted many variations in syllabic breaks. Whatever the rhythmic break within the line, which could be *dvipadī* (divided into two) in the first lines with which the narrative opens:

Nabīn bhābuk ek bhramaṇ kāraṇ
Bhārater nānā deśe kari paryaṭaṇ,

[A young thinker setting out on a journey
Travelled through Bharat's many countries,]

or *tripadī* (into three) in the line:

Dvija kan 'he sujan, *kara man samarpaṇ,*
Padminīr bichitra kathāy̆'

[The king said 'my good man, dedicate your mind,
To the strange tale of Padmini],

the punctuation remained more or less minimal, with commas or periods employed only at the point at which there would have been a break in the recitation.[29]

With Madhusudan, the pattern of punctuation took a revolutionary new turn. Enabled partly by the free line of blank verse, where the sentence continued into the following lines, Madhusudan's opening sentences stretched into three or four lines of verse that then often ended, after many semicolons, commas, and brackets, in an exclamation mark or question mark, and only very rarely in a *dā̃ṛi* or period point. Without going into an extensive analysis of the range of Madhusudan's works, just two instances may suffice here to give a sense of his use of punctuation. In a sonnet called '*Samāpte*' ['At the End'] in his *Caturddaśpadī kabitābalī*, a line towards the end of the poem reads:

Nārinu, mā, cinite tomāre
Śaiśabe, abodh āmi ! dākilā yaubane;
(yadio adham putra, mā ki bhule tāre?)

[I could not, ma, recognise you
In my childhood, ignorant as I was! You called in my youth;
(Although a son be prodigal, does a mother forget him?)]

Madhusudan must have been the first free user of the semicolon in Bengali poetry—and he is profligate in its use; the semicolon recurs in almost every other sonnet he wrote. The famous sonnet, '*Baṅgabhāshā*' ['Bengali'], has no less than four in the space of its fourteen lines. The rhythm and sense of his lines are almost entirely English in tone, and when he uses traditional modes of address such as '*he*', instead of using it as in Rangalal's use of it to end the line '*ke bachite chai hé,* or even as a form of address as in the above quoted line '*Dwija kon "hé sujan*...' or, again in the same poem, '*hena mūrkha āche ke hé*', Madhusudan anglicizes its usage in the Bengali line, using it rather to replace the poetic English 'oh!'. Thus the first line of '*Baṅgabhāshā*' reads: '*hé baṅga, bhāndāre taba bibidha ratan*', or 'Oh Bengal, your storehouse

[29] I thank Sibaji Bandhyopadhay for his guidance on these metres.

has many different gems', where the use of the Bengali '*hé*' for the English 'oh' is almost revolutionary in its aspect.

The famous lines Madhusudan composed for his epitaph were equally arresting in their intonation: '*dāñṛāo, pathikbar, janma yadi taba bange! tisṭha kkhaṇakāl*!' [Stop, wayfarer, if you were born in Bengal! Stand a while!] The shift to the drama of this line from the previously common use of the *payār* scheme, with its fixed medial and terminal pauses that led to a sing-song effect in recitation, cannot be underestimated. In an introduction to the works of Hemchandra Bandyopadhyay, writing about the lifeless nature of Hemchandra's use of blank verse, Pramathanath Bisi had pointed out that:

> The life of *amitrākkhar chanda* [blank verse] is in the use of punctuation when necessary. A variety of punctuation can be used to create a startling effect in *amitrākkhar chanda*; Madhusudan has done this. *Narrative, dramatic, lyrical* and *descriptive*—he has put this metre to its fullest use in all of these instances, and it does not feel tiresome anywhere. This has been made possible because of his unexpected use of punctuation. It is this that is the life force of the *amitrākkhar chanda*.[30]

Closer to Madhusudan's own time, Bankimchandra, writing in English, had also commented on what he called a 'variety of pause' in Madhusudan's lines in the *Meghnādbadh kābya*, saying briefly: 'Nor is the verse broken up into couplets complete in themselves, in the Sanskrit fashion, but, abounding like Milton's in a variety of pause, it seems to us musical and graceful, as well as a fitting vehicle for passionate feeling'.[31] This 'variety of pause', brought about by the effects of punctuation, was to go on to become one of the hallmarks of modern Bengali poetry. No modern poetry in Bengal was written in the years that followed that did not employ punctuation more or less in the manner of Madhusudan, and while Rabindranath reportedly had his reservations about the use of the semicolon in Bengali poetry, it is indisputable that as a result of this manner of punctuation, the cadence of the lines changed, the manner of its declamation changed,

[30] Pramathanath Bisi, 1971, 'Introduction' *Hemcandra-racanāsambhār*, Calcutta: Mitra & Ghosh, pp. iv–v.

[31] 'Bengali Literature', *Bankim rachanavali*, Vol. 3, p. 115.

the very nature of the poetry, it would not be an exaggeration to maintain, changed.

National Literature and the Mother Tongue

The nationalist understanding that a country's literature needs to be formulated in the authenticity of the mother tongue was first formulated mid-way through the nineteenth century in Bengal, curiously enough, in a symbolic moment in the life of Madhusudan Datta. Following the publication of Madhusudan's English narrative poem *Captive Ladie* in Madras in 1849, John Drinkwater Bethune, leading educationalist and advocate for women's education in Calcutta, wrote to Madhusudan's closest friend, Gaurdas Basak, that Madhusudan 'could render far greater service to his country and have a better chance of achieving a lasting reputation for himself, if he will employ the taste and talents, which he has cultivated by the study of English, in improving the standard and adding to the stock of the poems in his own language, if poetry, at all events he must write'.[32] This advice was endorsed by Gaurdas, who memorably added, 'We do not want another Byron or another Shelley in English; what we lack is a Byron or a Shelley in Bengali literature', the upshot of which was, according to standard texts of Bengali literary criticism, that Michael Madhusudan then turned away from the foreign to return to the welcoming arms of his native literature.[33]

Indian critics have dealt with this moment of the putting aside of the English language to creatively intervene in 'one's own' vernacular language somewhat heavy-handedly, and curiously in keeping with the colonialist imperative of reformers such as Bethune. Sometimes the disavowal of the English language in the creative enterprise of writers in the regional languages takes a simple and uncomplicated form; so Priya Joshi, writing about Bankimchandra's contribution as a 'widely influential novelist in India', speaks of 'two false starts' Bankim made in his career before he found his vocation as a Bengali novelist. 'Bankim's first false move,' she says, was that his first publication was a book of verse in 1856, and then the second, that he wrote his first

[32] Jogindranath Basu, *Māikel madhusūdan datter jībancarit*, p. 116.

[33] Ibid., p.118.

novel, *Rajmohan's Wife*, eight years later in 1864 in English. After this, 'each and every one [of his novels] was written in Bengali, rendering him accolades such as ... "the best Bengali novelist that Bengal has yet produced"'.[34] In this situation, the problem of the English language is solved by turning toward Bengali—'the solution he needed came partly from abandoning his reliance on British forms'—when a turn toward the Indian epic tradition in Bankim is seen as constituting Bankim's own 'efforts to indigenize the novel in the Subcontinent'.[35]

It would be salutary to remind ourselves, in this context, of the false start Bankim made in the Bengali language as well, writing the advertisement to his first Bengali novel, *Lalitā. Purākālik Galpa. Tathā Mānas* (1856) in such strange and terrible Bengali that it prompted Iswar Gupta, punning on the word 'bankim', to advise him never to use such 'bent/oblique language (*bankimbhāshā*) to express his feelings again'.[36] Brajendranath Bandyopadhyay and Sajanikanta Das, in their entry on Bankimchandra for the *Sāhitya sādhak caritmālā*, deploy their own adjectives: the advertisement to the novel, they say, was 'unreadable' (*apāṭhya*), 'deadly' (*bisham*), and 'fearsome' (*bhayābaha*).[37] In Joshi's developmentalist, teleological vision of Bankim's career, poetry as a genre and English as a language are seen as disabling devices, hampering the flowering of true creativity in the colonial subject; it is only when the writer turns from these 'false starts' towards presumably a truer start in his own language and what is seen today as the pre-eminent genre, that he truly comes into his own greatness, achieving immortality in the process.

A far more nuanced understanding of the moment of disavowal and return to the mother tongue is to be found in a text such as *Provincializing Europe*, itself a book that launches an acute and effective critique of European historicism. In it, an English poem by Madhusudan written in 1842 for the *Literary Gleaner* is quoted by Dipesh Chakrabarty in full, followed by the observation: 'Michael Madhusudan Dutt, the young Bengali author of this poem, eventually

[34] Priya Joshi, 2003, *In Another Country: Colonialism, Culture, and the English Novel in India*, Delhi, Oxford University Press, p. 147.

[35] Ibid., p. 152.

[36] Brajendranath Bandyopadhyay and Sajanikanta Das, 'Bankimchandra Chattopadhyay', *Sāhitya sādhak caritmālā*, Vol. 2, pp. 35, 37.

[37] Ibid.

realized the impossibility of being European and returned to Bengali literature to become one of our finest poets'.[38] If one were to read this 'impossibility' literally, as critics such as Bishnu Dey have done in their time, then of course it should be pointed out that it is doubtful whether Michael ever really stopped 'being European', or realized the invalidity of using European forms to create his own.[39]

Michael himself was responsible, however, in no small part, for the propagation of this imagery of return, reconciliation, and fulfilment when, in some of his most famous poems ('*Kabimātṛbhāshā*', '*Ātmabilāp*', '*Baṅgabhūmir Prati*', '*Baṅgabhāshā*'), he held forth passionately on his own neglect of, and return to his mother tongue, his motherland, his native shores, as here in the last mentioned poem that began: '*Hé Baṅga, bhāndāre taba bibidha ratan*'—

O *Baṅga*, your store has many gems;—
All of which (ignorant as I am), I held in contempt;
Intoxicated by the riches of others, I journeyed
To other countries, at an importunate moment, as a beggar.
Many days did I spend forsaking happiness!
Sleepless, I dedicated my body to starvation, gave
My mind to fruitless meditation, receiving the unacceptable;
Played with moss; having forgotten the lotus groves!
In a dream, your *Kulalaksmi* then said to me:

[38] Dipesh Chakrabarty, 2001, *Provincializing Europe*, Delhi: Oxford University Press, pp. 34–5.

[39] For a fuller discussion of Bishnu Dey's essay see the following section of this chapter. Responding to this point, Chakrabarty (email communication, 13/1/2009) explains further that

> if taken in a non-literal register, the impossibility referred to might conceivably be seen to exist rather in a feeling that many colonial writers—but definitely not all—experienced in their attempt to adopt the language of the master. Here 'impossibility' does not mean that they became impervious to European influences or that they ceased to feel attracted to European models, but has more to do with the sense in which Spivak used the word in her note on translating Mahasweta Devi in *Imaginary Maps*, where she says 'ethics is the experience of the impossible', meaning that the impossible is the experience of a passage you can never complete and yet one that you feel compelled to undertake again and again in a crossing where you never find yourself completely on the other side of the frontier. You end up being on both sides at once, which is why you might say that the frontier runs through you, creating your 'double consciousness'.

'O child, your mother's store is ranged with jewels
Why are you then in this beggar's state today?
Go back, you un-awakened, go back to your home!'
Happily did I obey the command; finding, in time
A mine in the form of my mother-tongue, fully a web of gems.[40]

Each of these poems, all of which are famous in Bengali literature, reiterate similar sentiments; more often than not, most Bengalis will quote verbatim from the lines above, or similar lines in the others, among the most well-known of which, perhaps, are the first lines of *Ātmabilāp* ('Heart's Lament'): '*Āśār chalane bhuli, ki phal labhinu, hāy, tāi bhābi mane?*' ('Deceived by the tricks of hope, alas, what fruits have I gained / I wonder?'), or those of the poignant *Baṅgabhūmir Prati* ('To Bengal'), prefaced with Byron's line, 'My native land, good night!', written five days before embarking on a ship to England: '*Rekho, mā, dāsere mane, e minati kari pade…*' ('Keep this slave in mind, mother, this I plead at your feet…').[41] This emotional bond with the motherland or 'mother tongue', exceedingly effective as a poetic image, was, however, hardly a literal statement—declaring an intent to abandon all that was foreign for all that was native—on the part of Madhusudan, as critics have been liable to read him.

This 'return' or turn towards a cultural practice that is perceived as 'one's own' is, of course, a seminal moment in Indian cultural history, occurring in various regional languages at various times, and involves a process of 'disowning and recovery' that was a fundamental trope in colonial creative experience.[42] The relationship to the mother tongue, in literary historical discourse, has been imagined in filial terms, where it is sometimes configured in the language of blood and sinew, an inheritance that cannot be disowned, while the English language is located at an ambivalent distance. The situation, however, in the creation of a modern secular vernacular language for literary composition has been a little more complicated than any easy binary of 'native' and 'foreign' will allow. As a closer look at the literary form of each of the writers here will show, the English language and its literary conventions were, in fact, an enabling device, not a disabling

[40] My translation. *Madhusudan rachanabali*, p. 159.

[41] Ibid., p. 567.

[42] See Amit Chaudhuri, 2008, 'Poles of Recovery', in *Clearing a Space*, pp. 39–57.

one. It is not possible to say, for instance, of either Bankim or Michael, that they somehow leapt over the hurdle of the English language to find their metier in their own tongues, for any perceptive analysis of the literary component in their work will show the persistence and profusion of English conventions in their Bengali work (along with both traditional and currently evolving ones from the Bengali) where these were, in fact, fundamentally facilitating rather than obstructionist apparatuses within the larger enterprise. The literary enterprise here has to be understood a little more densely than simply an attribution of a motive such as that a writer wanted to 'indigenize the novel in the Subcontinent' through his work.[43] Also, paradoxically, this moment of 'return' inaugurated not the triumph of a pure Bengali, but of a composite literature written as a participant in world literary culture, for it would not be unreasonable to point out that the literary arena, even while it wrestled with the nationalist burden of expectation as well as gloried in it, was, throughout its existence, also involved with the notion of modernity as it was located in a world culture of literary practice.

In these years, even as civil society hummed with speculation about whether Bankimchandra had read *Ivanhoe* or not before he wrote *Durgeśnandinī* (1865) (he maintained he had not), Michael had left no one in doubt about his graft of what he deemed the best of world literature, as in letter after letter he expounded theories that spoke of the wisdom of taking eclectically from the best of world literature, and of how he was preparing to embellish 'the tongue of my fathers' by studying Tamil, Hebrew, Greek, Telegu, Sanskrit, Latin, and English.[44] Famously placing his first Bengali play, *Śarmishṭhā nāṭak*, emphatically within a world tradition of modernity in literary practice, he wrote to his friend Rajnarain Basu:

> ...but if the language be not ungrammatical, if the thoughts be just and glowing, the plot interesting, the characters well maintained, what care you if there be a foreign air about the thing? Do you dislike Moore's poetry because it is full of Orientalism? Byron's poetry for its Asiatic air, Carlyle's prose for its Germanism?[45]

[43] Priya Joshi, see above.

[44] *Madhusudan rachanabali*, p. 538.

[45] Ibid., p. 541.

This creative exchange, however, which is fundamentally at odds with the idea that once Madhusudan began writing in Bengali he realized the 'impossibility of being European', was also one of the more common tropes in readings of the late nineteenth-century literary project, which was written as a narrative of the victory of a modern literature that survived the baneful influence of either the colonial (and foreign) or the popular (but vulgar) inheritance. Consequently, despite Madhusudan's various allegiances to Homer, Virgil, and Milton, which have been prominently marked, as has his equally eclectic borrowing from Kalidasa and all that he knew of the 'grand mythology' of his ancestors, his achievement in welding all these together to create an accomplished Bengali literature has been duly celebrated.

A modern approach to literature in Bengal can be traced, conventionally, from Rammohun Roy onward, with every succeeding practitioner making sometimes a significant and sometimes an infinitesimal change to the traditional received notions of literary endeavour and publication. These changes can be mapped in the new attitudes towards print and publication, between text and reader, and between author and text. But for the transition to be estimated more completely, we need to look also in the literary domain, at the shifting aesthetic and artistic parameters of literary practice itself. The punctuation and syntax of every line, it must be recognized, are symptomatic of Madhusudan's approach to the concept of the literary, which needs to be interrogated with close attention. This method of 'close reading', is not, however, to be understood as a return to the uncontaminated sphere of pure aesthetics; rather, it might be useful to look at the manner in which the insights of postmodernism and the cultural readings of capitalism in a critic such as Jameson have made room for an analysis that takes the sentence as 'the de facto unit of analysis' in *The Modernist Papers* (2008). Reviewing the book in the *Times Literary Supplement*, Eric Bulson summarizes:

> Jameson takes a materialist approach to Mallarme's Divagations and shows just how much experiments with the Livre (capital "L") were attempts to convey an alienated social experience. Commas, prepositions, blank spaces, paragraph breaks, conjunctions: the punctuation and syntax of every line are symptomatic of Mallarme's struggle to express himself. To understand just what this struggle involved, you concentrate on the

> sentence, the de facto unit of analysis for Jameson. The sentence (like the poem) is a constructed totality, one with the power to bring disparate objects and ideas into an associative relationship. 'So strong is the power of the sentence,' Jameson explains, 'that we fail to notice the heterogeneity of its contents or the arbitrariness with which they are placed in relationship'. Through this deformation of the textual apparatus Mallarme exposes the 'power' that language and syntax have to make even the most arbitrary relationships appear natural.[46]

In the context of reading Mallarme, this materialist approach helps Jameson to pay attention to textual detail without losing track of the effect of capitalism on literary form, which is his own unique project; how this might help us in reading Madhusudan, however, will depend on our ability to expose the 'power' that language and syntax have to construct social experience.

[46] Eric Bulson, 2008, 'Close Reading with Frederic Jameson', *Times Literary Supplement*, Sunday, 27 July.

(ii) Michael Madhusudan Datta and the Marxist Understanding of the 'Real Renaissance' in Bengal

'Our Real Renaissance'

In a Bengali essay called *Māikel o āmader renesans* ['Michael and Our Renaissance'] written in 1962, Marxist Bishnu Dey, one of the leading poets of his time, displayed to perfection the nationalist/chauvinist temper of the critics who had sought to separate the native inheritance from the foreign in the flowering of Madhusudan's genius. Quoting from a line that Lord Canning had written, 'I apprehend nothing to be so little useful as reasoning by analogy from Europe to India', Dey wrote (in a characteristically tensile, muscular, innovative Bengali prose that is hostile to translation) that Michael had entered the world of native poetry—

> … in his childhood, through his mother, and it was this childhood ingress that later gave this Europe-mad powerhouse the right to inquire into the very heart of Bengali poetry. Because, like many newly-educated babus of the past, Michael too had chased the mirage of Canning's analogy and had attempted to achieve that impossible aim from a very young age. But the Ramayana, the Mahabharata and Kabikankan Chandi remained unconquerable in the blood of this boy from Jashore-Khidirpur.[47]

Acknowledging that Michael had studied deeply in English, Latin, French, German, Italian, Greek, Sanskrit, and Persian poetry while discovering Europe, he reiterated that 'still, the influence of the undercurrent of Bengali kept flowing under all this, and made this strange Anglicized Madras-returned youth write his first noteworthy play in Bengali, and he had to write his first readable poem, too, in none other than his mother tongue'.[48]

[47] Bishnu Dey, 1962, '*Māikel o āmader renesans*', in Birendra Chattopadhyay (ed.), *Madhusūdan o uttarkāl*, Calcutta: Indiana, pp. 9–10.

[48] Ibid., p. 10.

Bishnu Dey's essay repeats this denial of the impact of other languages or cultural practices in the constitution of Michael's self in many different contexts of Madhusudan's life. In Dey's reading, just as all of Madhusudan's 'gulping down of European influences to the dregs' could not prevent the innate instinct of his own language from finding expression, similarly, his conversion to Christianity too was merely a materialistic move to manufacture a route to England.[49] This disavowal of Madhusudan's conversion is common to almost every commentator from Jogindranath Basu to the present day, and has been questioned only sporadically, by critics such as Pramathanath Bisi in 1941, or more recently by his most exhaustive biographer, Ghulam Murshid.[50] This was the time, Dey continues, when the call to 'return to the mother tongue' was echoing in the air, when Vidyasagar, Debendranath, Akshay Datta, Kaliprasanna Singha, and others were strengthening the path trod by Iswar Gupta to build Bengali. In a triumphant tone, Dey came to the conclusion that 'the English-minded Michael, in the interest of his own indomitable poetic talent, left his basically unsuccessful efforts at Englishness and returned home, and the prodigal son then wrote a Bengali play for the Belgatchia playhouse.' Taking his analogy one step further, Dey then asserts, 'Although his fluent knowledge of English and European literature remains amazing even today, still, he had understood that while in English—*my dear fellow*—it might be possible to write the most astonishing letters, to create literature you need the known language of blood (*rakter cenā bhāshā*)'.[51]

This sort of imagery, packed with metaphors of 'home', 'blood', 'sinew', or 'undercurrent', where poetry is shown to be welling up from the springs of the unconscious in Michael Madhusudan, is used by Dey throughout the essay. In sentences such as 'But in his every nerve and sinew there was the language's spoken rhythm, the memory

[49] Dey, '*Māikel o āmader renesans*', p. 11.

[50] Pramathanath criticized Jogindranath Basu for not being able to forget Michael's 'original sin' of converting to Christianity in *Māikel madhusūdan jīban bhāshya,* 1941, Calcutta: Ranjan Publishing House, p. i. Ghulam Murshid, 1995, *Āśār chalane bhuli: māikel jībanī,* Calcutta: Ananda Publishers. English translation by Gopa Majumdar, 2003, *Lured By Hope: A Biography of Michael Madhusudan Datta,* Delhi: Oxford University Press, pp. 41–55.

[51] Italicized phrase is originally in English. Dey, '*Māikel o āmader renesans*', p. 12.

of its native usage', Bengali poetry is to be found residing in the sinews and nerves, in the blood of a poet outwardly immersed in a different cultural landscape, coming to him unasked for, spontaneously.[52] 'The words come unsought', Michael had written, and Dey quotes this as well as another of his statements: 'The thoughts and images bring out words with themselves,—words that I never knew. Here is a mystery for you', to show how, in Madhusudan, the subterranean impulse of his race found an outlet despite the outer barrier of foreign influences in a manner that remained a puzzle to the poet's conscious self. Michael's immersion in Western European classicism is admirable, Dey says, but nevertheless 'That is why Michael, even within his tragically short maturity, realised his country's divided state, where the English awakening was unavoidable, yet nothing more than an empty and bitter space'.[53] Michael's life and work both, therefore, are read as a 'noble tragedy, another name for which is England's work in India', with Dey concluding,

> His tragedy lies in the drama of running after a false metaphor in the darkness of British-Indian history.... In the century that has passed since then, we have been unable to instil the glowing lesson manifest in him. Yet it is only if we can do so that our historical sight will be restored to us, and we will be able to compose our own inevitable and certain history, our real renaissance (*āmāder prakṛta renesans*).[54]

Bishnu Dey's own exhausted pursuit, in this essay, of the mirage of a history of modern Bengali creativity uncontaminated by colonial influence casts a powerful searchlight on a very dominant critical stance in nationalist thinking in the nineteenth and twentieth centuries in India. In thinking in the manner he did, he was not alone or isolated; rather, his views are the culmination of a long and hoary tradition of authors and critics in Bengal, starting from readings of Iswar Gupta, apropos whom the counter of 'authenticity' was first used to question the provenance of a creative work. Nineteenth-century Bengali literary writing abounds in instances of indignant feeling for a native inheritance that is being neglected and passed over, and the

[52] Ibid., p. 13.
[53] Ibid., pp. 22–3.
[54] Ibid., p. 26.

complaint of foreign influences was registered against the best-known Bengali practitioners of the craft. Thus while Bankim held up Iswar Gupta as an 'authentic Bengali poet', he himself had in turn faced Nabinchandra Sen's complaint that his novels were too much in the Western mould and did not appear to be genuinely Bengali in nature. Nabinchandra wrote:

> I said to him—'I have always told you, I don't like your never-ending offerings of lumpy heaps of English love (*bilātī piriter piṇda piṇdānta*) anymore. Always the same monotonous English novelistic husband-wife and mistress's love! I have told you repeatedly to paint the ideal love of our national life and national literature that is contained in the Ramayana and the Mahabharata—a father's love, a brother's love, a child-like love, love of one's subjects, and last of all, love of God. But you didn't listen to me.[55]

Much like the infamous Tebbit test in England in the mid-1980s, when the conservative leader Norman Tebbit asked that a test of citizenship should include an appraisal of which team an immigrant cheered for in a match between England and the immigrant's home country, the test of whether a literary work was authentic and representative included an evaluation of how inherently indigenous or native the work ultimately was.

One of the first to articulate this feeling in relation to Madhusudan was his own friend, Rajnarain Basu, who had said, despite calling him the Goethe of Bengali literature, 'Compared to other Bengali poets, national feeling (*jātīya bhāb*) was, perhaps, the least to be found in Michael Madhusudan. He might have clothed his poetry in Hindu garb, but underneath those Hindu clothes, the *coat-pantaloon* can be seen'.[56] Subsequently, Rabindranath, in conversation with Edward Thompson, had complained of Madhusudan: 'He was nothing of a Bengali scholar… he just got a dictionary and looked out all the sounding words. He had great power over words. But his style has not been repeated. It isn't Bengali'.[57] Ironically, the table was turned on Tagore by the literary historian Dineshchandra Sen, who privately let

[55] Nabinchandra Sen, BE 1366, *Āmār jīban*, *Nabinchandra rachanabali*, Vol. 3, Calcutta: Bangiya Sahitya Parishad, p. 68.

[56] Rajnarain Basu, cited in *SSC*, Vol. 2, p. 53.

[57] Quoted in Buddhadeva Bose, 1954, '*Māikel*', in *Sāhityacarcā* [Literary Practice], Calcutta: Signet Press, p. 35.

Thompson know that: 'His [Tagore's] mode of thinking is so essentially English that I appreciate his English translation of the *Gitanjali* far better than the original Bengali… . Among us those only who have lost all touch with the life of the people, reading only European books, are his admirers… . Bengal has not given Rabindranath to Europe—rather Europe has given him to the Bengalis…'[58] Later, in the 1960s, Buddhadeva Bose and Sudhindranath Datta went further, making the following statements: 'Rabindranath's works are European literature written in the Bengali language and they are the first of their kind', and 'In the hands of [Rabindranath] Bengali literature turned occidental in all but speech'.[59] Both these stalwarts, interestingly, led the charge on Madhusudan as well, which we shall discuss in more detail a little later.

The attempt to separate or to weed out the colonial or the Western strands from the matrix of our modernity has been, for many years, lent legitimacy and authority by the support structure of nationalism and its search for authenticity. A type of indigenist discourse was developed from the 1870s onward in which definitions of culture and religion acted as counters of authenticity, which was as much an affirmative as a pejorative discourse, deciding what would constitute cultural authenticity in a transformative period for a new intelligentsia. But any attempt to separate the vernacular from the cosmopolitan in a writer's cultural constitution, as we have seen, fails spectacularly, every time, with the very writer who complains about inauthenticity then facing a similar charge in his turn.

Clinton Seely, writing of Madhusudan's *Meghnādbadh*, quotes from Pramatha Chaudhuri, writing in 1919, who harks back to the same familiar note when he says, using a recurrent metaphor of the seed of foreign influence: 'Since the seeds of thought borne by winds from the Occident cannot take root firmly in our local soil, they either wither away or turn parasitic. It follows, then, that *Meghnādavadha Kāvya* is the bloom of a parasite… utterly devoid of any fragrance'.[60] Seely

[58] Cited in Dipesh Chakrabarty, 2001, *Provincializing Europe,* p. 158.

[59] Ibid.

[60] Cited in Clinton Seely, 2004, 'The Raja's New Clothes: Redressing Rāvana in *Meghnādavadha Kāvya*', in Ujjalkumar Majumdar (ed.), *Meghnādbadh kābya carcā* [Meghnadbadh: Poetry and Practice], Calcutta: Sonar Tori, p. 539.

is perceptive in following this up with a comment made in 1987 by the bi-lingual Kannada poet, A.K. Ramanujan, that serves to illustrate how writers themselves have defended their multicultural provenance: 'After the nineteenth century, no significant Indian writer lacks any of the three traditions: the regional mother tongue, the pan-Indian (Sanskritic...Perso-Arabic...), and the Western (mostly English). Poetic, not necessarily scholarly, assimilation of all these three resources in various individual ways seems indispensable'. 'Perhaps', Seely concludes, 'Dutt was just a bit ahead of his time'.[61] It remains, however, that Ramanujan's position was a defence in the face of critics in the same nativist/nationalist lineage; only the partly understandable worry of literary critics in an era of national struggle against colonialism has now been displaced into an attack more particularly on the global provenance of Indian writing in English.

The problematic notions of territoriality that mark any examination in India of a writer's sources had, by the time of Ramanujan, been displaced from the arena of vernacular literature to that of Indian writing in English; the defence, however, sounds remarkably similar right up to the present day. Thus Vikram Chandra, accused by Meenakshi Mukherjee of selling Indianness to the West, a commonplace charge in India since the 1990s, retorts that 'this anxiety about the anxiety of Indianness', was one that he constantly heard, 'in conversations, in critical texts, in reviews. And Indians who wrote in English were one of the prime locations for this rhetoric to test itself, to make its declarations of power and belonging, to announce its possession of certain territories and its right to delineate lines of control'.[62] In his justification, Chandra then goes to a seminal essay by Borges, called 'The Argentine Writer and Tradition' (1951) that Mukherjee, he maintains, had misleadingly quoted from at a seminar, in which she had reiterated her convictions about how writers such as Chandra were writing 'to exoticize the Indian landscape to signal their Indianness to the West, in the context of the Western market'. Looking up the Borges essay, however, Chandra concludes that

[61] Ibid.

[62] Vikram Chandra, 2000, 'The Cult of Authenticity', *The Boston Review*, Feb/March.

> the exhaustively cosmopolitan and erudite Borges is arguing in this essay for the freedom of artists to choose their tropes from wherever they see fit. Borges wrote, 'What is Argentine tradition? I believe that this question poses no problem and can easily be answered. I believe that our tradition is the whole of Western culture, and I also believe that we have a right to this tradition, a greater right than that which the inhabitants of one Western nation or another may have'.[63]

Madhusudan Datta, for whom such an insight and conviction would have been fundamental, was not, in fact, ahead of his time, but very much of it. In his life and works, he was emblematic of the career of the modern in India, which incorporated, from the very start, a mix of heterogeneous influences that was unapologetic about its graft of a variety of cultural inheritances. Rangalal Bandyopadhyay, his contemporary, and only a few years ahead of him in his own accomplishments, was similarly unapologetic about his borrowings from English conventions—it was only a little later that nationalist writers from the 1870s onward began to succumb to a cultural cringe caused by the potentially embarrassing reality of taking part in the creation of a modernity that was inalienably linked to the colonizer's cultural practices. Locating a similar impulse persisting even in the work of current historians, another writer, Amit Chaudhuri, has recently pointed out:

> Probably one of the principal reasons that the word 'modern' is problematic for Indians, that modernity remains, in South Asia, an unofficial and potentially embarrassing reality in spite of being a hegemonic and foundational one, is its filial involvement with the 'colonial'. For many South Asian historians today... the very terms, 'early modern' and 'colonial modern', are inflected with a nostalgia for what never did happen, or what might have—an indigenous, home-grown modernity, in whose narrative the problematic moment of colonialism never occurred... The secret, utopian longing, in India, for another, 'purer' modernity possibly explains why we fail to engage completely with the implications and radical achievements of this one.[64]

[63] Ibid.

[64] Amit Chaudhuri, 'Argufying: On Amartya Sen and the Deferral of an Indian Modernity', *Clearing a Space*, p. 105.

This 'secret utopian longing' for 'another "purer" modernity', 'an indigenous, home-grown modernity, in whose narrative the problematic moment of colonialism never occurred' also animates Bishnu Dey's polemic on Michael Madhusudan, with its muscular wistfulness, its aggressive longing that Bengalis should learn the lesson of Michael's false life in order to achieve, at last, in some impossible future, finally, 'our real renaissance'.

The Left's Revaluation of the Renaissance: 'an empty and bitter space'

It was in 1967 that Susobhan Sarkar published an English essay that sought to revise some of the notions in his original tract, *Notes on the Bengal Renaissance*, first published in1946, a book—almost a pamphlet really—that had quickly taken on the status of a cult manifesto.[65] While the formulation of an idea of an 'awakening', 'rebirth', or 'renaissance' in Bengal in the nineteenth century had been around since the late nineteenth and early twentieth century (in the writings of Keshab Sen, Sibnath Sastri, and Bipin Chandra Pal, among others), the formal academic structure was provided, indisputably, in 1946 and 1948 by Susobhan Sarkar in English and Benoy Ghose in Bengali. Although invariably clubbed together in later readings for their contribution to our understanding of the Bengal Renaissance, these were Marxists who belonged to opposite ends of the social spectrum.[66] The ideas of these two men, Rajarshi Dasgupta has noted, were part of a 'wider

[65] Susobhan Sarkar, 1967, 'The Conflict within the Bengal Renaissance', in *Bengal Past and Present*, Diamond Jubilee number, pp. 106–11. *Notes on the Bengal Renaissance*, originally published in 1946 by the People's Publishing House, Bombay; second edition published in 1957 by the National Book Agency, Calcutta; reprinted by Papyrus, Calcutta, 1979.

[66] Ghose himself commented on Sarkar's elitist background in his appendix, saying, 'It should be mentioned that those who took the model of the European renaissance from English historians and applied it indiscriminately to our country with great enthusiasm had perhaps been educated in upper-class colleges (such as the Presidency College), trampling over all the others to obtain the highest position in the competitive examinations, as a result of which 'history' was equated with 'him' and 'he' and 'history' became one, and its Marxist interpretation too was infallible. This is the confusing tragedy. That is, that this Marxist historical explanation itself should be the reason for the belief in the renaissance' (p. 163).

Marxist engagement with culture—marked by fervent participation of communists in literature, art, theatre, music, and various scholarly activities—famously known as the "progressive movement". Susobhan Sarkar and Benoy Ghose were not isolated figures'.[67] The defining historiographical frame that they provided, whose listing of a canon of great men was nationalist and patriarchal in tone and tenor, then began to be dismantled from '67 onward with the development and tragic denouement of the Naxalite struggle in the political sphere in Bengal.[68]

In his original 1946 manifesto, Susobhan Sarkar had located within the province of Bengal a cultural exceptionalism that made it the vanguard of the country's development, comparable to the story of Italy in the European Renaissance. By 1961, he had revised his original idea in Bengali essays written for the Tagore centenary and the left periodical *Paricaẏ*, but it was in 1967 that he first made a formal presentation of the changes in his thinking in English, using the Diamond Jubilee number of *Bengal Past and Present* to announce that this renaissance was deeply riven through the middle by a conflict between what he termed 'Westernism (modernism, liberalism) and Orientalism (traditionalism, conservativism)'; at the end, Sarkar came down on the side of the former. Refusing to throw out the baby with the bathwater, he warned the reader that the historian should 'steer between uncritical adulation and scornful rejection'. Revealingly, the word renaissance was first put into quotation marks and divested of its capital R in the sentence: 'The "renaissance" in Bengal lacked the tremendous sweep and vital energy of ... its European prototype', which was then followed, a few lines later, by the proclamation (with capital letters back in place): 'Yet the Bengal Renaissance has certainly

[67] Rajarshi Dasgupta, 2004, 'Inventing Modernity in the Colony: The Marxist Discourse on the Bengal Renaissance', *Contemporary India*, Vol. 3, No. 1, January–March, p. 25.

[68] For an excellent summation of the journey of the idea of the renaissance in the literature of Bengal till 1967, see the first footnote to Amales Tripathi, 'Bengali Literature in the Nineteenth Century' in N.K. Sinha (ed.), 1967, *The History of Bengal*, Calcutta: Calcutta University Press, pp. 510–11. I am indebted to Gautam Bhadra for leading me to this reference.

its own specific relative value'.[69] The main objections were presented succinctly in a sentence right at the start:

> A historical appreciation of the 'new life' in Bengal is possible, even after recognising its obvious weaknesses: it did move on the axis of the upper stratum alone of society, the 'bhadraloks'; it could not draw in the Muslim community and the backward Hindus; it failed to strike a consistent anti-imperialist note, in sharp contrast to the role of the intellectuals in the Russia of the same period.[70]

The elitist nature of the 'great awakening' in nineteenth-century Bengal also came in for criticism from the other great Marxist theoriser of the Bengal Renaissance, Benoy Ghose, who wrote his own original Bengali book on the phenomenon, *Bāṅglār nabajāgṛti* [*Bengal's Reawakening*] in 1948. Subsequently, his revaluations of the 'comprador' character of the Bengali bourgeoisie in 1970 and 1978 in essays appended to the original text of the book, however, reversed his own original thesis, following the ideology of the Naxalite student movement of the late 1960s in Bengal, which rejected the iconography perpetuated by the idea of the Renaissance, declaring that the 'Bengal Renaissance' was a wish-fulfilling fiction, constructed by a class that needed a basis for its hegemonic position in society. The move, which was essentially a displacement of the elite 'comprador' class of reformers and leaders from history in favour of the unknown, unnamed peasant and working-class hero, is beautifully illustrated in an introduction Ghose wrote to the first volume of *Selections from English Periodicals of 19th Century Bengal*, when he characterized the state of affairs in the nineteenth century in inappropriately Shakespearean language as 'dramatic sound and fury… signifying what? Was it "Renaissance" on the western model? That has yet to be assessed, perhaps wiping off much of the froth from the writings of our historians'.[71] By the end of the short introduction, which had begun with Rammohun Roy's taking up residence in Calcutta from 1815 (a frequent point of departure in the iconography of the Renaissance, also used by Susobhan Sarkar),

[69] Susobhan Sarkar, 1967, 'The Conflict within the Bengal Renaissance', *Bengal Past and Present*, Diamond Jubilee number, pp. 106–11.

[70] Ibid., p. 106.

[71] Benoy Ghose, 1978, *Selections from English Periodicals of 19th Century Bengal*, Vol. 1: 1815–33, Calcutta: Papyrus, p. xv.

the question mark had disappeared, and the focus was directed instead at the peasant rebellion of 1832–3 in Bengal. While Rammohun died in Bristol in 1833, he wrote,

> ...the peasant rebels of Bengal, fighting against the British soldiers from behind their improvised mud-and-bamboo 'fort' in a village, about thirty miles north-east of Calcutta, under the leadership of Titoo Meer, were gunned to death, and the survivors brutally tortured, burnt and hanged. The Rammohanites and the young radical Derozians of Calcutta did not even notice it in their papers. *The Enquirer* went into raptures over the Reform Bill which was finally passed in England in 1832, and 'Hail, freedom, hail! rang through' its 'impassioned sentences'.[72]

These lines were written in 1978, after an entire decade had passed since the first Naxal sympathisers took up guns to protest against system and State and had then been crushed by vicious police oppression; viewed against that backdrop, the description of the followers of Titu Mir being 'gunned to death, and the survivors brutally tortured, burnt and hanged' takes on a differently eerie significance. (The glorification of Titu Mir, interestingly, was also the deliberate mission at this time of Mahasweta Devi's Bengali novel on the subject.)

In 1985, a group of intellectuals in Calcutta published a volume in honour of Samar Sen, one of the leading Marxist poets of the 1940s in Bengal. Samar Sen's radical poetry was written over a decade, from 1934 to 1944; perhaps disenchanted with its capacity to redeem society, he stopped writing verse, which he had begun doing when he was only eighteen, at twenty eight, subsequently devoting a greater part of his latter life to the editorship of the *Frontier*. His charisma and significant appeal seemed to lie, it was apparent from the introduction to this volume, in his anti-capitalist social commitment, the integrity of his principles, and his radically contrary stance in relation to the mainstream. In these, he was representative of the central moral core of an ethic of radicalism that emerged in Bengal from the late 1930s. One of Samar Sen's best known poems, '*Pancam Bāhinī*' ['Fifth Column'], had captured the dilemma of the Bengal Renaissance to the thinking Left as far ahead as 1942, four years before Susobhan Sarkar's *Notes on the Bengal Renaissance*:

[72] Ibid.

We are Bengali; we have a Mir Jafari past, we are the fruit
Of Macaulay's poison-tree.
Many a day have I thought,
Sometimes in the sun's last tented evening in the open field of the sky,
Sometimes when the city sleeps in silence
I have thought many times;
Let the seeds not be borne into the future, let this poison tree end,
In the daily attack of the torturous insect
Or in pain, inch by inch,
Let this fruit be completely finished in our lifetime,
But let tomorrow come in the homeward worker's song
In the first pain of the young girl's sacrifice
In the simple cry of the new-born child;
After a century of pain
Let the new day come in civilization's ultimate purification of mind.[73]

This is the third and final section of the poem, which begins with an evocation of a pitch dark night of blackout during the Second World War on the streets of Calcutta and suddenly veers into this manifesto of guilt and shame, an acknowledgement of the failure of the compromised past, and an expression of a more hopeful future, a redemptive 'real renaissance', significantly to be realized in the voices and experiences of the disempowered and disenfranchized, the subaltern worker, the girl-child, the infant. The optimism lasts only for these five lines, however, as the last part of the poem turns again towards dejection, with the realization that the 'bad blood' of Mir Jafar (the man who betrayed the last independent ruler of Bengal, Sirajuddaula, to Robert Clive at the Battle of Palashi [Plassey] in 1757) cannot be transcended:

But winter over, the snake comes out,
Mir Jafari bad blood lies hidden again
In the common clerk's room, in the nooks and corners of many households,
In the merchant's mattress, in the heart of *ahiṃsā*'s den.
In our garden the shrub of the *phaṇimansā*[74] grows;
Secretly, preparations are made for the worship of *Manasā*.[75]

[73] My translation. Samar Sen, 2001, '*Pancam bāhinī*' ['Fifth Column'] in *Samar sener kabitā* [Samar Sen's Poems], Calcutta: Signet Press, p. 95.

[74] *Phaṇimansā*: prickly pear, a small wild herb akin to cactus.

[75] *Manasā*: Hindu snake-goddess.

Dejected I turn, the drone of the blind house-fly in my ear.
Occasionally, in the stormy wind, I hear another song:
Nāhi deṅge hāmārā Hindustān.[76]

The poison-tree, or *bishabṛkhkha*, would inescapably remind readers of Bankimchandra Chatterjee's famous novel of the same name, published in 1873; the phrase was common parlance to denote a poisonous inheritance.[77] In Samar Sen's poem, the poison tree is Macaulay's legacy, and its fruit are no doubt 'the class of intermediaries' he had envisaged as English in opinion and in intellect, who would interpret India to the colonial rulers; the image of the seed recurs in the plea: 'Let the seeds not be borne into the future'. Treachery, as in Mir Jafar, and false consciousness, as bequeathed by Macaulay, are what constitute the middle-class Bengali for Samar Sen in 1942; it is no coincidence, then, that Bishnu Dey in 1962 follows an almost identical paradigm in his essay on Madhusudan and the false analogy of translating from British contexts into Indian ones.

The 1985 volume in tribute to Samar Sen contained an essay by Partha Chatterjee called 'The Fruits of Macaulay's Poison Tree'. At no place in the essay but in the title itself is Samar Sen's poem alluded to, and where it stands without any reference mark, to be recognized only by the already informed. Coming at the end of the whole movement of the disowning of the Bengal Renaissance that had begun with the poem, it attempted to sum up the Left's trajectory of disillusionment with the nationalist construction of the Renaissance in the nineteenth and twentieth centuries; its argument was also summarized in the fifth section of the first chapter of *Nationalist Thought and the Colonial World: A Derivative Discourse?*, which too was published in 1985. Here, in the Samar Sen Festschrift, however, its very first lines are: 'The time has come once again to talk about the "Bengal Renaissance". And also

[76] 'I will not give up my Hindustan': lines spoken previously in the poem by Muslim labourers.

[77] For instance, the same phrase can be seen in the text of the sixteenth-century Bengali woman poet Molla's version of the Ramayana, where, in the third book, referring to 'Rama's insane jealousy of Ravana and suspicion about his innocent wife, she wrote: 'Poison-fruit of the poison creeper, seeds of the poison tree'. [*Bish-latār bish-phal go, bish-bṛkhkheṛ bīj*]. See Nabaneeta Dev Sen, 'Flowering of the Poison Tree', in Chinmoy Guha (ed.), *Time, Space, Text: Mapping Cultural Paradigms*, 2008, Calcutta: Academic Staff College and Department of English, University of Calcutta, p. 131.

to talk about ourselves', which ironically, and perhaps unintentionally, paraphrase Lewis Carroll's 'The time has come, the Walrus said, / To talk of many things…'[78]

First setting out Susobhan Sarkar's 1946 thesis, Chatterjee then follows the attempt by Left-wing historians in the 1970s to question that formulation or to invert the equation between cabbages and kings. The trajectory traced, however, concentrates entirely on English language academic publications, leaving out the hugely influential Bengali literature on the subject, without mention of which the story remains inevitably incomplete. In English-language historiography, the charge against Susobhan Sarkar's original thesis was led, in an oedipal turn, by his son, Sumit Sarkar, in articles on the Derozians and Rammohun Roy in 1973 and 1975, respectively. The slaying of the father, however, could also be turned around and read as its opposite, as an affirmation of the later position of Susobhan Sarkar, for Sumit Sarkar seemed to be developing upon the argument already repeatedly presented by his father, also in articles on Rammohun Roy and Derozio and Young Bengal, showing how the 'progressive' elements that had been read into these nineteenth-century figures were 'deeply contradictory' and in many instances flawed by an innate identification with the colonial masters and 'alienation from the masses'.[79] A similar argument was further developed in Asok Sen's *Iswar Chandra Vidyasagar and His Elusive Milestones* (1977), which carried a couple of verses from Bishnu Dey's poem '*Parabāsi*' as the dedication:

> Where are those woods gone? Yet there are no settlements,
> Only the bare plains, only the howl of the dry wind.
> …

[78] Partha Chatterjee, 1985, 'The Fruits of Macaulay's Poison Tree', in Ashok Mitra (ed.), *The Truth Unites: Essays in Tribute to Samar Sen*, Calcutta: Subarnarekha, p. 70.

[79] Susobhan Sarkar, 'Economic Thought of Rammohun Roy' (1965), 'Religious Thought of Rammohun Roy' (1967), 'Derozio and Young Bengal' (1958) in *On The Bengal Renaissance*, 2002, Calcutta: Papyrus; Sumit Sarkar, 1975, 'Rammohun Roy and the Break with the Past' in V.C. Joshi (ed.), *Rammohun Roy and the Process of Modernization in India*, Delhi, and 'The Complexities of Young Bengal', 1973, in *Nineteenth-Century Studies*, October. The parallel drawn with Russian intellectuals, and the perception that our intelligentsia failed to make the great leap made by the Russians occurs in both father and son.

> ...
> How long do we roam about carrying our tents?
> When does the alien set up his own house? (Dey's own translation)

This lament of dry wind in the bare landscape, and the enforced alienation of the outsider poet in his own homeland is evocative of Samar Sen's depiction of the wasteland of Calcutta and its intellectual life in *Pancam Bāhinī*, and is captured in a language that gestures, immediately, towards Eliot. Asok Sen is no exception to the mood of despair; the 'impotence and falsity' of 'middle-class Bengal' were juxtaposed, in his book, with the figure of Vidyasagar, always an 'outsider' in Calcutta, whose creative force was nonetheless unable to transcend the 'social situation arising from the whole complex of England's work in India'.[80] (Notice the echo of Bishnu Dey in the last phrase, when Dey had said that Michael's life was 'noble tragedy, another name for which is England's work in India'.) Sen's argument therefore, as Chatterjee put it, was that while the 'nineteenth-century intelligentsia may have genuinely welcomed the new ideas of reason and rationality, and some may even have shown considerable courage and enterprise in seeking to "modernize" social customs and attitudes', unfortunately, it was all undermined by the fact that 'the fundamental forces of transformation were absent in a colonial society'.[81]

The argument, strangely enough, seems to replicate the charge made by Harachandra Dutt at the Bethune Society meeting in 1852 that Bengalis could have no genuine poetry because they were a colonial society—a charge Rangalal Bandyopadhyay sought to dispute with the publication of his first book of verse. The achievements of those born before Independence, presumably then, are hollow, as they could not have achieved their true shape or destiny in a colonial frame; consequently, the roll call of the greats as they are lined up in

[80] Asok Sen, 1977, *Iswar Chandra Vidyasagar and His Elusive Milestones*, Calcutta: Riddi-India, p. 4. The phrase 'England's work in India' recurs on p.103.

[81] Another critique of the nineteenth-century 'renaissance' that re-evaluated a literary work held to be a champion of peasant rights was, as Chatterjee pointed out, Ranajit Guha's analysis of Dinabandhu Mitra's *Nīldarpaṇ* (1974), where Guha showed that Dinabandhu's critique of the planters was rooted in liberal-humanist assumptions that were based on 'an abiding faith…in English law and in the good intentions of the colonial administration taken as a whole'. Chatterjee, 1985, 'The Fruits of Macaulay's Poison Tree', p. 75.

the narrative of the Bengal Renaissance, from Derozio to Michael to Rabindranath, from Rammohun to Vidyasagar to Vivekananda, are all permeated by a false consciousness in relation to the colonial economy. But Independence itself, for the Left, was infamously termed a 'false independence' ('*ye azādi jhoota hai*' was B.T. Ranadive's formulation in 1948), and the Naxalites in Bengal in the late 1960s and early 1970s were harking back to precisely that vision of an armed uprising ushering in the revolution that the Telengana peasant rebellion of 1946-51 represented. The iconoclasm of these Left historians' review of the Bengal Renaissance in the 1970s was in some way fundamentally connected to, Chatterjee failed to mention, the political chaos of the Naxalite movement (1967–71) in Bengal, particularly in the party youths' rejection of colonial educational systems and the destruction of statues of nationalist leaders and nineteenth-century social reformers known as *mūrti bhāṅgār āndolan*; the statues or busts that were targeted were of Gandhi, Rammohun Roy, Iswar Chandra Vidyasagar, and Vivekananda, among others. In an article published in 1970 in a journal called *Deśabratī*, the CPIM(L) theoretician Saroj Datta, who had revived the 1948 Ranadive line, wrote a vindication of these youths' activities, 'In Defence of Iconoclasm', asserting, 'This is not a negative action. They are destroying statues to build new statues. They are demolishing Gandhi's statue to put up the statue of the Rani of Jhansi; they are destroying Gandhighat to build Mangalghat' [after the woman who fought the British army in 1857 and Mangal Pandey, the subaltern sepoy who fired the first shot in the 1857 rebellion].[82] Charu Majumdar, the political leader in the eye of the storm, also championed the youths' desecration of statues: '…without destroying this colonial education system and the statues set up by the comprador capitalists, the new revolutionary education and culture cannot be created'.[83] When some criticism was made in the autumn of 1970 by a party colleague, Sushital Ray Chowdhury, to make a distinction between Gandhi on the one hand and Rammohun, Vidyasagar, or Rabindranath on the other, once again it was Saroj Datta whose eloquence summed up the violent mood of the radicalized youth when

[82] Saroj Datta, 1970, 'In Defence of Iconoclasm', *Deśabratī*.

[83] Charu Majumdar, cited in Sumanta Banerjee, 1980, *In the Wake of Naxalbari: A History of the Naxalite Movement in India*, Calcutta: Subarnarekha, p. 238.

he said, at a meeting of party workers in a village in Hooghly, 'The masses never make mistakes.... Revolution is bound to signify excess'. 'Forget the past', he said, 'forget the old poets'. It is only the new poets of the revolution 'who have emerged from the peasant's struggle, who are the fighting poets'.[84]

The Left's response to the Renaissance, like its response to political activity, was therefore splintered, by the 1970s, into factions, and Asok Sen and Sumit Sarkar were in fact attempting to redeem in some measure—and only in some measure—the vigorous destruction of the icons of the Renaissance that hardliners like Saroj Datta in the political sphere, and Benoy Ghose, Badruddin Umar, or Benoykrishna Datta in the intellectual sphere had advocated, the last named famously categorizing the Bengal Renaissance by the untranslatable term '*kākjyoṯsnā*', which means the illusory hour of approaching dawn when the crows are deceived into thinking it is already day. By introducing the clauses of 'complexity' or 'elusive[ness]' in their readings of the Renaissance icons, Sen and Sarkar were trying, in fact, to salvage a few fragments from the wreck.[85] Although acknowledging that civil society had not yet emerged in the European sense in colonial Bengal, still, the achievements of Vidyasagar were atypical of his class, Asok Sen argued, concluding that 'the weakness of Vidyasagar's class situation led to his failure; but his individual struggle implied an endeavour to redeem his society from its narrowness'.[86] Partha Chatterjee, meanwhile, at the end of his essay on Macaulay's poison tree in 1985, was prescient enough to trace the end of the 'renaissance' to the formation of the Left Front government in West Bengal in 1977, where according to him it met 'its final impasse'; at the same time, many other Bengali intellectuals, from Narahari Kabiraj and Dilip Biswas to Amiya Sen, Rajat Ray, and

[84] Saroj Datta, from a version of the speech carried in *Pūb Ākāś Lāl* [*The Eastern Sky is Red*], a CPIM(L) publication.

[85] Benoykrishna Datta, n.d., *Unabiṃsa satābdir svarūp,* Calcutta: Saraswat Library, p. 36. Badruddin Umar had denounced Vidyasagar as entirely subject to the limitations of the class character of the Bengali middle-class in *Īśvar candra bidyāsāgar o uniś śataker bāṅgālī śamāj* [*Iswar Chandra Vidyasagar and Nineteenth-Century Bengali Society*] in 1974. Pradyumna Bhattacharya had defended Vidyasagar in a review of Umar's book in the journal *Paricaẏ*. I am grateful to Anjan Ghosh for pointing this out to me.

[86] Asok Sen, 1977, *Iswar Chandra Vidyasagar and His Elusive Milestones*, p. 149.

even Sumit Sarkar himself in later essays began a reclamation of sorts of lost ground, asserting that it would not be wise to entirely negate the achievements of the phenomenon labelled the Bengal Renaissance.

Devaluation through Nomenclature: From Sri Madhusudan to Michael

Bishnu Dey's essay on Michael and the Renaissance, significantly, then, was written at a time when the first revaluations of the 'Bengal Renaissance' were already well underway in Calcutta, at least in Bengali literary writings. Already, since the 1940s, various Left-leaning literary Bengali intellectuals had begun to question the elitist formulation of the narrative of the Renaissance in Bengali journals and magazines of the time, and Bishnu Dey, who belonged, in fact, to the group around the leftist journal *Paricay* where Susobhan Sarkar's first revaluation was published in 1961, would have been well aware of the current of this thought in 1962, when he wrote his essay on Madhusudan.

It is my contention, in this context, that at the same time that the iconography of the Bengal Renaissance had begun to be put into place in the academic formulations of Susobhan Sarkar and Benoy Ghose, in a parallel development, literary critics and poets were engaged in the dismantling of at least one of the seminal figures of that 'renaissance', Michael Madhusudan Datta. Considering that the 'nineteenth-century cultural harvest' of Bengal 'was mainly literary', as Amales Tripathi conceded, it is worth pointing out, perhaps, a development in literary culture which took upon itself the mission—primarily through its own investment in the 'modern' or the modernist—of destroying the halo around a seminal figure of the renaissance such as Madhusudan at the same time that the idea of the 'renaissance' itself, intact with its European analogy, was being disseminated among Marxists and the general populace. We have already noted Samar Sen's denunciation of the Bengali middle class as 'Mir Jafari' and as the 'fruit of Macaulay's poison tree' in '*Pancam bāhini*' in a 1942 formulation that was to resonate across the living rooms of educated Bengal, lodging in the interstitial spaces of the intellectual re-evaluations that were to follow in the 1970s. But what has escaped attention so far, especially in relation to its import upon the subsequent deconstruction of the idea of the Bengal Renaissance among Left historians, is the steady destruction of the iconic stature of Madhusudan beginning in the 1940s, of which Bishnu Dey's 1962 essay was a culmination of sorts. My intention, in thus holding up the example of Madhusudan's devaluation, is not to construct a teleological and simplistic narrative of how the bringing down of an icon of the renaissance in the literary sphere impacted upon the bringing down of the entire edifice of the renaissance itself, but to point toward the similarity of resonances in both cases in an attempt to understand the manner in which the literary was intermeshed with the political.

Madhusudan had, till 1940, been feted by middle-class Bengalis across the spectrum as a legendary poet of great endowment and tragic ambition, his towering personality definitively constructed no less by his talented biographers, Jogindranath Basu in 1893 and Nagendranath Som in 1921, as by a dedicated army of commentators, beginning famously from his contemporary, Hemchandra Bandyopadhyay, in 1862 to a series of textual interpretations from stalwarts such as Gyanendramohan Das and Dinanath Sanyal among many others in the 1910s, 1920s, and 1930s. From the first year of the 1940s, however, the brilliant aura around the figure of Madhusudan began to be muddied by critics whose modernist provenance was an even more powerful impulse than the Marxist. Together, the impulse to modernism and Marxism that led irrevocably, in the final instance, to the cultural politics of Naxalbari in 1967 (whose proximity to the world political student unrest of 1968 is itself something that should not go un-remarked upon), saw to the eventual dethroning of the legend of Michael Madhusudan and a decline in his reputation that has been irremediable to this day.

One of the most interesting shifts that marked this decline and fall was the change in the use of the name by which Madhusudan was generally referred to; this changed, along with the change in estimation, from Madhusudan in Jogindranath Basu to the affectionate Madhu in Nagendranath Som's title, *Madhu-smṛti* (which punned on the word *madhu* to not only mean 'recollections of Madhu' but also 'sweet recollections'), to the reverential *Kabi Śrī madhusūdan* (1947) in Mohitlal Majumdar's title, where the appellation, '*Śrī madhusūdan*' had an immediate reference to the name by which the god Krishna was also known to the ordinary Bengali. Abalakanta Majumdar wrote *Mahākabi madhusūdan* [The Great Poet Madhusudan] in 1943, while

Sasankamohan Sen and Brajendranath Bandyopadhyay used simply *Madhusudan* (1921) and *Madhusudan datta* (1955), respectively.

Madhusudan himself had dwelt upon the double character of his names, separating the Bengali Madhu from the English Michael in a letter written just before he travelled to England in 1862, saying, 'No more Modhu the '*kabi*' old fellow, but Michael M.S. Dutt Esquire of the Inner Temple Barrister-at-law!! Ha!! Ha!! Isn't that grand?'[87] Significantly, however, when he finally did qualify as barrister, he performed another of those turns that have, by now, become such a characteristic part of his life story, changing the spelling of his name from the colonially anglicized Dutt to Datta, which was phonetically more assimilated to the Bengali or the Sanskrit. That this was a self-consciously nationalist and sentimental move is evident from a letter he wrote to Vidyasagar from London: 'I went to the court of common Bench in Westminster to put my name down in the list of English Barristers.... I have changed the spelling of my name and given it the true Sanskrit form. I am "published" Barrister as Michael Madhusudan Datta, Esquire. You might drop the vulgar form "Dutt".'[88] He signed the letter 'Ever your obliged, Michael M. Datta', and retained that signature even in his last desperate letters to Vidyasagar toward the end of his life.

In the literary world of Bengali letters, however, it remains a matter of peculiar significance that, from the 1940s onward, Michael Madhusudan Datta, as he had called himself, began increasingly to be called, simply, 'Michael'—a change that only one critic took the trouble to explicate. In 1941, Pramathanath Bisi launched an attempt at the demystification of the legend of Madhusudan in a biography called *Māikel madhusūdan jīban bhāshya* [*A Commentary on Michael Madhusudan's Life*]. In its introduction, in a meditation on his own impulses in writing the biography, he declared:

> All of them [Madhusudan's biographers], from Bankimchandra to the respected Mohit-babu [Mohitlal Majumdar] and my friend Banaphool, have written *Sri Madhusudan*; in these circumstances, I have written *Māikel Madhusudan*—some may consider this a barbarism. But they have written of the poetic existence of Madhusudan, that is why they can write

[87] *Madhusudan rachanabali*, p. 566.

[88] Ibid., p. 699.

> *Sri Madhusudan*. I sat down to give an idea of Madhusudan's complete existence—and this completeness incorporates both good and bad, big and small, all mixed up—in the midst of which the word Michael is also one element. I have not turned Michael into a god; I have shown his faults and failings, in fact, I have even laughed and made fun of him; I don't think this means I have belittled him—instead, I think this has allowed me to think of him as a man and respect him for it; one can laugh at a man, and love him; gods cannot be laughed at, and therefore cannot be loved in the same way.[89]

In the totality of Madhusudan's life and work, then, 'the word Michael is also one element'. The use of 'Michael' here, then, is strategic, and meant to bring down the subject from its pedestal; the intent is both humanist and modern, but not iconoclastic, for there is no attempt to question the legacy of the poet or the poetry itself; in fact, the biographer is struggling to dislodge the giant shadow thrown by the reputation of the poet to be able to approach, through intimacy and satire, the living pulse of the man.

Writing five years later in 1946, it was Buddhadeva Bose (1908–1974), a contemporary of Bishnu Dey and the leading critic and poet of his generation, who was determined to reveal the speciousness of everything Madhusudan had achieved—especially in contrast to Rabindranath—in a searing essay called, simply and startlingly, 'Michael'.[90] The essay began with a simple proposition: Michael's fame was not commensurate with Michael's achievements. 'Although Vidyasagar himself had curled his lip, still, Michael's reign had been established among his contemporaries from even before *Meghnādbadh* was published. And since then, for almost a hundred years now, we have heard unceasingly that Michael is a great poet, the saviour of Bengali literature, and the liberator of Bengali poetry.' But this fame, he then alleges, rests more on the dramatic eventfulness of the poet's life than on his poetic accomplishment. 'To tell the truth', he goes on, 'Michael's glory is Bengali literature's most famous rumour, its most

[89] Pramathanath Bisi, 1348 BE (1941), *Māikel madhusūdan jīban bhāshya* [*A Commentary on Michael Madhusudan's Life*], Calcutta: Ranjan Publishing House. This was first published serially in *Sanibārer Ciṭhi* and then in *Baṅgaśrī* before being rewritten for this edition.

[90] Buddhadeva Bose, 2007 (1954), 'Michael', in *Sāhityacārcā*, Calcutta: Dey's Publishing, p. 23.

indestructible superstition'.[91] In a couple of breath-taking sentences, he then proceeds to demolish Madhusudan's lifetime's accomplishments:

> The modern Bengali reader, after reading Michael's Complete Works, will be forced to come to the conclusion that his plays are unreadable and not fit to be performed in a theatre of any class whatsoever, that the *Meghnādbadh kābya* is lifeless, that apart from three or four, the sonnets are mere grandiloquence, in fact, even in his best work, the *Bīraṅganākābya*, the only sign of life is to be found in Tara's speech. It is astonishing to think that the life-force that can be seen so plentifully in Michael's English letters has not been transmitted into any work apart from the two farces—and even the two farces are not complete plays in every respect, but merely dark sketches made by the green hand of a novice, largely the result of his immaturity. But has anybody ever dared to say these things?[92]

This act of iconoclasm was unprecedented for its time; a literary equivalent of the *mūrti-bhāṅgār āndolan* that attempted to deal a body blow to the reputation of the poet in the literary world far more effectively than the vandalizing of the statues was ever to achieve in the political. The only element in Madhusudan that the essay saw fit to praise was his use of '*chanda*' or metre, and in this he seemed to be echoing Rabindranath's comment on the 'accomplished sound and flowing pace' of Madhusudan's *chanda.*[93] In doing so, his opinion here reflected the overall tenor of the essay as a whole, which was informed by a partiality for the accomplishments of Rabindranath in contrast to Madhusudan that somewhat diminished the force of its argument. Rabindranath himself had infamously critiqued Madhusudan at the age of 21 in the journal *Bhāratī*, when he had rubbished Madhusudan's accomplishments as being forced, artificial, and workmanlike, a savagery that he had later apologized for as being the result of the indiscretion and arrogance of his youth. According to Buddhadeva, that retraction was, in fact, false; it was the earlier stance that had been truthful with the candour only the young are capable of.

Certainly, Buddhadeva Bose was right about the tremendous regard in which Madhusudan was held by his contemporaries, both

[91] Ibid.

[92] Ibid., p. 23.

[93] Rabindranath Tagore, *Āshāḍh* 1301 BE, '*Kabi Bihārilāl*', in Tarun Mukhopadhyay (ed.), 2004, *Bihārilāl cakrabartī racita kabya*, Calcutta p. 145.

the learned and the lay reader. Sibnath Sastri described the moment memorably, contrasting the power and force of Madhusudan's aura to that of the declining Iswar Gupta:

> When Madhusudan dawned upon the sky of Bengali literature, the mellow light of Iswarchandra Gupta's talent had still not disappeared. There we were—immersed in the Gupta poet's wit and entertainment, when, right in front of us, what an enormous pulsating light began to rise. We shall never forget that amazing night in Bengali literature. As a Sanskrit poet had once said—'On the one side, the moon was sinking in the sky. On the other, the sun was leading the day into our sight'.
>
> This was the sort of scene in Bengali literature at that time! Madhusudan's powerful rays came and fell upon Iswarchandra's pleasant radiance. Readers of Bengali literature joyfully entered a new world.[94]

As for the lay reader, Madhusudan himself had happily recounted their support in his letters, from the 'Banian's assistant in a mercantile firm' who wrote to him of his blank verse—'I read your book with feelings of admiration and have no hesitation in affirming that its poetry is of such high order that I have never seen anything like it yet attempted in Bengali', to the 'literary shopkeeper' at Chinabazar whom he saw 'deeply poring over Meghanad', who told him that it was 'poetry that would make my nation proud'.[95]

Rabindranath had, twenty-five years after his first youthful comments, singled out Madhusudan as an example of the fortuitous union of Western thought with the Indian mind in the essay '*Sāhityasṛshti*'; referring to that late piety, Buddhadeva Bose asked: 'Isn't the real reason behind that not the fact that it was impossible for him to refer to "*Mānasi*" or "*Sonār tari*" or "*Kāhinī*" in that context?' The long and the short of Buddhadeva's argument then, was that it was not Madhusudan who first brought 'an infusion of Western blood into the comatose arteries of Bengali literature' but Rabindranath. 'To say so might make me seem like an awful religious renegade' he continues, 'but it is absolutely true to say that the Western mode was brought into Bengali literature not by Michael, but by Rabindranath'.[96]

[94] Sibnath Sastri, 2003, *Rāmtanu lāhirī o tatkālīn baṅga-samāj*, Calcutta: New Age Publishers, p. 222.

[95] *Madhusudan rachanabali*, pp. 553, 569.

[96] Buddhadeva Bose, 2007 (1954), '*Māikel*', p. 25.

In his support, Buddhadeva Bose could find only one modern poet, Sudhindranath Datta, who has been bold enough to articulate his thoughts honestly. Sudhindranath had declared that old Bengali literature was 'generally unreadable', and similarly, he was unafraid to say that Michael 'may have loved the Bengali language, but he didn't understand its nature; that is why he has remained merely the servant of *Baṅgabhāratī*, not her saviour'. 'I too had once said,' Buddhadeva continues, 'that Michael did not know Bengali. That he did not know it might sound like an exaggeration, but it is true that although it was his mother tongue, Michael had ignored it since his childhood and never entered its inner core'. Here, an asterisk indicates a footnote in which he then triumphantly quotes from Edward Thompson's book on Tagore, first published in 1946, that quotes Rabindranath, as we have already seen, saying of Michael, 'he just got a dictionary and looked out all the sounding words. He had great power over words. But his style has not been repeated. It isn't Bengali'.[97]

The test of authenticity, here, is undertaken in the service of the modern rather than the national, as it so often was. Bose is more of a modernist than a nationalist, and although involved in the anti-Fascist league and a Left sympathiser, he was certainly not a card-carrying Marxist, so the critique, although enmeshed in the aura of Left politics, which had a powerful cultural impetus at the time, was primarily articulated as a literary disagreement. Pramathanath Bisi was more actively political, having worked for the Congress in the freedom movement, later even becoming legislator and member of the Rajya Sabha from that party, and Bose's destruction of Michael's reputation was not something Bisi could swallow. In an introduction he wrote to the collected works of Madhusudan in 1959, *Māikel Racanāsambhār*, whose very title, appropriately, epitomizes the shift from Sri Madhusudan to Michael that he himself had inaugurated with his biography in 1941, he made an obvious reference to Bose's polemic without naming any names:

> Many critics have expressed adverse opinions about Madhusudan's influence—they seem to think that Madhusudan's influence did not extend beyond his death or till a few years after his death. This is an

[97] Ibid., p. 28.

> absolutely unjust statement… . Rabindranath, in his mature years, drew the curtain of 'immortal poetry' over his immodest opinions at sixteen, but why should that stop the status-hungry literary critic? The fact that the *Meghnādbadh kābya* has withstood every attack for over a hundred years and is still standing on the strength of its own glory—does that itself not prove that the *Meghnādbadh* is 'immortal poetry' and Madhusudan an immortal poet?[98]

Following from this, Bisi then goes on directly to the comparison with Rabindranath:

> Judged exclusively on the importance of literary talent, Madhusudan is not inferior to Rabindranath, but if Rabindranath's talent has had a wider manifestation (it must have had), then the reasons for that lie largely in social and pedagogic culture (*sāmājik o śikkhāgata saṃskār*). The influence of such a hugely talented individual might recede temporarily, but it cannot disappear; with time it will surely become strong again. Once Rabindranath's universal appeal has receded somewhat and Bengali poetry will once again search for a new way, then there will be no other way than to take recourse in Madhusudan.…The immense achievements of Madhusudan are waiting for that day.[99]

Contrary to Bisi's expectation, however, Rabindranath's 'universal appeal' shows no signs of receding to this day, more than fifty years since these lines were written, though the Bengali celebration of that appeal has moved away from the literary world to that of popular culture, where, as any examination of the celebrations of his birth anniversary on *panciśe baisākh* (the twenty-fifth day of Baisakh) in the city will show, it has metamorphosed into a bizarre statist organization of Rabindranath-centric programmes characterized by carnivalesque excess.

Buddhadeva Bose's endorsement of Rabindranath at the cost of Madhusudan, however, was contextual, and needs to be understood in the light of certain literary battles that were fiercely fought in the Bengali literary world in the decade preceding his essay. Bose's essay, '*Māikel*', was written in 1946, five years after Rabindranath had died in 1941. All through the preceding decade, starting from the 1920s,

[98] Pramathanath Bisi, 1959, Introduction to *Māikel racanāsambhār*, Calcutta: Mitra & Ghosh.

[99] Ibid.

modern Bengali poets had initiated and then vehemently put forth a critique of Rabindranath centred upon a perceived lack of social realism, modernism, and a sense of the city in his works. The criticism had come both from the left as well as from those, like Bose, whose provenance, in the struggle to get away from the overwhelming presence of the older poet, was more modernist than Marxist. While the Left-leaning critics such as Debiprasad Chattopadhyay, Nihar Ranjan Ray, and Bhabani Sen pointed out, somewhat literal-mindedly, that Rabindranath, scion of one of the wealthiest and most distinguished and powerful families in Calcutta, lived in an ivory tower and so could know nothing of 'reality' and was, therefore, 'a bourgeois poet', on the other hand, the group around the journal *Kallol*, such as Achintakumar Sengupta and Buddhadeva Bose, spoke of the experience of the city and its link to modern existence, complaining that Rabindranath was incapable of articulating in poetry any sense of the daily-ness of urban-lived experience, for which they had to turn instead to Baudelaire, Eliot, Pound. Samar Sen and Bishnu Dey both wrote poems that reworked, in an ironic mode, noted lines from Rabindranath into their own evocations of the crowded metropolis, in the context of buses, machinery, traffic jams, roads, and prostitutes on Kalighat Bridge.[100]

This hostility to the blind spots in Rabindranath, however, began to recede by the time the poet was nearing his death. The poets who had rebelled so vociferously against him had, in fact, been formed by his work and were beholden to it and the world it created in more ways than they had been willing to acknowledge. Buddhadeva Bose, for instance, visited the ailing poet in Santiniketan and wrote movingly of his experience in *Sab peyechir deśe* [Wish-fulfilling Country], conceding, later, his devotion to the poetry of the older poet despite his criticisms of him. Five years after Rabindranath's death, therefore, in 1946, when the essay 'Michael' was written, it is perhaps not unwarranted to presume that he was holding up Rabindranath as an example to Madhusudan perhaps out of a sense of guilt and expiation at the distress caused to the now deceased poet in his last years by the unnecessary rigour and harshness of their materialist

[100] For a fuller discussion, see Dipesh Chakrabarty, 2001, 'Nation and Imagination', *Provincializing Europe*, pp. 160–1.

and realist demands; such rigorous tests, the essay on Madhusudan seemed to show, were even more spectacularly failed by poets such as Madhusudan.

Cosmopolitanism and the Nature of the Modern Aesthetic

The generations from the 1930s to the 1960s that attempted, as I have shown, to dismantle Madhusudan's iconic status in Bengali literary modernity were noentheless linked to the figure of Madhusudan in one last and all-encompassing category—that of cosmopolitanism. The intellectuals of 1930s' Calcutta imbibed the most diverse of cosmopolitan influences in order to forge their own idiom in poetry; yet the most overwhelming impulse of the time was to escape the overarching influence of Rabindranath, in the flight from whom these modern poets of the twentieth century perhaps failed to see the correspondences between their own world view and that of not only Rabindranath himself, which has been well documented, but also Madhusudan. In the same breath as he ridiculed Madhusudan's emulation of Milton, Buddhadeva Bose, who called Madhusudan's work Popish rather than Miltonic, found in the nineteenth-century Baudelaire a poet worthy of emulation. Modernists such as Eliot and Pound helped these poets speak of the city; at the same time, Jibanananda Das invoked the Surrealists in a tradition of cosmopolitanism that continued right through to the *Kṛttibās* writer Sarat Mukhopadhyay's wonderfully named *Ryambo, bhārleine Ebaṅg Nijasva* [*Rimbaud, Verlaine and My Own*] (1963). This manner of confronting the rush of history with a symbolic appropriation of the cosmopolitan, which serves as a site of attraction, is a modern response that was common to both Madhusudan and Buddhadeva, although the latter might have denied that commonality. Modernity's inescapable momentum caught both men within its vortex of change, and both men enter the modern world through a cosmopolitanism that is all encompassing, despite its different locations for them individually and artistically. Cosmopolitanism, in this sense, is therefore an attitude of survival, and always an ongoing process, politically contested and historically unfinished, a form of personal and collective self-fashioning.

Nor was the impulse to cosmopolitanism a trend among the poets alone in this period. This was a time, like Levi Strauss's New York in the 1940s where Surrealist art and structural anthropology were both commonly concerned with 'the human spirit's "deep" shared springs of creativity', when the social sciences and poetry in Calcutta were both still animated with a drive to describe critically 'the local orders of culture and history'.[101] If it was Surrealist art that informed structural anthropology in New York, in Calcutta, in the 1930s and 1940s, poetry, socialism, and the social sciences came together in a fortuitous union, one unusual instance of which can be seen in the felt emotion approaching poetry in Benoy Ghosh's preface to his book *Bāṅglār nabajāgṛti*, which employed, nonetheless, a rigorously sociological methodology in the main text. Writing in the revised edition published in April 1979, he said, generally failing to demarcate between poetry and politics:

> Thirty years ago, when I wrote *Bāṅglār Nabajāgṛti*, my heart and mind were constantly reverberating to the resonance of what is called '*thirtees leftism*' (sic). It was the last part of the English decade of the forties. Those years—although the Second World War was over then—seem like an amazing era. Revolution, socialism, communism, it was then all in our grasp, and the hands that grasped were naturally young men's fists. *Caudwell-ism*, *Auden-ism*, *Isherwood-ism*, *Strachey-ism*, *Palme Dutta-ism*, and all other isms led us to the wonderful variety of *Marx-ism*, along with Victor Gollancz, the Left Book Club etc., and their combined effect, on the mind of youths like us in far off Bengal's Calcutta city, was like that of a rainbow-coloured dream that sounds like a fairy tale today. Only thirty years have passed, but what should have been the difference of one generation seems, in 1978-79, like the difference of many generations. That is why, within the passing of a single generation, *Bāṅglār Nabajāgṛti*, which had once seemed to be the historical truth, seems today to be merely 'a myth' [*ekṭi atikathā*].[102]

This specific path through modernity is one among many others, a result of similar historical visions, and of responses to a truly global space of cultural connections and dissolutions that had only recently become available for Bengalis from the nineteenth century onward.

[101] James Clifford, 1988, *The Predicament of Culture*, p. 243.

[102] Benoy Ghosh, 2009, Preface to *Bāṅglār nabajāgṛti*, Hyderabad: Orient Blackswan.

In studies of Bengali modernity, there is a division between the works of literary critics and that of social scientists—the parameters of 'art' and 'science' do not intermesh in any significant way. However, the insights of social scientists on text, society, and the changing aspects of literary production need to be complemented with literary critical readings that deal with the internal matters of line breaks, of punctuation, of Bankim's 'variety of pause'. Once that is done, and in a manner far more exhaustive and detailed than has been possible here, it will, perhaps, be possible to see the correspondences that link many modern writers to Madhusudan in a variety of ways. Then it might still be possible to contradict Buddhadeva Bose's view that Madhusudan's works were repositories of a 'sterile treasure' (*nirbīj aiśarya*) that did not herald the future of literary endeavour in Bengal; that he may have charmed everybody in his time, from princes to shoe-makers, but still could not save the day.[103] While dismissing him as an 'apprentice poet' still searching for his true voice, Buddhadeva conceded that perhaps some of the things Rabindranath had achieved had also been achieved by the elder poet, pointing us towards a verse from the *Brajāṅganā*, where he quotes the lines ending '*Ār ki yatane kusum ratane brajer bālā?*' commending them for their metre, blind to the glaring resonance between the phrase Michael uses and Rabindranath's famous song '*Tomāy sājābo yatane kusum ratane*'.[104]

Perhaps the denial of Madhusudan, which preceded the denial of the Bengal renaissance, should be read instead as a denial of the inescapable father, made obvious in strange turns and a puzzling blindness. Thus Bishnu Dey felt compelled to name his collection of essays *Māikel, Rabīndranāth o anyānya* in 1967 (a title that seems to echo Sarat Mukhopadhyay's *Ryambo bhārleine ebaṅg nijasva* of 1963) although, searching through it for further essays on Michael, I found only one essay on Madhusudan in the entire collection—the same one discussed above—yet Michael needed to be part of the title of the book. Perhaps then, in the end, it might be possible to say instead, in the words of a contemporary poet, Alokeranjan Dasgupta, 'By now, the definition of modernity has changed so many times, but Madhusudan still remains. For us, who live in today's world, he is indispensable'.

[103] Buddhadeva Bose, '*Māikel*', p. 34.

[104] Ibid., p. 35.

Explaining further, he adds, 'Modernity's first and last refuge is the individual, or the freedom of the individual. Before Madhusudan, perhaps there was a hint of that in Gyandas, and a partial glimmer of it in Bharatchandra-Ramprasad or Ramnidhi Gupta, but it was in Madhusudan that it found its material expression'.[105] Dwelling in detail on particular lines and stanzas, Alokeranjan is stunned by how Madhusudan had achieved a particular 'interiorised' rhyme long before Rabindranath, concluding, '*Brajāṅganā* is talkative, *Caturddaśpadī* reticent. *Brajāṅganā* is the overwhelmingly egotistical speaker [*kathikā*] of the unique first moments of modernity in Bengali poetry, *Caturddaśpadī* is that modernity's first certain, self-aware writer' [*lipikā*].[106]

In this chapter, I have tried to recontextualize strategies of reading and representation, which change historically in response to evolving and shifting cultural paradigms, showing how readings of a particular writer or a period are orchestrated through a multiplicity of exchanges in politically charged situations. All authoritative readings, whether made in the name of literature or the social sciences, are historically contingent and need to be submitted to periodical reorganization. This is one such attempt, and like all others, must necessarily remain incomplete, as it is an exploration rather than a seamless idea in the service of a unified vision of history. I am not attempting to redeem Madhusudan, nor am I interested in resurrecting the idea of the Bengal Renaissance; the effort, rather, is to bring out the local, political contingencies of the readings in the past, and to propose thereby that any reading is subject to a temporal vision which decides, only temporarily, on the dynamism or the tragedy of historical agents or moments whose meaning we must each learn to decipher according to our diverse conjunctures and specific occasions of interpretation.

[105] Alokeranjan Dasgupta, 1962, 'Madhusudan and the Modern Mind', Birendra Chattopadhyay (ed.), *Madhusūdan o uttarkāl*, Calcutta: Indiana, pp. 78, 81.

[106] Ibid., p. 85.

5 (i) Hemchandra's *Bhārat saṅgīt* (1870) and the Politics of Poetry: A Pre-History of Hindu Nationalism in Bengal

The real spirit of the Bengali poems and songs cannot be conveyed in English translations. One must read them in the original to get an idea of their true significance and of the fire it kindled in youthful hearts. But poor though the translations are, they would serve to demonstrate, beyond any doubt, that the militant nationalism—the so-called terrorism—was not the wild pranks of a few misguided youths, but the result of a great national reawakening which profoundly swayed the people at large.

—R.C. Majumdar[1]

Although Hembabu had become famous by virtue of a variety of excellent poems, still, whenever his name is mentioned, Bengalis recall his Bhārat saṅgīt and Bhārat bilāp—just as Grey would have become immortal even if he had written nothing other than Elegy Written in a Country Churchyard, just as Wolfe would have been counted as a poet if he had written only the Burial of Sir John Moore, just as Pope's 'Eloisa to Abelard' was enough to make him known as a poet, just as, if Shakespeare had written only Hamlet his incomparable talent would have been obvious to the world, in the same way, if Hemchandra had left us only Bhārat bilāp or Bhārat saṅgīt, he would still have been accorded a high status among poets as an outstanding poet—there is no doubt about that.

—Anonymous, *Āryadarśaṇ*, Calcutta[2]

[1] R.C. Majumdar, 1975, *History of the Freedom Movement*, Vol. 2, Calcutta: K.L. Mukhopadhyay, p. 154.

[2] Cited in Manmathanath Ghosh, 1919, *Hemcandra*, Calcutta.

As the artist builds to a plan, so is a nation fashioned by its own dreams.
—Sister Nivedita[3]

Writing in 1870, Hemchandra Bandyopadhyay (1838–1903), in one of his most celebrated poems, *Bhārat saṅgīt*, imagines a young man standing on a mountain top, wearing a Hindu *nāmābalī* (scarf), blowing upon a trumpet, and calling his countrymen to wake from their slumber. Dressed thus in unabashedly Hindu garb, this young man 'with the stance of a sannyasi' is depicted as enveloped in an astonishing light as he exhorts his fellow men to forget distinctions of caste, to forget their chanting, their prayers, their meditation, and to join together in the worship of arms. 'Become experts in the deployment of weapons, go mad in the *rasa* of warfare' the poet declaims, 'This is not the time for meditation; unsheathe your swords ... Descendants of Aryans, your eyes have been deceived at the sight of a few sentries standing guard; can it be that a nation of twenty crore should remain in chains, slave to the foreigner?'[4]

This vision predates Bankimchandra Chatterjee's famous depiction of militant Hindu sanyasis in the novel *Ānandamaṭh* (1882), which Ashis Nandy describes as 'arguably the most important political novel ever written in India', by a full dozen years.[5] *Ānandamaṭh* was famous for propagating a powerful image of a community of militant Hindu ascetics who worship the nation as a mother goddess and are ready to fight and die for their country, and for its song, *Bande mātaram*, which subsequently echoed through almost every rally, meeting and protest march among campaigners for Indian independence. In it, the adoration of an ideal motherland in the first verse (*sujalām suphalām malayajaśītalām śasya śyāmalām*) gave way, in the next, to an aggressive imagery of combative strength:

Who hath said thou art weak in thy lands,
When the swords flash out in twice seventy million hands
And seventy million voices roar

[3] Sister Nivedita, 1907, *Modern Review*, Calcutta.

[4] Hemchandra Bandyopadhyay, 1870, *Bhārat saṅgīt* (First published in the *Education Gazette*, Calcutta) in Sajanikanta Das (ed.), 1963, *Kabitābalī*, Calcutta: Bangiya Sahitya Parishad, p. 115.

[5] Ashis Nandy, 2001, *Time Warps*, New Delhi: Permanent Black, p. 25.

Thy dreadful name from shore to shore?
With many strengths who art mighty and stored,
To thee I call, Mother and Lord!

Thou who savest, arise and save!

To her I cry who ever her foeman drove
Back from plain and Sea
And shook herself free.[6]

This translation of Bankim's song was done by the neo-Hindu nationalist and poet Aurobindo in 1909; three years earlier, in 1906, thirty-six years after Hemchandra's original vision of a Hindu youth upon a mountain top calling his countrymen to arms, Aurobindo wrote '*Bhawani mandir*' (Temple of the Mother), which began, eerily but tellingly, with a vision that derived many of its elements from the imagery in *Bhārat sangīt*:

Om Namas Chandikayai

A temple is to be erected and consecrated to Bhawani, the Mother, among the hills. To all the children of the Mother the call is sent forth to help in the sacred work...

We will therefore build a temple to the white Bhawani, the Mother of Strength, the Mother of India; and we will build it in a place far from the contamination of modern cities and as yet little trodden by man, in a high and pure air steeped in calm and energy...

We will therefore have a Math [monastery] with a new Order of Karma Yogins attached to the temple, men who have renounced all in order to work for the Mother...[7]

The martial sentiment in *Bande mātaram* is echoed in *Bhawani mandir*'s vision of the mother goddess of the country as 'the mother of Strength... pure Shakti'. 'For what is a nation?' asked Aurobindo, 'What is our mother-country? It is not a piece of earth, nor a figure of speech, nor a fiction of the mind. It is a mighty Shakti, composed

[6] Aurobindo Ghose's English translation (1909). This is the verse translation; another translation by Aurobindo of the poem into powerful prose, first published in the *Karmayogin*, also exists. See Sri Aurobindo's translation (1972) of Bankimchandra Chatterjee's *Bande mātaram*, in 'Translations, From Sanskrit and Other Languages', *Sri Aurobinda Birth Centenary Library*, Vol. 8, Pondicherry: Sri Aurobindo Ashram.

[7] Ibid., p. 60. I am indebted to Partha Chatterjee for first having pointed this out to me.

of the Shaktis of all the millions of units that make up the nation'.[8] In his notes, Aurobindo mentions that although it was written by him, *Bhawani mandir* was more his brother Barindrakumar Ghose's idea than his. In the context of the extremist movements that flourished at the time, he also clarified that 'It was not meant to train people for assassination but for revolutionary preparation of the country'. Barin attempted, initially, to find a suitable place in the hills to implement this dream, but fell ill while travelling and returned to Calcutta. Aurobindo said that with time he 'thought no more about it ... [but] Barin who clung to the idea tried to establish something like it on a small scale in the Manicktala Garden'.[9] Thus the dissemination of certain extremist and revolutionary ideals through a few influential literary texts inaugurated a philosophy of extremist politics that travelled, in no time at all, from the literary arena into life.

This chapter intends to examine the legacy of an image that the poet Hemchandra inaugurated at the very inception of nationalist literary discourse in Bengal; was this prescient image, which would become fundamental to a certain type of anti-colonial politics, any different in nature from other influential ideas propagated by the likes of Bankimchandra or Aurobindo? Within the space of the years that separate *Bhārat saṅgīt* in 1870 (which sounded the first call to militancy) from *Ānandamaṭh* in 1882 (which embodied that militancy in the image of the Mother) and from *Bhawani mandir* in 1906 (which combined both these elements in its potent blueprint for action), had something died and was something else born? Was Hemchandra's vision rooted in cosmopolitan, metropolitan, and essentially egalitarian forms of thinking, or was it in tune with the Hindu chauvinism of the later Bankimchandra or the extreme political rhetoric of Aurobindo? Sudipta Kaviraj has remarked that 'In the conventional historiography of nationalism, Bankimchandra's fame, and to Western secularists his ignominy, lies primarily in his responsibility for dreaming up the icon of the nation—feminine, maternal, territorial, natural, but offensively Hindu....', yet at the same time, Jagadish Bhattacharya has also

[8] Sri Aurobindo, 1997, *Bhawani Mandir* in *Bande Mataram: Early Political Writings*, Pondicherry: Sri Aurobindo Ashram, pp. 61, 65.

[9] Aurobindo Ghose, 1953, *Sri Aurobindo on Himself and On the Mother*, Pondicherry: Sri Aurobindo Ashram, pp. 85–6.

pointed out that the *Bande Mātaram* was written at a time in his life when Bankimchandra was a declared atheist.[10]

A study of the relation between nineteenth-century literature and militancy in Bengal reveals, intriguingly, that *A Journal of Forty-eight Hours of the Year 1945*, by Kylash Chunder Dutt, the first novel written by a Bengali in English, envisaged an armed uprising of Bengalis against oppressive British rule a century later. Another fictional work in English on the same theme was Shoshee Chunder Dutt's *The Republic of Orissa: Annals from the Pages of the Twentieth Century*, while the armed rebellion of Indians against the British was also the theme of S.C. Dutt's *Shankur: A Tale of the Mutiny of 1857* (1892) and S.M. Mitra's *Hindupore* (1909).[11] Any interrogation of the conflicting attitudes prevalent at the time, however, will show that it is very difficult to construct any straightforward picture of what, in the nineteenth century, constituted the Hindu right and what the liberal centre; that images associated with an extreme Hinduism could originate in the mildest of political persuasions, complicating our notions of the origins of a particular strain of strident political Hinduism as it exists today.

One of the most discussed and controversial themes in twentieth-century Indian history and politics has been the character of Hindu nationalism as an ideology and political language. A number of studies on the origins of Hindu nationalism, as it occurred both nationwide and in Bengal, have been undertaken over the years, but those that have examined the role of literature in political life have usually emphasized the importance of one central figure, such as Bharatendu Harishchandra in Benaras or Bankimchandra Chatterjee in Bengal, in their narratives.[12] Bankimchandra, more than any other figure, has

[10] Sudipta Kaviraj, 1998, *The Unhappy Consciousness: Bankimchandra Chattopadhyay and the Formation of Discourse in India*, Delhi: Oxford University Press, p. 142.

[11] Kylash Chunder Dutt, 1835, *Calcutta Literary Gazette*, 6 June; Shoshee Chunder Dutt, 1845, 'The Republic of Orissa: Annals from the Pages of the Twentieth Century', *Bengal Hurkaru*, 25 May.

[12] See, for instance, Vasudha Dalmia, 1996, *The Nationalization of Hindu Traditions: Bharatendu Harishchandra and Nineteenth-century Benaras*, Oxford: Oxford University Press, and for Bankim, see Partha Chatterjee, 1986, *Nationalist Thought and the Colonial World: A Derivative Discourse?* Delhi: Oxford University

been almost universally identified as the disseminator of sectarian sentiments through influential literary works that were of a 'deeply communal nature' in late nineteenth-century Bengal, principally because of the enormous influence of his novel, *Ānandamaṭh*, and its song.[13] However, a closer look at the politics of other literary and political leaders and intellectuals of the time critiques the monolinearity of this perspective, and, by re-instating the various cross-currents of contemporary intellectual thought, restores the polyvocality of civil society. The diversity and range of opinions even within the narrow spectrum of thought on the role of Hindu religion in national life in nineteenth-century Bengal is obvious, for instance, when we compare and contrast the attitudes of the poet Hemchandra Banerjee and his mentor, the great intellectual Bhudev Mukhopadhyay (1827–1894), with those of the critic Akshaychandra Sarkar (1846–1917) and his friend and mentor Bankimchandra Chattopadhyay (1838–1894)—all of whom belong to a particular milieu characteristic of upper middle-class Bengali culture in the nineteenth century. Certain choices made by these authors in their delineation of a nation in the making, and the descriptions of the sort of nation and its citizens that formed their ideal, lead us to the problematic question of the interdiscursivity between early formulations of Bengali poetry and criticism and exclusivist Hindu rhetoric, and the extent of its existence.

Hemchandra's *Bhārat saṅgīt* was published in 1870, and he died in 1903: chronologically, therefore, Hemchandra wrote in an age of greater political passivity and inaction than the years of the Swadeshi movement that immediately followed, when Bengal's partition by Curzon in 1905 was opposed with a concerted wave of such passionate activism that the act had to be officially repealed in 1912. Sumit Sarkar has characterized this period as a 'hiatus between the myths of renaissance improvement and nationalist deliverance', a time that 'encouraged moods of introspection and nostalgia' among the

Press, or Sudipta Kaviraj, 1995, *The Unhappy Consciousness*, or, more recently, Chetan Bhatt, 2001, *Hindu Nationalism Origins, Ideologies and Modern Myths*, 2001, Oxford: Berg, pp. 26–31.

[13] Shivarama Padikkal, 1993, 'The Emergence of the Novel in India', in T. Niranjana, P. Sudhir, and V. Dhareshwar (eds), '*Interrogating Modernity: Culture and Colonialism in India*', Calcutta: Seagull Books, p. 227.

bhadralok.[14] To a great extent, the formative impression made upon this period by Rajnarain Basu and Nabagopal Mitra of the Hindu Mela also needs to be taken into account to fully appreciate the mood of those years, while Rabindranath, the most successful writer-activist of this period, wrote extensively on the Hindu component of our national life in his most revivalist phase, remarking, in *Svadeśī-samāj*: 'Will not Hinduism be able to bring every one of us day by day into bonds of affinity and devotion to this *Bhāratbarsha* of ours—the abode of our gods, the hermitage of our *rishi*s, the land of our forefathers?'[15] Also, in the Indian context, histories of Hindu nationalism tend to concentrate on the early years of the twentieth century leading to Independence; Christophe Jaffrelot's book, *The Hindu Nationalist Movement in India*, for instance, takes as its starting point the year 1925, when the Rashtriya Swayamsevak Sangh was first formed. The ideological developments in the nineteenth century that made it possible for such political formations to come into being, however, were operating, at least in Bengal, from the latter half of that century onward. This period, that constituted what could be called the 'prehistory' of Hindu nationalism, was one in which the idea of the 'Indian nation' was still in its early stages of construction.[16]

It is my contention that certain influential ideas and images of the nation were envisaged in *poetic* practice long before such conceptions found currency even in the political rhetoric that preceded political activism. The idea of the 'Indian nation' was, in fact, first imagined into existence through a repeated articulation in 'poetical rhetoric', that is, in lines of poetry that came into existence in Bengal in the English language in the early nineteenth century and in Bengali verse in the late nineteenth, a few years before similar instances are to be found anywhere else in India.[17] The importance of poetry to

[14] Sumit Sarkar, 1998, *Writing Social History*, Delhi: Oxford University Press, p. 300.

[15] Rabindranath Tagore, 2002, '*Svadeśī-samāj*', *Rabindra rachanabali*, Vol. 2, Calcutta: Vishvabharati Press, p. 533.

[16] John Zavos, 2000, *The Emergence of Hindu Nationalism in India*, New Delhi: Oxford University Press. The book deals with the political organization of Hinduism in this early period.

[17] I have discussed this idea of 'poetical rhetoric' also in 'An Ideology of Indianness: The Construction of Colonial/Communal Stereotypes in the Poems of

nationalist discourse in late nineteenth-century Bengal has generally and consistently been overlooked, yet many of the debates around which contemporary politics was structured were first played out in the literary arena, between literary critics, creative writers, and their readers, between dramatists and their audiences. Contrary to popular academic belief, it was not the novel that first and most influentially narrativized the nation; it was poetry and drama that seized the incipient and imaginary idea of India and presented it in the public sphere as a necessary and vital embodiment of the aspirations of the middle classes. The imagery that portrayed the nation in influential Bengali works throughout this period, however, was often inflected with Hindu overtones, used unconsciously or otherwise, to depict a nation that needed not only to be awakened, but also to be armed.

This chapter, then, intends to briefly examine the works and politics of some of the most influential writers of late nineteenth-century Bengal in relation to their attitudes towards the Hindu religion and the imagined nation; to lend it coherence, it will be structured around the publication of Hemchandra's revolutionary poem, *Bhārat saṅgīt*, alongside references to other related works by him, while looking at crucial debates in the public sphere on the nature of nationalism between 1870 and 1903, which were not only the years of Hemchandra's working life, but also the crucial years in which certain aspects of our nationalism were being forged. While Rabindranath Tagore's objections to the aggressive politics of coercion and violence in the swadeshi movement are well documented by analysts looking both at his novels and essays,[18] this study intends to broaden the ambit of the discussion somewhat by examining, for instance, the objections made by an eminent literary critic, Akshaychandra Sarkar, to the nature of nationalism in *Bhārat saṅgīt*, which he defined as narrow and self-serving when contrasted with the ideals of traditional, or *sanātan*, Hindu dharma.

Henry Derozio', 2004, *Studies in History*, Vol. 20, No. 2, New Delhi/Thousand Oaks/ London: Sage Publications, p. 169.

[18] See Ashis Nandy, 1994, *The Illegitimacy of Nationalism: Rabindranath Tagore and the Politics of Self*, Delhi: Oxford University Press; Partha Chatterjee, 2003, *Rābīndrik neśan ki?* [What is Rabindranath's 'Nation?'], *Bāromās*, Pūjā śamkhyā.

Hemchandra and *Bhārat saṅgīt*

Born into a poor but respectable Brahmin family in the Hooghly district, Hemchandra's entrance into the senior school division of the Hindu College when he was fifteen was sponsored by a kind and wealthy neighbour. An industrious student, he did consistently well in school, and then at Presidency College (1855), obtaining scholarships and certificates of honour at all levels. In 1857, he was in the first batch of examinees, alongside Bankimchandra, of the newly instituted entrance examinations for Calcutta University, and in the second batch of students who gave the B.A. exam, passing in the first division along with two others in 1859. A subsequent degree in law allowed him to join the high court as a lawyer and pursue a successful vocation; the government appointed him chief government lawyer in 1890. His literary career began in 1861 with the publication of *Cintātaraṅginī*, a long poem written after the suicide of a close friend. The very next year he became the first Bengali to annotate and introduce a literary work by another Bengali poet more famous and more talented than himself—Michael Madhusudan Datta's *Meghnādbadh kābya*. A long and illustrious career in poetry was thus innocuously inaugurated, and Hemchandra proceeded to become well known as one of the leading poets of the time in Bengal. His position as unofficial poet-laureate was cemented by Bankimchandra when he wrote, at the time of Madhusudan's untimely and tragic early death:

> But the throne of the poet of Bengal is not empty. That is the Bengali's star of good fortune in this sea of sorrow. Madhusudan's trumpet is silent, but may Hemchandra's veena attain immortality! He who was seated on the throne as Bengal's poet has travelled to the other world, but while Hemchandra is here we cannot weep that our mother Bengal's lap is bereft of good poets.[19]

From 1868 onward, Hemchandra was publishing poetry in leading journals such as Bhudev's *Education Gazette*, Bankim's *Baṅgadarśan*, Akshaychandra's *Nabajīban*, and Dwijendranath's *Bhāratī*, as well as

[19] Bankimchandra Chatterjee, cited in Brajendranath Bandyopadhyay, 'Hemchandra Bandyopadhyay,' in *SSC*, Calcutta: Bangiya Sahitya Parishad, 1372 BE, p. 14.

individual volumes such as *Bṛttasaṃhār* (1875), his best-known work, which was followed by *Āśā-kānan* (1876), *Daśamahābidyā* (1882), and *Cittvabikāś* (1898). Apart from these major works, he had translated from Dante's *Divine Comedy* and Shakespeare's *Tempest* and *Romeo and Juliet*, and published various compilations of his poems as well as the occasional farce or satire. In the Preface of his first publication, a long narrative poem called *Bīrabāhu kābya* (1864), he said, 'I have composed this narrative with the sole intention of showing the commitment and resolution of a brave band of Hindu heroes in the past in their resolve to defend their own country.' The poem's language is emotional, with the country personified as a mother who does not heed the distress of her children:

Mother, O mother, country of my birth!   how many ages more
will you spend at this age as a captive?
Tell me how many ages more   will foreign groups oppress you
with a merciless and cruel bent of mind?
How much longer will you sleep   wake, mother, wake, wake -
see how your sons and daughters cry themselves blind.
Our bodies are white with dust   and roll on the ground
take us into your lap for once and let us call you mother.
Whose mother are you   and whom do you have on your lap;
pushing aside your own son whose son do you rear?
Whom do you give your milk to   that is not your child,
you are taming a black cobra with milk in your home.[20]

While the honesty of this impassioned plea is certainly not in doubt, it is worth pointing out here that the same poet published, a few years later, a volume called *Bhārateśvari mahārānī bhiktoriār jubili utsab* [The Jubilee Celebrations of Queen Victoria, Empress of Bharat] (1887). This was then also printed in a special edition, in Royal four-page format and in various coloured ink, as a gift to the Queen; here, English translations of the poems followed the originals in Bengali. Yet, a year before, in 1886, Hemchandra had also famously recited a poem called '*Rākhi-Bandhan*' at the second session of the Indian National Congress in Calcutta, incorporating within the poem a section from Bankimchandra's song *Bande mātaram*. Hemchandra's opinion on the

[20] Hemchandra Bandyopadhyay, *Bīrabāhu kābya* (1864) in Pramathanath Bisi (ed.), 1971, *Hemcandra Racanāsambhār*, Calcutta: Mitra & Ghosh, pp. 336–7.

British presence in India may be seen in statements such as: 'Know it as gospel truth that the enlightened policy of the English nation is the *sine qua non* of the emancipation of India' or 'for the future of India there is no other course open to the destiny of her life. With them [the English nation] she must rise or fall'.[21] Such inconsistencies were, perhaps, typical in the moderate political mindset of the period, in which the assumptions of faith that the socially progressive and politically ambitious middle class had in British institutions coexisted with an increasing despair and accumulating frustration that found first utterance in the guise of poetry and song. *Bande mātaram* itself did not acquire its immense status until quite a few years later, as Aurobindo Ghose pointed out in 1907:

> It was thirty-two years ago that Bankim wrote his great song and few listened; but in a sudden moment of awakening from long delusions the people of Bengal looked around for the truth and somebody sang Bande Mataram. The Mantra had been given and in a single day a whole people had been converted to the religion of patriotism.[22]

Apropos the publication of *Bhārat saṅgīt*, Akshaychandra Sarkar commented somewhat acerbically, 'Right from the beginning of the year 1277 [1870] our poet was hell-bent upon giving direction to our national life. The famous "*Bharat Sangeet*", I think, was presented at the very start of the year.'[23] First published in the government-owned *Education Gazette*, edited at the time by Bhudev Mukhapadhyay (1827–94), the poem was strident in its tone, starting with a description of the march of the various nations of the world towards progress and emancipation, portraying an America driven by aggressive imperialist ambitions in a manner that sounds surprisingly apposite today:

> 'Do not still sleep, lift up your eyes,
> Look, look and behold this universe

[21] Quoted in H.M. Das Gupta, 1935, *Studies in Western Influence on Nineteenth-Century Bengali Poetry 1857–1887*, Calcutta: Chuckervutty, Chatterjee & Co., pp. 45*n*1, 50*n*1.

[22] The English Works of Sri Aurobindo, Centenary Edition, Vol. 17, p. 389.

[23] Akshaychandra Sarkar, 1911, *Kabi hemcandra*, Calcutta: Bangiya Sahitya Parishad, p. 9.

How beautiful, how curious,
With its diverse and different peoples.

....

There is America, newly risen,
Aiming to swallow the world.
Made impatient by her own strength
She roars, and the world trembles:
It is as if she wishes to pull and tear it to pieces
So that she can build it anew.

And there, at the centre, always worshipped
Always brave, mother to courageous sons,
Eternally young, the Greek world
Lights up the earth with the rays of her glory,
Thrashes the ocean, tramples the mountain range
And floats away in jest.

Arabia, Egypt, Persia and the Turks
Tartars, Tibetans—where else should I look?
China, Burma, uncivilized Japan,
They too are free, they too are important;
To be a slave, contemptibly,
It is only Bharat that still sleeps.
Sound the trumpet, sound it to say
Everybody is free in this vast universe
Everyone is awake and takes pride in honour;
It is only Bharat that continues to sleep.'

The entire opening section is within quotation marks, as it is part of a song being sung by a young man, whom Hemchandra then proceeds to describe:

After speaking thus, raising a trumpet to his mouth
Upon a mountain top, wearing a sacred Hindu scarf
Summoning lightning in the light of his eyes,
A youth then continued to sing.

He had large eyes, a noble forehead,
Fair body, and the stance of a sannyasi,
Standing upon a mountain top, wearing a sacred Hindu scarf
Summoning lightning in the light of his eyes, his
Body bathed in the lustre of an incomparable light.

The trumpet roared with force,
"Two hundred crore human lives
In this land of Bharat are the foreigner's slaves,
They lie there tied in chains!
The men that conquered Aryavarta—
Are these men descendants of the same race?
Only a few sentries stand guard
But their eyes are deceived at the sight![24]

The poem continues with an invocation of the glorious past, when 'our ancestors', the Aryans, had conquered the country. The martial abilities of the Aryans have given way now to a state of enslavement among Indians, and the youth resumes his song towards the end of the poem to urge the people that it is still not too late to unsheathe their swords, awaken, and reclaim their days of lost ability.

Bhudev Mukhopadhyay, who was said to have inspired the poem, had apparently been reluctant to publish it, but eventually did so upon being reproached for not publishing it by Hemchandra in a poem called *Bhārat bilāp*, written after *Bhārat saṅgīt* but published before.[25] Bhudev's son Mukundadeb tells us that Bhudev had asked for a softer approach, and was directly responsible for giving the poem a 'historical character'. Objecting to the references to the British, he wanted the original mention of 'a few white sentries standing guard' changed, so that Hemchandra subsequently altered the word *śvetpraharī* in the concerned line.[26] When the poem eventually appeared in a collection, it sported a head note beginning: 'In India when the Mughals ruled…' which was not there in the original, and Shivaji's name, mentioned in the poem then, was missing later from the lines: 'Standing on the mountain-top, wearing a *nāmābalī*, /Stood Shivaji, calling lightning to his eyes…'

A huge controversy erupted upon the poem's publication, so much so that it was changed in certain places before it appeared in a collection; the second and third edition of Hemchandra's selected poems, *Kabitābalī*, not daring to carry the poem at all. Akshaychandra

[24] Hemchandra Bandyopadhyay, *Bhārat saṅgīt*, in *Kabitābalī*, ibid., pp. 115–17.

[25] '*Bhārat bilāp*', 1870 (1277 BE), *Education Gazette*, *Jaistha*, May–June.

[26] Mukundadeb Mukhopadhyay in *Bhūdeb carit*, cited in Manmathanath Ghosh, 1325 BE, *Hemcandra*, Calcutta: Gurudas Chattopadhyay & Sons, p. 229.

asserts that the government was concerned enough to specifically have had the poem translated. When Robinson, the translator, translated the word 'yaban' to mean foreigner, and transcribed Shivaji as 'Sewji', the governor-general wrote to Bhudev asking him to explain the inclusion of such verses in the Education Gazette. Bhudev apparently maintained that the translator had erred in rendering Shivaji as Sewji, and especially by referring to the word 'yaban', which was derived from Yunani and now meant Muslim, to denote a foreigner. But he maintained that the beauty of the poem made it deserve its place in such a publication.[27]

Hemchandra's iconic imagery in this poem was prophetic in more ways than one, for not only did the motif of renunciation and militancy embedded in the image of the youth upon the mountain top become inspirational, but the figure of Shivaji too was to become a celebrated marker of Hindu heroism in nationalist politics by the turn of the century. Tilak had originally initiated the first Shivaji festival in Maharashtra in 1895 with the hope that it would spread all over India; in 1902 Sakharam Ganesh Deuskar was the first to organize a Shivaji Utsav in Calcutta, and this became an annual ceremony in which Shivaji's ideal of a single Hindu rashtra was celebrated, with Rabindranath writing a famous poem called 'Shivaji-Utsav' for the festival of 1904. However, all that was about thirty years after *Bhārat saṅgīt* finally made its way into a collected edition of Hemchandra's poetry; and when it did there was an elaborate note preceding the poem that avoided mentioning Shivaji's heroism too directly.[28]

After so much controversy, it would be reasonable, then, to assume that *Bhārat saṅgīt* was read at the time by almost every

[27] Akshaychandra Sarkar, 1911, *Kabi Hemcandra*, pp. 9–10.

[28] The head note read: 'At a time in India when the Mughals dominated and the Mughal armies had gradually swamped *Bhāratbarsha* entirely and then proceeded to attack the region of Maharashtra, a Maharashtrian Brahmin named Madhavacharya, terribly saddened by the misery of his country, went about the cities and the mountains of the land singing songs that spoke about bravery and excited enthusiasm towards defending the freedom of his land. His songs have been extremely popular and dearly loved among Maharashtrians ever since the time of Shivaji. After Madhavacharya's death, these songs have been sung from one place to another by other singers. I have written *Bhārat sāṅgīt* in emulation of that custom.' Hemchandra Bandyopadhyay, 1963, *Bhārat sāṅgīt*, in *Kabitābalī*, p. 115.

educated Bengali in the country. Indeed, R.C. Dutt mentioned that Hemchandra's 'patriotic lyric on India is known by heart to a large circle of readers...[29] How large that circle was may be gauged from the fact that the first edition of his *Kabitābalī* (21 November 1870) had a print run of five hundred copies which sold out so quickly that a second edition of 1500 copies was printed the next year, followed by many successive reprints.[30] Rajnarain Basu, in his famous 'Lecture on Bengali Language and Literature' in 1878, had commented: 'His composition, *Bhārat saṅgīt*, is absolutely astonishing. It completely suffuses the soul with the fire of love for one's country, and excites the mind to the highest pitch'.[31] An eminent woman writer, mentions Manmathanath Ghosh, described the upheaval at the time in these words:

> The day his *Bhārat Saṅgīt* was first published in the Education Gazette, that was some day! I have heard from my elders that this one poem by Hemchandra had, at the time, created the same effect as when an earthquake makes a country heave and shake from one end to the other. There was not an eye that did not shed continuous tears upon reading this poem, there was not a heart that did not tremble, was not moved, that did not light up with its force. In a manner of telling, it was this one single poem that firmly ensconced Hemchandra in the literary establishment.[32]

The political controversies surrounding the poem, from the start, therefore, closely shadowed its poetical merits, and after Rangalal Bandyopadhyay's immortal lines, '*svadhīnatā hīnatāẏ ke bāñcite cāẏ he, ke bāñcite cāẏ*'? *Bhārat saṅgīt* was the next great landmark in the nationalist literature of modern Bengal, becoming famous for its vision of insurrection against British or foreign rule.

[29] R.C. Dutt, 1963, *Literature of Bengal* cited in the Introduction to *Kabitābalī*, p. vii.

[30] Manmathanath Ghosh, *Hemcandra*, p. 249.

[31] Rajnarain Basu, 1878, *Bāṅglā bhāshā o sāhityabishayak baktṛta*, Calcutta.

[32] Manmathanath Ghosh, *Hemcandra*, p. 231.

The Sudden Popularity of the Term *bhārat*

That the title of *Bhārat saṅgīt* reflects a national aspiration in its use of the term '*bhārat*' rather than '*bāṅgā*' or ''*bāṅgālī*' is self-evident, and the popularity of the term Bharat at this time is attested to by Hemchandra's *Bhārat bilāp, Bhārat saṅgīt, Bhārat bhikshā*, and *Bhārat kāminī*, all of which had been preceded by Iswar Gupta's poems of the 1850s: *Bhārat santāner prati, Bhārater abasthā, Bhāratbhūmir durdaśā*, and *Bhārater bhāgya biplab*. This particular nomenclature, therefore, preceded a contemporary excitement, even obsession, with the term in the age of the Hindu Mela, set up in 1867, a significant arena with regard to the development of Hindu nationalism. While the idea for it was taken from Rajnarain Basu's influential *Prospectus for the Promotion of National Feeling Among the Educated Natives of Bengal* (1866), the Hindu Mela was put into practical effect by Nabagopal Mitra, the Tagore family, and Manmohan Basu.[33] In his reminiscences, Rabindranath wrote:

> A mela called the 'Hindu Mela' was created with the help of our family. Nabagopal Mitra was appointed its main organizer. That was the first time that we attempted to experience a sense of respect for *Bhāratbarsha* as our *svadeś* [own country]. Mejdādā composed his famous national song '*Mile sabe Bhāratasantān*' ['Come together, children of Bharat'] at this time. At this mela, patriotic songs eulogising the country were sung, poems that expressed love for our country were read, country crafts and physical exercises displayed, and talented countrymen were rewarded.[34]

The famous song by Rabindranath's brother Satyendranath mentioned here is in itself a remarkable rehearsal of the sort of concerns that Hemchandra was preoccupied with in *Bhārat saṅgīt*. Written in 1868 for the second year of the Hindu Mela, it was an unquestionable influence on *Bande Mātaram* as well as *Janaganamana* (both Bankim and Rabindranath were effusive in their praise of it) and was, perhaps, India's first national song, celebrating victory to the motherland:

[33] Manmohan Basu was the editor of a weekly, *Madhyastha*, which was first published in Calcutta in 1872. A public speaker of some worth, his speeches were collected in *Baktṛta-mālā* (Calcutta, 1873), while his lectures on Hindu culture were published as *Hindu āchār byabahār* (Calcutta, 1887).

[34] Rabindranath Tagore, 1962, *Jībansmṛti*, Calcutta, p. 78.

Children of Bharat unite, with one heart and mind,
And sing of Bharat's fame.
Which other land can be compared to this land of Bharat?
Which mountain can equal the Himadri?
Bearer of fruits, crops, forceful rivers, goodness,
Storehouse of a hundred mines—of such jewels and gems.[35]

A rousing chorus, 'Let there be victory for Bharat / Victory for Bharat, victory / Sing, victory to Bharat / What do you fear, why fear / Sing victory to Bharat' punctuated every verse, while the song ended with an invocation of the legendary bravery of the Indian people. Satyendranath's and Hemchandra's vision of Bharat, however, remained within the confines of Bengali Hindu nationalism (it was the Sanskrit of the *Bande Mātaram* song that gave it an all-India application, as Nabinchanra Sen had pointed out to Bankim at the time[36]), for although the term 'Bharat' was being held aloft with a nationalist intent, and the geographical and historical markers in them were mostly pan-Indian, the poems did not travel as widely beyond Bengal.

Satyendranath's song, albeit the most popular, was still only one of the many patriotic songs, poems, and lectures that were composed and presented on the occasion of the Hindu Mela, whose ultimate aim, claimed Ganendranath Tagore, was 'not ordinary religious work, nor material happiness, nor fun and frolic—this was for our country [*svades*], for our land of Bharat'.[37] Pramathanath Bisi, commenting upon the Hindu Mela, had said that it was self evident from the Mela's intentions, the meaning of its songs, the title of its newspaper, and so on, that at the time, 'everybody understood "national" and Bharat to mean the same thing…'.[38] Even more pertinently in the context of the use of the term Bharat, we find Abanindranath Tagore remarking:

Nabagopal Mitra laid the foundation stone of a new age. All around us was Bharat, Bharat; the paper *Bhāratī* began to be published. Nobody

[35] Satyendranath Tagore, 2001, *Bāṅgālīr gān*, edited by Durgadas Lahiri, Calcutta: Pashchimbanga Bangla Akademi, pp. 612–3.

[36] Nabinchandra Sen, 1366 BE, *Āmār jīban*, Vol. 2, edited by Sajanikanta Das, Calcutta: Bangiya Sahitya Parishad, p. 163.

[37] J.C. Bagal, 1968, *Hindu melār itibṛtta*, Calcutta: Maitri, pp. 7–8.

[38] Pramathanath Bisi, 1965, *Citracaritra*, Calcutta, p. 121.

used the term *bāṅgā* in those days. National feeling (*bhāratīyabhāb*) was initiated from that time onward, and it was from that time that everybody learned to think of Bharat.[39]

Meanwhile, Manmohan Basu, as we have seen, wrote of Nabagopal's nationalist aspirations with much humour, recalling that 'In those days, he had ended up being labelled "national Nabagopal"'.[40] Yet it is important to note here that this insistent celebration of the national did not take on the character of hostility toward British rule. Geeta Chattopadhyay has remarked that 'in the Hindu Mela, there was no ideology of opposition or racial hostility (*jāti-baira*) toward the foreign rulers. At least, the subject of *jāti-baira* certainly did not exist. Yet remembrances of the proud past heritage of the country and its present misery were repeatedly brought up'.[41]

Hemchandra, in his poems *Bhārat bilāp* and *Bhārat saṅgīt*, was the first to bring into the public sphere an element of direct confrontation with the British that had been absent so far from the nationalist literature surrounding the Hindu Mela. Contemporary observers discussed this feeling of hostility, called *jāti baira*, animatedly at the time, as I shall show a little later. In *Bhārat bilāp*, published a couple of months before *Bhārat saṅgīt* in the *Education Gazette*, an astonishingly direct attack was launched upon the British presence in India. The narrator of the poem is depicted standing one evening on the shore of the Ganges and gazing upon a capital city full of imposing buildings, a great fort, and a pleasure garden. Whose city is this, asks the poet of the residents of Bengal; which people enjoy such a capital city?

If you do not know, come here
And you will see how in a variety of vehicles
The king-like men go in diverse dispensations
        Their feet do not touch the ground for pride.

'Rule Britannia' is being played afar
Carriage after carriage o'er spreads the ground
The inhabitants of Britain go forcefully forward—
        Where is Indra and Indra's power now!

[39] Abanindranath Tagore, 1962, *Gharoyā*, Calcutta, p. 72.

[40] From Manmohan Basu's journal, cited in Geeta Chattopadhyay, 1983, *Bāṅgla svadeśī gān*, Delhi: Delhi University, p. 8.

[41] Geeta Chattopadhyay, ibid., p. 12.

Oh destiny of mine, why cannot we
Move forward just like them
Forcefully, in order to say that this is ours
    This land of our birth, this land in which we live?

Fearfully we go, fearfully we glance
We fall upon the ground when we see a white person
We cannot speak, we cannot shout out loud—
    Such is the terror in our hearts.[42]

Once again, Hemchandra revised some of the lines in this poem before it was collected in an anthology, changing, for instance, a section in which he had specifically mentioned by name the oppressors of his native land as 'the Pathans, Mughals, and residents of Britain', to read, subsequently, 'Pathans, Mughals and ill-intentioned Persians' who had all 'trampled upon the wretched Hindu'. He also changed entirely the last verse of the poem, which Akshaychandra had cited as specifically directed as a reproach to Bhudev for not publishing *Bhārat saṅgīt*; in it, Hemchandra had originally written:

Fearfully I write, what more should I write,
Or you would have heard this *bīṇā* of mine
Resound thunderously, and once again
    Would have overflowed this pained heart of Bharat.[43]

While the personification of Bharat was being evoked thus in poetry and song, modern Bengali historiography had already moved, irrevocably, from being the 'history of kings', as in Mrityunjay Vidyalankar's *Rājābalī* (1808), to the 'history of this country', as in *Bhāratbarsher itihās*, the title given by at least three different writers, Tarinicharan Chattopadhyay in 1858, Kedarnath Datta in 1860, and Krishnachandra Ray in 1870, to their textbook histories of India.[44] Partha Chatterjee has argued in the context of these history texts that a pre-colonial mindset gave way now to a European understanding of

[42] Hemchandra Bandyopadhyay, *Bhārat Bilāp* (first published in the *Education Gazette*, Calcutta, 1871) in *Kabitābalī*, ibid., pp. 23-5.

[43] Akshaychandra Sarkar, *Kabi Hemchandra*, pp. 9-10.

[44] Partha Chatterjee, 1998, *Nation and Its Fragments*, Delhi: Oxford University Press, p. 95.

one's country in terms of territory, statehood, and people.[45] A study of Hemchandra's nationalist poetry shows, however, that since 1870, alongside this territorial/historical realm, the term Bharat had also begun to be transformed into an emotive/affective idiom in literature and song from Hemchandra's *Bhārat saṅgīt* and *Bhārat bilāp* onward. The use of the term Bharat became current now, and came to be understood in a different sense from its usage in the older Puranic or Vedic literature in Sanskrit. For the first time, histories of India with 'Bharat' in the title had begun to be written for school rooms; while these textbooks popularized the notion of Bharat as a nation state, at the same time, that idea began to be given emotional content in patriotic lyrics of a kind that were, in India, entirely new.

'The Religion of Patriotism'

Militant Hinduism in *Bhārat saṅgīt* was personified in the war-like Aryans (identified as 'our forefathers'), and in the young man with 'the stance of a sannyasi', standing upon a mountain top wearing a '*nāmābalī*'. While the use of Aryan heritage has its own specific narrative in the history of ideas in modern India, the imaginary figure envisaged by Hemchandra also occupied a significant, if ambiguous, symbolic space in nationalist discourse; as I hope to show, the figure with the Hindu scarf is a sign more resistant to straightforward interpretation than we might today suppose it to be. The controversial demand in *Bhārat saṅgīt* of organized rebellion was inalienably linked, in the nationalist imagination in late nineteenth-century Bengal, to the reconfiguration of the figure of the sannyasi. Indira Chowdhury has commented briefly upon the inadequate scholarship attending to Vivekananda's appeal 'in terms of his redefinition of masculinity within the image of the sannyasi' and has attempted to redress the balance; however, her focus is on Vivekananda, and to some extent upon Bankimchandra, and attendant social discourses.[46]

The actual historical originals of the iconic figure of the sannyasi-fakir had first been extensively written about in the pages of the *Asiatic*

[45] Ibid.

[46] Indira Chowdhury, 1998, *The Frail Hero and Virile History: Gender and the Politics of Culture in Colonial Bengal*, Delhi: Oxford University Press, p. 121.

Researches by H.H. Wilson in 1828, where he listed the various types of ascetics while describing the many austerities practiced by them; remarkably, Derozio's long narrative poem, *The Fakeer of Jungheera*, published in the same year, romanticized the figure of the bandit king-cum-fakir in its tale of the love between the Muslim fakir and a Brahmin girl snatched from the funeral pyre. Literary representations of the ascetic, therefore, seemed to have idealized the colonial administrative image of them as disreputable fraudsters from very early on, later investing in their mysterious persons some of the romance and danger of extremist revolutionary politics. According to R.C. Majumdar,

> The militant nationalism of Bengal was founded upon the twin rocks (*sic*)—the ardent patriotic call of Swami Vivekananda based on the philosophical teachings of Vedanta and *Gita*, and the religious devotion to motherland preached by Bankim Chandra through *Ānandamaṭh*. These works became the sacred canon of a small group of young patriots who were ready to sacrifice their all at the altar of their motherland. Many of them literally left their hearth and home and joined the secret societies in the spirit of the Sanyasins of *Ānandamaṭh*.[47]

Meanwhile, he continued, 'The revolutionaries used *Bhavani-Mandir* … as a suitable background for the organization of revolution. Even Bipin Chandra Pal, a Brahmo, openly preached that the national life should be based upon religious beliefs and the Hindus, Muslims and others in India should form distinct cultural units of a "composite nationalism"'.[48]

This emphasis upon the role of religion in our national life was a characteristic feature of the last quarter of the nineteenth century. Pal was not alone in being a rationalist Brahmo and straying towards religiosity; he had been guided in this enterprise by Bijoy Krishna Goswami (1841–1899), who had travelled in the hills from one sannyasi to another in quest of his spiritual guru, and whose neo-Vaishnavite inclinations led Pal into proclaiming Srikrishna 'the Soul of India'. Another distinguished Brahmo leader of the time, Keshab

[47] R.C. Majumdar, 1975, *History of The Freedom Movement in India*, Vol. 2, Calcutta: K.L. Mukhopadhyay, p. 150.

[48] Ibid., p. 158.

Sen (1838–1884), was blamed for the decline of Brahmo influence in Bengal by Sibnath Sastri, who said:

> As far as I can recollect after much thought, it was from this time [1872: the controversy over the Native Marriage Act] that the hold of the Brahmo Samaj upon the people of the country began to loosen... . Mr Keshabchandra Sen in a sense forsook the leadership of the youth and lost himself in yoga, devotion [*bhakti*], renunciation [*bairāgya*]... he began to cook his own food and began to wear saffron; he became immersed in preaching renunciation... . Young people now seemed to turn their back on the Brahmo Samaj and move towards politics and national improvement.[49]

Hemchandra's views reflecting these trends are evident in his two English publications, *Life of Srikrishna,* written while he was still a student in 1857, and *Brahmo Theism in India,* 1869, in which he demonstrated the inevitable decline of Brahmoism in the future and the enduring legacy and superiority of Hinduism. Once again, in the first book, he seems to precede all the other thinkers of nineteenth-century Bengal who sought to construct an ideal god in Krishna, most notably Bankimchandra in his influential *Kṛsnacaritrā* (1886) and *Dharmatattva* (1888), and Nabinchandra Sen in his trilogy, *Rāibatak-Kurukshetra-Prābhās* (1887, 1893, 1897). The magnetic appeal of Ramkrishna at Dakhineswar in these years also conclusively points toward the educated Bengali middle-class's search for salvation, and the path to salvation seemed to lie either in militant revolution or in spiritual renunciation, while occasionally, the two came together in a fruition that galvanized not only the pages of contemporary literature but also political life.

Brahmabandhab Upadhyay, maverick Christian crusader and ardent preacher of the Vedanta, who both converted to Catholicism and ran away to join the army of the Maharaja of Gwalior in his youth, is one example that amply illustrates the point. Advising the readers of his immensely popular journal, *Sandhyā* (started in 1904), 'Whatever you hear, whatever you learn, whatever you do—

[49] Sibnath Sastri, 2003, *Rāmtanu lāhirī o tatkālīn baṅga-samāj*, p. 274.

remain a Hindu, remain a Bengali',[50] he used his extremist journal to inculcate a race hatred that was intended to deliberately break the spell or *māyā* of British power and prestige while aiming for complete independence. *Sandhyā*, *Nabashakti* (ed. Monoranjan Guha Thakurta, 1907–8), and *Bande mātaram* (eds Aurobindo Ghosh, Shyamsundar Chakrabarty, and Hemendraprasad Ghosh, 1906–8) were all journals that advocated extremist politics; but by far the most bloody minded was the *Yugāntar* (ed. Barindrakumar Ghosh, Abinash Bhattacharya, and Bhupendranath Datta, 1906–8). Criticizing the policy of passive resistance, the *Yugāntar* openly called for violent revolution: 'Without bloodshed the worship of the goddess will not be accomplished... And what is the number of English officials in each district? With a firm resolve you can bring English rule to an end on a single day... Begin yielding up a life after taking a life'.[51] The point being made here is that the anti-colonial discourse of militant nationalism in Bengal drew its imagery from poets such as Hemchandra, who had articulated almost exactly the same sentiments in *Bhārat saṅgīt* thirty years earlier at the very inception of nationalist literature in India:

> Nowadays you are a hundred crore more than before,
> Why shouldn't you be able to rescue your native land,
> You could with laughing ease rule
> From Sumeru to Kumari
> You could raise the flag of victory on this earth
>   If a few of you woke up and took a vow.
>
> Then at the feet of a different race
> Why do you stay grovelling all
> Why don't you tear apart these shackling chains
>   And make up your minds to be free?[52]

The numerical superiority of the Indians in relation to the presence of a few sentries (originally 'white sentries') standing guard that occurs at the start of the youth's song, along with the mention of

[50] Quoted in Prabodhchandra Sinha, n.d., *Upādhyāy brahmabāndhab*, Calcutta, pp. 81–3.

[51] '*Svarājya-Sthāpan*', *Yugāntar*, Vol. 1, No. 49 (3 March 1907) in Angsuman Bandyopadhyay (ed.), 2001, *Agniyuger agnikathā: yugāntar 1906-1908*, Pondicherry: Sri Aurobindo Asram, p. 383.

[52] *Bhārat saṅgīt*, in *Kabitābalī*, p. 118.

the population in India being 'several crore' greater today than when the Aryans ruled were elements that became integral to nationalist rhetoric in India. First imagined thus in this early poem in 1870, this refrain of strength in numbers would be repeated ceaselessly (most famously in the *Bande Mātaram* song) in songs, poems, essays, and speeches, becoming a fundamental trope of nationalist politics in pre-Independent India. 'Will Bharat remain thus asleep?' ('*Bhārat ki sudhu ghumāye rabe?*') asked the poet in the last line of *Bhārat saṅgīt*, and this question seemed to animate real-life revolutionaries into answering the question far sooner than anticipated, perhaps, with the birth of militant Hinduism's first modern cadre, the secret societies or terrorist cells that were imbued with the spirit of religious emotionalism.

jāti-baira: the Poetic Nationalism of Racial Hostility

Meanwhile, Akshaychandra Sarkar had finished formulating his thoughts on the national life of the Bengali in *Kabi Hemcandra* by 1904, when the book was completed, although the hesitant committee that had commissioned it did not publish it till 1912. Akshaychandra, whose stature may be gauged from Bipin Chandra Pal's description of him as 'not only my teacher in literature, but also the man whose paper, the *Sādhāraṇī*, taught me the "a b c" of politics right through to the last lesson', had many objections to the nature of nationalism in *Bhārat saṅgīt.*[53] Hemchandra's nationalism, according to Akshaychandra, was shallow, and confined to the realm of ethnic hostility to the British, to *jāti-baira*; it did not have the characteristic of true adherence to the Hindu religion, which was the only true form nationalism could and should take.

Jāti-bairitā was a phrase first used in the journal *Śiksha-darpaṇ o saṅgit-sār* edited by Bhudev in 1864, and elaborated upon by Bankim in an essay in the *Sādhāraṇī*, which Akshaychandra edited, in 1873. The fact that the ordinary Englishman is superior to the ordinary Bengali is not in doubt, Bankim had said, and for amity to exist between the two sides, it was necessary for the inferior side to remain humble, obedient, and dutiful towards the superior side. However,

[53] Kalidas Nag (ed.), 1887, *Akshay sāhitya sambhār*, Vol. 1, Calcutta: Indian Associated Publishing Company, p. iii.

We may be obedient, but we are not humble, and never will be. That is because we are an ancient race (*jāti*). To this day we read the Ramayana and the Mahabharata, we act according to the laws set down by Manu and Yagnavalkya, we bathe, and then worship God in the world's most incomparable language. Until we forget all these things, we shall not be able to be humble. We might pretend to be modest outwardly, but cannot be humble in our hearts. Therefore, this *jāti-baira* is a result of our current situation.

As long as the relationship is one of subject and conqueror between the native and the foreigner, we shall remember our past pride, and the hostilities (*jāti-baira*) will not be checked. And we pray with our heart and soul that until we become equal to the English, the influence of this hostility (*jāti-baira*) remains as strong as it is now. As long as these hostilities exist, there will be a feeling of competition... It is our good fortune indeed to have commenced hostilities with the English.[54]

Akshaychandra quotes extensively from the text of Bankim's explication of the term *jāti-baira*, and then proceeds to define the limits of Hemchandra's nationalism:

Bankimbabu has said 'It is our good fortune to have commenced hostilities with the English'. That 'good fortune' had its source in the poetry of Hembabu. *Jāti-baira* existed. But it was not perceived to be a blessing; as a result, it did not have pomp. The Brahmin pundit had it in his dilapidated school-room, the English novice had it—after listening to Ramgopal Ghosh's lectures, while reading the Hindu Patriot, and in the poetry of Rangalal. But *jāti-baira* had not yet acquired such grandeur; it had not spread so wide.[55]

Akshaychandra was quite right about the influential nature of the hostility engendered against the British at this time. Hemchandra wrote in an age when nationalist agitation was gathering clarity and force, and his own involvement in such matters was comprehensively present in his poetry, so much so that many contemporaries hailed him with great enthusiasm as the poet of *jāti-baira*.[56]

[54] Bankimchandra Chattopadhyay, 1280 BE [Oct–Nov 1873], '*Jati-baira*', in the *Sādhāraṇī*, 11 Kartik, quoted in Akshaychandra Sarkar, *Kabi hemcandra*, p. 66.

[55] *Kabi Hemcandra*, p. 68.

[56] Kshetra Gupta (ed.), 1965, *Hemcandrer nirbācita racanābalī*, Calcutta: A.K. Sarkar, p. 37.

It was this popularity that Akshaychandra wished to question when he remarked that the hostility (*jāti-baira)* of the Marathas towards the Mughals in the verses of *Bhārat saṅgīt* (for the Maratha leader Shivaji had been the original hero) spread 'among the enervated Bengali's schools and colleges, courtrooms and zamindari offices, and in the inner chambers of civilization'.[57] But although the reach of Hemchandra's influence was wide, it was still, in a crucial sense, restricted, for, as Akshaychandra pointed out, 'in spite of the feeling of hostility (*jāti-baira*) in courts, colleges, and civilized society that it has been our good fortune for Hemchandra's talent to have induced, it is still limited to those areas alone. The word has not reached the bazaars, the fields, the riverside, or the road; the man in the market does not know who Hembabu is, the farmer in his field has never heard or caught a whiff of his name. The young village girl who bathes in the river does not comprehend'—and here he quotes from *Bhārat saṅgīt*—'that "Bharat is still sunk in slumber"'.[58]

This Gandhian concern with the common man, with the farmer and the labourer, the poor and the dispossessed, that Akshaychandra articulates here did not find political expression until much later, emblematized most emphatically in Gandhi's shedding of his three-piece suit for the loincloth as an expression of solidarity with the masses. Anticipating that later political turn to touch the soul of India, Akshaychandra saw, long before the Congress politician did, that *jāti-baira* belonged to the educated Bengali alone, and was not enough. Completing his thought from the section earlier quoted, invoking the village girl at the river, he concluded, 'There are so many people out there on the road, long stick in hand, thin cotton [*gāmchā*] tied around, who do not know what "Bharat" is'.[59] Nehru made a similar discovery many years later when, as he famously recounted in *Discovery of India*, he realized that the peasants he met in the countryside did not know what they meant when they shouted 'Bharat Mata *ki jay*—Victory to Mother India', unable as they were to answer his question as to who this Bharat Mata was whose victory they desired.[60]

[57] *Kabi Hemcandra*, p. 69.

[58] Ibid., pp. 48–9.

[59] Ibid., p. 69.

[60] Jawaharlal Nehru, 1946, *The Discovery of India*, New York: John Day, pp. 48–9.

In a preceding section of the book *Kabi Hemcandra* called 'The Bengali's "National Life" and Hemchandra', Akshaychandra had explained why he was dissatisfied with what Bengalis understood by the term '*jātīya jīban*' or national life:

> First of all, we do not properly understand this term, The National Life of the Bengali. Perhaps the leaders of the Congress understand the term 'The National Life of the Indian'; we certainly do not comprehend it. If the national life of the Bengali is a constituent part of the national life of the Indian, then that is even more incomprehensible. Instead of saying this, if we say the national life of the Bengali is a part of Hindu life that too does not help much. How much a part? Only that part which is geographically in Bengal? In Bengali history? Then is Kashi (Benaras) not a part of our national life? And Ram-Lakshman? Are they too nothing? What sort of a national life is that? I don't understand it.
>
> The real thing is that the time has come when we must understand what we mean exactly when we use terms such as 'nationalism' (*jātīyatā*), 'national life' (*jātīya jīban*), or 'the welfare of the country' (*deś-hitaishītā*).[61]

This criticism, however, was not made from the point of view of a detached observer of the political scene. Akshaychandra was 'prominently connected with the Indian Association in its early days, and took a leading part in ensuring the success of the second session of the Congress in Calcutta in 1886. He was a leading figure in connection with the Rent Bill agitation and worked in earnest cooperation with the Editor of the paper (*Bengalee*) as a sturdy champion of the rights of ryots'.[62] While he worked hard with the government on the issue of zamindari panchayats, he ceased cooperation with the authorities the moment the matter involved traditional Hinduism, fiercely opposing the Widow Remarriage and Age of Consent Bills. A committed proponent of the swadeshi cause long before it became fashionable, he is reputed never to have bought a foreign item for twenty-six long years from 1891 to 1917; when Indian umbrellas could not be obtained, he did not use an umbrella for all these years, even forsaking European medicine for the first seven years of his vow.

The pointed reference to the Congress in his criticism of a particular type of politics perhaps had its origins in Hemchandra's presentation

[61] *Kabi Hemcandra*, p. 59.

[62] Cited in *Akshay sāhitya sambhār*, Vol.1, p. v.

of one of his poems, *Rākhi bandhan* (which he hailed for having incorporated a section of Bankim's *Bande mātaram* within it), at the second session of the Indian National Congress in Calcutta that he too had been involved in administrating. Akshaychandra's criticism of Hemchandra's nationalism is distinct, however, from Aurobindo's pointed criticism of Congress policies of conciliation in a series of articles in the *Indu Prakash* in 1893–4, called 'New Lamps for Old', where the rhetoric instead seems to echo Hemchandra's directive to shed the old and bring in the new in terms of modes of resistance.

Hinduism versus Nationalism

Akshaychandra based his understanding of nationalism upon his allegiance to the Hindu religion, not only making a clear distinction between the sacred and the secular, but extolling the superiority of the Hindu in every instance. 'What is this thing called the welfare of the nation (*deś-hitaishītā*)?' he asks, 'Does that mean saying that Malda-Murshidabad are better places than Kashi-Puri-Sridham? I'm afraid I do not understand that'.[63] Sites of Hindu pilgrimage are far above the unimportant political/secular sites associated with Muslim hegemony, and the core of our national life, he says, needs to be located within them. His criticism of Hemchandra, therefore, is centred on the notion that in Hemchandra's poetry, the 'welfare of the nation' is not unequivocally situated in a conception of the superiority of Hinduism.

It should be noted, though, that when Akshaychandra had emphasized that for him, 'He who looks after his own dharma is the true "patriot"; one's own country, one's own jāti, sanātan rites and rituals, he loves all of these…' he was differing from his guru Bankimchandra in an essential way.[64] Bankim's Hinduism was both self-conscious and reconstituted: in fact, in order for Hinduism to survive in history, he felt it was essential for it to be reconstructed rationalistically in a manner very different from its traditional form. Sudipta Kaviraj makes the point that the symbols that Bankimchandra had taken from the repertoire of Hinduism were 'actually highly

[63] *Kabi hemcandra*, p. 60.

[64] Ibid., p. 63.

unorthodox'.[65] For Bankimchandra insisted that the only way forward was either to forsake Hinduism altogether, which was unadvisable, or to 'take only the essence of it, that part with which society can move forward, and uplift itself, and follow that'.[66] Kaviraj has argued too that Bankim, 'remarkably, does not give any encouragement to usual forms of chauvinism' and that 'The Bande Mataram is not statistically communal. Muslims provide, on any serious demographic enumeration, the majority of those twice seven crore uplifted hands, or the arithmetic of the song collapses'.[67] Amales Tripathi too has defended Bankim from the condemnation that the 'exclusive Hindu tone and imagery' of his works offered 'Hindu communalism a defence and Moslem communalism an excuse', maintaining that this view is shrouded in 'cobwebs of misunderstanding'.[68]

In an essay called '*Debatattva o hindudharma*', Bankimchandra did not, like Akshaychandra, equate rites and rituals with dharma; he placed dharma above rites and rituals. Giving an example of two kinds of Brahmins, he shows one to be a cruel and corrupt landlord who 'incants Hari's name even in the act of forging documents; is this man a Hindu?' The other Brahmin is a man who

> takes his food from all castes; does not refuse dining with Muslims and Christians. He does not observe a single ritual of worship. But he never tells lies… and honours God inside himself. He never deceives anyone, does not covet other's goods.… Of these two who is a Hindu in reality? … One has strayed from dharma, the other from religious rituals. Are the rituals religion, or is dharma religion?'[69]

He concludes, emphatically, that he does not believe in

> some sort of difference between Hindus and Muslims. If someone is a Hindu he is not automatically good, and a Muslim evil.… He who has the quality of dharma on his side, along with other qualities, is superior

[65] Sudipta Kaviraj, 1995, *The Unhappy Consciousness*, p. 142.

[66] Bankimchandra Chatterjee, 1998, *Bankim rachanavali*, Vol. 2, Calcutta: Sahitya Sansad, pp. 707–8.

[67] Sudipta Kaviraj, 1995, *The Unhappy Consciousness*, pp.131–2.

[68] See Amales Tripathi, 1967, *The Extremist Challenge: India between 1890 and 1910*, New Delhi: Orient Longman, p. 3.

[69] Bankimchandra Chatterjee, '*Devatattwa o hindudharma*', *Bankim rachanavali*, Vol. 2, p. 707.

> whether he is a Hindu or a Muslim. Even with other qualities, he who lacks dharma, whether a Hindu or a Muslim, is inferior.[70]

In this particular aspect of his thinking, Bankim shared his world-view with the earlier mythic imagination of Mrityunjay Vidyalankar in *Rājābalī* (1808), who had asserted likewise that kings are rulers on earth only as long as they follow dharma and to forsake dharma is to invite divine retribution, whether you were the Hindu king Prithviraj or the Muslim emperor Aurangzeb.

On the other hand, it must be conceded that Bankimchandra had no compunction in describing the Muslim in the most prejudiced and unacceptable language imaginable. Disputing the Muslim historian's version of Bengali history as false, he maintained that 'he who does not judge for himself, but accepts as history the narratives of these blind, racially arrogant, lying, Hindu-hating Muslims, is not a Bengali'.[71] It is the vituperative descriptive rhetoric he employs in his delineation of the Muslim—'that killer of the sacred cow, that shaven-headed Muslim'—that has led to his enduring reputation as a communally prejudiced thinker who sowed the seeds of Hindu chauvinism through the powerful use of language in both his essays and his novels such as *Sītārām* and *Ānandamaṭh*.[72] The noted Bengali historian, Akshaykumar Maitreya, had pointed out that Bankim's depiction of Siraj-ud-daula as well as the brave Muslim general Mohammed Taki Khan was a gross distortion of historical fact in two of his books, *Sirājaddoulā* and *Mīr Kāsim*.

Hemchandra's social politics incorporated a conservative belief in traditional value systems not dissimilar to those advocated by Akshaychandra, who had taken such exception to his understanding of patriotism in *Kabi Hemcandra*. A heated controversy on the role of intellectuals in Bengali society had broken out when Keshab Sen, the then leader of the Brahmo Samaj, attacked Hemchandra publicly for observing orthodox Hindu rites at the funeral services of his father. If such well-known figures did not set an example by repudiating such antiquarian and patently absurd rituals, Kesabchandra demanded

[70] Ibid.

[71] Bankimchandra Chatterjee, '*Bāṅgālīr itihās sambandhe kayekti kathā* [A Few Words on the History of Bengal], p. 291.

[72] For a detailed discussion, see Chapter Six.

to know, what was the future of modernity in Bengal? Hemchandra replied by writing, in English, a tract entitled 'Brahmo Theism in India' in which he pointed out to the Brahmos 'how impracticable it is to found a popular religion on the basis of a metaphysical theology'.[73] Defending Hinduism for its 'extraordinary vitality', Hemchandra explained that it owed its longevity to 'two facts—its character, and the law which regulates the propagation of religions'.[74] These factors had helped it to out manoeuvre Buddhism, Christianity, and Islam. Of the latter, he wrote, in a language common to many Bengali intellectuals of his time: 'For five centuries, at least, Mahomedan infidels swayed over India with an iron sceptre; and yet did Hinduism set at defiance the Koran and the sword of Mahomet'.[75]

In *Kabi hemcandra*, Akshaychandra puts a name to his understanding of the Hindu faith; as he puts it:

> Country, jāti, language, rites and rituals, all of these are contained in the *sanātan* dharma. If you have to protect your dharma, you have to protect all of these. He who looks after his own dharma is the true 'patriot'; one's own country, one's own jāti, *sanātan* rites and rituals, he loves all of these. To be only a devotee of your country (*deś-bhakta*) has no meaning.[76]

Sanātan could loosely be translated to mean the eternal and continuing forms of Hindu religion and tradition, and Akshaychandra had elsewhere written a separate book on the subject, called *Sanātanī*, in which he explained his understanding of traditional Hinduism with the help of extended quotations from Monier Williams and Robertson's *Disquisitions on Ancient India*. A concept which, alongside that other new construct, nationalism, was being formulated and debated vigorously at this time, *sanātan* Hinduism was interpreted in different ways in different parts of the country. As Vasudha Dalmia has pointed out, 'what crystallized as the *sanātanī* position at the end of the nineteenth century, was, in fact, part of a process of interaction with the discursive formations which challenged it (the missionary

[73] Hem Chundra Banerjee, 1869, *Brahmo Theism in India*, Calcutta: I.C. Bose & Co., p. 49.

[74] *Kabi Hemcandra*, p. 29.

[75] Ibid., p. 28.

[76] Ibid., p. 63.

and the 'neo-Hindu') or with those, in which it sought and found support (the Orientalist explications)'.[77] Without going into a detailed exposition of the origins and implications of the term, let it suffice to say that here, Akshaychandra emphatically places it *above* all forms of nationalism, differing thereby from Aurobindo, who, interpreting nationality as a higher form of spirituality, had famously asserted in 1909: 'I say no longer that nationalism is a creed, a religion, a faith; I say that it is the Sanathana Dharma which for us is nationalism. This Hindu nation was born with the Sanathana Dharma; with it, it moves and with it, it grows...'[78]

The defence of traditional Hinduism was an old project in Bengal, almost as old as the reformist impulse itself. The Gaudiya Samaj, for instance, was formed in 1823 to promote the sanctity of the Hindu scriptures and social customs and to promote learning, while the Dharma Sabha had organized itself in 1830 not only around the primary objective of mobilizing public opinion against the banning of sati, but also to prevent the government from interfering in matters of religion and to protect *sanātan dharma* or traditional Hinduism. In Rajnarain Basu's last book, *Bṛddha hindur āshā* [An Old Hindu's Hope], first published in Bengali in 1886 in Akshaychandra's journal, *Nabajīban*, he spoke of the organization of Hindus into a Mahasamiti in which Muslims would have no place; he suggested, though, that they were free to form a Maha-Mussalman Samiti and cooperate with the Hindus in political matters. The flag of this Samiti would bear the inscription: 'God and the Motherland: Triumph of Sanatan Dharma'.[79] Before this, in 1872, Rajnarain had delivered a famous lecture on the superiority of Hinduism to all other religions, entitled *Hindu Dharmer Śreshṭhatā*, in which he had claimed that 'The Hindu

[77] Vasudha Dalmia, 1995, '"The Only Real Religion of the Hindus": Vaisnava Self-representation in the Late Nineteenth Century', in Vasudha Dalmia and H. von Stietencron (eds), *Representing Hinduism: The Construction of Religious Traditions and National Identity*, New Delhi: Sage Publications, p. 177.

[78] Aurobindo Ghosh, 'Uttarpara Speech', 30 May, 1909, first published in *Karmayogin*, June 1909, in the *Sri Aurobindo Birth Centenary Library*, Vol. 2, Pondicherry: Sri Aurobindo Ashram.

[79] Sibnath Sastri, 1959, *Rāmtanu lāhirī o tatkālīn baṅga-samāj*, p. 273.

religion contains, like the ocean that washes the shores of India, gems without number and will never perish as long as the country exists'.[80]

Bhudev, Rabindranath, Akshaychandra: Correspondences

The phenomenon that Akshaychandra was defining himself against in his valorization of the eternal and ongoing beliefs of traditional Hinduism—and it could not be more emphatically underlined that his entire polemic here is essentially a reactionary one—was that of the 'Bengal renaissance', which was overwhelmingly under the influence of a powerful section of reformist and rationalist Hindus dominating the social and political landscape in Bengal at the time. Akshaychandra's attitudes toward Hinduism shared something with the theories of Bhudev Mukhopadhyay, by far the most well-known exponent of traditional Hinduism at this time. Remarkable correspondences may be noticed between the lives and beliefs of the two. Bhudev's relationship with his father was very similar to Akshaychandra's with his, about whom he had declared, in his dedication to *Pushpānjalī* (1876): 'You are my progenitor and teacher. I have not learnt even one per cent from books or anyone else of what I learnt from you'.[81] Unlike Akshaychandra's father, Ganga Charan Sarkar, Bhudev's father was unacquainted with Western learning; both, however, led exemplary personal lives imbued with a deep regard for traditional Hindu culture that was central to the world-view of their sons. Bhudev was from a Brahmin family that considered the code of conduct prescribed for the Brahmins as worthy of imitation by everyone else; Akshaychandra was a Kayastha who fervently held that 'The Brahmin is still at the head of Hindu society. The revival of the Brahmin is the first necessity; if the Brahmin rises, all the rest will be rescued the more easily', even setting up a school for the promotion of traditional Brahmin rites.[82] Both believed in the merit of the caste system, in the rites and rituals that maintained the sanctity of the old system, in *adhikārbhed* and the *barṇaśramdharma*. Both were uncompromising nationalists. Bhudev

[80] Cited in Ibid.

[81] Quoted in Mukundadev Mukhopadhyay, 1917–27 (BE 1324–34), *Bhudeb-charit*, Vol. 3, Calcutta, p. 449.

[82] Cited in Brajendranath Bandyopadhyay, p. 14.

was the first to conceive of the country in the form of the mother goddess in *Pushpānjalī* (1876); a characteristic statement shows an innovative displacement of the location of patriotic sentiment within traditional Hindu mythology:

> When I was a student of Hindu College, a European teacher told us that patriotism was unknown to the Hindus, for no Indian language had any word to express the idea. I believed his word and was deeply distressed by the thought. I knew then ... the mythical account of Sati's death [cut to pieces by Vishnu's disc, Sati's body parts landed in fifty-two places that became centres of pilgrimage for all Hindus], but that knowledge did not help me refute the teacher's statement or console myself. Now I know that to the descendants of the Aryans the entire motherland with its fifty-two places of pilgrimage is in truth the person of the Deity.[83]

A man of tradition by his own declaration, Bhudev had, in his *Sāmājik prabandha*, offered to defend the most indefensible aspects of Hindu society, such as child marriage and the caste system. Yet Bhudev advised Hindus, as Bankimchandra did, to come to terms with change in an analytic and self-conscious manner, speaking of '*samāj*' in an entirely new way, equating it, not, as in the old days, to one's neighbourhood, village, caste, or sect, but relating it to the abstract modern conception of society.[84] Like Akshaychandra, he too had asserted that contemporary India lacked a sense of identity. While nationalism was 'certainly an elevated feeling within the human heart, it was not the most important. National feeling, or *jātīya bhāb*, is a mixed thing, containing both the good and the bad'.[85] This was what Akshaychandra shared with him, apart from a fervent respect for Hinduism as a way of life: a commitment to a higher ideal than mere patriotism.

When Bhudev identified what comprised *svajātīyatā* or people of the same *jāti*, however, he insisted that it was a quality conferred upon people who share the same natural and historical world, and

[83] Bhudev Mukhopadhyay, *Adhikarbhed o swadeshanurag*, in Pramathanath Bisi (ed.), 1968, *Bhūdeb racanāsambhār*, Calcutta: Mitra & Ghosh.

[84] Sudipta Kaviraj, 1995, 'The Reversal of Orientalism', Vasudha Dalmia (ed.), *Representing Hinduism: The Construction of Religious Tradition and National Identity*, New Delhi: Sage Publications, p. 278.

[85] Bhudev Mukhopadhyay, 1375 BE, *Bhūdeb racanāsambhār*, p. 261.

the same sorrow and happiness (*samadukkhasukhatā*), which comes from inhabiting the same history, and not from formal faith alone. Muslims, therefore, and Christians, are identified as tied to Hindus by similarities that exceed the differences. In his references to Muslims, this arch-conservative ritualist was generous to the point that it has been said, perhaps a trifle exaggeratedly, that apart from Rammohun Roy, no other Bengali writer of the nineteenth century showed such an openness toward Muslim society and religion.[86] His dream, in the treatise *Svapnalabdha bhāratbarsher itihās*, was the establishment of a regenerated and united Hindu Maratha kingdom in India, yet in an essay called '*Dharmāchārya*' he had maintained, 'Among all the prophets or men of god who have appeared in this world, it is Mohammed who one comprehends as the most superior'.[87] In the sphere of his own fiction, he had made the legendary Muslim, Sabuktigin, the hero of his novel *Saphal svapna,* while in another historical novel, *Aṅgurīya binimaẏ*, he had depicted Shivaji smitten by love for Aurangzeb's daughter; both books reveal a deep respect for Islam. In his imaginary history of India, a character had said: 'If a child is born of the mother's womb and another child is fed at her breast, are not the two in a brotherly relationship? Certainly, according to every scripture. Hence the Hindus and Muslims who live in India share a brotherly relation'.[88] Similarly, in *Ātmaparicaẏ*, Rabindranath had said: 'It is not impossible to imagine a Hindu family, in which a Christian brother, a Muslim brother and a Vaishnav brother are brought up together by the same parents, and it is not difficult to imagine this but instead this thought is what is natural—because this is what is the real truth, and therefore auspicious and beautiful'.[89] The similarities between Rabindranath's social and political thought and Bhudev's here are so striking that Pramathanath Bisi thought there were entire passages in Bhudev that Rabindranath would have accepted without needing to change a single comma or semicolon.[90]

[86] Pramathanath Bisi, Introduction to *Bhūdeb racanāsambhār*, p. vi.

[87] Ibid., p. vii.

[88] Bhudev Mukhopadhyay, '*Svapnalabdha bhāratbarsher itihās*', *Bhudev Rachana Sambhar*, pp. 345–6.

[89] Rabindranath Tagore, '*Ātmaparicaẏ*' (1912), in *Rabindra rachanabali*, vol. 9, p. 599.

[90] Ibid., p. xxi.

Like Akshaychandra and Bhudev, Rabindranth Tagore too, in essays such as 'Nationalism' and novels such as *Ghare bāire*, had famously rejected, at the height of the violent political convulsion of the swadeshi movement, the demands of narrow nationalism. Akshaychandra's politics, however, was different from Rabindranath's in one crucial aspect—his imagination had room in it only for a sectarian understanding of *sanātan* Hinduism that was grounded in an exclusivist and partisan view of the nation. While Akshaychandra was formulating his thoughts on the national life of the Bengali in *Kabi Hemcandra*, which he had completed writing by 1904, Rabindranath Tagore had published two essays, '*Nation ki?*' [*What is 'Nation'?*] and '*Hindutva*' in the pages of the *Baṅgadarśan* in1902. Distinguishing there between the European nation and the Indian state of affairs, Tagore prioritized the civilizational qualities of Indian society, where the Hindu system found place for different races to live together amicably.

Hinduism seemed to be, for Rabindranath, an idea that transcends any systemic definition, and a civilizational attribute that far outshone the virtues of nationalism. 'What is hindutva?' he asked, replying, 'That is exactly what I am showing you, and at the same time, I also want to inform you that what European civilization calls national greatness is not the only ideal of greatness that exists. Our vast social ideals were far greater and higher in comparison'.[91] Although he repeatedly went back to what he understood to be the essence of Hinduism, Rabindranath was unsparing in his numerous attacks on the ritualism and casteism of traditional Hindu beliefs, stating, in an almost direct contradiction of Akshaychandra, at the inception of the Benaras Hindu University, 'there are some people who take pride in the distinctiveness of our race but they see that distinctiveness in a very narrow way… . That is why I am anxious about those who want to establish a Hindu university, what is the idea of Hinduism with which they want to work?'[92]

[91] The title of '*Hindutva*' was changed later to '*Bharatbarshiya samaj*'. See *Rabindra rachanabali*, Vol. 2, p. 622.

[92] Rabindranath Tagore, '*Hindu biśvabidyālay*', cited in Partha Chatterjee, '*Rabindrik "nation" ki?*, in *Bāromās* (*Pūjā śaṃkhyā*, 2003) p. 12.

In a series of lectures collected in the *Rabindra rachanabali* under the title *Bhāratbarsha*, Rabindranath had articulated, among other things, his conception of what constituted the Indian nation. Attempting, at every juncture, to formulate an idea of India in opposition to the Western and the colonial, he returns, interestingly, to some of the same Hindu images we have been examining, when he said, for instance, in a lecture titled '*Nababarsha*', also written in 1902:

> Victory shall come; it is Bhāratbarsha that will be victorious. Victory shall belong to the Bharat that is ancient, that is concealed, that is vast, that is generous and that is silent; we—who speak in English, who disbelieve, who tell lies, who boast—year by year we shall dissipate, disappear, like the waves in the ocean. Silent, *sanātan* Bharat will not suffer any loss as a consequence. Covered in ashes, maintaining a vow of silence, Bharat sits at the crossroads on a deerskin; when we have finished with all our briskness and sent our sons and daughters on their way in coat and frock, then Bharat will still be peacefully waiting for our grandsons. That wait will not be in vain, for they shall go to this sannyasi with folded hands and say: grandfather, give us the mantra.[93]

This turn to a romanticized, pastoral past and a yet unblemished spiritual essence in order to mould a coherent identity in the present was a valorization of the traditional against the foreign, of the values of the colonized in contrast to the colonizer. In both Rabindranath and Hemchandra, the image of the sannyasi, irrespective of whether he is war-like or peaceable, is no more than an idiom, a signifier of core cultural values.

The early symbolic revivalism of such sentiments as expressed by Rabindranath gave way, later, to a more self-conscious awareness of the inclusive nature of Indian society. A few years later in 1909, Gora, in the novel of the same name, is shown singing the patriotic songs of Hemchandra in his youth. Gora's exclusivism is oriented by, and directed towards, the past, but events conspire to shake the foundations of his self-definition and nationalism when it is revealed at the end that he is an orphaned Irishman. Neither Hindu nor Muslim nor Brahmo, this adopted Bengali is thus freed at last, free to be a true patriot, free to love and serve his country irrespective of his origins. Hemchandra's

[93] Rabindranath Tagore, '*Nababarsha*' [*New Year*] in the *Rabindra rachanabali*, Vol. 2, Calcutta: Visva-Bharati, 2003, p. 703.

vision of the direction in which India needed to move forward shared something with this depiction of the shedding of caste and community on the road to self-definition. In a section of Hemchandra's *Bhārat saṅgīt* that Akshaychandra took serious exception to, the young man with the look of a sanyasi too calls out to the people of India to forget all distinctions of class and caste:

Just once, forget all your different castes,
Kshatriya, Brahmin, Vaishya and Sudra unite,
Take a firm vow to raise up in this universe
    Your own flag of greatness.
Chanting, meditating, building of sacrificial fires
Praying, worshipping sacred fires and created images
None of these will help you at all in any way
    Worship a quiver of arrows instead.
.....

Those days are no longer there
When Bharat could be rescued through invoking her gods
It will not do—will not do, draw your swords,
These are not the monsters of the past.[94]

'*E sab daitya nahe temon*': 'These are not the monsters of the past'—this line became immortal in Bengali literature, echoing through subsequent novels and plays. Quoting the above lines, Akshaychandra had concluded: 'Such advice—to follow a method that is bereft of all dharma, belief, or devotion—no one had issued such advice to the people of our country with such arrogance before this'.[95] In such lines are contained the tragedy of the educated Bengali, he says, for in our country, our life has always resided in our dharma. 'We cannot aspire to build a new life for ourselves by negating our faith and our beliefs, Indians stay as well as move forward only in dharma'.[96]

This emblematic line of Hemchandra's—'*E sab daitya nahe temon*'—demarcates an important moment in the history of Bengali culture, for no other poet till then had signalled such an emphatic and dramatic break with the past. Until then, poems or plays on the theme

[94] Hemchandra Bandyopadhyay, *Kabitābalī*, p. 120.
[95] *Kabi Hemcandra*, p. 59.
[96] Ibid.

of national sentiments had emphasized the past glories of the country, and harped upon the coming regeneration of the nation in the future that would re-enact those achievements. Nobody had said till then that those old ways would not do, that the old system did not work, that a violent rupture with the past needed to be accomplished for the nation to move forward. The hypnotic drum-beat of the repeated phrase '*habe nā, habe nā, khol tarbār*' ['It will not do, it will not do, draw your swords'] signalled the need for a new strategy, a new way forward, and gestured towards a failure of the old in a manner that was not to be found in other patriotic verse of that time. Its resonant tones drown out the protest Akshaychandra makes, which, with hindsight, seems outdated and irrelevant in the context of the direction travelled by modern Indian society.

This moment of rupture, this break with tradition and the *sanātan*, takes on different meanings from different perspectives. For us, as we examine the original impulses behind Hemchandra's creation of the symbols of Hindu militancy, Hindu exclusivism might be read as residing in the symbolic accessories of Hemchandra's image; to Akshaychandra, looking upon it at that moment, it seems to signify a turn that brought home to him in some subconscious way the cultural redundancy of his own position. Hemchandra's delineation of a Hindu youth urging the people to draw their swords might seem, today, to belong to a particularly virulent strain of political Hindu nationalism, but to his contemporary Akshaychandra, it seemed too much like secular nationalism, degrading Hindu rituals and asking instead for the worship of arms and the establishment of liberty and equality in a Western sense. Hindu exclusivist rhetoric in the nineteenth century thus proves to be, with the passage of time (which both obscures and clarifies), not as simple and homogeneous an entity as we might be tempted to believe in the current context.

(ii) Cutlets or Fish Curry?: Debating Indian Authenticity

> *I want to argue that authentic speech, where it is conceived not as a political strategy within a specific political and discursive formation but as a fetishised cultural commodity, may be employed ... to enact a discourse of 'liberal violence', re-enacting its own oppressions on the subjects it purports to represent and defend.*
>
> Gareth Griffiths[97]

To Serve Politics and Literature

When Akshaychandra Sarkar was commissioned to write the first book on Hemchandra Bandyopadhyay after his death, it was expected to be an eulogy and an appreciation of a respected and well-known figure. Instead, *Kabi Hemcandra* [*The Poet Hemchandra*] was a denunciation so vigorous and acerbic in its tone that the 'Society for the Preservation of Hemchandra's Memory' hesitated and prevaricated, and finally released the book in 1912, a full eight years after it was first written up in 1904. Upset admirers of Hemchandra rallied around to urge Manmathanath Ghosh to write another book, which then appeared in 1919. One of the leading critics of his time, Akshaychandra's tone in this book was grudging at best, but perhaps, with hindsight, not unexpected in one of the most incisive and orthodox minds of that society.

Sunitikumar Chattopadhyay, who had described Akshaychandra's works as 'classics in the domain of modern Bengali literature, particularly in literary criticism', had exclaimed, in the introduction to the first collected edition of Akshaychandra's works, 'This is no less than an unprecedented, matchless, "sparkling" seven-stringed gemstone

[97] Gareth Griffiths, 1994, 'The Myth of Authenticity' in Chris Tiffin and Alan Lawson eds. *De-Scribing Empire*, London: Routledge.

necklace on the neck of mother Bengal'.[98] Political commentator, literary critic, editor, collector, and anthologist of medieval Bengali verse, Akshaychandra was a towering figure in his time, influential in his opinions, trenchant in his criticism, formidably learned in various fields. He had taken and passed the B.L. examinations from Presidency College, where he had met Bankimchandra, but was actually a student of what was then known as an 'Honours in Arts—M.A.' in Philosophy. Kalidas Nag has recounted, in his introduction to the *Akshay sahityā-sambhār*, that he was unfairly marked and failed in the M.A. examination because the Presidency College Principal, J. Suttcliffe, took exception to his appearing in both the B.L. and M.A. examinations in the same year. His knowledge of Western philosophy, though, was legendary; disputing a point on the philosophy of Mill with Sir Gurudas Banerjee, he had famously conceded, 'Yes, I am orthodox in my reading of Mill, but it is better to be orthodox after having read him than to brag without having read him'.[99] In his memoir, *Pitā-putra* [Father and Son], Akshaychandra mentions how in his youth, when his head was full of the disputations of Western philosophers such as Mill, Comte, Spencer, and so on, his father would argue with him as an equal adversary. 'Mill's *māyābād* (Permanent Possibility of Sensation), Comte's Positivism, Herbert Spencer's social theory, these would be the subjects of the most nuanced argument between us, father and son'.[100] A thorough knowledge of the Western canon was what many nineteenth-century figures in fact had in common; what distinguished Akshaychandra was his privileging of his own tradition and irritation at those who failed to make the distinction between an 'other' culture and 'one's own', as he felt, inestimably superior lineage closer home.

Any account of Akshaychandra has to take into consideration the influence of his father, Ganga Charan Sarkar, upon him; the relationship between these two men, in whom a thorough schooling in English texts coexisted with a deep reverence for, and vast knowledge of, Sanskrit

[98] Sunitikumar Chattopadhyay, 1888, '*Sāhityācārya akshaycandra smaraṇe*' (In Memory of Akshyachandra), in Kalidas Nag (ed.), *Akshay sāhitya-sambhār*, Calcutta: Indian Associated Publishing Company, p. viii.

[99] See Kalidas Nag, ibid., p. iii.

[100] Akshaychandra Sarkar, ibid., pp. 1–82.

and Bengali traditions, illuminates not only Akshaychandra's own proclivities but also gives us a sense of a particular type of orthodox temperament which was of some importance in those formative years of modern Bengal. A student of D.L. Richardson, Ganga Charan excelled in his renditions of Shakespearean verse; a sub-judge at Dhaka, he was an active member of the *Dacca Hindu Dharma Rakshini Sabha*. Two of his lectures, *Hindudharma bishaỳe baktṛta* [Lectures on Hinduism, 1879] and *Baṅga sāhitya o baṅga bhāshā* [Bengali Literature and Language, 1880] neatly encapsulate the twin driving forces behind Akshaychandra's love for Bengali and the traditional Sanatan Dharma. Meanwhile, the old-fashioned orthodoxy of this family may be gauged from the celebratory recounting in the memoir of an act of sati by Akshaychandra's grandmother, told to him by his father, who had witnessed the glorious moment at the age of five.[101]

Akshaychandra had studied at the Hooghly College and then enrolled to study law at Presidency, completing his degree in 1868; there, in the third year, he had Bankimchandra Chatterjee as a fellow student, though he became a friend and follower of Bankim's only later.[102] In a letter to his friend Jagadishnath Ray, Bankimchandra had written of Akshaychandra, apropos the founding of *Baṅgadarśan*: 'I have got a lot of contributors, who have promised to write and can write, in Dinabandhu, Hemchandra, Krishnakamal Bhattacharya, Taraprasad Chatterjee and a young man whom you don't know, but whose intellectual life, I think, I have greatly influenced, for good or for evil, and whose inherent gifts presage something great for him in the future. His name is Akshay Sarkar'.[103] Founder-editor of a well-known Bengali political weekly called the *Sādhāraṇī* (1873), Akshaykumar had said of its aims and objectives in the first edition:

[101] Ibid.

[102] His description of his fellow student is worth quoting: 'Bankimchandra used to arrive at the Presidency College law section galleries from his three-storeyed house, located on the western side of what is now the City College, with his orderly holding up his umbrella. Goodlooking, well-built, of slender frame, he had an aquiline nose, bright eyes, and a small smile playing around the corners of his mouth. But that smile was accompanied by a tremendous sense of dignity. He would come, sit quietly at one side, not speak to anybody. None of us were, at the time, acquainted with Bankimbabu.' Cited in Brajendranath Bandyopadhyay, 1956, *SSC*, pp. 5–7.

[103] '*Paricitī*', *Akshay sāhitya-sambhār*, p. xi.

> The *Sādhāraṇī* takes the side of the Hindu *jāti*, of the Bengali. It prays for the stability of the current government, the welfare of the ordinary people, and most of all, for the good of the subject… Although I have said it desires the stability of the government, while it does that, it also recommends certain fundamental changes in methods of ruling. The sad thing is that the English have not understood the meaning of the word 'king' as yet. They are busy with governance, busy making laws, as busy spending money as they are in making money, but they remain unmindful of the chief duty of the king, which is the satisfaction of his subjects.[104]

The *Sādhāraṇī* was printed at the *Baṅgadarśan* press at Kanthalpara, and in his autobiography, Akshaychandra said, in retrospect, that the journal was born in order to 'serve politics and literature consistently and on an equal footing, and that is what it attained… Bankimbabu's *Baṅgadarśan* gave the Bengali babu a taste for educating himself into reading Bengali, and, in order to cater to his taste for politically oriented literature, the *Sādhāraṇī* was born'.[105] Yet it has been said that it was Akshaychandra even more than Bankim who carried forward the practice of review articles and essays on literary criticism in the modern Bengali journal; his own innumerable contributions to the art of literary criticism often taking the form of extended essays such as, for instance, *'myākbeth o hyāmlet'* ['Macbeth and Hamlet'], where he discussed why in spite of both plays being about the murder of a king, they were so essentially different. The journal shared its name with a school for the propagation of English education that he ran for ten years.

After the demise of the *Sādhāraṇī*, Akshaychandra went on to edit a monthly called *Nabajīban* for five years from1884 that published such stalwarts as Bankimchandra, Hemchandra, and Nabinchandra in its pages; it was here that Bankim's most important thoughts on the meaning of Hinduism, the *Dharmatattva*, began to appear serially from 1884. When Bankim retired from active journalism, it was Akshaychandra who he chose as a successor for the *Baṅgadarśan*, but the proposal fell through for financial reasons.[106] His qualities as an editor were recognized in his lifetime by his peers; both Jogendrachandra

[104] Ibid, pp. 9–10.

[105] Ibid.

[106] Nabinchandra Sen, *'Āmār jīban'*, *Nabinchandra rachanabali*, Vol. 1, p. 459.

Basu, editor of the famous *Baṅgabāsī* and Ramendrasundar Tribedi, one of Bengal's leading essayists, were his apprentices at one time. One of his more enduring legacies involved the painstaking collection, along with Saradacharan Mitra, of early medieval devotional verse in *Prācīn kābya saṃgraha*, described as 'one of the earliest specimens of modern research into Bengal Vaishnavism',[107] which Rabindranath acknowledged as the source material for his first, in his own words 'unauthorized' entry into the world of literature, *Bhānu siṃher padābalī*.

> When Mr Akshaychandra Sarkar was engaged in the task of bringing out the *Baishnab Padābalī* serially, I was at a very young age... I went through the newly published *Padābalī* a few years before I turned sixteen when I went to my *mejdādā* [Satyendranath] in Bombay. Let us say I had just stepped into fourteen. I was still not considered old enough to read the fragments of the *Padābalī* openly. Yet I was their only reader in our house. My brothers never noticed when these disappeared from their desk... . Ascending after this to the next step, I considered forging them. From Akshaybabu, I had heard of the boy-poet Chatterton. I desired to emulate his feat.[108]

Associated for a long time with the Bangiya Sahitya Parishad, where he was assistant editor for some years, Akshaychandra's was a distinctive and individual voice, direct and to the point, his gift for image and metaphor ably reinforcing his arguments with vivid and telling force.

Kabi Hemcandra

In his slight book titled '*Kabi Hemcandra*', which was eventually published in 1912, Akshaychandra Sarkar devoted a substantial amount of his energies addressing the troubled issue of the authenticity of Hemchandra's corpus, which he treated in relation to the work of Bengal's most well-known preceding poet, Iswar

[107] Amiya P. Sen, 1993, *Hindu Revivalism in Bengal*, Delhi: Oxford University Press, p. 86.

[108] This last mentioned Akshaybabu, however, is Akshaychandra Chaudhuri, not Sarkar, a friend and classmate of Jyotirindranath Tagore. See Rabindranath Tagore, *Jībansmṛti*, *Rabindra rachanabali*, Vol. 9, pp. 407–514.

Gupta.[109] Using Akshaychandra's critique as a gateway to the world of nineteenth-century disagreement and debate on the topic (the book itself generated passionate indignation and controversy), I shall try to indicate, through a detailed discussion of Akshaychandra's objections and predispositions in relation to Hemchandra's work, the ideological predilections and nationalist tropes that were deployed in literary discourse in an attempt to self-consciously fashion a modern Indian national identity. Tied to this articulation of a modern Indian identity for a newly imagined nation were questions of authenticity. Repeatedly, the questions that were asked included: was Hemchandra's poetry authentic? How did it compare with what was claimed as the more authentic verse of a preceding poet like Iswar Gupta? Could a poet so deeply immersed in Western literary convention produce authentic Indian poetry?

The chapter on Hemchandra's poetic authenticity, '*Hemcandra o Īśvar Gupta*', is central to Akshaychandra Sarkar's book, both literally, located as it is in the middle pages, after the biographical details and at the start of the literary discussion, and figuratively, as it articulates an important newly evolving awareness of the constituents of one's own Indianness and a definition of that which is foreign or alien to it. Written originally as an essay for the periodical *Nabajīban* in 1893 eighteen years before the publication of *Kabi Hemcandra* in 1912, Akshaychandra reprinted the essay in that book with some additions, as he felt that the topic was still relevant: 'The country is filled with hypocrisy; to tell the truth is a great responsibility' ['*Bhaṇḍāmite deś bhariyā uṭhila; satya kathā balā bisham dāy*']. He begins with an unequivocal assertion, that

> Although he is saddened to say it, and hesitant too, yet it is still true that Iswarchandra Gupta was Bengal's last poet. Madhusudan is Bengal's Milton, Hemchandra Pindar, Nabinchandra Byron, and Rabindranath Shelley: well and good, but what then is Iswarchandra Gupta of Bengal? Iswar Gupta—is Bengal's Iswar Gupta. To this fact can be traced criticism of Iswar Gupta, and praise for him to the same fact. His poetic quality is the Bengali's own. Even if that might resemble the poor man's small change, still, it is his own. And because it is his own, it is very dear.

[109] Akshaychandra Sarkar, 1912, *Kabi Hemcandra*, Calcutta: Bangiya Sahitya Parishad, p. 20.

> Is Hemchandra's poetry then not our own, and is it not dear to us? [110]

Akshaychandra answers by admitting that yes, indeed, Hemchandra too is our own, and especially dear to us, but there is something that needs to be said. Imagine then, that:

> Your better half sits by herself and intently embroiders flowers upon some velvet, and so makes a beautiful cap for you. She presents this to you; you smilingly wear it, and, still smiling, show it to ten of your friends outside. That cap is part of your beloved, and part of your self: how dear it is to you! But the wool is all of it English wool; the flowers are English flowers; the English creeper twists around in an English scheme in the design. From within that which is one's own (*nijasva*), a sort of otherness (*parasva*) peeps out in every layer.[111]

This is the first among a number of startling and innovative images used repeatedly by Akshaychandra to reinforce his thoughts in this essay. It is immediately followed by a continuation of the imaginary scene he had started with: 'And then you take those ten friends of yours and sit down to a meal'. An elaborate description follows of a domestic setting, where the wife serves the food she has cooked personally to their guests. The smell of the cooking fills the room with its fragrance; the pilau contains both almonds and raisins and other foreign commodities, but that is no more than the '*masalā*' necessary for its preparation. It has all been mixed together in a sublime mixture, and the wife, as she sits with her head half-covered with her sari and her gold bangles clinking on her arm, is also part of the whole picture—which includes (and here he makes a list) the commodities, the method by which the food has been prepared, as well as the manner in which it is served—which in its entirety is entirely our 'own' (*nijasva*). He concludes, therefore, that 'even if there is anything foreign (*parasva*) about it, that element has sunk without a trace, it has been absorbed in the immensity of that which is *nijasva*, our own. Iswar Gupta's poetry may not be that fragrant pilau, but it is certainly liquid fish curry. His poetry is our own, it is of our self, it is dear to us, and we love it greatly'.[112]

[110] Ibid.

[111] Ibid., p. 20.

[112] Ibid., p. 21.

This stream of associated imagery is brought to a culmination by a last thrust, and Akshaychandra finishes his diatribe in a reasonable tone:

> I do not ask you to throw away the embroidered cap and pilaus made by your wife and spend your days having fish *soup*. But when I see cutlets being appreciated more than fish curry, I am truly unhappy. And yet as the days go by, that is exactly what has been happening. The Bengali's authentic Bengali poetry has taken shelter in the margins. English fragrance, English rhythm, its wool is English, its flowers are English, a sort of foreign (*parasva*) poetry has occupied centre-stage and does business. Do you not feel sad? Maybe you do not. But we do.[113]

In this debate over the authenticity of Hemchandra's poetry, Akshaychandra Sarkar ends his discussion with an additional section written expressly for his book *Kabi hemcandra*. Here he admits, with a great deal of honesty, that although he had not thought anything of it at the time of writing, ever since Hemchandra's death, he had been struck by moments of remorse (*Hemcandrer mṛtyur par āmāder mane kintu keman ektā khap khapāni haiteche*). What he had said about Iswar Gupta was hundred percent true, but what he had said of Hemchandra was merely a sort of preface or prologue to the matter, and he needs now to put the record straight:

> Certainly there is an otherness (*parasva*) about Hemchandra. That is only natural. There are many Persian manners in Bharatchandra, but who tries to catch those? And who is disturbed by it? … In the same way, Hemchandra is, in this matter, even more successful than Bharatchandra.… Hemchandra is truly the goddess *Sarasvatī*'s godson. With her blessings he has been able to turn what is foreign into what is Hem. And that Hemness he has handed down to us. As possessors of it, we think of his gift as our own and are grateful, and we thank him for it. [114]

Colin Graham, in an essay on 'Ireland and the Trope of Authenticity', comments: 'Authenticity may resist definition, but its materiality in textuality is undeniable. In this it shares with imaginings of nationalism an important reliance on its various media: what Benedict Anderson calls 'the technical means for "re-presenting" the

[113] Ibid., pp. 21–2.
[114] Ibid., p. 22.

kind of imagined community that is the nation'.[115] Like nationalism, authenticity also has an ambiguous relationship with 'origins'; it is 'the "genuineness" of "genuine origins" that authenticity highlights rather than the materiality of origins; and "genuineness", in a perfectly circular resistance to theory, is known by its authenticity'. Concluding his discussion of the analogy between nationalism and authenticity, Graham says: 'As with the nation in Benedict Anderson's famous formulation, authenticity wishes to be conceived of as "moving steadily up (or down) history", and as with the nation, authenticity 'proves' itself through its simultaneous and contradictory textual existence and refusal to be defined'.[116] Graham also invokes Jacob Golomb's *In Search of Authenticity* (1995) as a text that constitutes a major attempt to read authenticity as an integral part of Western philosophical, humanistic traditions. Authenticity, Golomb noted, is bound to notions of authority: 'One is historically authentic when one creates one's own history by utilizing and recreating one's past and the past of one's people, projecting them with anticipatory resoluteness towards one's future... [Authenticity] is the loyalty of one's own self to its own past, heritage and ethos'.[117] This project of creating one's own history was indubitably one of the earliest preoccupations of the colonized in British India: not only in historiographical, but also in literary and cultural terms and contexts.

The juxtaposition, in the chapter in *Kabi Hemcandra* entitled '*Hemchandra o īśvar Gupta*', of the figures of the poets Iswar Gupta and Hemchandra to highlight the contrast between the two implies a continuum, as if the one immediately precedes or follows the other. There is, however, a critical gap in the picture, for in between these two major Bengali poets of the nineteenth century comes the formative figure of Rangalal Banerjee, who was arguably the first English-educated Bengali poet. Rangalal is crucial because he was instrumental in ushering in, quite self-consciously, a new sort of poetry to Bengal, a poetry born of the colonial encounter, and composed to conform to what Rangalal considered the purer and loftier standards

[115] Colin Graham, 2001, 'Blame It on Maureen O'Hara: Ireland and the Trope of Authenticity', *Cultural Studies*, Vol. 15, No. 1, January, pp. 60–1.

[116] Ibid., p. 63.

[117] Jacob Golomb, 1995, *In Search of Authenticity*, London: Routledge, p. 117.

of taste contained in English poetic conventions. Akshaychandra's harking back to Iswar Gupta, then, is actually an act of reclamation and reconstruction. He composes his tirade against Hemchandra here almost as if he does not know of the existence of Rangalal; by eliding Rangalal from the scene so effectively, Akshaychandra achieves the impossible: he manages to establish the antecedents of modern Bengali verse in what he perceives as the traditional and the non-Western, and thereby tries to determine what future course it should take. That this struggle was entirely ineffective for the time being, encountering as it did, apart from Hemchandra, the combined efforts of Madhusudan, who admired Milton and Virgil and Kalidas, and Nabinchandra, whose *Palāśīr yuddha* [The Battle of Plassey] (1875) was modelled on the historical scenes of Byron's *Childe Harold*, and even written in a metre new to Bengali poetry, which was a variation on *Childe Harold*'s Spenserian stanza, is now history.

The origins of authenticity as a cultural necessity may be seen to lie in what David Lloyd sees as the labelling of colonized cultures as 'inauthentic' by the colonizer. 'On the side of the colonizer, it is the inauthenticity of the colonized culture, its falling short of the concept of the human, that legitimates the colonial project'.[118] Here, in late nineteenth-century Calcutta, this perceived 'inauthenticity of the colonized culture' was packaged all-pervasively for the educated classes not only in the ascendance of what Robert Young calls 'racialism—that is, theories of race offered as a form of scientific knowledge about mankind', whose explicit theorization began 'in the late eighteenth century, [and] were increasingly scientificized in the nineteenth'.[119] The idea of the superiority of the white race was also present in Western theories of the culture of science and the concept of history, both of which had to be acquired by Indians desirous of progress. Its effective internalization gave rise to a vicious self-denigration among reactive cultural nationalists in the latter half of the century, as evidenced in the belief, for instance, that being a subject race, Bengalis

[118] David Lloyd, 1993, *Anomalous States: Irish Writing and the Post-Colonial Moment*, Dublin: Lilliput.

[119] Robert Young, 1995, *Colonial Desire: Hybridity in Theory, Culture and Race*, London: Routledge, pp. 91–2.

could not produce a genuine poet.[120] There occurred simultaneously, as a corollary effect in response to this damaged self-esteem of the colonized, a concerted effort among prominent Bengalis to create, from among their own, categories of excellence conforming to Western standards and design, an enterprise envisaged as 'tools of survival under the colonial political economy' by Ashis Nandy, and as 'an indigenous nationalist project for counter-appropriation' by Ranajit Guha.[121] So, long before Bankimchandra issued his famous ultimatum that Hindus would remain a subject race so long as they did not write their own history, early Indian modernists like the Derozian Krishna Mohun Banerjea, once again invoking the foundational trope of authenticity, had felt that if Europe had transcended its past by acquiring a historical consciousness, India, which showed a 'lamentable want of authentic records in … literature', could do so too.[122]

Westernization and Cultural Nationalism

Interestingly, it was the prominent members of the landed moneyed classes who took the lead in matters relating to literature, commissioning professional middle-class writers to fashion a new drama and a new poetry for Bengal. Rangalal mentions his indebtedness to two powerful patrons: the zamindar of Kundi, Babu Kalichandra Raichaudhuri, who had encouraged and stimulated him in his endeavour, and Raja Satyacharan Ghoshal, who, pained at the popularity of vulgar and profane poetry among children, the elderly, and women, had requested him again and again to compose poetry using more cultivated parameters. At exactly the same time, Madhusudan Datta was asked to produce an English translation of Harsha Deva's *Ratnavali* (Rangalal's poem was published in the Bengali month of *Āshāḍh*, 1858, which roughly corresponds from the middle of June to the middle of July; while *Ratnavali* was first performed in July 1858) by Raja Jyotindramohan Tagore. A note

[120] See Chapter Three.

[121] Ashis Nandy, 'World Historians and Their Critics', *History and Theory*, Connecticut: Wesleyan University, p.58; Ranajit Guha, 1998, *Dominance without Hegemony*, Delhi: Oxford University Press, p. 3.

[122] Nandy, p. 65.

congratulating him for the play expressed the hope that 'you may live long and continue to show the nations of Europe what inestimable gems we have in our ancient language'.[123]

This endeavour to showcase the heritage of India for the West began, of course, with William Jones and his team at the Asiatic Society from the last years of the eighteenth century onward. By the time the nineteenth century had entered its second half, earlier styles of adaptation to Western colonial rule had given way, according to Ashis Nandy, to an 'odd form of reactive Westernization which wore the garb of cultural nationalism':

> Riding the growing political participation and exposure to new forms of communication, both of which had been effectively deployed for social reform in the earlier generation, cultural nationalists soon became a significant presence in Indian public life. They were the first Orientalists that the Orient itself produced in defence of the Orient. They depended mainly upon the knowledge that nineteenth-century Europe produced about India, and on their revaluation of the country's martial past.[124]

Nandy identifies this typical response of the late nineteenth century with the figure of its most towering representative, Bankimchandra Chatterjee, among others, in an attached footnote on the 'Kiplingesque antipathy' of this era towards 'Anglicised, city-bred, effeminate babus'.[125]

Hemchandra Bandyopadhyay, against whom Akshaychandra directed much of his polemic, was certainly one of these new creatures, being both anglicized and city-bred, and he himself was nervous and apologetic about his own affiliations. In the advertisement that accompanied his most accomplished work, *Bṛtta-saṃhār* (1875), he is regretful about the fact that 'since my childhood I have studied the English language, and the Sanskrit language is unknown to me, so it will not be surprising if this book is marked in many places by faults caused by my inexperience in Sanskrit and my allegiance to the

[123] *Madhusudan rachanabali*, 1993, Calcutta: Sahitya Sansad, p. 75.

[124] Ashis Nandy, 2001, 'Contending Stories in the Culture of Indian Politics', *Time Warps: The Insistent Politics of Silent and Evasive Pasts*, New Delhi: Permanent Black, p. 18.

[125] Ibid.

sentiments of English writers'.[126] The difference a few years made in this context is worth remarking upon. Hemchandra wrote this abject plea in 1875; preceding him, in 1858, Rangalal had proudly proclaimed, in the preface to his *Padminī upākhyān*: 'Over and above all else, I have given careful consideration to English poetry (*imlaṅḍīo kabitā*), and writing poetry along the more cultivated parameters (*biśuddha praṇālīte*) of that poetry is an old practice of mine.... .'[127]

The passage of time, however, was not kind to such allegiances to English poetic convention. This is evident from the fact that when Kasiprasad, who described himself as the first Hindu gentleman to write English verse, published his poems in 1830, that act had been hailed universally, and had been imbued in nationalist sentiments along the lines of 'what you can do, I can also do', a sentiment that animated many initial colonial responses, from historiography to poetry. Invited to record the impulses that led to his endeavour, he had written:

> I have always found it easier to express my sentiments in [the English] language than in Bengali, but whether it is because I prefer the associations, sentiments, and thoughts which are to be found in English poems to those that are met with in Bengali poetry, I cannot decide. I can only say that I have bestowed more time and attention upon English books than any others.[128]

From poetry in the English language in Kasiprasad, to Bengali poetry written according to English poetic convention in Rangalal, to Hemchandra's apology for not knowing enough Sanskrit and knowing too much English, the trajectory of linguistic chauvinism along nationalist lines that was to convulse political and literary life in both pre- and post-Independence India was proceeding apace, until, in a few more years, it became morally indefensible to either write in or be influenced by the language of the colonizer.

In Hemchandra's time, however, a new poetry was being self-consciously forged by a new generation of men in an idiom new to

[126] Hemchandra Bandyopadhyay, Preface to *Bṛtta-saṃhār*, cited in Brajendranath Bandyopadhyay, *SSC*, Vol. 3, p. 32.

[127] Rangalal Banerjee, 1951, *Padminī upākhyān*, p. 10.

[128] Rev. James Long, 1848, 'Autobiography of Kasiprasad Ghosh', *Hand-Book of Bengal Missions*, Appendix D, London, p. 510.

indigenous literature. Hemchandra gave his entrance examination in the same year that the University of Calcutta was established, 1857, and was among the three students who passed their B.A. in the first division in 1859. Bankimchandra had preceded him the year before, in the first batch of B.A. examinees in 1858, showing how literally men who went to the same English college and studied the same English texts were among those who were occupied in creating a new literature for Bengal.[129] The influence of English studies upon Hemchandra is revealed in the use of epigraphs that ranged from Byron to Spenser and Goethe to Longfellow, a common practice borrowed from English poetic convention at the time, to publications such as *Chāyāmayī* (1880), in which, in his own words, he had 'attempted to capture a slight aura of the famous European poet Dante's unrivalled poem the 'Divina Comedia' in this small book'. In his translations of Shakespeare's *Romeo and Juliet* (*Romeo-Juliet*, 1895) and *The Tempest* (*Nalinī-basanta nāṭak*, 1868), he makes the same apologetic gesture, calling them mere shadows of the originals rather than translations, due to the 'inestimable differences' between the two languages.

It was not uncommon to find translations of Western poetry within even the most nationalist of verses at this time; thus Hemchandra's epigraph to *Bīrabāhu kābya* pointedly quoted from Byron: 'Italia! Oh Italia!.... Oh God! that thou wert in thy nakedness, / Less lovely or more powerful and coulds't claim / Thy right, and drive the robbers back, who press / to shed thy blood, and drink the tears of thy distress'.[130] Bengali nationalism, thus, was openly and unabashedly using the colonizer's language to pillory his rule; the Bengali language and English literature having come together in a common purpose in a manner unacceptable not only to later linguistic chauvinists but also,

[129] The (now-vanishing) creative interrelationship between writers in the Indian languages and an education in English has been commented upon by Amit Chaudhuri, who shows how many of 'the most influential writers in the regional or vernacular literatures of modern India' mirror the trajectory of Madhusudan Datta's career (and indeed of Bankimchandra and Hemchandra as well), encompassing writers of as diverse backgrounds as Qurratulain Hyder (Urdu), O.V. Vijayan (Malayalam), U.R. Ananthamurthy (Kannada), Mahasweta Devi (Bengali), and Ambai (Tamil), to name only a few living examples, who 'have all been students, even teachers, of English literature'. Amit Chaudhuri, 'Poles of Recovery,' *Clearing a Space*, pp. 39–57.

[130] Cited in Brajendranath Bandyopadhyay, *SSC*, pp. 26–7.

for different reasons, to contemporary purists such as Akshaychandra Sarkar.

śikkhita baṅgālī [the educated Bengali]

Vaishnav devotional poetry, epic poetry by the Bengali writers of the Mahabharata and Ramayana, Kashidas and Krittibas, the religious Kali songs of Ramprasad, the love songs of Nidhu babu, and the poetry of Bharatchandra—these are the predecessors Akshaychandra would have reverenced as in the authentic and genuine Bengali tradition. Akshaychandra's objection was that this traditional literature had been forgotten; continuing his harangue on the educated new Bengali in the section 'Hemchandra and Madhusudan', always using the term 'educated Bengali', it must be remembered, slightingly, he says, echoing Bankim, 'The educated Bengali has five important poets. Madhusudan, Hemchandra, Nabinchandra, Rabindranath, and Girishchandra'.[131] The inclusion of Rabindranath in these lists would surprise many Bengalis today; perhaps because all Bengalis think of themselves as cultivated Bengalis nowadays, and wouldn't realize that that was, in any way, different from being a 'genuine' Bengali.

The phrase in Bengali that Bankimchandra unleashed in his criticism of the new poets of the nineteenth century is a term that Akshaychandra too will deploy repeatedly: '*śikkhitā Baṅgālī*' meaning 'the cultivated or educated Bengali'. Such critiques are also to be found, however, in the accusations levelled at Derozio and Young Bengal, when these intellectuals were criticized for being 'denationalized' and 'hyper-westernized' while denying the validity of their entire cultural heritage.[132] This cultural heritage that these nineteenth-century critics were looking back to with such pride had, however, only recently been collected, annotated, explained, and re-presented to the public in the latter half of the century. Old and medieval Bengali literature could be easily accessed in the form of printed books only towards the end of the century in such works as Dineshchandra Sen's *Baṅga bhāshā o sāhitya*, published in 1896. In this project, Akshaychandra himself

[131] *Kabi Hemcandra*, p. 51.

[132] Dineshchandra Sen, 1911, *History of Bengali Language and Literature*, Calcutta: Calcutta University Press, p. 883.

was an early player, as one of his more enduring legacies involved the painstaking collection, along with Sarada Charan Mitra, of early medieval devotional verse in *Prācīn kābya saṃgraha* (published serially from 1874–77), following in the footsteps, in fact, of a man he much admired, Iswar Gupta, who had first attempted to present the literary history of Bengal to the ordinary Bengali when he published, in his paper the *Saṃbād prabhākar*, specimens of traditional Bengali poetry with extensive notes between the years 1853–5.

'What sort of an animal is the educated Bengali?' asks Akshaychandra in the course of his discussion on Hemchandra, almost echoing Bankim's celebrated diatribe on the Bengali babu in his *Confessions of a 'Young Bengal'* in answering:

> The educated Bengali is an 'agnostic', a follower of the incomprehensible, without belief in the straightforward word. The educated Bengali does not believe in religion (dharma), does not believe in action (karma), does not believe in the *śāstras*, does not believe in society; has no belief in the teacher, nor in the student.
>
> The educated Bengali disbelieves everything, and has reposed his faith in sorrow. Hemchandra is the poet for this Bengali, and he has fulfilled his life's promise singing songs of this sorrow.[133]

Thus the matter is resolved in Akshaychandra's argument, and presented as a fait accompli.

This discussion on the nature and meaning of authenticity thus culminates in a discussion on nationalism. Akshaychandra's understanding of both these issues, authenticity and nationalism, is governed by his concern for the traditional, and for him, tradition is ultimately located in the Hindu religion. Unconscious of the fact that his polemic was, by its very definition, a Western construct, characterized as it is by the relentless cut and thrust of argument, definition, and debate in a structurally English mode, contained in the essay form in a print publication addressed to a new reading public, he concludes *Kabi hemcandra* with one last arrow from his allegorical quiver.

In the penultimate paragraph of his study, he returns, once again, to the poet Iswar Gupta, who had once said he would rather worship

[133] *Kabi hemcandra*, p. 34.

dogs that were native than gods who were foreign. Akshaychandra praises the sentiment, observing that that sort of love for one's own people, that strength of love of one's country was absent from Hemchandra. If Hemchandra had had it, writes Akshaychandra, he could never have written of 'the disgraceful Hindu of depraved character' (*kulāṅgār Hindu durācār*).[134] 'His hand would have trembled before he could write such words; he would have become tongue-tied before he could have uttered them. If this sort of writing proves love for one's people, then what does one call hatred for one's people?'[135] And then Akshaychandra ends with the image that for him defines his discussion on the national life of the Bengali.

> In times when the love of one's religion was strong in this country, then there had existed no need to shout and scream about one's devotion to one's country, one's love for one's people. Nowadays all this is perhaps necessary; because: 'When Ram is without his Sita, it is the monkey whom he loves.' And perhaps it is the monkey who will ultimately help us to rescue Sita. Perhaps singing the praise of our country and people will result in a genuine love for our religion.
>
> These monkeys have been brought here, or perhaps they already existed in the bushes, and now they have been brought out, and made to jump, by Hembabu. This is what is called 'Rejuvenating the dejected state of our national life'. If you can use these monkeys, Sita will be rescued; if you cannot, their jumping about will be all that remains.[136]

Akshaychandra had used the image of the monkeys repeatedly in the various sections of his discussion on the nature of Hemchandra's nationalism. About *Bhārat saṅgīt*, the poem around which much of this discourse is constructed, he had said that, due to that poem, 'a sort of flaming, illuminating, "national life" had been organised and driven forward. But that illumination, that enthusiasm, all of it belonged to the monkeys. However, the monkeys were beloved of Ram because they were the ones, he thought, who might bring Sita back to him'. At the end of his book and in his concluding remarks on Hemchandra,

[134] He is referring here to the refrain in Hemchandra's poem *Bhārat Kāminī*, where Hemchandra had chastized the Hindu male for his tyranny towards the Hindu widow.

[135] *Kabi hemcandra*, p. 70.

[136] Ibid.

it is the monkeys, once again, that Akshaychandra invokes. He would not have wasted so much time and effort on Hemchandra's poetry unless he had felt that one day, *jāti-baira* would ultimately compel one to love one's religion. It would come, or perhaps it had already begun to come, in bits and pieces. 'We are still Sugrib's companions. Come, let us now pledge allegiance to Lord Ram, and take care to rescue our own religion.'[137]

It was only after the advent of Gandhian politics that the first effective resistance to militant nationalism was articulated in India. It was Gandhi, who, through the strategies of non-cooperation and non-violence, first attempted to turn India's freedom movement into a contribution to world peace, saying, 'Violent nationalism, otherwise known as imperialism, is the curse. Non-violent nationalism is a necessary condition of corporate or civilized life'.[138] Akshaychandra had no solution at hand in his time, but in spite of radical differences in their politics, he seems to share a sort of temperamental affinity with Gandhi (as well as, of course, Tagore) in his aversion to violence, although his politics was of a different order than either of theirs. Anticipating Gandhi in his dislike of 'brute strength' as the solution for our national problems, he had described educated Bengalis, in his own elliptical style, as 'those whose only recourse is brute strength, whose only method is imperial; they are the ones who say—hit and thrust, who receive—slaps and blows, who unsheathe—their swords, who dust themselves with—powder'.[139] Physical violence, then, like talcum powder, is a modern import into Indian life: in this rejection of the symbols of modernity, Akshaychandra allies Hemchandra's poetry, along with militancy and powder, with the modern and un-traditional. Thus the matter is resolved in Akshaychandra's argument, and presented as a fait accompli: 'Hemchandra is the poet of the educated Bengali; the educated Bengali normally has no belief in religion; so Hemchandra's poetry too is without it. In some places his remarkable power of remembrance results in a love of his country, at

[137] Ibid., p. 83.

[138] M.K. Gandhi, 1969, *Collected Works*, Vol. 25, New Delhi: Publications Division, Government of India, p. 369.

[139] *Kabi Hemcandra*, p. 83.

others the strength of his hostility (*jāti-baira*) leads to affection for his people. But that is all'.[140]

The series of innovative images that Akshaychandra had employed at the beginning of his essay on Hemchandra's authenticity of an embroidered cap, fragrant pilau, and cutlets, thus leads to discussions on the nature and meaning of national character, which he tries to construct in contrast to Hemchandra's cosmopolitan, liberal, English-speaking values. In the penultimate paragraph of his study, he returns, once again, to a valorization of the poet Iswar Gupta, who had advocated a hatred of the foreign that ultimately came to stand for an undisguised exclusion not only of the Western but also of the Muslim, which was defined in oppositional terms to the native and the Hindu. Inevitably, the vexed issues of authenticity and the subtext of nationalism contained in the choices made by every individual writer at the very inception of the discourse that formulated a modern language of nationhood illuminate and clarify, in however small a manner, the contemporary and continuing struggle to define the character of the modern Indian people and their literatures.

[140] Ibid., p. 64.

6 (i) History in Poetry: Nabinchandra Sen's *Palāśīr yuddha* (1875) and the Question of Truth

One day, lord L … visited the Babu and his family in Calcutta, and having surprised Aru with a novel in her hand, he told the two girls, 'Ah! You should not read too many novels, you should read histories.'

Toru replied, 'We like to read novels, lord L …'

'Why?'

The bright young girl replied smilingly, 'Because novels are true, and histories are false.'

—Clarisse Bader[1]

Nārad kahilā hāñsi, 'sei satya ya racibe tumi
Ghaṭe ya ta sab satya nahe, kabi taba manabhūmi
Rāmer janmasthan, Ayodhyār ceye satya jeno.

[Narad smiled and said [to Valmiki]: That is the truth which you compose
The event is not the complete truth. O Poet, it is your mind
That is the birthplace of Ram, more truly than Ayodhya.]

—Rabindranath Tagore[2]

[1] Toru Dutt was the first Indian woman to publish English poetry to great critical acclaim; she also translated French poetry and wrote a novel in French. This quotation is taken from the introduction to the original French edition of her novel, *Le Journal de Mademoiselle D'Arvers* (1879) by Clarisse Bader, reprinted by Penguin in 2005.

[2] These famous lines by Rabindranath were in the news in 2007. News reports said:

> After drawing flak from the Bharatiya Janata Party (BJP) for questioning the existence of Lord Ram, West Bengal Chief Minister Buddhadeb Bhattacharya yesterday blamed the media for 'putting his remarks out of context'. Bhattacharya said he had

In the process of writing about how modern Western history essentially began at the moment of differentiation between the present and the past, Michel dé Certeau noted without disagreement that in India, 'new forms never drive the older ones away'.[3] Already, right at the start of *The Writing of History*, Certeau had established that in historiography, as in modern Western culture, '*intelligibility is established through a relation with the other*; it moves (or "progresses") by changing what it makes of its "other"—the Indian, the past, the people, the mad, the child, the Third World' (original emphasis).[4] The otherness of India is then compounded, a few pages later, by the assumption that in India, that first step, wherein historiography separates its present time from a past, does not exist.[5] After all, Dumont had certified, in 1964, that there, the 'march of time' does not need 'to be certified by distances taken from various "pasts"', that on the contrary, 'a "process of coexistence and reabsorption" is the "cardinal fact" of Indian history'.[6] Just like 'the Merina of Madagascar', in India too, history is very far from 'being an "object" thrown behind so that an autonomous present will be possible, the past is a treasure placed in the *midst* of society that is its memorial…'[7]

> quoted a line from Rabindranath Tagore's *Bhāshā o chanda* (Language and Verse), which said, '*Kobi tabo monobhumi ramer janmasthan, Ayodhar cheye satya jeno*' (The poet's mind is the birthplace of Ram, which is more real than Ayodhya)… At a meeting held in Kolkata on Thursday [6 December, 2007] to mark the 15th anniversary of the Babri Masjid demolition, Bhattacharya said, 'Ram was born in the imagination of poets and Ram Setu is a natural formation under the sea'.

Accessed on 12 September 2012: http://twocircles.net/2007dec08/buddhadeb_blames_media_ram_controversy.html

[3] Michel dé Certeau, 'Introduction', 1988, *The Writing of History*, Tom Conley (trans.), New York: Columbia University Press, p. 4.

[4] Michel dé Certeau, 'Introduction', p. 3.

[5] Although conceivably, it could be the American Indian he has in mind when he says 'Indian' here, following from his discussion, in the preface, of Jan Van der Straet's etching for *Americae decima pars*, 1619, where Vespucci is shown confronting the Indian America; this confusion of the Americas for India has, of course, an old and venerable history. Nevertheless, India would still figure as a constituent of the Third World, the last mentioned entity on his list.

[6] Certeau, 'Introduction', p. 4. He is quoting from Louis Dumont, 1964, 'Le Probléme de l'histoire', *La Civilization indienne et nous*, Paris, Colin, Coll. Cahiers des Annales, pp. 31–54.

[7] Ibid.

This denial of an autonomous time of the present to Indians, where the self-conscious construct of history is not in evidence in India even as late as 1975, when Certeau's text was first published in French, is an old Orientalist perception, stretching back, as Rao, Shulman, and Subrahmanyam suggest in *Textures of Time*, a thousand years to 'the great polymath scholar al-Biruni', who complained that 'the Hindus do not pay much attention to the historical order of things…', an allegation that they believe is almost certainly wrong.[8] Refuting the notion that history 'was an "alien" import brought in … by colonial rule', Rao, et al. show, through a literary close reading of texts in various genres, from folk epics to court poetry, 'that history in South India has been written in many genres and that writing history is not a matter of strict adherence to formal characteristics and types', unlike in modern Western history as it emerged in the same period.[9] The methodology employed by these historians, in this most recent attempt to establish an autonomous time of modernity in which historiography exists in the early modern period in India, is in fact a sophisticated inversion of the older nineteenth and early twentieth-century attempts to fill the lack of history and the historical consciousness in India as perceived by Western historians from the mid-eighteenth-century onward. Attempting to construct an autonomous time of the present, behind which Indian history stretched into the mists of antiquity, was, in fact, one of the earliest preoccupations of Indian historians from the nineteenth century onward. This chapter will attempt to trace some of the early attempts, in Bengal, to separate myth from history by amateur and professional historians struggling to define 'history' and its relation to literature and to truth.

History, not Poetry

When the nineteenth-century Bengali poet Nabinchandra Sen's stirring epic poem, *Palāśir yuddha* [The Battle of Palashi] was finally released in the public sphere on 15 April 1875 in Calcutta, a huge storm erupted in the literary world almost instantly. After several well-

[8] Rao, Shulman, and Subrahmanyam, 2001, *Textures of Time: Writing History in South India 1600–1800*, New Delhi: Permanent Black, p. 1.

[9] Ibid., p. 3.

known journals of the time brought out extensive reviews, Bengal's most eminent man of letters, Bankimchandra Chattopadhyay, published a detailed discussion in his own periodical, *Baṅgadarśan.* By September of the same year, it was put up as a play by a group called 'The New Aryan Theatre', where the famous actor/director Girishchandra Ghosh is said to have first made a name for himself when he acted the part of Clive.[10] The controversies and disputes that arose with the publication of this work were so great in number and so complicated in nature that they continued well into the turn of the century, returning time and again to haunt the author at every juncture.[11] But by far the most pointed charge among the many that Nabinchandra faced in his lifetime was made in 1897 by the historian Akshaykumar Maitreya, who, for the first time, raised the question, apropos *Palāśīr yuddha*, of the relationship of history to poetry and to truth.

In his book *Sirājaddoulā* (which had been appearing serially in the journals *Sādhanā* and *Bhāratī* from 1896), Maitreya devoted an entire section of the crucial chapter describing the actual battle at Palashi in 1757 (called The Battle of Plassey by the British) to Nabinchandra Sen's work. He said there that he had written to the poet asking him why he had invented imaginary depravities for the character of the Nawab Sirajuddaula in the poem, and whether he had any historical information on the subject. In reply, an interlocutor (the editor of '*Sāhitya*', Sureshchandra Samajpati) said, on behalf of the poet, 'Not a single line [was based on historical fact] (*ek lāino nay*). *Palāśīr yuddha* is poetry, not history—that is what he has permitted me to write you.' Maitreya continues, 'Not everyone realises that *Palāśīr yuddha* is not history! A lot of people will not easily have the courage to surmise that a patriotic, erudite man of letters like him would have followed his poetic muse so far as to unnecessarily stain Siraj's character from head

[10] Nabinchandra Sen, 1985 '*Āmār jīban*', *Nabinchandra rachanabali*, Vol. 1, Calcutta: Bangiya Sahitya Parishad, p. 359.

[11] These ranged from literary criticism that judged it with reference to Hemchandra Bandyopadhyay's mythological epic, *Bṛtta-saṃhār*, to a feud between East and West Bengali writers, to its selection as a text book, to the British government's queries about certain objectionable passages.

to toe with scandals created in his own imagination—many people accept his *Palāśīr yuddha* as history!'[12]

In his turn, when Akshaykumar Maitreya's *Sirājāddoulā* was reviewed by Rabindranath Tagore in 1897, Rabindranath had only one complaint against the historian:

> In only one department has he [Maitreya] broken the laws of history. Although he has not tried to conceal any of the flaws in Siraj's character, nevertheless, he has taken his side with a shade too much of enthusiasm. Instead of presenting his material calmly with the sole aid of historical witness, he has revealed his own opinion at the same time with a little too much impatience and ardour. Fighting a rigid and hostile prejudice and facing blind and unfair received opinion at every step, he has naturally become extremely agitated. But the peace that resides in truth has been destroyed in the process, and the reader has occasionally been a little troubled by the thought, quite without foundation, of favouritism.[13]

'The laws of history' and 'truth' come together again in this passage, and Akshaykumar Maitreya's excitability is deprecated; certainly Maitreya seems to have made something of a career out of violently attacking many established reputations in the various genres of poetry, the novel, and art.[14] In his view, writers of fiction were supposed to invent everything in their narratives—characters, events, plots, and themes—while the historian invented nothing but certain rhetorical flourishes or poetic effects to tell a 'true story'. But as for the writer at the conjunction of history and poetry, who was depicting past events under the rubric of the novel or the poem—did his practice belong to history or to literature?

[12] Akshaykumar Maitreya, 2006 (1897), *Sirājaddoulā*, Calcutta: Dey's Publishing, p. 265.

[13] Rabindranath Tagore, 1395 BE, 'Sirajuddaula', *Itihās*, Santiniketan: Visva-Bharati, p. 129.

[14] Akshaykumar Maitreya took issue with Abanindranath regarding certain pieces the latter wrote in *Bhārat śilper kathā*, while he charged Surendranath Ganguly with ahistoricality in 'The Flight of Lakshman Sen' in *Modern Review* (Jan 1909) pp. 61–3. For a fuller discussion, see Tapati Guha-Thakurta, 1992, *The Making of a New 'Indian' Art: Artists, Aesthetics and Nationalism in Bengal, C. 1850-1920*, Cambridge: Cambridge University Press, p. 220.

The relationship between historiography and literature is a tenuous and difficult one. 'In part', Hayden White has suggested that

> this is because historiography in the West arises against the background of a distinctively literary (or rather 'fictional') discourse which itself took shape against the even more archaic discourse of myth. In its origins, historical discourse differentiates itself from literary discourse by virtue of its subject matter ('real' rather than 'imaginary' events) rather than its form. But form here is ambiguous, for it refers not only to the manifest appearance of historical discourses (their appearance as stories) but also the systems of meaning production (the modes of employment) that historiography shared with literature and myth.[15]

In India in the nineteenth century, where the discourse of myth belonged not to the 'archaic' past but the recent past, and the newly constructed site of a scientific Indian historiography seemed ever to be in danger of slipping back into 'fictional' discourse, Akshaykumar's agitation can perhaps be understood a little more sympathetically than Tagore did when he condemned him for violating the 'laws of history' which demand objectivity, or 'calm'. Recent theories of discourse solve the problem in their own way when they dissolve the distinction between realistic or historical discourse and fictional discourse based on the presumption of hardly any ontological difference between their respective referents, the real and the imaginary. Instead, what is emphasized is their common aspect as semiological apparatuses that produce meanings by the systematic substitution of signifieds for those extra-discursive entities that serve as their referents. In these semiological theories of discourse, narrative is held up as a particularly effective system of discursive meaning; for to conceive of narrative discourse in this way allows us to account for its universality as a cultural fact. It also adds perspective to the debate on 'historical objectivity' by showing that there really is no such thing as 'complete objectivity'.

The distinction between historical and fictional discourse has been discussed also by Jacques Rancière, the French political philosopher, who has written, in *The Names of History*, about the 'poetics of

[15] Hayden White, 1987, *The Content of the Form: Narrative Discourse and Historical Representation*, Baltimore: Johns Hopkins University Press, p. 45.

knowledge' that constitute the discourse of history, and of the 'set of literary procedures by which a discourse escapes literature, gives itself the status of a science, and signifies this status'.[16] Distinguishing the characteristics that give certain texts the status of history, he writes:

> ... history can become a science *by remaining history* only through a poetic detour that gives speech a regime of truth .... It doesn't give this to itself in the form of an explicit philosophical thesis, but in the very texture of narrative: in the modes of interpretation, but also in the style of the sentences, the tense and person of the verb, the plays of the literal and the figurative.[17]

History, it seems, has to attain a degree of scientificity before it can be called history. This scientificity is resident in the truth-value of its narrative, which then distinguishes it from the purely literary or the purely political.

Nabinchandra Sen's *Palāśīr yuddha* confounded the public because it contained at once both the logic of narrativity and the appearance of truth, thus resembling, in its essential poetic structure, the new discourse of history. In its form, however, and style, in the texture of its narrative, and the play of the literal and the figurative, it remained embedded within the field of poetry, which was constructed, at the time, as belonging to the higher moral plane. This was not only because poetry, following Vico in the early eighteenth and Hegel in the nineteenth century, was considered as 'originary' and 'primordial', as belonging to a time prior to that of prose; indigenous theories of *rasa*, which came to Bengali intellectuals not only from the high Sanskritic texts of Abhinavagupta or Anandavardhan, but also through the Vaishnav influence, were equally important in formulating a living tradition for late nineteenth-century writers such as Bankimchandra or Nabinchandra.

The matter was further complicated by the fact that Nabinchandra's *Palāśīr yuddha* had been published in a textbook version by Sanyal and Co. of Calcutta, with a Preface attached to it that vouched for it as

[16] Jacques Rancière, 1994, *The Names of History: On the Poetics of Knowledge*, translated by Hassan Melehy, Minneapolis and London: University of Minnesota Press, p. 8.

[17] Ibid., p. 89.

'the history of Bengal' and attested to its suitability as a textbook for use in schools. In a footnote, Maitreya quotes from the Preface to this 'history' book edition: 'Not only has a complete poem like this a merit of its own superior to that of mere compilation of fugitive pieces but as it is also the history of Bengal of the period in verse, the introduction of such a book into our schools will be doubly beneficial to the students and an encouragement to real talent as well as to the literature of Bengal'.[18] Maitreya took exception to this, asserting:

> It may be that 'the poet's path knows no impediments', but in his selection of historical portraiture he cannot in all places act without restraint. If the poet had stuck to 'real history' (*prakṛta itihās*) while writing about this unfortunate young king who was tricked, imprisoned, and then met with an untimely death, his composition would have touched our hearts much more. In fact, it would perhaps have been better had the poet taken refuge in his own imagination, then his imagination would not have been so much in the mould of Macaulay at every step. Macaulay's Battle of Plassey is also poetry—it is not history. If the poet had not clung to him with all the eagerness with which a blind man clutches his cane then the unfortunate Sirājāddoulā's ghost could have been protected from the harsh hand of so many baseless attacks. That is the only reason that has compelled me to write an analysis of the calamitous mistakes made by one of our country's most celebrated poets.[19]

The phrase, 'the poet's path knows no impediments', literally 'the poet's path has no thorns' (*nishkanṭak*), that Maitreya quotes in this passage is from Nabinchandra's one page appendix to *Palāśīr Yuddha*, where he gives the reader somewhat sketchy details of his sources for certain historical events portrayed in his narrative, concluding, in the last instance, 'whether this story is true or false its author could not tell me, nor is it necessary for the poet to know; for his path knows no impediments'.[20] This last phrase so irritated Maitreya that he quoted it many times in his text within quotation marks, sometimes ironically, sometimes sarcastically, repeatedly drawing attention to the absurdity of such an assertion. The distinction between history and poetry, where Macaulay's history is sarcastically identified as poetry because,

[18] Maitreya, *Sirājāddoulā*, p. 265.

[19] Ibid.

[20] Ibid., p. 264.

presumably, it bears so little resemblance to 'truth' or factuality, is based not merely on a certain formalization of the style, frame and method of history-writing in early twentieth-century India, when, following Western historians from Hegel onward, prose was identified as the most appropriate medium suited to a history that claimed to embody truth. Macaulay's history is prose, but lacks credibility as history because it does not tell the truth. On the other hand, Nabinchandra's so-called history is also not history, not because it is written in verse, but because it fails, once again, the test of truth.

History as 'a Method of Science'

A closer look at Akshaykumar Maitreya's own understanding of the role of the historian explains this impatience with the famous poet's interpretation of poetic license. In an appendix to *Sirājāddoulā*, Maitreya attaches an article in English first delivered as a lecture at the Calcutta Historical Society and later published in their journal, called 'The Black Hole Story' ('*Andhakūp-kāhinī*').[21] Here, right at the start, he lays down his own preferences in historical method. 'I must confess, at the outset,' he says, 'that I find it more reasonable to adopt the critical methods of investigation recommended by "the historians of the modern school in Europe" than to follow the time-honoured practice of swallowing all extravagant stories without any sort of investigation.' For these European historians are not mere 'iconoclasts', having 'shown by example that if they are obliged to destroy any old fetish of faith they destroy it only to replace fiction by truth'.[22] (Since he was speaking here in the context of the outrageous stories surrounding the Black Hole episode, it should perhaps be pointed out that his allegation regarding the 'time-honoured practice of swallowing all extravagant stories' was aimed, paradoxically, at English rather than Indian historians.) Maitreya continues that in this critical method, the 'main thing' for the historian is 'not the art of accumulating material, but the sublimer (sic) art of investigating it,—of discerning truth from falsehood.' J.S. Mill had pointed out, he said, the necessity of going 'to the fountain-head' for our 'knowledge of history', but the

[21] Ibid., pp. 307–21.
[22] Ibid., p. 307.

'modern critical method' goes a step further even than that, for it tests even first-hand information for its unbiased veracity. Maitreya then substantiates this with the example of how Clive had written a letter to the Mughal emperor after Palashi about Sirajuddaula's retreat, which, though a first-hand report, was deliberately misleading. The story of the Black Hole of Calcutta therefore needs to be carefully investigated afresh, 'according to the well-established system of modern critical method, *which is a method of Science*' (my emphasis).[23]

Attempting to set the record straight, Maitreya's defence of Siraj's character had begun with a rebuttal of the poet's description of the night before the battle at Palashi—the lilting lines composed by the poet depicting a drunken Siraj enjoying the company of a dishabille dancing girl might have been exceedingly enjoyable to a majority of Bengali readers, he said, but it was very far from the truth. The scene, when it was subsequently enacted on a well-lit stage with the help of prostitutes, must have helped many a person along the road to moral decrepitude, Maitreya asserts, but rather than the character of Siraj, the illuminated theatre only served to show up an exact reflection of the new Bengali filthy-rich.[24]

Maitreya begins this section, in fact, with a description, from historical sources, of the night preceding the Battle at Palashi. That the English soldiers had undertaken a long and arduous march through the night in heavy rain to reach Palashi, and that Clive had not slept that night in expectation of the coming battle had been attested to by British historians such as Orme; Maitreya actually misattributes a line from *Palāśīr yuddha* ('*ki haẏ ki haẏ raṇe, jaẏ parājaẏ!*') spoken, in the poem, by Siraj rather than Clive, to portray that moment of anticipation for Clive. The night as it passed for Siraj is then described—he too did not find the time for sleep, counting the hours in solitude and loneliness until dawn in his tent. Assessing the situation, a cunning thief departed with the hookah kept in front of him, and when a startled Siraj pursued, he found that his guards had deserted him. A stricken Sirajuddaula then murmurs to himself—'Alas, they count me as dead even before I have died'. The footnote to this section mentions: 'Scrafton's Reflections.—A different version

[23] Ibid., p. 308.

[24] Ibid., p. 264.

of this incident has been described in Stewart and it has also found a place in various other histories'.[25]

Maitreya then goes on to assert that Sirajuddaula had given up drink before he ascended the throne in accordance with a vow he made at his grandfather Alivardi's deathbed—this inalienable fact had been acknowledged as true even by the English historians who were his enemies. Footnotes quoting from both Scrafton and C.S. Beveridge prove his point, but, Maitreya sarcastically continues, it needed his fellow Indian poet to write of that contemplative solitary moment in the tent in the following manner:

> Pour the wine into the golden cup, pour again
> Come and make your offerings to these flames of desire
> Drink, pour, pour, and drink! The ocean of love
> Shall overflow, modesty's island will be exiled.
> Oh you dishabille beauty! Wine glass in hand
> Where do you dance and go?—To the Nawab?
> Go then, wearing a smile on your lips,
> Your plait, like a serpent, swaying behind you.
> Let the dance go on, let the feet loose their balance,
> Let the banner of love fly—tomorrow we go to war.[26]

This portrait of a besotted, befuddled Nawab is to be found, apparently, in Charles Stewart's description, in his pioneering *History of Bengal* (1813), of the Nawab Shaukatjung in his tent at Nawabgunj; Maitreya concludes therefore that Nabinchandra had read Stewart and 'unhesitatingly' used the description of Shaukatjung for his own portrayal of Sirajuddaula—for after all was not 'the poet's path free of all impediments'?[27] In a footnote to a later edition, however, Maitreya then concedes that after the first edition of his book *Sirājāddoulā* appeared, Nabinchandra had told him that he had not, in fact, read Stewart before he wrote *Palāśīr yuddha*.

There were further calumnies attributed to Sirajuddaula that Maitreya then lists one by one so as to show up the inaccuracies in Nabinchandra's poem. A rumour entertained by the common people

[25] Ibid., p. 263.
[26] Ibid., p. 264.
[27] Ibid.

with reference to Sarfaraz Khan, that he had, in a distracted frame of mind, happened to see the face of Jagat Seth's daughter-in-law, and in penance, had given up his life at the battle of Giriya, is embellished and attributed to Siraj by Nabinchandra, Maitreya asserts. In fact, the descendants of Jagat Seth himself do not acknowledge this story to be true. Again, with reference to the battle at Hooghly, Nabinchandra writes of Siraj, 'a blade of grass held between his teeth', fearfully escaping the battle. In reality, Maitreya writes, this young king, who from childhood had been reared sword in hand in one tent of war or another, and who had been unfairly tricked and defeated at Palashi, was not even present at Hooghly. It was the English who had attempted at the dead of night to gain unfair advantage at Hooghly but had been repulsed, and Clive had retreated with his head bowed on that occasion. Finally, it was the Nawab Mir Quasim who had imprisoned Raja Krishnachandra Ray and his son at Munger fort, but the poet Nabinchandra flies in the face of chronology and shows Siraj as responsible for this deed. In the appendix to *Palāśīr yuddha*, the source for this story remains unnamed as 'a friend, well-known in the literary world', and that is how, Maitreya concludes, the poet escapes responsibility. Akshaykumar Maitreya then ends this long discussion with a lament: 'In a country in which narrative poetry has undertaken the responsibility of history-writing, is it any wonder that Siraj-scandals should become cumulatively indelible?'[28]

Akshaykumar's concerns, which belong to the realm of traditional Western historiography, are best encapsulated in the remarks made by Hayden White in his Preface to *The Content of the Form*:

> Since its invention by Herodotus, traditional historiography has featured predominantly the belief that history itself consists of a congeries of lived stories, individual and collective, and that the principal task of historians is to uncover these stories and to retell them in a narrative, the truth of which would reside in the correspondence of the story told to the story lived by real people in the past. Thus conceived, the literary aspect of the historical narrative was supposed to inhere solely in certain stylistic embellishments that rendered the account vivid and interesting to the

[28] Ibid., p. 265.

reader rather than in the kind of poetic inventiveness presumed to be characteristic of the writer of fictional narratives.[29]

It was Nabinchandra's transgression of this brief that caused Akshaykumar such intense annoyance: the kind of 'poetic inventiveness' that Nabinchandra displayed was a characteristic of fiction, not of history or historical narrative. At the time that Maitreya was writing, Indian historiography in the Western sense of the term was still in its formative stage. History as an academic discipline had begun to be institutionalized from the time of Rajendralal Mitra (1822–1891), admiringly described as 'the man who raised studies in Indian history and culture to a scientific status' by a later historian.[30] Rajendralal's major works stretched from his study of the Pala and Sena kings of Bengal in 1855 to the psychological tenets of the Vaishnavas in 1884, and notwithstanding his immense achievement, it still remains that he was a singular figure in his time. It was only with the next generation of scholars such as Haraprasad Sastri, whose career was more or less coterminous with a galaxy of other amateur historians such as Akshaykumar Maitreya and Ramaprasad Chanda, that history-writing began to acquire a professional community and a disciplinarian outlook that was then further reinforced by the work of Rakhaldas Bandyopadhyay and Jadunath Sarkar. The very notion of the professional historian thus solidified into being at a gradual pace between the 1890s and 1915, the period in which Maitreya wrote some of his most influential works.

Throughout this period, well-known writers of poetry and prose intervened in the construction of the nation's history in their own right. Bankimchandra's drive in reconstructing the history of Bengal, his famous edict that a nation cannot come into existence until it has a history, his numerous essays between 1872 and 1884 toward building up the edifice of history-writing ('*Baṅgadeśīya kṛshak*' [The Bengali Peasant], '*Bāṅgālīr bāhubal*' [The Bengali's Strength], '*Bāṅgālār itihās*' [The History of Bengal], '*Bāṅglār itihās sambandhe kayekki kathā*' [A Few Words on the History of Bengal], and '*Bāṅglār*

[29] Hayden White, 1987, *The Content of the Form: Narrative Discourse and Historical Representation*, Baltimore/London: The Johns Hopkins University Press, pp. ix–x.

[30] Bimala Prosad Mukerji, 1958, 'History', in A.C. Gupta (ed.), *Studies in the Bengal Renaissance*, Calcutta: National Council of Education, p. 368.

itihāser bhagnāṅgśa' [Fragments of Bengali History], and above all, his powerful historical novels, which created a unique awareness of India's past at a popular level, have been repeatedly acknowledged by commentators. This tradition continued in the figure of Rabindranath Tagore into the twentieth century, who, apart from his numerous historical poems, plays, and novels between 1898 and 1912, wrote significant prefaces and introductions to contemporary Sikh, Maratha, and Muslim histories, contributing eighteen serious articles on history, now collected and published as a separate book called *Itihās* [History]. Apart from these there exist other articles such as *Bhāratbarsher itihās* [Indian History], *Bhārat-itihās-carcā* [Indian Historiography], and *Bhāratbarsher itihās dhārā* [The Flow of Indian History], which attest to his interventionist interest in Indian history and culture.[31]

Quite obviously, then, it was an accepted convention that a distinguished man of letters in Bengal should be concerned also with the writing of its history—this much was never a matter of dispute. Essays or articles written about history or history writing were undoubtedly the entitlement of the writer in nineteenth-century India (in complete contrast to the situation presently), but what happened when literary texts represented history? How far could a literary representation claim to be a 'history' of a period or a country? The lines between literature and history that had so far been blurred, causing *Palāśīr yuddha* to be read now as a narrative poem and now as a history textbook, began now to be drawn with increasing firmness. Gradually, by about the turn of the century, as the discipline of history began to become institutionalized, the authenticity of historical representation in some of the most influential literary works of the time began to be challenged—and in this matter, Akshaykumar Maitreya was undoubtedly one of the first to show the way. The strenuous defence of history as a 'method of science' that we find in Maitreya has therefore to be understood in the context of a powerful literary scene in which eminent novelists like Bankimchandra and popular poets like Nabinchandra were the agents who first depicted the history of India to its people in stirring lines of poetry and prose.

[31] Ibid., pp. 361–85.

The Transcendence of Eternal Truth

For Hegel, early in the nineteenth century, poetry is figured in terms of development in the history of Spirit (*Geist*). In this history, poetry emerged first, prior to prose, and was characteristically united in 'the original presentation of truth, a knowing which does not yet separate the universal from its living existence in the individual…'[32] Prose comes later, and splinters this unity into a relativity that is constitutive of History, for History feeds upon prose. The conditions for the production of History are then made complete, after the advent of prose, by the state, 'which not only lends itself to the prose of history but actually helps produce it'.[33] Hegel's characterization of poetry as the 'original presentation of truth' was in concordance with a Romantic conception of the poetic that dominated the nineteenth century, elevating all that was 'literary' to a domain above the merely historical. It was a view that animated Jadunath Sarkar, a student and teacher of English literature before his turn to history, in his preface to Bankimchandra's *Ānandamaṭh*, where he spoke in terms of what he called '*cirasatya*' or 'eternal truth'. This quality, he felt, inhered in the elevated sphere of the successful work of art, and transcended the demands of the merely 'historical'.

Jadunath Sarkar, in the 'Historical Introduction' he wrote to some of Bankimchandra's novels for their 'Centenary Edition' publication by the Bangiya Sahitya Parishad, launches into a detailed discussion of what constitutes literature, and what history, with specific reference to the conception, an entirely new one in Bankim's time, of the 'historical novel'. This discussion was a continuation, in a manner, of extensive argumentation among many eminent Bengali historians following Akshaykumar Maitreya in the first few decades of the twentieth century on the status of literature and history with reference to Bankimchandra's historical novels. Bankim himself, in his introduction to *Rājsiṃha*, had not wanted any of his 'historical novels' to be read as such, adding that *Rājsiṃha* was, in fact, actually the first historical novel he had written. Of these, the novel *Sītārām*

[32] G.W.F. Hegel, 1975, *Aesthetics*, Vol. 2, Oxford: Clarendon, p. 973.

[33] G.W.F. Hegel, 1975, *Lectures on the Philosophy of World-History*, translated by H.B. Nisbet, Cambridge: Cambridge University Press, p. 136.

alone had invited reams of indignant commentary from the likes of Satishchandra Mitra, author of *Yaśore khulnār itihās* [The History of Jashore and Khulna] (1922), Ramaprasad Chanda, Akshaykumar Dasgupta, Rakhaldas Bandyopadhyay, and others. Satishchandra Mitra, whose work on the history of the eponymous king Sitaram was the most extensive and authoritative, made a charge against Bankim in 1922 that replicated, almost word for word, Akshaykumar Maitreya's original complaint against Nabinchandra Sen:

> So the Emperor of Literature has asked us to disbelieve the historicality of his novel. But will the self-forgetful (*ātma-bismṛta*) Bengali reader listen to his advice? Or will he place the novelistic story above history and stain the face of Sitaram with black? It is because the novel is engaged in bringing about the ruin of history that I have had to say so many things.[34]

That the Bengalis were 'a self-forgetful race' [*ātma-bismṛta jāti*] was a statement made famous by Haraprasad Sastri in his seventh address to the Bangiya Sahitya Sammelan in 1914; commenting upon this statement, that had subsequently attained the status of a proverb among Bengalis, Bhabatosh Dutta characterized that age as the age of the 'search for history'.[35]

In direct contradiction of the stand taken by fellow historians such as Satishchandra Mitra, Jadunath Sarkar maintained that all seven novels from *Durgeśnandinī* to *Sītārām* were, indeed, historical—some had more historical characters, some less, but in all of them 'the society, the houses, the thought processes, the rites and manners of past times has been truthfully reflected. However, historical truth has not been preserved at each and every step in these books; because Bankim has deliberately painted over such pictures of truth with the colours of an extraordinary light'.[36] Bankim's own understanding of the historical novel was rather constricted and limited, Sarkar complains, bolstering his argument of his own understanding of Bankim's historical novels

[34] Satishchandra Mitra, 1965, *Yaśore khulnār itihās*, Vol. 2 Calcutta: Dasgupta and Co., p. 598.

[35] Bhabatosh Datta, 1978, *Haraprasād śāstrī o bāṅglār itihās*, Calcutta: Sanyal Prakashan, p. 261.

[36] Jadunath Sarkar, 1345 BE, Historical Introduction to Bankimchandra Chatterjee, *Ānandamaṭh*, edited by Brajendranath Bandyopadhyay and Sajanikanta Das, Calcutta: Bangiya Sahitya Parishad, p. iii.

with examples from the categories of the arts such as painting and photography. According to Sarkar, the 'creative mystery' and 'literary form' of these novels show us the way towards understanding them. For here, Bankim has given us quite a bit of historical truth in his depiction of events, characters, manners, and speech, but he has deliberately not reduced this delineation to the level of purely 'true photography'. Sarkar explains:

> Almost every picture is a lifeless delineation of man's external appearance; but in the hands of the great artists—like Leonardo da Vinci, Rembrandt or Sir Joshua Reynolds—the famous portraits seem to show us the souls of those men and women through the expressions on their faces, the look in their eyes; once you see them you cannot forget them, and the more you see them, the more they give rise to new feelings in the spectator's mind. Bankim's novels have just this quality, and that is why they will remain immortal.[37]

'How close is *Ānandamaṭh* to historical truth?' asks Sarkar, echoing the amateur historian, Akshaykumar Maitreya, who had asked exactly the same question *apropos* Nabinchandra's *Palāśīr yuddha*. The professional historian, paradoxically, then proceeds to give a startlingly different answer, asserting, essentially, that the truth of historicism is limited, while the truth in Bankimchandra's historical novels is above the historical truth and in the realm of that which is eternally true, for which his word was '*cirasatya*'. Sarkar claimed that although the characters in *Ānandamaṭh* are not historical characters, in the portrayal of politics, society, and the main events of the time it represents, it is certainly entirely borrowed from history. Sarkar then furnishes supporting historical evidence from all the sources at his disposal, both medieval and modern, to show Bankim's fidelity to the historical. 'It might be true,' he concedes, that 'if people investigate every particularity of dates and events they may find, in this genre of novels, much that is wanting and self-created; in fact, in comparison even with the current prescribed school-textbook histories they may appear wrong or a bit lacking in many places. But these contain man's living picture.' Could it be said that in *The Names of History*, Ranciere, using very dissimilar techniques, attempts a similar re-reading of

[37] Ibid.

Michelet's *History of the French Revolution*? Substituting Sarkar's 'dates and events' with 'words', Ranciere locates the revolutionary moment in Michelet's work in a metaphor 'by which the narrative of the event becomes the narrative of its meaning'. Michelet's words constitute 'an essential poetic structure of the new historical knowledge', that Rancière champions in *The Names of History* as being 'very much a question of the truth, insofar as the truth signifies more than the exactitude of the facts and figures, the reliability of the sources, and the rigor of the inductions, insofar as the truth concerns the ontological modality to which a discourse is devoted'.[38]

Forty-three years after Akshaykumar Maitreya first complained about creative license in relation to historical truth, strenuously arguing for the 'scientific' status of the latter, we find Jadunath Sarkar, one of the most eminent professional historians in Bengal, turning the tables on him by arguing for the primacy of creativity in relation to historical truth. 'Why do these novels [of Bankimchandra] not incorporate the most minute and exact truths from history? Because, Bankimchandra did not at all want to give us a photograph of those eras; he wanted to create them in the form of prose-poetry, as instruments for the education of the people'.'[39] For Sarkar, the great validity of Bankimchandra's project lay not only in the realms of creativity, but also in the morally unimpeachable impulse towards patriotism and national regeneration that was behind Bankim's impulse in these works. Referring to '*Bhārat-kalanka*', '*Bāṅgalār itihās*', and '*Bāṅgalār itihās sambandhe kayekti kathā*' earlier in the Introduction, Sarkar had already put forward the thesis that Bankim had not rested content merely with the success of his 'domestic novels' because he was, 'in his heart of hearts, in every sinew of his body even, a lover of this land, a devotee of the people'.[40] Thus Bankimchandra's achievement in these novels consisted in 'taking a few material truths from history, adding to these his incontestable talent in imaginatively creating characters, and pouring into it all his high-minded idealism, thus breathing life into these novels and gifting Bengali literature an astonishing thing'.[41]

[38] Rancière, *The Names of History: On the Poetics of Knowledge*, pp. vii, 49.
[39] Jadunath Sarkar, Historical Introduction to Bankimchandra Chatterjee, p. iv.
[40] Ibid.
[41] Ibid., p. vii.

Sarkar makes a distinction here between what he calls 'a "stony, scientific" history' and Bankimchandra's historical novels, which are the 'life of the age'.[42] The words 'stony, scientific' are coupled together and within quotation marks, but there is no accompanying note to explain the origin of the term. Sarkar takes for granted the familiarity the reader must have had at this time with the term because of the raging controversies surrounding the issue in Bengali historiography since 1910. The words 'stony' and 'scientific' were first put into controversial circulation by Haraprasad Sastri, who, in the introduction to his 1919 historical novel *Bener meye*, had used both words in close proximity:

> *Bener Meye* is not history; therefore it is also not a historical novel. Because, nowadays, in the time of 'scientific' histories, one cannot write history without recourse to stony evidence (*pāthure pramāṇ*). We have bodies made of flesh and blood, we are not made of stone, nor do we ever want to be. *Bener Meye* is a story. Just like many other stories.[43]

The entire thrust toward 'scientific' history writing was led at the time by Rakhaldas Bandyopadhyay, whose reliance on the dateable archaeological artefact and preoccupation with precise dating and epigraphic evidence had perhaps lent itself to the adjective 'stony' or *pāthure* being used by Haraprasad. Akshaykumar Maitreya and the group belonging to the *Barendra-Anusandhān Samiti* [Society for Historical Enquiry at Barendra] were among the more ardent believers in the use of rock inscriptions and copperplate edicts, using these as their primary evidence in the *Gauṛ lekhamālā* [Inscriptions of Gouda] in 1910, which they considered the only reliable indices of historical proof. Paradoxically, the most fervent champion of scientific history and archaeology, Rakhaldas Bandyopadhyay, had then declared, in the introduction to his monumental *Bāṅgalīr itihās* [Bengal's History] (1915), that what he had written was merely the 'skeleton' of a history, rather than a construction of a 'narrative of people's faith

[42] Ibid., p. viii.

[43] Haraprasad Sastri, 1984, Preface to *Bener meye* in the *Haraprasād śāstrī racanā saṃgraha*, edited by Satyajit Chaudhury, Vol. 1, Calcutta: Pashchim Banga Rajya Pustak Parshad, p. 609.

and thought'.[44] In order to do that, like Haraprasad, he had turned to the historical romance, writing a book revealingly titled *Pāshāṇer kathā*, or The Stone's Story, which 'was a narrative written in the image of history, not a history written in the scientific method'.[45] A decade after Jadunath Sarkar wrote his Historical Introductions to Bankim's novels in 1939, the issue was still alive and kicking, and the historian Niharranjan Ray resurrected the imagery of a dead history when he wrote in 1949, in his own introduction to his *Bāṅgālīr itihās* [The History of the Bengalis]:

> My Bengal and Bengalis are not there in the pages of any old *puñthi* [manuscript], nor in any royal epigraph and decree; that land and the people are what exists before my eyes and resides in my heart. The ancient past is for me as real and as alive as today's present. And it is that palpable living past that I have endeavoured to bring forth in this book, not the skeleton of a dead history.[46]

As this brief discussion shows, many eminent historians in Bengal, starting perhaps with Romesh Chunder Dutt, had written historical novels since the 1870s, some of them, such as Dutt, with direct encouragement from Bankim. This attempt by the historians to make of history a living thing was manifested both in historical novels, as well as in the writing of history itself, and Jadunath Sarkar's Historical Introductions to Bankim, therefore, take up and continue with some of the same issues that we have been tracing so far. Painstakingly pointing out the numerous factual inaccuracies in *Ānandamaṭh* (the *santāns* were North Indians, not Bengalis; illiterate—not capable of quoting from the Bhagavad-Gita; Shaivite, not Vaishnav), he still concludes (and note how he conflates the highest creative impulse in these novels with 'poetry'): 'I accept all this. But the nectar [*amṛtras*] that is there in *Ānandamaṭh*, *Debī chaudhurāṇī* and *Sītārām* is not present in other historical novels a hundred times closer to "truth". That nectar [*rasa*] flows from its source in the high-minded idealism

[44] Rakhaldas Bandyopadhyay, Preface to the first edition of *Bāṅgālīr Itihās*, Vol. 1.

[45] Rakhaldas Bandyopadhyay, 1914, Preface to *Pāshāṇer kathā: A Historical Romance*, Calcutta: Bengal Medical Library.

[46] Niharranjan Ray, '*Nibedan*', 30 Ashvin, 1356 [16 October 1949] in *Bāṅgālīr itihās, Ādi parba*, translated by Tapati Guha-Thakurta, 2004, in *Monuments, Objects, Histories*, New York: Columbia University Press, pp. 133, 335.

of Bankimchandra's heart... . This is the sign of the greatest poetry; herein lies the immortality of *Ānandamaṭh*, *Debī chaudhurāṇī* and *Sītārām*'.[47] Harnessing support, in conclusion, somewhat eclectically from Buddhist inscriptions to the Bhagavad-Gita, Sarkar ends his discourse in an ecstatic crescendo, using the most popular image of an emergent Hindu nationalism of the time, that of the militant ascetic in the hills, an image inaugurated in Hemchandra Bandyopadhyay's *Bhārat Saṅgīt* (1870), used in Bankimchandra's *Ānandamaṭh* (1882), and in Aurobindo's potent blueprint for action, *Bhawani mandir* (1906):

> It has been forty-four years now since Bankimchandra has been taken from us. But he who has drunk the secret 'rasa' of *Ānandamaṭh* has seen, with his inner eye, the *rishi* who initiates us into national awareness [*svajātīyatā*] standing upon a mountain-top in the Himachal, his body bathed in light, calling to the entire people:
>
> Awaken from selfishness, awaken from poverty,
> Awaken from all stiffness, oh awaken,
> In a powerful, uplifted splendour.
>
> *This* is the answer to the question: whither freedom?[48]

Anti-Muslim Rhetoric

If Akshaykumar Maitreya had been angry about Nabinchandra Sen's depiction of Sirajuddaula in his first work in 1896, in a later publication, *Mīr Kāsim* (1904), he was absolutely apoplectic about Bankimchandra's portrayal of Mohammed Taqi Khan in his novel *Candraśekhar*. In a chapter entitled 'The Battle at Katoya', Maitreya, following the methodology of his first book, initially carefully presents the historical accounts of this battle, citing sources such as Malleson's *Decisive Battles of India* and Ghulam Husain Tabtabai's *Sair al-mutakkherin*, depicting, in emotionally charged language, the bravery of Mir Qasim's foremost general, Mohammed Taqi Khan, who had fought with such courage and aggression that he had single-handedly almost turned the tide of the battle in favour of the Nawab until his

[47] Jadunath Sarkar, Historical Introduction to Bankimchandra Chatterjee, p. x.
[48] Ibid., Chapter Five.

unfortunate death in an English ambush. Following this, he turns his attention to the gross misrepresentation of historical fact in the scenes in *Candraśekhar*, which he does not name, that dealt with Taqi Khan, asking, at the outset: 'Why have such infamous and baseless allegations been put up against someone as loyal and brave as Mohammed Taqi? Why was it necessary to cast such an indelible stain upon so patriotic a Muslim king as Mir Qasim?' The blame, as usual, lies at the door of the literary impulse, and he answers, 'Perhaps it is the novel that is culpable, as the historical mode has been put aside in the interests of the creation of beauty. Let history be abandoned—the novel has certainly become brighter!'[49]

The novel *Candraśekhar* shows the character of Mohammed Taqi Khan going personally to kill the 'beautiful seventeen-year old wife of Mir Qasim', renamed (and Maitreya is sarcastic about this) from Daulat un Nisa as 'Dolni Begum'; Maitreya comments, 'Even in the days of the "cow-slaying, shaven-headed" ["*go-hatyākārī, kshaurita-cikur*"] Muslim's rule, the Faujdar was never sent personally for executions—a professional executioner was always employed for the purpose.' (Here he identifies in a footnote the phrase within quotation marks—describing the Muslims as 'shaven-headed cow-slayers'—as occurring in a historical essay by Bankim where the mere mention of a Muslim historian calls forth such a phrase.[50]) The narration in the novel continues with Taqi Khan, smitten by the ripe beauty of Dolni, ending up propositioning her, to which she reacts by kicking him. The unlikely end to all this in the novel is Dolni's subsequent death by self-poisoning, and Taqi Khan being slain by Mir Qasim's sword. 'The novel is thus made appetising', Maitreya concludes, outraged, and 'when it is acted on the stage, the applause is resounding! The genuine contempt in which the Hindu heart holds the "shaven-headed, cow-slaying" Muslim is also revealed. But alas! Neither Taqi Khan nor Mir Qasim can be recognised any more as historical characters'.[51]

[49] Akshay Kumar Maitreya, 2004, *Mīr Quāsim*, Calcutta: Puthipatra, p. 94.

[50] Bankimchandra Chatterjee, 1998, *Bāṅgālīr itihās sambandhe kāyekti kathā* [A Few Words on the History of Bengal] *Bankim rachanavali*, Vol. 2, Calcutta: Sahitya Sansad, p. 291. Since Muslims did not shave their heads completely, 'shaven-headed' might have been a representation of the vulgarized word commonly used for converts, '*ṛeḥe*', which itself could have conceivably been a legacy from converts to Buddhism.

[51] Akshaykumar Maitreya, *Mīr Quāsim*, p. 96.

This sacrifice of history at the altar of the creative impulse offended Maitreya, and impelled him to a strident condemnation of the communal feeling that he detected residing in the heart of so many works by Bengali stalwarts in their respective fields. Certainly, he has no rival among the protagonists of the so-called Bengal Renaissance in the disinterestedness of his objective idealism; in his defence of history and historical accuracy, it can be said without a doubt that Akshaykumar Maitreya did not take sides. He too was motivated by a patriotic impulse similar to the high idealism Jadunath Sarkar identified as a validation of Bankimchandra's immense gift, for he repeatedly marshalled his argument in favour of historical 'truth' with a view to strengthening the nation.

> British writers proclaim the triumph of British heroes who are dedicated and dutiful in poetry, history, literature and the novel—at every place they maintain the historical character intact, and these examples then serve to illuminate their national life. The literary guru of New Bengal has read, from beginning to end, the history of a dedicated, dutiful, and self-sacrificing Muslim hero, resident of Bengal, such as Taqi Khan, and yet when he composed his novel he concealed the natural beauty of the historical character and disfigured it with the stain of chicanery, betrayal, and cowardice.[52]

Mohammed Taqi Khan's defeat was, according to Maitreya, 'a vanquishing of the entire Bengali race', and his memory has been lost among our people.

> Otherwise it would not have been possible for the name of somebody as dutiful and brave as Mohammed Taqi Khan to be defiled in a novel. It is only where the common people of the country do not feel any pain in their hearts at painting so unrestrainedly black a stain upon so brave a character that the novel has gained such genuine enthusiasts; it is only in such a country that the stage has reverberated with the sound of clapping; it is only in such a country that people have the courage to fight with historians in order to establish the absolute authority of the poet's clan.[53]

In a rousing climax of indignation and righteous wrath, Akshaykumar then declares, in conclusion:

[52] Ibid.

[53] Ibid., p. 97.

> Nevertheless, the independent historian will announce this as an indelible stain upon the Bengali. If Muslim society had life in it, this would not have been possible even in this country. A prostitute kicking Taqi Khan in front of so many—this is an indelible stain on the theatre of Bengal! [54]

Maitreya underlines the deliberate nature of Bankimchandra's distortion of Taqi Khan's character by mentioning in a footnote that while Bankim had been posted in Murshidabad on official duty, he had read, in the famous scholar Dr Ramdas Sen's library, the English translation of *Sair al-mutakkherin* with much care, marking the text in places, and even mentioning, in the introduction to the novel, his reading of this then relatively lesser-known text. Since that text, both in its English and Urdu editions, explicitly and in great detail mentions the bravery of Taqi Khan (describing how twice he had been impeded; once when his horse was shot, and then upon a bullet entering his shoulder, but he had pressed on regardless, exhorting his men to fight, and making advances, when a sudden discharge by hidden English soldiers caused a bullet to pierce his brain and killed him instantly, creating a turnaround in fortunes that resulted in the battle, and subsequently Bengal, being lost), and since Akshaykumar has quoted extensively from this text in the section preceding this, Bankimchandra's inventions do appear unforgivable, culpable, and remorseless to the reader. Why then did Jadunath Sarkar not address this particular charge in his introduction to *Candraśekhar* at all, and why did he defend Bankimchandra from the charges of historical inaccuracy, and from the allegation of communal ill will?

The answer seems to lie in Sarkar's perception of the role of creativity and the creative artist in relation to history or the historical novel. The fact that literature differs significantly from historiography in dealing with historicality was the point Jadunath was making in Bankimchandra's defence, and this very issue has been taken up for discussion by Ranajit Guha as recently as in 2002, in his *History at the Limit of World History*.[55] In that book, taking the example of Tagore, Guha identifies 'wisdom' as the most essential category in a 'truly creative writer', whose task it is to renew the past creatively through

[54] Ibid., pp. 97–8.

[55] Ranajit Guha, 2002, *History at the Limit of World-History*, Delhi: Oxford University Press.

language in a manner not available to the academic historian. Hegel's concept of world-history is governed by a 'narrowly defined politics of statism'; to escape it, one must turn away from the narrative of public affairs that is the concern of the historian towards the poet's eye that engages with the past as a story of man's being in the everyday world. Using one of the poet's last recorded essays, *Sāhitye aitihāsikatā* (1941) as a manifesto, Guha feels it is Tagore's intention here to declare: 'Historicality, too, demands facts', but the historicality that resides in the creative impulse is somehow free of 'the bounds of historiography'.[56] Guha quotes from Heidegger to establish that the factuality involved in the work of the creative artist is 'ontologically totally different from factual occurrence of a kind of stone', a metaphor that uncannily echoes the whole Bengali debate on 'a stony scientific history'. The concept of 'facticity', which, according to Heidegger, 'implies that an "innerworldly" being has being-in-the-world in such a way that it can understand itself as bound up in its "destiny" with the being of those beings which it encounters in its own world', is then harnessed by Guha to explain that the poetic moment resides in this understanding of facticity, which is opposed to the 'object-historical conventions of historiography'.[57]

Tagore suggests, according to Guha, that 'it is only by confronting historiography with creativity' that 'we can hope to grasp what historicality is about... . As the two sides are lined up, it turns out to be a confrontation between, on the one hand, the externality and publicness of academic historical representation and, on the other, the inwardness of the self's labour of creation and its claim to what accrues inalienably from it.'[58] In this contest, for Guha, it is the creative process that wins, for that is the side which argues for 'a notion of the past so big and broad' that it allows for 'history ... [to] fulfil its promise in the plenitude of historicality.'[59] Jadunath Sarkar might not have put it in quite these words, and whereas Guha emphasizes Tagore's 'inward eye' or 'inner soul' compared to Sarkar's highlighting of Bankim's 'high-minded idealism', the end result describing the

[56] Ibid., p. 79.
[57] Ibid.
[58] Ibid., p. 87.
[59] Ibid., p. 90.

transcendence of the creator or the work of art is remarkably similar. The words used by Sarkar to describe Bankimchandra's triumph in the historical novels ('taking a few material truths from history, adding to these his incontestable talent in imaginatively creating characters, and pouring into it all his high-minded idealism, thus breathing life into these novels and gifting Bengali literature an astonishing thing.') are strikingly of a kind with those of Rabindranath that Guha uses to validate the creator above the historian: 'The creator gathers some of the material for his creation from historical narratives and some from his social environment. But the material by itself does not make him a creator. It is only by putting it to use that he expresses himself as the creator'.[60] Where the two might have differed fundamentally however, would have been in their understanding of the role of the historian, for Sarkar never confuses the historian with the litterateur, while Guha clearly says that it is to the neighbouring field of literature that the historian must now turn to avoid the pitfalls of the academically pedantic historian. Sarkar, one might be reasonably certain, might never have gone so far, only claiming, for the creative artist, a higher plane and a greater achievement than any historian could hope to accomplish.

This national and cultural self-consciousness of the status of art, which presented itself as a principle of integration overriding all others, is in large part to be accounted for by the pre-eminence accorded to it throughout the long nineteenth century. Overturning the usual notions of this period as a time of convention and conformity, Harold Bloom and Lionel Trilling have remarked, in the context of the English literary scene, 'Nothing so much shaped the identity of the Victorian Age as its consciousness of being *modern*' and this, of course, was only the continuation 'of a defining trait of the preceding cultural epoch of the nineteenth century' in the Romantic period, which also was marked by a lively awareness of progress and change.[61] A defining feature of this awareness of modernity in the colonial context in the time of Nabinchandra was the view of art and its function that was held by the great writers and critics of the time. In England, Coleridge had represented poetry as the mediator between man and the universe,

[60] Ibid., p. 98.

[61] Lionel Trilling and Harold Bloom, 1973, 'Victorian Prose', *The Oxford Anthology of English Literature*, Oxford: Oxford University Press, p. 4.

while Shelley had said that the true basis of ethical life was in the exercise of the imagination as it was brought into activity by poetry; poets were the unacknowledged legislators of the world. A little later in the century, the great prose stylist Thomas Carlyle wrote an epochal essay, 'On Heroes, Hero-Worship, and the Heroic in History', (1840) in which he set his intensely held view that the decisive element in all cultural achievement is the individual person of genius, while John Stuart Mill wrote 'What Is Poetry', an essay that shows him to be one of the best readers of poetry of that age. Nabinchandra Sen might or might not have read one or the other of these influential works—a direct correspondence does not need to be drawn. What matters, rather, is a general awareness in this time of the power of poetry, which gathered into itself the hegemony of spirit that hitherto been found in the domain of religion, in an accelerating commitment to what Hegel called, in his *Philosophy of History*, 'secular spirituality', a commitment that, in the colonial context, was indispensable in creating a space for the commitment to nationalism.

Nabinchandra Sen's lofty response to Maitreya, that *Palāśīr yuddha* was not history, but poetry, therefore, was precisely meant to indicate perhaps that his poem was not concerned with dispelling false beliefs about the past; instead, it endowed real events with the kinds of meaning that only literature is enabled to give. In this view, art and literature, wherever and however they are produced, are paradigmatic in that they claim an authority different in kind from that claimed by both science and politics. This notion of the authority of 'culture', always a problematic notion, was what gave Nabinchandra Sen the space to transcend, in an Arnoldian formulation, the nitty-gritty of historical fact to create an autonomous zone of creativity, a zone that Tagore invoked in a different way when he stated, 'in his own field of creativity, Rabindranath [referring to himself]' was 'tied to no public by history', a view that also seems to inform, essentially, Jadunath Sarkar's perception of universal truth or *cirasatya*.

(ii) The Curious Case of Nabinchandra Sen and the Textbook Committee: An Investigation into Hindu/Muslim Representations

Some of the more fanciful teachers would compare me to Clive. The comparison has been vindicated. Clive had established British rule in India through the Battle of Palashi; and its rulers know me as the one who is destroying the Indian kingdom through my 'Battle of Palashi'. Clive was made famous by the Battle of Palashi; I too have been made famous by the 'Battle of Palashi'. Then how am I any less?

—Nabinchandra Sen[62]

The sense of belonging—belonging to the present nation—involves the creation and replication of a sense of 'them' and 'us' through icons, stories, and narratives. This siring of communities and narratives about long-existent collectivities often takes place simultaneously. And this pair has a duplex—both 'twin' and 'duplicitous'—claim to history and to particularist remembrances of times past.

—Shahid Amin[63]

In a discussion of the stereotypical images by which we recognize the Muslim citizen of India, Shahid Amin points to 'a larger process of "fabrications" of the past' by which 'groups, large and small, simultaneously "construct, manufacture, invent and forge" ... their identities'.[64] This urge to construct ourselves through definitions of the other has only the most tenuous link to history, for although

[62] Nabinchandra Sen, *Āmār jīban*, Vol. 1, *Nabinchandra rachanabali*, p. 17.

[63] Shahid Amin, 2005, 'Representing the Musalman: Then and Now, Now and Then', in Shail Mayaram, et al. (eds), *Muslims, Dalits and the Fabrications of History: Subaltern Studies XII*, New Delhi: Permanent Black, p. 9.

[64] Ibid.

past events are often picked upon, 'this imagination thrives on "facts" without contexts and events without history, and it soars ahead, usually unchallenged, unruffled by contradictions'.[65] One of the most fertile fields of the imaginative construction of communities has been the arena of literary culture—alongside and interactively with oral narratives and popular representations, the fledgling industry of the modern Indian literatures saw eminent men of letters try to construct the past of a community through their literary writings in the late nineteenth century. Hindi literature in Northern India at this time, for instance, developed through the works of men such as Bhartendu Harishchandra, Balkrishna Bhatt, Radhacharan Goswami and Pratap Narayan Mishra, who reflected the most profound sense of urgency in grappling with the Hindu-Muslim question. Their works exhibited a perception that there was a correlation between Hindu-Muslim unity and the country's destiny, while at the same time employing unprecedented venom against Muslims that went entirely against the first impulse. Amin, in extension of the work done by Sudhir Chandra, who has shown, in some detail, the historical construction of the idea of the nation in literary Hindi texts of the late nineteenth century, feels that popular Hindu remembrance was, in fact, being 'fabricated' by these litterateurs quite consciously.[66] To understand how writers manufactured community pasts through narratives of historical nationality is essential for an appreciation of the cultural politics of an era in which literature was understood to exist on a plane far removed from the nitty-gritty of practical life. One of the most startling pieces of evidence on how communities and their pasts were 'fabricated' in a particular narrative by an author, sometimes against his will, can be found, as a matter of fact, in the strange case of Nabinchandra Sen's alterations to his epic poem, *Palāśīr yuddha*. While one section of the Hindu intelligentsia of Uttar Pradesh in the late nineteenth century was busy, as Sudhir Chandra has shown, creating colonial Hindu texts that extolled the virtues of British rule (whether as empty ritual or not) while condemning their Muslim contemporaries as well as their

[65] Ibid.

[66] Shahid Amin, 2005, 'Representing the Musalman', p. 16; Sudhir Chandra, 1992, *The Oppressive Present: Literature and Social Consciousness in Colonial India*, Delhi: Oxford University Press.

erstwhile Muslim kings in Hindi literary texts, in Bengal, a similar drama was being played out with minor differences.[67]

Here, it is actually possible to furnish documented proof of the manner in which changes were deliberately made to the text of a poem in order to undermine both the Muslim character and historical role, ostensibly to placate aggressive neo-Hindu adversaries in powerful positions in the textbook committee in Calcutta. Nabinchandra Sen's *Palāśir yuddha* (1875) was a key text in the literature of nationalism, and changes as vital as the ones that were made to it eventually by its author have a significance not wholly out of proportion to the importance of the text itself in the cultural nationalism of early twentieth-century Bengal. Nirad C. Chaudhuri mentions, in the Introduction to his *Clive of India*, a personal reminiscence that is revealing inasmuch as it shows that the battle of Plassey was personified, in the minds of children growing up in a provincial outpost of East Bengal in the first decade of the twentieth century, with Nabinchandra's *Palāśir yuddha*:

> Moreover, to Indian nationalists, both Clive and Warren Hastings became symbols of British usurpation and oppression, and they, together with the battle of Plassey, passed into the literature of nationalism… . Here I would give a personal detail. I myself as a boy of ten took the part of one of the Jagat Seths in the scene of conspiracy against Siraj-ud-daula from a Bengali epic poem which we acted out on the home stage; my elder brother lay flat on it and declaimed the dying speech put into the mouth of Mohanlal, who did not die in the battle of Plassey.[68]

Commenting, in the book, on the events following the battle at Palashi in 1757, Nirad Chaudhuri's biography of Clive delved into the historical reasons for Muslim humiliation and resentment at their losses in the face of British martial superiority. A hatred for the English had animated many Muslim rulers in the last days of the Mughal Empire in India, and many Muslim commanders and nobles chafed at the indirect power of the English in those early days after the battle at Palashi. Referring to the fact that the Muslims, in very little time, forgot 'the oppression of Siraj' and looked back to him 'with sympathy', Chaudhuri asserted that:

[67] Sudhir Chandra, 1992, *The Oppressive Present*, pp. 117–59.

[68] Nirad C. Chaudhuri, 1975, *Clive of India: A Political and Psychological Essay*, London: Barrie and Jenkins, p. 11.

> Curiously enough, this Muslim resentment against the English and sympathy for Siraj was acquired in the last quarter of the nineteenth century by the new Bengali Hindu intelligentsia created by British rule, who could admire Siraj with impunity, being immune from his oppression. This was first exhibited in literature, with the publication in 1874 of a long poem in Bengali entitled 'The Battle of Plassey', by a Bengali Hindu poet, Nabinchandra Sen. Reviewing it, the great Bengali novelist Bankim Chandra Chatterji, the creator of the new Hindu nationalism, wrote: "When Nabin Babu's patriotism flows out, he does not speak in a restrained manner; it gushes out like lava. If those who are Bengali by birth will not read the heartfelt lamentations of the Bengali people, they have been born Bengali in vain." By that time, the Bengali Hindus had identified themselves with Siraj. The Muslims, who had been delivered from Siraj, were bound to do so from the time of his death.[69]

It was this conservative Hindu irritation with Nabinchandra's sympathy for Siraj that was to land the poet of *Palāśīr yuddha* in so much trouble with his peers, which in itself was a story not fully made public even with the appearance of the final edition of his autobiography in 1914, where it lay buried in the copious extent of its five volumes. Nirad Chaudhuri, consequently, seems unaware of the neo-Hindu aggression Nabinchandra faced at the turn of the century which mirrored exactly his own attitude to the poem, which took the form of an irritation that coloured even Bankimchandra's equivocal response to it with a greater approbation than was actually expressed. As a matter of fact, Chaudhuri was wrong about the Muslims identifying themselves with Siraj 'from the time of his death'—that identification, as I shall try to show in this chapter, came much later, in the late nineteenth century; contemporary Muslim historians such as Ghulam Husain Salim, Ghulam Husain Tabtabai, and Yusuf Ali Khan, writing after his death in the late eighteenth century, did not hesitate to depict Siraj's oppression, ignorance, and intoxication with power.[70] This chapter will attempt to delve into some of the more virulent objections made

[69] Ibid.

[70] Ghulam Hussain Salim, 1975, *Riyazu-s-salatin*, translated by Abdus Salam, Delhi: Idarah-i-Adabiyat-i-Dihli; Ghulam Hussain Tabtabai, 1902, *A Translation of the Sëir Mutaqherin, or A View of Modern Times*, Calcutta: R. Cambray; Yusuf Ali Khan, 1969, *Tarikhi-i-bangala-i-mahabatjangi*, edited by Abdus Subhan, Calcutta: Asiatic Society.

to Nabinchandra Sen's *Palāśīr yuddha* on purely communal grounds, showing how alterations were made to the text of a poem that was a seminal text to nationalist Bengalis, learnt in school and read widely (its sales were next only to Bankimchandra's works), irrevocably changing the reader's response upon reading the poem from a sense of sorrow at a shared historical past into a communitarian and parochial understanding of separate future destinies.

National Epic or Moment of Shame?

Palāśīr yuddha had been first conceived by the poet Nabinchandra Sen in 1864, when, as a young seventeen-year-old student at Presidency College, Calcutta, he had spent a summer vacation in Rajshahi with a friend, who had, on the way, pointed out the field at Palashi to him and told him many fantastic tales about it. Four years later, in 1868, he wrote the first version for a few literary friends at Jessore, chief among whom was the fiercely nationalist editor of *Amritabazaar patrika*, Sisirkumar Ghosh, whose patriotic fervour Nabinchandra wholeheartedly confessed to being influenced by at the time. It was only in 1873, however, that Nabinchandra managed to do some substantial work on the poem, expanding it now into a full-fledged narrative. Bankimchandra was one of the first to read and enthusiastically greet the poet upon reading it, hailing it as the greatest work yet written in the Bengali language, 'next, if at all, to *Meghnād*'. After several mishaps with the production and publication, due primarily to the prevarication of Bankimchandra, who was supposed to have published it from the *Baṅgadarśan* press, *Palāśīr yuddha* was finally released in the public sphere on 15 April 1875.[71]

In Nabinchandra's own words, 'there was great excitement and agitation (*hulusthul*) in the Bengali literary world' from the moment the book appeared.[72] Three well-known periodicals, the *Āryadarśaṇ*, the *Bāndhab*, and the *Sādhāraṇī*, immediately came

[71] Nabinchandra Sen, 1875, *Palāśīr yuddha*, Calcutta: Printed at the Nutan Bharat Press by Sri Ramnrisingha Bandyopadhyay; 1985, Preface, *Palāśīr yuddha*, in *Nabinchandra rachanabali*, edited by Sajanikanta Das, Calcutta: Bangiya Sahitya Parishad, pp. 4–5. All further references to *Palāśīr yuddha* are from this edition.

[72] *Āmār jīban*, *Nabinchandra rachanabali*, Vol. 1, p. 358.

out with laudatory reviews; Bankimchandra followed these up with a lengthy review in his own journal, the *Baṅgadarśan*, all in the same year.[73] Bankim's review was less enthusiastic than his initial comments comparing it to Madhusudan Datta's already great classic, *Meghnādbadh kābya*; Nabinchandra himself commented that Bankim had 'changed his tune'.[74] Bankimchandra avoided the issue now by disingenuously proclaiming that it would be unfair to Nabinchandra, in fact, to compare his work to that of Madhusudan or Hemchandra's mythological epics, as his was, essentially, a 'modern' (*ādhunik*) work about historical events in which the actors were humans like ourselves. 'So the poet remains chained to this world like a caged bird, he cannot rise up in the sky and sing. Therefore it is not possible to say that Nabinbabu has been fortunate in his selection of subject matter.' In the end, then, the only praise that Bankim could muster was to crown Nabinchandra the Byron of Bengali poetry; and, as if aware that this could be interpreted as damning with faint praise, strenuously assert in the same breath that this was not a comparison to be taken lightly ('*E praśaṃsa baṛa alpa praśaṃsa nay*').[75]

This issue of the subject matter of *Palāśīr yuddha* being an inappropriate one is hinted at in the most oblique manner by Bankimchandra, but with the passage of time it would become more and more apparent exactly what the imputation behind this charge meant. In *The Bengal Magazine* of 1876, its editor Rev. Lal Behari Day was a little blunter. 'We are of the opinion', he said, 'that the subject is unhappily chosen, as the celebrated battle which the poem describes reflects no lustre on the Bengali nation, and there can be no true epic except on the theme of national glory'.[76] National glory, obviously, could not be seen to inhabit a scene that Akshaykumar Maitreya, castigating partisan Hindu depictions, would subsequently read, in *Sirājāddoulā* (1897), as a tragic instance of betrayal and bravery as the last independent king of Bengal fought for his kingdom, for in such a reading, national glory would be seen to reside in the Muslim

[73] *Āryadarśaṇ*, 1282 BE: *Jaistha*; *Bāndhab*, 1282 BE: *Jaistha/Āshāḍh*; *Sādhāraṇī*, 1282 BE: 14 and 28 *Āshāḍh*, and *Baṅgadarśan*, 1282 BE: *Kārtik*.

[74] Sajanikanta Das (ed.), *Amar jiban*, ibid., p. 358.

[75] Cited in Nabinchandra Sen, *SSC*, Vol. 3, p. 26.

[76] Lal Behari Day, 1876, in *The Bengal Magazine*, January, p. 282.

nawab's defence of his realm; the 'Bengali nation', if it was constituted of Hindu Bengal, played an inglorious role in that episode.

That a section of the Bengali *bhadralok* world perceived Nabinchandra to be more on the side of the Muslims than was seemly remains thinly disguised in the words of these reviewers; this was to be revealed much more nakedly in private correspondence. When the all-powerful textbook committee in Calcutta met to recommend *Palāśīr yuddha* as a school text the third time around (it had already been on the list twice previously), three influential Bengalis, part of a corrupt nexus, vehemently opposed its inclusion in the syllabus. Nabinchandra Sen records how these men, whom he christened the triad of Mahadev-Nandi-Bhringi, were defeated at that particular meeting by the efforts of Gurudas Banerjee and Haraprasad Sastri.[77] Incensed at their humiliation, the man Nabinchandra christened 'Nandi', unable to contain his rage, wrote a letter to him just after the meeting detailing the reasons for his position. Nabinchandra subsequently described 'Nandi' as the dwarfish man Rabindranath had written the satirical poem *Hiṃtiṃchaṭ* about; as a satellite who merely reflected Bankimchandra's talents; as a hanger-on at Bankim's evening drawing-room conversations, reproducing Bankim's private opinions in empty elaborate prose pieces. Nevertheless Nabinchandra adds that he had respected him for his grasp of the Bengali prose style, and that this same man had praised *Palāśīr yuddha* to him when it had first appeared.[78] This man, as Nabinchandra described him, and especially on the evidence of the Tagore poem, was Chandranath Basu. Chandranath wrote a short letter, the heart of which proclaimed:

> In connection with the textbook committee meeting I had voted against your *Palāśīr Yuddha*.... I don't understand your *Palāśīr Yuddha*. In *Palāśīr Yuddha* the Muslims lost Bengal. Why should the Hindus be excited about that—what is the rationale for that? For that matter, why does Mohanlal himself grieve? Is it because he is a servant of the Muslims? You are a Hindu, how can you bear that? And by showing Mohanlal expressing such regret aren't you being disloyal to the British government? Disloyalty to the British government permeates your book in many other places,

[77] Mahadev-Nandi-Bhringi refers to Lord Shiva, also known as Mahadev, and his two favourite layabout companions Nandi and Bhringi.

[78] *Āmār jīban, Nabinchandra rachanabali*, Vol. 3, pp. 264, 268.

> if not openly, then certainly in a concealed manner. I have not told the committee about this.
>
> I don't understand why the Hindu's heart should be rocked by waves of emotion at the thought of the battle of Palashi. Is it because a few Hindus gifted Bengal to the English there? If that is the case, do you really believe that if the English had lost at Palashi a Hindu kingdom would have been established in Bengal or Bharat? If that is the belief that animates your writing of *Palāśīr Yuddha* then I must say that you have not made your intention clear at all. I have tried to understand *Palāśīr Yuddha* in various other ways, but have not understood it.[79]

Nabinchandra wrote a short evasive reply to this missive, but was so angry about its contents that he took the letter to Sir Gurudas Banerjee, chairman of the textbook committee, who was also a friend of Chandranath Basu's, and threatened to go to press with the story of the corruption in the committee's working (which consisted of prescribing books written by themselves and their relatives and acolytes in order to profit from the lucrative returns that the textbook trade brought) and publish the full text of the letter. As such a move would implicate the chairman as well, the threat was never put into action, and Chandranath sent a second letter to Nabinchandra full of apologetic noises and veiled entreaties.

Chandranath Basu (1844–1910)—in alluding to whom Nabinchandra was driven to quote from *The Tempest*: 'For some of you there present / Are worse than devils'—was a leading spokesman of conservative Hindu society in late nineteenth-century Calcutta.[80] He made his name first through articles in the pages of the *Baṅgadarśan*, where he was nurtured by its editor, Bankimchandra, who is said to have initiated him, originally a writer of good English prose, into writing in Bengali. An early essay in English, 'On the Importance of the Study of History' in the *Calcutta University Magazine* of 1864 was praised for its prose style, while another essay, 'Present Social and Economic Condition and Its Probable Future' of 1869, preceded Bhola Nath Chunder's theory of economic drain that in turn had led to the

79 Ibid., p. 265.

80 Ibid., p. 546.

development of economic nationalism among historians of Bengal.[81] The conservative Brahmin pundit Sasadhar Tarkachuramani, who had become something of a rage among Hindu revivalists in Calcutta at the time, converted him to orthodox Hindu beliefs, reviving his faith in the Hindu gods that he had lost with his English education.[82] His contributions to the *Baṅgadarśan* and the *Baṅgabāsī* were influential and read widely, and books such as *Hindutva–hindur prakṛta itihās* (1892) [Hindutva—The True History of the Hindus] established, polemically, ideas that he propagated more popularly in satirical novels such as *Paśupati-saṃbād* [*Pasupati*-News] (1884). As one of the foremost writers and spokesmen for Hindu orthodoxy in Bengal, he argued, like his more illustrious and respected predecessor, Bhudev Mukhopadhyay (whose ideas were permeated by a catholicity of opinion and social inclusiveness missing from Chandranath), for the pre-puberty marriage of Hindu women and against widow remarriage, advocating a scrupulous regard for the caste system, ritual observances, and vegetarianism based on obscure Hindu *shastric* doctrines.

'Hindu! Hindu!—Slave! Slave!'

Nabinchandra Sen's attitude towards Hinduism is worth exploring in the context of Chandranath's charges. Writing in a period historians often refer to as one of Hindu revivalism, Nabinchandra wrote a trilogy that became one of the most influential interpretations of Hindu texts in modern Bengal after Bankimchandra's *Kṛṣnācaritra* (published serially from September 1884 in *Pracār*) and *Dharmatattva* (published serially in *Nabajīban* from July 1884). Other essays by Bankim on the subject subsequently appeared as *Debatattva o hindu dharma* and *Śrīmadbhagabatgītā*. While all of Bankim's works on Hinduism were written in prose, Nabinchandra's famous Krishna trilogy, *Raibatak* (1887), *Kurukshetra* (1893) and *Prabhās* (1896), on the other hand, was composed in the just-inaugurated popular medium of blank verse or the *amitrākkhar chanda*. These works presented Nabinchandra's

[81] Amiya P. Sen, 1993, *Hindu Revivalism in Bengal 1872-1905: Some Essays in Interpretation*, Delhi: Oxford University Press, pp. 212, 216.

[82] Brajendranath Bandyopadhyay, 1397 BE, *SSC*, Calcutta: Bangiya Sahitya Parishad, p. 14.

own conceptions about the life and work of Krishna, and his approach to the subject veered between a cosmopolitan interpretation of Krishna as a historical character and something like an inner spiritual quest. Considered his most accomplished work by later critics, superseding *Palāśīr yuddha* in poetic achievement and epic and philosophic vision, this trilogy was described by Brajendranath Bandyopadhyay as 'the golden key at whose touch the complex facts of Hindu spiritual philosophy were transformed into an enjoyable and tasteful thing'.[83] Nabinchandra himself proclaimed unabashedly and repeatedly in his autobiography that he had written these works immersed in a spiritual ecstasy, often submerged in his own tears at the mystical contemplation of divinity.

Nabinchandra's attitude toward the Hindu traditions is beautifully demonstrated in an exchange with the younger poet Rabindranath Tagore. Rabindranath, who had then just published the poems of *Sonār tāri* (1894), spent a day with him at Ranaghat on his way by train to Kushthia for some work related to their family landholdings. In the course of the day, after Rabindranath had sung a beautiful composition of his own in the form of a Hindu devotional *kīrtan*, Nabinchandra, struggling to contain his tears, had expressed his curiosity about the Brahmo Rabindranath's opinion on Radha-Krishna, especially in view of the large number of songs composed by him on the theme of the Radha-Krishna *līlā*. Rabindranath replied:

> 'I have often thought about whether I am an idolater or not. Especially with regard to the *Bhāgabaṯ*, my thoughts are different from those of other Brahmos. I consider the *Bhāgabaṯ* to be one of the highest forms of *allegory*'. I said—'If you derive satisfaction from thinking about it as an allegory, there is no harm in that. You are free to see it in that way. But when I see the made-up Krishna come on to the *yātrā* stage, I cannot control my tears; do not break that black clay image of mine. Keep that for me'. While speaking thus, tears came into my eyes. I saw that my heartfelt emotion had touched his heart too. Tears welled up in his eyes as well.[84]

[83] Brajendranath Bandyopadhyay, 1391 BE, *SSC*, Vol. 3, Calcutta: Bangiya Sahitya Parishad, p. 24.

[84] The word allegory is italicized to indicate the use of the English word in the Bengali text. *Āmār jiban*, *Nabinchandra rachanabali*, Vol. 3, pp. 63–4.

This unabashed reiteration of the tearful emotions stirred by the contemplation of mystic love had its roots in the traditions of medieval Bengali Vaishnav Bhakti; what was remarkable was how this sentiment coexisted, in the trilogy, with the modern impulse to explain, to rationalize, to interpret, and thereby, finally, to inscribe the essence of Hindu spirituality in contemporary discourse.

Apart from those who praised the trilogy for its many excellent qualities, *Raibatak–Kurukshetra–Prabhas Nabin Chandra Rachanabali* each ran into stiff criticism from various quarters. *Raibatak* had, in fact, run into difficulty right at its conception, with Bankimchandra warning him against the ambitiousness of the endeavour, advising caution, criticizing sections, and praising a few parts of the first draft. After it was published in its entirety, Hemchandra Bandyopadhyay praised its use of blank verse, but doubted if it catered to popular taste, while a detailed and perceptive essay, written in the style of Akshaychandra Sarkar, appeared in the pages of the *Sādhāraṇī*, followed sometime later by an excellent appraisal by Brajendranath Seal in the *Calcutta Review*.[85] Nabinchandra himself was of the opinion that it had won the hearts of the thinkers and intellectuals of Bengal, if not of the general reading public or of the spokesmen for the orthodox. The middle and last book in the trilogy further widened the rifts that had already appeared with the publication of the first—the Brahmo camp remained opposed, the conservatives continued to take umbrage, and literary readers expressed some dissatisfaction at the fact that the themes were becoming increasingly indistinguishable from those of Bankimchandra's essays on Hinduism.

In a section toward the end of his autobiography, called '*Hindudharma and Hindusamaj*', Nabinchandra wrote explicitly about his own feelings on matters relating to Hinduism in a tone that combined impatience and scorn:

> The deafening shout of 'Hindu, Hindu' that assails our ears today—I do not know what that word 'Hindu' means. I have heard that the word 'Hindu' is not to be found in any Sanskrit dictionary or book. No grammar confirms the existence of this word. Even the 'gentlemen' [*mahāśay*] who taunt the English-educated class of their countrymen

[85] *Nabinchandra rachanabali*, Vol. 2, pp. 471, 475. The *Sādhāraṇī* review was written by Thakurdas Mukhopadhyay.

as 'Babus' have not been able to explain to the wretched 'Babus' what the word means. Some say 'Hindu' is a Muslim word—it means slave. After the Muslim conquest when the people of Bharat lost their freedom or became slaves, the victors named their religion (*dharma*) and society (*samāj*) Hindudharma and Hindusamaj. If that is the true explanation, then I must say calling the *dharma* and *samāj* of these 'gentlemen' 'Hindu' is an appropriate appellation indeed.[86]

Further reflections follow on how the words Hindu and Hindustan may have evolved from the inability of Muslims to pronounce the letter 's', so that when they reached the river Sindhu they referred to it as the Hindu river, and the land as Hindustan or land of the Hindus. He continues,

> Other theories include the opinions of those who point out that unlike the Buddhist, Christian or Muslim religions, ours has an infinite number of prophets and texts, so how can it be named after any one? Still others say our religion does have a name. It is called *Aryadharma* or *Sanātandharma.* Then why don't we stop screaming 'Hindu!—Hindu!—Slave!—Slave!' and accept one of these two names? Perhaps because then the gentlemanliness of these 'gentlemen' is gone.[87]

With a startlingly unconventional pragmatism, the ruination of the Hindu, Nabinchandra finally reflects, lay in the *chaturvarna* system of caste division. One might reasonably suppose, he argues, that a weaver's son will weave cloth with a speed and skill not inherent in the son of a non-weaver, but the moment caste becomes a question of birth, the result is just the opposite. 'For if the Brahmin's son can become a Brahmin despite being the most abysmally ignorant animal, then why should he suffer such privations to practice Brahminical virtue and work?' The decline of Hinduism and the Hindu race is then pinned on the decline in the Brahmin community, which has reached such a stage, that 'compared to all other races (*jāti*) they are the most ignorant and fallen…'[88] This section on Hindu dharma is then concluded with the presentation of a very long and complex

[86] *Nabinchandra rachanabali,* Vol. 3, p. 587.
[87] Ibid.
[88] Ibid., p. 589.

history of intense factionalism and petty rivalry between his family and some Brahmin families of Chittagong and its protracted outcome.

The zeal for education, progress, and modernization that Nabinchandra exhibited in his personal life (whether in his novel insistence on an educated and mature bride or in the numerous instances in his autobiography in which he deplores the lack of civic sense, rationality, and desire for change in the villages and towns of his various postings) co-existed, throughout, with a deep regard for the spiritual emotionality of his response to his religion. In practice this translated into observations such as that which he made approvingly on his son's religious feeling:

> Last year in the month of *Baiśākh* when he returned from England, on reaching home on the evening of the seventh day of *Bāsantī pūjā* ...after three years he looked upon the idol and cried, 'Ma! Ma!' This time too, like the last, he wore saffron robes and sang *kīrtan*s (devotionals) for three days. A barrister's *kīrtan* and a B.A. and B.L. as priest and worshipper—Bengal must never have witnessed such a scene anywhere else.[89]

Here he was presumably referring to his son, who had qualified as a barrister, and to himself as priest, B.A. and B.L.—taking pride in every aspect of this description.

It was, therefore, perhaps unsurprising that in the trilogy, the modernizing impulse, the drive to fashion the legends of the Mahabharata into a long narrative poem in blank verse, interpreting, in the process, the immemorial spirituality of Hindu texts for the present age, existed in an uneasy relationship with the ecstatic worship of traditional culture. Thus the trilogy that he wrote as a sincere devotee also claimed, for instance, in the Orientalist mode of William Jones, that Krishna's older brother Balaram was the same as the Greek hero Hercules, and that the Pandavas left for a trip around the Red Sea and the Mediterranean after the Great War of Kurukshetra, theories that understandably managed to upset even the most accommodating among the Hindu critics of the Krishna trilogy such as Hirendranath Datta. A review in the *Amritabazaar patrika* that Nabinchandra found out had been written by Hirendranath had said, in part, '... The historical reader may be apt to find fault with the poet's heresies

[89] *Āmār jīban*, *Nabinchandra rachanabali*, Vol. 3, p. 616.

in making Balaram lead an expedition of civilizing and proselytizing colonization to Greece and identifying him with the Greek Hercules and also making the Pandava Princes depart upon a divine errand around the Red Sea and the Mediterranean Sea....'[90] In the second edition of *Prabhās*, he tried to justify these departures by appending historical evidence in support of his theories from the Bible and ancient Greek chronicles.

Muslim Antipathy, British Ire

What was far more surprising than the Hindu reaction to his heretical notions in the trilogy was that, following the previous publication of *Palāśīr yuddha*, it gradually became apparent that many Muslim writers branded him as anti-Muslim on the evidence of that poem. Writing bitterly of his experience with the government, which stalled his promotion to first grade on the evidence of his seditious writings in *Palāśīr yuddha*, he was exasperated enough to mention: 'On the other hand, the new Muslim writers abuse me for being a Muslim-hater. Yet my many Muslim friends know that I believe in Hindu-Muslim unity more, I suppose, than any other ill-fated Bengali'.[91] Far from being an empty boast, this assertion was grounded in lived reality if we consider the fact mentioned at the very start of his autobiography while discussing family genealogy, that a branch of his family had converted to Islam at some point in history, and that their descendants were still pre-eminent among the Muslims of Chittagong. 'Although they are Muslim', he then avers, 'we still regard them with the same respect and love as others of our family'.[92] At another point in the narrative he recounts a situation involving his Muslim relatives:

> Suddenly, the *tehsildar* of the *khāsmahal*, Badial Alam, appeared. He had married a girl from that branch of our family that had become Muslim. I used to treat him with the same affection as a Hindu relative. His wife was as beautiful as an *apsarā*. She respected me more than my own sister. She was Asad Ali Khan's daughter; I have referred to him earlier in this book. I used to call Asad Ali 'Chacha'. 'Jamila Khatun' was his eldest daughter.

[90] *Nabinchandra rachanabali*, Vol. 5, Preface to *Prabhās*.

[91] *Āmār jīban*, *Nabinchandra rachanabali*, p. 577.

[92] Ibid.

A few days after this, she died, leaving Noakhali immersed in grief, and depriving me of one of life's consolations.[93]

That certain Muslims were against him in the context of his poem had first been intimated to him by a friend who wrote to him to give an account of the textbook committee meeting that met in 1897 to consider the inclusion of *Palāśīr yuddha* as a school text. The letter began: 'Another battle of Palashi was enacted today on the issue of your *Palāśīr yuddha*'. Giving an account of the proceedings, in which, curiously, the letter-writer seems to side with the British victory at Palashi, the friend concluded: 'The four people who had been against it on that day were still opposed to it. But thanks to your good fortune and my conjuring skills, today there were seven more people present apart from them. So at this battle of Palashi commander Mohanlal was defeated and Mir Madan disabled'. Then he adds, 'The Muslims were against you. Certainly it is true that they were the ones defeated at the Battle of Palashi'.[94] The argument that Nabinchandra had maligned the Muslims was made, as I have shown in the previous chapter, most effectively a little later by Akshaychandra Maitreya. Muslim writers would have had occasion to feel aggrieved at the unhesitating acceptance of the degeneracy both of Siraj's character and of later Muslim rule in general. Nabinchandra was not constrained in the context of Siraj's shortcomings either, and the hyperbolic imagery and overheated tone of many of these descriptions could certainly arouse dismay.

The charge of being anti-Muslim in their writings was one that haunted the Bengali Hindu elite at the core of the business of literary rejuvenation in the nineteenth century, often quite justifiably. Bankimchandra Chatterjee was one of those most commonly assumed to have sinned in this regard, and Jadunath Sarkar, in an article entitled '*Baṅkimcandra o islāmiya samāj*', written in 1939, had defended Bankim from the charge that 'by vilifying them' in *Ānandamaṭh*, and 'pouring the poison in his own heart' upon the Islamic religion, Bankim had 'created an animosity' against the Muslims.[95] Examining

[93] *Nabinchandra rachanabali*, Vol. 2, p. 368.

[94] *Āmār jīban, Nabinchandra rachanabali*, Vol. 3, p. 548.

[95] Jadunath Sarkar, 1345 BE, *Baṅkimcandra o islāmiya samāj*, *Māsik Basumatī*, *Āshāḍh*, pp. 481–4. I am grateful to Gautam Bhadra for alerting me to this essay.

the issue calmly, as he puts it, Sarkar put forward his defence point by point. The first of his defences was historical accuracy. He argued, quoting from Macaulay and Vincent Smith, that the historical verity of the oppressive nature of Muslim rule in the country at that particular period is unimpeachable; quoting from Ghulam Husain's *Sëir Mutaqherin*, a book 'popular with everybody', he illustrates how Husain depicted these outrages—and suggests that he too then should be tarred with the same brush. Then, dealing with the allegation that the characters Bankim created spoke in an unnecessarily hostile and anti-Muslim manner over and above the demands of literary characterization, he said:

> if one thinks about it calmly, one will realize that Bankim is a novelist, he is not sitting down to write a history, and in his writing of fiction, he will make each character speak according to the rules of poetry and drama... If the farmer speaks in the language of the pandit, if the murderer begins to speak a learned language with Vedantic references, then such a book will become laughable.[96]

The English phrase in brackets—'dramatic necessity'—used by Sarkar to explain why the *santāns*, in the heat of the battle, are abusive and vituperative, is reflective of his early training in English literary studies; further, he continued, if a Muslim writer such as Mir Musharraf Hussain is critical of Muslim characters, will he be tarred by the same brush? He too, is only following the rules of poetry, just as Bankimchandra has done. Similarly, in Scott's *Ivanhoe*, when the Grand Master says to the Jewish character: 'Back, dog, I touch not the misbeliever save with the sword', does that make Scott an anti-Semite? Scott was merely following the rules of '*nātyaśāstra*' is how Sarkar puts it, and just as this does not prove that Scott was a Christian dogmatist, Bankim too cannot be shown to be a Hindu bigot.[97]

This debate over Bankimchandra's alleged communalism occurred forty years after his death, and was of an academic nature inasmuch as it left the original body of work untouched; Nabinchandra Sen, on the other hand, faced a response to *Palāśīr yuddha* that was so hostile and so urgent, that he was compelled to sit down and change line after line

[96] Ibid.
[97] Ibid.

in his poem to suit the tastes of his interlocutors. The irony lies in the fact that it was not the critics who accused him of being anti-Muslim that he sat down to try and placate, but those who cried that he was too sympathetic to the plight of the last Muslim king of Bengal. These were Chandranath Basu and his like-minded neo-Hindu associates in powerful positions in the textbook committee, who had, after being defeated in their endeavours a couple of times, prodded the British government officials into belatedly waking up to the fact that the poem was, after all, very anti-British in many parts. In 1899, a sudden development saw the Official Secretary to the Government of Bengal, F.A. Slack, write a letter to Nabinchandra detailing several 'objectionable passages' in the book and demanding the 'elimination of these passages from any future Edition of that book'.[98] A translation of these four passages was then appended to the letter, done in all probability by Chandranath Basu again, who functioned as translator to the Bengal government from 1887 to 1904. The first two of these are in a speech made by Rani Bhabani, countering the traitorous proposition, put forward at a secret meeting of Bengal's most powerful men, that Siraj be deposed and dethroned. Ironically, the government and its acolytes picked instances which isolated certain phrases, whereas in its entirety, especially in the context of the narrative, the reader is inclined instead to see the speech for what it was—a dramatic, powerful, and spine-tingling indictment of chicanery and cowardice in political life.

Consider the opening scene of the first canto of the poem. It is midnight. The world is silent, the skies are lowering and dense, and an evil snake-like lightning tears restlessly across the clouds. Celestial women seem to suddenly open the windows of heaven to see the condition of Bengal, but, fearing Siraj, immediately shut them again; one's eyes are blinded by their beauty. The clouds momentarily animate the skies, but then, made fleet-footed by fear, are vanquished (Stanza 1). Time, as night, weeps quietly on the shoulders of Bengal; fearing the Nawab, silently she cries. Wet with the tears of night, the garments of sorrowful Bengal are drenched. The air is still; the child at the mother's breast, the couple on their bed, the lord in fear of his life, the wife in fear of losing her chastity, all wonder where salvation lies.

[98] *Āmār jīban, Nabinchandra rachanabali,* Vol. 3, p. 554.

Sleep, the giver of rest, fearing the Nawab's cruelty, has left the house of Bengal and gone (Stanza 5).

We move, after this opening segment, to the house of the Seths, the richest moneylenders in Bengal at this time. Surprisingly, there is no sound of the sitar, of the pakhwaj, of the raag *Megha-malhār* being sung; the house is unlit, the windows shut, no light penetrates the deep darkness. A thin ray of light penetrates the cave-like gloom and leads us to a room in a temple. There, astonished, we find seated those whose achievements have made Bengal proud, and in whose hands lie the future of Bengal; heavy of heart, sad in spirit, silent as the midnight hour and the lonely place they inhabit (Stanza 10). One by one, each of those present rise to speak. The most powerful voice is that of Jagat Seth, implacable in his resolve, fierce in his opposition, arrogant and proud. Berating the reasons for Bengal's eternal servitude, he describes the desire for revenge that animates him, intoning: 'Revenge—revenge—revenge is all / All I have left now is revenge!'[99] [These lines are quoted by Nabinchandra in his autobiography as the raison d'être for the enmity of the members of the textbook committee who were against him[100]] Raja Rajballabh follows this with a speech on the inequities of Siraj's rule, mentioning the atrocity of the Black Hole as a prime example of the cruelty and inhumane lust for blood that distinguishes Siraj's character. Raja Krishnachandra adds to the list of Siraj's failings, describing him as worse than a dog, a coward, a drunkard. Following the infamous historiographical myth, Bengal is described as having lost its freedom seven hundred years ago when seventeen Turkish horsemen defeated the weak Sen king (a depiction that was to infuriate Akshaykumar Maitreya). The Pathans and the Moghuls have come and gone, but Bengal is still in chains. The English have returned to avenge the Black Hole tragedy, and the time is right to displace the young tyrant with the help of Clive.

At the end, after all have spoken, Rani Bhabani is invited to take her stand. The Rani, previously described as 'fair, with a slender neck and large eyes, / shining like a star in the painted sky' (st.12), was, as Nabinchandra must have known only too well, the stuff of legend. When Ranajit Guha, in *A Rule of Property for Bengal*, described her as a

[99] *Palāśīr yuddha*, Canto I, Verse 28, p.13.

[100] Quoted in *Āmār jīban*, *Nabinchandra rachanabali*, Vol. 3, p. 546.

figure who, for generations of Bengali patriots, personified 'the image of a brave, lone Boadicea defending the last outpost of independence', the reference he makes in the footnote is to Nabinchandra's 'highly unhistorical portraiture' in his 'famous poem', *Palāśīr yuddha.*[101] It was, however, at least historically true that this popularly styled queen was one of the largest landholders of Bengal, the size and value of her property in one of the most fertile districts of Bengal placing her at the very top of the landed aristocracy. Guha adds, 'Her charity had its colossal expression in the building of temples and digging of sweet water lakes and thus made her the very symbol of benevolence...'[102]

The Rani's speech, in the poem, is almost double the length of any of the other speakers, running on for almost seven pages in the narrative. Almost all of her exhortations are anti-British, and she advances a theory that is, essentially, more accepting of Muslim rule than subjugation by the British. This unremittingly hostile tone is sustained over several passages, and the Rani's speech ends with her anticipating a most terrible fate for India. Strangely, the government did not dwell any further on sections of Rani Bhabani's fearful speech that had repeatedly invoked the British in terms of violence, destruction, terror, and calamity. After expressing a moment of motherly concern for the unfortunate Siraj, she asks the maharaja not to advance down the path of conspiracy, which will only mean an exchange of masters, but to wait and take the broad road ahead toward Independence. In sympathy, the thunder roars outside, splitting the sky with a canon-like roar at which the mansion trembles, rain and storm commence, and nature assumes its most violent aspect.

The famous passage spoken by the Rani on the advent of the British that was quoted as seditious was inimitably rendered in Indian English by the government translator; Nabinchandra quotes him: 'Why for nothing let in the crocodile by cutting a canal or setting fire to your house with your own hands?' ['*Kena miche khāl kāṭi ānibe kumīre/ pradānibe sthir gṛhe svahaste anal?*'][103] But this, in effect, should have

[101] Ranajit Guha, 1981, *A Rule of Property for Bengal: An Essay on the Idea of Permanent Settlement*, Delhi: Orient Longman, p. 58.

[102] Ibid.

[103] This translation is the original submission quoted by Nabinchandra. *Āmār jīban, Nabinchandra rachanabali,* Vol. 3, p. 554.

been the least of the government's worries. What was remarkable about the Rani's theories was the consistent perception of the British as more dangerous, more alien, and in the end more harmful to India than any previous colonizer, and the express hope that Maratha power would, if things were allowed to take their own course, eventually establish an independent Hindu kingdom in India. Bhudev Mukhopadhyay, in *Svapnalabdha bhāratbarsher itihās* [*The History of Bhāratbarsha as Seen in a Dream*] (serialized in the *Education Gazette* from 1875, the year that *Palāśīr yuddha* was published) had taken much the same position, both as regards Muslims and regarding the ideal outcome of Maratha suzerainty. This strange coincidence of views has not been remarked upon by commentators, but the resemblance is uncanny. While Bhudev had imagined the crown of India being handed over, after the third battle of Panipat, to the Maharashtrian king, Raja Ramchandra, Nabinchandra, in turn, made Rani Bhabani say: 'When we see how powerful the Maratha-lord has become in the South, it is obvious that in a few days more, the lord of Maharashtra shall become the overlord of Bharat. Once again then, Bharat will be rescued'.[104] As regards the Muslims, both writers benevolently give them a place in the family tree, albeit inferior to the Hindu, but related to them nonetheless. Nabinchandra makes the Rani assert: 'I know the Muslims are a different race, as the British too are; yet the difference is like that between heaven and hell. The Muslim has lived in India continuously for the past seven hundred and fifty years, and in the course of this long interaction, love and intermarriage has grown between the two, the conquered and the conquering'. Most tellingly, just as Bhudev had likened the Muslims to foster-brothers of the Hindu, suckled at the same breast, Nabinchandra too implies that the Muslim is related to the Hindu, using the metaphor of the mighty Ashwathha tree to denote the Hindu, at whose foot the Muslim branch flourishes.[105]

Nabinchandra's reaction to the charges made by the British Government was that they were trumped up and unsustainable, and that twenty-two years after the poem had been published it was impossible

[104] *Palāśīr yuddha*, Canto 1, p. 23.

[105] Brajendranath Bandyopadhyay, 1944, 'Bhudeb Mukhopadhyay', *SSC*, Vol. 3, Calcutta: Bangiya Sahitya Parishad, pp. 55–6. Nabinchandra Sen, *Palāśīr yuddha*, Canto 1, verse 50.

to believe that the poem could bring any harm to the British Empire if it had not already done so in all these years. He was being harassed and persecuted by his own jealous countrymen, he wrote, and certain Englishmen at the helm of affairs had succumbed to the propaganda against him. While trying to make sense of this sudden development, Nabinchandra had later discovered that apparently, at a trial for sedition in Bombay against the great political leader Lokmanya Tilak, the counsel for Tilak had argued in the Bombay High Court that what he had said in his putatively seditious speech was to be found in many school texts all over the country. It was in response to this allegation that the then governor-general Lord Curzon had asked for all Indian school texts to be scanned for traces of sedition.[106] It could also well be surmised that Nabinchandra's active participation in the political life of Calcutta, and his well-known behind-the-scenes activity at the Congress conclave of 1890 might have alerted the authorities to his potential as a politically involved participant. He mentions himself that he was the one person who had friends in every camp, and details how he intervened to bring the warring factions of the *Amritabazaar* group (under the brothers Sisir Kumar Ghosh and Motilal Ghosh) and the *Bengalee* group (under Surendranath Banerjee) together for the Calcutta Congress. He thought that the Congress meeting that year was a tremendous success due to his efforts, mentioning that he himself went to the scene of the meeting only after it was over, which too was promptly reported to the government in the secret reports of the detectives. His feeling at the time was that he would be in trouble with the government following his role in organizing the Congress, and in this he was proven right. The events that followed comprise the narrative we have been following so far—the sudden reinspection of the text of *Palāśir yuddha* by the school-book committee, and then subsequently, the letter from the chief secretary detailing the objectionable passages.

Apparently, soon after this, charges were to have been brought against him by the state prosecution, an eventuality that Nabinchandra claimed was staved off by the intervention of sensible British deputy magistrates who had argued that such a move, twenty-two or twenty-three years after the event, would be unsuitable. The most implacable

[106] *Āmār jīban*, *Nabinchandra rachanabali*, Vol. 3, p. 557.

opposition, however, existed at the very highest level, in the person of lieutenant governor Woodburn himself. This august personage (referred to pejoratively in Bengali by Nabinchandra as 'burnt wood' [*poṛā-kāshṭho*]) had, when petitioned by Nabinchandra for being passed over for promotion, apparently thundered back at him that far from his having a complaint against the government, it was the government that had a 'greater grievance' against him, and that he would ensure there would be no promotion for him as long as he remained Lieutenant Governor.[107]

Alterations, Emendations, Reductions: The Word 'Yavana' and Other Matters

Promotion to the first grade finally came to Nabinchandra in 1903, a year after which he retired from service, having worked thirty-six years without applying for an extension. In the meanwhile, Nabinchandra had sat himself down and changed every instance that gave offence to the government, as well as many other portions that referred to Siraj in any way so as to imply an exalted status or influential position. From the last independent king of Bengal who held the future of India in his hands, Sirajuddaula was reduced to a Muslim tyrant whose removal spelt an end to Muslim power and polity. The editors of the Bangiya Sahitya Parishad edition of *Palāśir yuddha* have pointed out that Nabinchandra changed the spellings and words of almost every stanza in the text of the poem each time it appeared in a new edition throughout his lifetime. Sometimes these changes were technical in nature, but, as a list compiling the changes between the first edition of 1875 and the tenth edition of 1907 shows, not all of them were responses to aesthetic concerns.[108] The first type of change included replacing, for instance, the word 'French *jāti*' with '*Pharāshī*', which is the Bengali word for French, or changing the spellings of individual words; but such instances, in fact, are few and far between and quite inconsequential in their effects. Far more astonishing are the immense number of small changes that created an overall impact that can only be understood by a closer look at the different versions.

[107] Ibid., p. 575.

[108] For this list, see *Nabinchandra rachanabali*, Vol. 4, *Palāśir yuddha*, pp. 6–11.

First, the four passages referred to by the government were, of course, altered into a more acceptable phraseology. In the first passage, the objectionable idiom, about inviting the crocodile into your home was deleted and a more innocuous phrase about dethroning the lord of the land of Bengal used instead. The second passage was barely altered at all. The text still describes the British attacking the Maratha army like tigers maddened by the taste of blood; only the word 'result' (*pariṇām*) in the last sentence 'the result makes me shudder [with apprehension]' (*pariṇām bhebe mama śarīr śihare*) is replaced by the equally provoking phrase, 'How horrible! I shudder to think of it.' [*Ki bhishaṇ! bhebe mama śarīr śihare*] The third passage on the government list, a reference to the grief of Bengalis at the defeat at Palashi is toned down and changed into vague references to the destiny of Bengal and what is written in her fate. Lastly, the scene of Siraj's beheading that forms the last couplet of the work is changed. But once again, as in the second instance, the alteration is so slight that the essential sentiment remains unchanged. The lines that originally depicted the last hope for Bengal's freedom flowing out with the blood shed at the moment of Siraj's decapitation are marginally adjusted to read: 'The candle in the room goes out; and with it, Bharat's last hope is turned into a dream!'

Nabinchandra's poem, although titled after the battle at Palashi, is actually about the tragic fate of the degenerate king Sirajuddaula, and could have easily been called, instead, 'The Tragedy of Sirajuddaula, Last King of Bengal'. Essentially, the poem commiserates with the nineteen-year-old monarch who is shown to be the very worst example of all that could be debased in a character, and yet, whose betrayal and beheading inspire pity and terror in the beholder. In this portrayal of the anti-hero as protagonist, Nabinchandra seemed to have been, apparently unconsciously, influenced by Milton's portraiture of Satan in *Paradise Lost*, or, closer home, to Milton's greatest Bengali disciple Madhusudan's epoch-making depiction of Ravana as the hero of *Meghnādbadh kābya*. Nabinchandra, writing fifteen or so years later, might not have been quite so clear-sighted about his own allegiances as Madhusudan was, but he was certainly ambiguous enough in his handling of the fate of Siraj to arouse the antipathy of some of his conservative Hindu countrymen.

After the charges made by the government, Nabinchandra changed his text, substantially in two instances, and insubstantially in two others in response to the four specific instances cited by the government. However, what he also did, over many years and subsequent editions, was to change many words, phrases, and sometimes even a few lines throughout the length and breadth of the poem, thus altering its character in the most implicit but devastatingly effective manner. One of the most remarkable of his changes was to replace, in many places, the word Bharat with '*yaban*'. Traditionally, in Sanskrit sources, the word was one that implied the outsider or 'the other'; in the *Manusmriti*, the Yavanas referred to are the Indo-Greeks who ruled in North-West India in the second century BCE, and the term came to be especially associated with the sciences of the Greeks, particularly mathematics and astronomy.[109] By the time of Akbar, however, certain Hindu texts used *Yavana/Mlechha/Turuska* interchangeably to denote the Muslims in the context of military exploits, although these are not projected images of an undifferentiated 'other'. '*Yavana* and *Mlechha* were already generic terms with reference to "outsiders" in the early medieval context', B.D. Chattopadhyay has commented, although he is careful to point out also that 'there could be various empirical realities in political relations between Yavana and non-Yavana powers, and there could be various representations too'.[110] In Indian languages, the term 'Muslim/Musalman' did not, it would be historically accurate to say, evolve into a category of reference until the nineteenth century, when it slowly took its current form in the context, in fact, of the concurrent framing of the term 'Hindu'. We have seen Nabinchandra's irritation with the term Hindu, which did not exist in Indian languages until then, and it would be fair to say that the term 'Musalman', as a rubric to refer to all Muslims, also came into being at around the same time as the opposite binary of 'Hindu' in the nineteenth century. Until then, all invocations to people belonging to the Muslim community would have been organized along the principles of particular references,

[109] Dermot Killingley, 2007, 'Mlecchas, Yavanas and Heathens: Interacting Xenologies in Early Nineteenth-Century Calcutta', in *Beyond Orientalism*, Delhi: Motilal Banarasidass, p. 127.

[110] Brajadulal Chattopadhyay, 1998, *Representing the Other? Sanskrit Sources and the Muslims*, New Delhi: Manohar, pp. 30, 82.

depending on caste, class, sect, ethnicity, and region. The British, of course, were the earliest users of the terms 'Hindu' and 'Musalman' to refer to the respective communities, and Rammohun Roy, for instance, used the terms 'Hindu' and 'Mohammedan' in answers to questions posed by the Select Committee of the House of Commons in 1831.[111]

Arguably, it was the modern Bengali writer who had reinvented the ambiguity of the term Yavana to stand in for either the British or the Muslim foe—both Hemchandra (in *Bhārat saṅgīt*) and Bankimchandra (in *Ānandamaṭh*) ran into trouble with the government over the use of the word. Hemchandra had used it to imply the British in lines of poetry that spoke of a clarion call to arms to expel them from the land, and had to camouflage his political intent by having Bhudev Mukhopadhyay, editor of the *Education Gazette* in which the poem had appeared, clarify that the term did not mean 'foreigner', as the government translator Robinson had said, but referred specifically to the Muslim. A decade or so later, Bankimchandra changed all the references to the English or *Iṅgrej* in the first edition of *Ānandamaṭh* to, selectively, either '*yaban*' or Musalman. Nabinchandra, in this poem, uses it quite obviously to refer to the Muslim; still, by not using the term 'Musalman', which was, after all, available to him, he was both following indigenous convention as well as leaving a space of ambiguity for himself.[112] By the turn of the century, the indeterminate nature of the term had diminished, becoming narrower in its reference until it came to stand steadfastly for the Muslim inhabitant of India, a fact that Muslims themselves grew increasingly aware of, as their complaints against Nabinchandra made evident. In a different case altogether, an anonymous Muslim reviewer of Brajasundar Sanyal's *Caṇḍīdās carit* (1896), in the periodical *Nabanūr* in 1904, protested against the use of the term '*yaban*' or Yavana for Muslims. 'It is obvious', the review stated,

> that all the Hindu writers feel unduly elated if they can demonstrate a hostile attitude towards Musalmans... Can it really be the case that Hindu

[111] Rammohun Roy, 1832, *Exposition of the Practical Operation of the Judicial and Revenue Systems of India*, London: Smith Elder & Co.

[112] The term 'Musalman' was known by the thirteenth century, but not used commonly in written sources that used other generic terms such as Yavana to refer to Muslims. Chattopadhyay, *Representing the Other?* p. 29.

writers will not give up using the word *yaban* to mean Musalman? Then shall we too use the term *kāpher* to denote 'Hindu'? But Muslim society is still reluctant to endorse and encourage injustices of this sort. However, if these writers continue to show their heartlessness (*hṛdaẏhīnatā*) in this way much longer, then Muslim society too will not accept this without a fight.[113]

If we look at the cumulative effect of the changes Nabinchandra made to his poem, deleting the word 'Bharat' and replacing it with 'Yavana', it is startling to see how they work to devalue the significance of Siraj's rule and the battle he lost in the context of the narrative. The fourth canto, in its original first edition version, referred to Bharat at least nine times, all of which were deleted and changed in the final edition. Titled simply, 'War', this canto was the one that actually described the battle as it took place on the fields of Palashi on that fateful day in June 1757. In the very first verse, describing dawn at the battlefield, the poet had said: 'Gone are the happy days of Bharat; / As if painting destiny on the bloody sky, / The sun rose slowly and sadly'. Now, in the existing Bangiya Sahitya Parishad edition of the poem, we read: 'Gone are the happy days of the *yaban* / As if painting *yaban*-destiny on the bloody sky, / The sun rose slowly and sadly'. What the change from 'Bharat' to '*yaban*' accomplishes in the context of the poem is a change of perspective: from a national loss and moment of national shame at the defeat at Palashi, the battle is now read as a final disaster for the Muslim rulers only. Rather than being the nationalist epic that the young Nabinchandra had set out to write mourning his own history, the poem then becomes the work of a poet elegizing a moment in history while at the same time distancing himself from it. Ironically, and almost certainly unintentionally, the writer then assumes the role of a poet narrativizing the tragic fate of the *yaban* king—in this guise, he is occupying a secular space of culture created by modernity that allows him to chronicle both the heinous character as well as the awful betrayal of a Muslim king from the disinterested territory of creative space.

This section also contains the speeches by Mohanlal that made Chandranath Basu express such irritation with the poet and that

[113] Review of Brajasundar Sanyal, 1904, *Caṇḍīdās carit* in *Nabanūr* (3rd year, 3rd number). I am indebted to Gautam Bhadra for this reference.

Nirad Chaudhuri implicated as unhistorical. Apart from the warlike grandeur of his heroism, Mohanlal's speeches, at the end, also reflect on the future awaiting his countrymen. At the end of the day's fighting, awakening from his faint, wounded and bloodied, he asks the sunlight not to fade, for with the waning of the day 'will come eternally the saddest of days in Bharat's destiny!' He continues, 'In this darkness of sad subjection, / Do not drown this land of Bharat forever and go, O Sun!' Almost identically to the earlier changes, here too, the word Bharat is replaced in later editions by the word '*yaban*', denoting Muslim, and the land of Bharat, '*Bhārat-bhūmi*' in Bengali, is replaced by '*yaban-rājya*' or Muslim kingdom in the next line.

In a nod to the sentiments of his colonial masters, Nabinchandra also changed lines that had *not* been picked up for specific mention that referred to the coming of British rule as a dark and depressing era of servitude. Earlier in the poem, in the first canto, Rani Bhabani refers to the English as strangers. 'We do not know', she says, 'where they stay, across the distant ocean'. She continues, 'If you think about it deeply you will see that they are not like us either in religion or race, in features or in manners...' In the first edition, however, this line had read, startlingly, 'Fathered by the monkey in the womb of the demon [*bānar-ourase janma rākkhasī udare*], they are terribly unlike us in features or in manners'. When reflecting upon the stalling of his promotion in the civil service, Nabinchandra had in fact asserted that his chief detractor in the textbook committee had quoted this very line to the Lieutenant Governor, saying that even if there was nothing actually 'seditious' in the text of the poem, Nabinchandra had nevertheless referred to Englishmen in this manner. This was the reason, according to Nabinchandra, why the letter that was sent to him by the Inspector of the Presidency Division and the textbook committee had said 'these and other *passages of similar import*' (original emphasis).[114] Apart from this infamous line, other instances included changing a couple of lines spoken by Mohanlal, who had, in the original version, exhorted the sun not to return to Bharat again until her years of slavery were over. In the revised edition, these lines were

[114] *Āmār jīban, Nabinchandra rachanabali,* Vol. 3, p. 568.

changed to read: 'Tomorrow when the door of the East shall open, / You shall see a new vision of Bharat'.[115]

Much more pernicious, however, was the manner in which Nabinchandra played down the depiction of the emotions aroused in the country at the spectacle of the fate of the Muslims who had ruled it. While in his earlier version, Nabinchandra had portrayed the young king Sirajuddaula as having held the future of India in his hands, and this moment in history—the moment of his defeat—had been depicted as one that would bring a reign of servitude to Indians, now that picture was altered indelibly. By reducing the words Bharat or *Bhārat-bhūmi* or *Bhārat-bhāgya* to read *Yaban* or *Yaban-rājya*, (changes not asked for by the government or the textbook committee), Nabinchandra seemed to be disassociating Siraj and the Muslims from any integral role as constituents of the land or of the destiny of Bharat. Portraying the actions of Muslims in a manner so as to arouse the pity of his countrymen was proving to be so unpopular among his constituency of readers that he decided, quite consciously, to downplay his previous ideas. In the same speech of Mohanlal's in which the sun is addressed at dusk, where the reference to Bharat's eternal servitude is changed to suggest instead that in the morrow a new dawn shall arise, further references to the state of Bharat are replaced with references to the Muslim state. Mohanlal addresses the evening, on whose brow the gem-like stars already shine. But, he speculates, are those spots of blood that have appeared on the forehead of the sky when, on hearing Bharat's sad news, it was struck repeatedly in anguish? Dusk has descended prematurely to hide the face of Bharat, which is lowered in sorrow! Here, in these lines, once again, the word Bharat is changed to *yaban*. Consequently, the poem now narrates how, on hearing the *yaban*'s sad news, dusk has descended prematurely to hide the face of the *yaban* kingdom, which is lowered in sorrow.[116]

Despite these changes, however, the rest of Mohanlal's speech, over the last five or six pages, still contains an overview of five hundred years of Muslim rule that is certainly not entirely negative or prejudiced. Reflecting on the change of regime, from Muslim to British rule, Nabinchandra makes Mohanlal say that for Bharat, like

[115] *Palāśir yuddha*, p. 91.

[116] Ibid.

the wild bird shut in the cage, there is no happiness or unhappiness—to the captive, both are the same. That is why, echoing Satan's speech in *Paradise Lost*, Mohanlal asserts that to be free in hell is better than to be captive in heaven, or why the free beggar under the tree is happier than the un-free king. This is the end of Muslim power in India, Mohanlal prophesies—from now on, whether wealthy, middle-class or poor, Muslims will remain dormant (literally, asleep). In an almost automatic manner, Muslim excess and tyranny is bemoaned to start with, but immediately, he says that while we acknowledge the countless sins of Muslim rule in every chapter of history, is it not true, alas, that they had also, in places, a collection of gem-like achievements that history guards lovingly? All their kings were not ferocious sinners—for every Aurangzeb or Alauddin, was not there a Babar or Akbar? He pictures the massive Mughal Empire sinking into darkness and Delhi and Murshidabad, their great cities, turning into graveyards of Muslim pride—at this point in history, he reflects, what is the point of dwelling on the darker side?

Unconsciously echoing British historiographical attitudes toward the Indian character, he mentions that it is Bharat that is to be blamed for bringing ruin to this race, for all those who live in this land for too long are reduced to effeminacy and lassitude. The Mughals were incomparably wealthy and courageous—their kingdom, that stood on such firm ground for five hundred years—who knew it would fall, in a moment of Bengali treachery, into the hands of merchants? The sun that set at Panipat will not rise again soon. In the penultimate lines, in another distancing move, the sentiment that had originally read, 'Bharat's tears shall fall every moment and eventually remove all these sins' is changed to 'How strange it is that the end of an era causes blood to flow like a stream!'[117]

So what was originally conceived as an epic poem of loss and betrayal, of a country vanquished and still waiting to be free, was changed—or an attempt was made to change it—in the course of twenty-three or more years, to a disinterested account of a particular battle. A poem originally written by a patriotic young man moved by the story that had been enacted once upon a time upon a battlefield in Palashi was tampered with and altered, subtly and not so subtly,

[117] Ibid., pp. 93–9.

by an older and more cautious poet with a reputation and a bank balance to defend. Nabinchandra had said, when he asked the Chief Secretary Mr Buckland some questions in the context of his non-promotion: 'I wrote *Palāśīr yuddha* when I was a young man. Am I to be punished for it now, in my old age?'[118] But the changes that Nabinchandra had made to the text of his poem, regrettably, had little to do with the charges of sedition, but rather more to do with popular opinion among an influential section of his countrymen, who were unwilling to see the defeat at Palashi as a defeat for all Indians, or to concede that the moment of British conquest spelt doom for all concerned. Separating out the consequences for Hindus and Muslims, Nabinchandra attempted, in his revisions, to divide the poem along communal lines, seeming to concede that the moment of defeat was catastrophic for the Muslim rulers and community, who would never recover from this blow, but not so for the Hindus, who perceived this to be the dawning of a new age.

[118] *Āmār jīban, Nabinchandra rachanabali,* Vol. 3, p. 572.

7 Rabindranath's Early Style and Reconstruction of the Past

> *My (circular) point [is] that beginnings are first and important but not always evident, that beginning is basically an activity which ultimately implies return and repetition rather than simple linear accomplishment, that beginning and beginning-again are historical whereas origins are divine, that a beginning not only creates but is its own method because it has intention. In short, beginning is* making *or* producing difference*; but—and here is the great fascination in the subject—difference which is the result of combining the already-familiar with the fertile novelty of human work in language.*
>
> —Edward Said[1]

Beginnings

In an essay written in 1894 on the occasion of the death of the poet Biharilal Chakrabarty—a little-known lyric poet at the time of his death—Rabindranath wrote not only about Biharilal's achievements, which he did in some detail, but also of his own original lonely impulse toward poetic composition. Biharilal's enduring fame in the annals of Bengali literature rests upon his installation as precursor to Rabindranath by Rabindranath; in that incarnation he has been the subject of essays and editorials written by various distinguished twentieth-century Bengali literary commentators, from Mohitlal Majumdar to Kalidas Ray, all of who have followed almost to a line the opinions already expressed about Biharilal by Rabindranath himself. Speaking of his first encounter with the poetry of

[1] Edward Said, 1975, *Beginnings: Intention and Method*, New York: Columbia University Press, p. xvii.

Biharilal as a young boy in the pages of an obscure journal called the *Abodhbandhu*, Rabindranath had famously identified this poet as the 'bird of dawn' (*bhorer pākhi*), saying:

> In that early hour, very few were awake, and the literary gardens were not yet resonant with a variety of birdsong. In the early morning light, only one bird of dawn had begun its sweet song. That song was its own.
>
> I cannot speak of history, but that was the first I had heard a poet's own voice in Bengali poetry...This was perhaps the first expression, in modern Bengali literature, of a poet's own voice. At that time, or a little before, Michael's *Caturdaśpadī* had occasionally expressed his heart's feelings—but very rarely—and the short form of the sonnets made them rigid and constrained, without the spontaneous flow of a song of pain.[2]

In a clear reference to the poetry of Hemchandra Bandyopadhyay and Nabinchandra Sen, he then went on to distinguish the voice of this lyric poet from that of his predecessors. 'Unlike the poets of that time who were newly educated in the English language', Biharilal, he said, did not write 'epic poetry full of scenes of war or rousing patriotic poems or even traditional narrative verse (*paurāṇik upākhyān*) in the manner of the older poets'. Instead, 'he sat alone and wrote in his own rhythm of his own feelings'. In those utterances of Biharilal's, there was, Rabindranath insisted again, 'no concern for the welfare of the world or the welfare of the country, no attempt to please gatherings at meetings. That is why his melody took an intimate form and entered the heart, attracting the reader's trust quite easily'.[3]

The image this passage builds upon, of the solitary poet sitting by himself, writing 'in his own rhythm, of his own feelings', was quite patently one that was the nearest to Rabindranath's own self-image. Speaking of his own early urge as a boy attracted by the poetic impulse, he had already, at the start of the essay, begun with a sketch of his own teenage self discovering the lyric poetry of Biharilal one Calcutta afternoon:

[2] Rabindranath Tagore, '*Kabi Bihārīlāl*', *Āshāḍh* 1301 BE. Reprinted in *Sāradāmaṅgal o sādher āsan*, 2004, edited by Tarun Mukhopadhya, Calcutta: Karuna Prakashani, p. 146.

[3] Ibid.

> I still remember, having escaped school, sitting in a south-facing room in the long, lonely afternoon, reading the Bengali translation of *Paul-Virginie* in the *Abodhbandhu*, my heart pierced with intense sorrow as I read. At that time I was unacquainted with nature as it existed outside Calcutta and the descriptions I read in *Paul-Virginie* of the sea beach and the forests seemed to me like an indescribable dream, and that vision of the union and sorrowful separation of Paul-Virgine in the forest-shadowed, wave-pounded seaside used to sound to me like the most beautiful song.[4]

Rabindranath then develops upon this theme over the course of the rest of the essay, speaking of how Biharilal was the first poet to speak to him in intimate tones. 'Just as *Paul-Virginie* had first introduced me close at hand to nature and man, so too in Biharilal's poetry, in the same way, I found an intimate friend'.[5] The meaning of nature and its significance for him as a future poet is dwelt upon, and he quotes copiously from Biharilal's poetry in the essay, showing how it contained its yearning in melodious metre and language. Speaking of Biharilal's best-known work, the *Sāradāmaṅgal*, Rabindranath invoked Shelley's 'Hymn to Intellectual Beauty' (1816), quoting the lines:

> Spirit of Beauty, that dost consecrate
> With thine own hues all thou dost shine upon
> Of human thought or form

reiterating, a little later, that what Shelley meant when he spoke of intellectual beauty as 'Thou messenger of sympathies, / That wax and wane in lover's eyes' was the same as the goddess that was incarnate in Biharilal's Saraswati.[6]

[4] Ibid., p. 145. *Paul et Virginie* is a novel by Jacques-Henri Bernardin de Saint-Pierre, first published in 1787, on the eve of the French Revolution. Its Enlightenment views were essentially those also espoused by Rousseau, in that it held up the natural world and the nature of man as joyous and free, which was exhibited in the book in its characters and its setting in Mauritius, then a French colony. Thomas Carlyle, writing of it in his magnum opus, *The French Revolution* (1837), described it in language not dissimilar to Rabindranath's calling it '[a novel in which] there rises melodiously, as it were, the wail of a moribund world: everywhere wholesome Nature in unequal conflict with diseased, perfidious art; cannot escape from it in the lowest hut, in the remotest island of the sea'. Thomas Carlyle, *The French Revolution*, Chapter 8, 'Printed Paper': Second last paragraph, Sentence 3.

[5] Rabindranath Tagore, '*Kabi Bihārīlāl*', ibid., p. 146.

[6] Ibid., p. 153.

Rabindranath wrote this essay in the Bengali year 1301, in the month of *Āshāḍh*, or in June–July 1894; much of what he said here was reiterated in his autobiographical *Jībansmṛti* (1912) written many years later. In 1894 he was thirty-three years old and in full flow as a mature poet, creating at the same time in these years some of the first and finest short stories written in the language while looking after his father's estates in the verdant beauty of riverine East Bengal. Landscape and lyric poetry also came together in this period in the inspirational collections of *Mānasī* (1890) and *Sonār tari* (1894), which, together with the ground-breaking short stories, present a cornucopia of creative production unmatched by any other contemporary. Many of the definitions he set down about the nature of 'true' poetry in his essay on Biharilal, we can see, were forcefully emblematic of his own work at the time, and he was at pains to emphasize, repeatedly, that the origin of the lyric impulse to poetry came to a poet through nature and the imagination, consciously or unconsciously echoing the Romantic manifesto in the process.

In the preface (*abataraṇikā*) to the *Rabindra rachanabali*, in the seventy-eighth year of his life, which he felt was reaching its end, he returned again to the theme of how he became a poet, encapsulating the experience once again in an image of a lonely boy:

> However those [early] writings were, there is a story behind them—that is of a boy, shy, lonesome, isolated, whose play was all in his own mind. He was outside of the strictures of society, outside of the discipline of school. The discipline at home too, was light…
>
> So began my fragmentary poetic compositions in uneven rhyme, like meteor-showers; a boy's wilful, untidy, shaky constructions. The impulse to break with conventions was innate to that isolated boy.[7]

Concluding the paragraph quoted from above, where he speaks of himself in both first and third person, he dwelt upon both the criticism and the encouragement he had received from his elders, concluding, 'That is why, although I was not indulged, and I had to make my way

[7] Rabindranath Tagore, 1409 BE, 125 *Sulabh Saṃskaran*, *Abataraṇikā*, *Rabindra rachanabali*, Vol. 1, p. 16.

through the opposition of convention, *I built up my own writings in my own way*. (my emphasis)'[8]

The image of the poet that he produced with such precision in writings such as these was one of the lonely creator, working from within himself, creating poetry through communion with nature and beauty, but above all, in communion with himself, his own interiority and isolation emphasized repeatedly. It was, of course, a Romantic vision, resonant of Wordsworth's powerful emphasis in the Preface to the *Lyrical Ballads* that the origins of poetry lie in the emotions and memories of the poet.[9] Rabindranath's early debt to the Romantic vision of poetry was spelt out in a number of essays written at this time; what is significant is that it was a debt he wished to cancel—by omitting those essays in which he had dwelt upon his literary gleanings from the Romantic poets or English literary convention—when putting together his own life's works in the form of the Collected Works or *Rabindra rachanabali*. When this was first published by a dedicated team of scholar-academics at Santiniketan in 1939, Rabindranath wrote an Introduction for it in which he spent an inordinate amount of time explaining why he felt his own early work needed to be left out of such a compilation.

Anticipating many of the issues that he would reiterate in another essay on the historicality of literature that was one of his last pieces to be published in 1941, '*Sāhitye aitihāsikatā*', Rabindranath returned obsessively in the *Rachanabali* introduction to the question of history and its relation to literature. 'The property of history and the assets of literature are not of the same kind', he wrote, for:

> History wants to remember everything, but literature forgets a lot. The printing-press is the chief assistant of the historian. Literature contains the predilection to be selective, to which the printing press is a major obstacle. A poet's field of work may be compared to a constellation. In the vast, obscure light there sometimes glows brightly some complete and integrated creations. Those are poetry. I want to acknowledge only those among my compositions. The rest, which are like gaps of faint vapour, are

[8] Ibid., p.17.

[9] 'Poetry is the spontaneous overflow of powerful feelings: it takes its origin from emotion recollected in tranquillity.' William Wordsworth, 1815, Preface to *Lyrical Ballads*, London.

not evidences of literature. The historian is like an astronomer; the vapour, the stars, the gaps, he doesn't want to leave anything out.[10]

In the space of the three pages of the introduction, Rabindranath returns to this complaint obsessively. If in one place he says that, at his age, he feels it his duty to preserve only those writings that have attained the status of literature, dumping the rest, for after all, 'to recognise the forest, one needs to clear the woods', then in another, he compares these early writings to railway coaches of unfinished manufacture—they should not have been allowed to leave the factory shed. However, many of the poems at the beginning of the *Rachanabali* too were such—'just as mist is not rain, so too, these poems are not poetry', he said, specifically naming the poems in '*Sandhyā-saṅgīt*' in this context.[11] He speaks here of some of his songs that had been criticized by Bipinchandra Pal—those were childish writings that should never have been judged in such a manner. 'They were passed off in literary society with the help of the printing press in order to supply history with material. If you try to remove them, history objects on the basis of its own prior claim'.[12]

Rabindranath's objection to the oppressions of history and historians was premised, as I have shown elsewhere, upon his irritation at this time with the materialist, modernist, and Marxist literary criticism of the time.[13] The open antagonism the Calcutta critics of the 1920s and 1930s expressed toward what they perceived to be the transcendentalism of the older poet was infamous in its time. It led the aged poet to say, with a devastating matter of factness, in the Preface to the *Rachanabali*: 'No other writer has ever had to endure a disrespect that was so continuous, so unabashed, so unkind, and so unchecked as I have'.[14] Not only did Rabindranath express his feelings toward the tyranny of history in the Introduction and Preface to the *Rachanabali*, he also spoke of it in his private correspondence with

[10] Rabindranath Tagore, *Bhūmikā*, *Rabindra rachanabali*, Vol. 1, p. 9.

[11] Ibid.

[12] Ibid., p. 10.

[13] See Rosinka Chaudhuri, 2012, '*The Flute*, *Gerontion*, and Subalternist Misreadings of Tagore', *Freedom and Beef Steaks: Colonial Calcutta Culture*, New Delhi: Orient Blackswan, pp. 175–201.

[14] *Rabindra rachanabali*, Vol. 1, p. 17.

the editor, Charuchandra Bhattacharjee. Bhattacharjee's introduction to a new edition—dated September/October 1953, twelve years after the death of the poet—of the official Visva-Bharati publication of the Collected Works of Rabindranath began with a disclaimer:

> There is one more thing which the poet had referred to in his Introduction. He had wanted to discard many of the compositions he had written at an early age as they were very immature, not giving them a place in this *Rachanabali*. In this regard, he let us know—'Copious quantities of those writings that I wish to disinherit you want me to recognise at your combined insistence. My shame will be made immortal and it will bear my signature. Therefore when I stand before future generations, I will not be able to take off my dunce's cap. You people argue, the dunce's cap that you fashion out the detritus of history, one has to wear it and stand in the court of eternity in the interests of history. The poet's head is bowed in shame by this. History too discards much that is immaterial to become true history. Man's ancient ancestors went around with a long extension protruding from their backs—every man will acknowledge that constantly judging this fact later doesn't enlighten us about man's history'. [15]

The beleaguered editor then concludes that they have finally found a way out of this problem. 'All those writings that he had wanted to discard will find a place in the appendix'. Consequently, Volume Seventeen of the *Rachanabali* is a compilation of Rabindranath's earliest writings, mainly from 1874 to about 1885, but some written later, all of which he had himself declared unworthy of inclusion in his canon, and which he had wished to discard in the face of history.

The whole point about beginnings, of course, is that they are always chosen. In his last published book, *On Late Style* (2006), Edward Said reflected upon one of his own first works, *Beginnings: Intention and Method* (1975), dwelling upon the many aspects of what he calls 'the self-making process'. The whole notion of the beginning, he said there, was about 'the moment of birth and origin, which in the context of history is all the material that goes into thinking about how a given process, its establishment and institution, life, project, and so on, gets started'.[16] The construction of a beginning is the first step in the self-

[15] Ibid., p. 7.

[16] Edward Said, 2006, *On Late Style*, London: Bloomsbury, p. 4.

making process, and is common to all cultures and traditions. His book, *Beginnings*, therefore, had explored

> how the mind finds it necessary at certain times to retrospectively locate a point of origin for itself as to how things begin.... To locate a beginning in retrospective time is to ground a project ... in that moment, which is always subject to revision. Beginnings of this sort necessarily involve an intention that either is fulfilled, totally or in part, or is viewed as totally failed, in successive time.[17]

Self-fashioning was the term introduced by Stephen Greenblatt (*Renaissance Self-Fashioning*, 1980) for what Said calls 'the self-making process', to describe the course of constructing one's identity and public persona according to a set of interrelated social principles. Authors themselves participate in the work of construction, often writing masterpieces of autobiographical self-justification (Rabindranath's *Jībansmṛti* or Coleridge's *Biographia Literaria*) for a centrepiece in which that self-construction is enshrined. In Western culture, as Said suggests in passing above, that moment in retrospective time which is set as the beginning of a project or a life in writing is 'always subject to revision', either by the writers themselves or usually by their critics. Here, however, Bengali literary critics have by and large overwhelmingly endorsed Rabindranath's *own* construction of his beginnings—in writings that range from *Jībansmṛti* to *Sahitye aitihāsikatā*—repeating the story he created and repeatedly reiterated, of the lonely child immersed in his interiority, awakening at the touch of natural beauty. A critic such as Prabodhchandra Sen, who has written extensively on the subject of early Rabindranath, returns (even while acknowledging that 'beginnings always have prior beginnings', which are Rabindranath's own words) to Rabindranath's *Jībansmṛti* itself as the best source of information for the period that 'preceded the dawn' in his life's works. That dawn is dated, according to him, at 1877, at the start of Rabindranth's involvement, at sixteen, with the family periodical, *Bhāratī*, when he began to publish prolifically in prose and verse in the pages of that journal, which had been set up expressly for that purpose.[18] It would take about another four or five years, however,

[17] Ibid., pp. 4–5.

[18] Prabodhchandra Sen, 1998, '*Rabīndranāther bālyaracanā*,' ['Rabindranath's

for the poet to attain the subjectivity that characterized his best and most luminous poetry, as he himself had always maintained.

'An Enormous Hole in the Fabric of History'

In an introduction to the collected works of Hemchandra Bandyopadhyay, *Hemcandra-racanāsambhār*, the editor of the volume, noted literary critic Pramathanath Bisi, began his discussion of that poet's works by reporting a couple of experiences. Fifty years ago (which would have been in 1921), he said, he had one day asked Rabindranath, 'you have written about Bankimchandra, Madhusudan, Biharilal and others, but why have you been silent on the subject of Hemchandra and Nabinchandra?' The reply had been both dismissive and terse: 'They had nothing to say'. The conversation stopped there. Following this, Pramathanath then describes an experience at a syllabus committee meeting for Bengali literature at the postgraduate level many years later. As a committee member, he had arrived at the meeting to see that the planned syllabus had omitted Hemchandra and Nabinchandra, because those who had planned it had felt that 'nobody read the poetry of Hem-Nabin anymore, as nobody wrote in that manner and in that sort of language nowadays'. An outspoken member of the committee had then remarked—'in that case, one should first eliminate the *Caryāpad* from the syllabus as nobody reads that anymore, and even if they read it they do not understand it, and of course there is no question of writing in that manner. There was no answering this uncomfortable truth, and therefore Hem-Nabin remained a part of the syllabus'.[19] The same committee member then said,

---

Childhood Writings], in Gargi Datta (ed.), *Bhorer pākhi o anayānya prabandha* [The Bird of Dawn and Other Essays], Calcutta: Ananda Publishers, p. 59.

[19] Pramathanath Bisi, 1971, Introduction to *Hemcandra racanā-sambhār*, Calcutta: Mitra & Ghosh, p. i. The *Caryāpad* was a twelfth-century manuscript fragment believed to be the earliest extant specimen of Bengali literature. A collection of short songs by Buddhist teachers of the Sahajiya cult, it was discovered by Haraprasad Sastri in 1916 and edited under the title *Bauddha gān o dohā*. Its discovery pushed back the history of Bengali literature by several centuries and it was incorporated in the Bengali syllabus as the starting point of Bengali literature in Calcutta University. It remains a prescribed text for university students of Bengali to this day.

> Hem-Nabin's poetry may not be of the highest standard, but if you leave it out, you create an enormous hole in the fabric of history (*itihāse masta ektā ched pore yāy*). You cannot always think only of incorporating works of the best quality in the syllabus; even if the standard of a work is lower, if that work is a part of history, then there is no option but to include it.[20]

Rabindranath's brusque reply to Pramathanath Bisi regarding his attitude to Hemchandra and Nabinchandra should not have surprised the well-read critic. Rabindranath had already expressed this opinion in print on many occasions, as any dedicated reader of his would have known. However, if Pramathanath had asked the question hoping to elicit from the poet an admission that his first poetic compositions had indeed been written under the direct influence especially of Hemchandra, which they indisputably had, then Rabindranath's terseness is understandable. Even a cursory glance at the seventeenth volume of the *Rabindra rachanabali*, which contains all that Rabindranath had felt ought *not* find a place in his Collected Works, which included published and unpublished poems rescued from notebooks and journals from 1874 onward, when he was just thirteen, shows the direct impress of the famous older poet upon the teenage boy. Remarkably, these early poems—among which are '*Abhilāsh*' [Covetousness] (published anonymously in the *Tattvabodhinī patrikā*, November-December 1874), '*Hok bhārater jay*' [Victory to Bharat] (published in the *Bāndhab*, January–February 1875), '*Prakṛtir khed*' [Nature's Grievance], '*Hindumelāy upahār*' [Gift for the Hindu Mela] (published in the *Amritabazaar patrika*, 25 February 1875), '*Dillī Darbār*' [Delhi Durbar], and '*Bhāratī*' [Of India] (published in *Bhāratī*, July–August 1877)—are almost overwhelmingly political. Written exactly in the style of his famous and influential predecessors whom he later so deplored, Nabinchandra Sen and Hemchandra Bandyopadhyay, many of these rousing patriotic poems were written for political occasions such as the Hindu Mela, where they were read out loud before large audiences, reminding us that one of his stated reasons for liking Biharilal's poetry was that it made 'no attempt to please gatherings at meetings'.

Two poems, in particular, show the direct influence of Hemchandra Bandyopadhyay's famous nationalistic poems. These were '*Prakṛtir*

[20] Ibid.

khed' and '*Hindumelāy upahar*', written when Rabindranath was fourteen, in 1875. The first was published anonymously initially in the *Tattvabodhinī Patrikā*, edited at the time by Jyotirindranath Tagore, friend, patron, older brother, and enthusiast, and then revised for a second appearance in a periodical called *Pratibimba* [Reflections]. (This was a poem whose lines Rabindranath had recited from memory a full sixty-four years later when asked about its authorship by Sajanikanta Das.[21]) It described the piteous condition of the country, '*Abhāgī bhārat*' [wretched Bharat], in widow's garb, being addressed by Nature, who speaks of her distress and grief. In one instance, the poet has Nature ask that this fertile land be transformed into desert, destroying all in its sorrow.

Read out by Rabindranath at the second meeting of a society called *Biddvajan Samāgam* or 'Learned Gathering' on 9 May 1875, the recited poem was described in Akshaychandra Sarkar's weekly, *Sādhāraṇī*, as being 'extremely pleasing' as 'during its reading tears fell from our eyes at the remembrance of the current pitiable condition of *Bhāratbhūmi*.[22] At the meeting the previous year, the first item had been a recitation of some of Hemchandra Bandyopadhyay's rousing patriotic poems by a youth, and the enormous shadow of Hemchandra Bandyopadhyay upon both '*Prakṛtir khed*' and '*Hindumelāy upahar*' has been acknowledged by commentators. Prashanta Pal endorses Prabodhchandra Sen's opinion, that 'Just as Hemchandra's '*Bhārat saṅgīt*' influenced the poem '*Hindumelāy upahār*', so did Hemchandra's poem '*Bharat bilāp*' spread its shadow over the poem '*Prakṛtir khed*',' pointing out that the patriotic poetry Rabindranath was writing at this time was closely modelled upon the tone, language, and metre (*bhāb-bhāshā-chanda*) of Hemchandra's poetry.[23] The metre Rabindranath used for this poem was used by Hemchandra in his poem '*Hatāśer ākkhep*', and Prashanta Pal points to an interesting movement from the first to the second version of the poem ['*Prakṛtir khed*'] from the type of Hemchandra to that of Biharilal's *Sāradāmaṅgal*, which Rabindranath had admitted to admiring greatly

[21] Prabodhchandra Sen, *Bhorer pākhi*, p. 107.

[22] Akshaychandra Sarkar (ed.), 1875, *Sādhāraṇī*, *Jaishṭha* [May–June].

[23] Prashantakumar Pal, 2007, *Rabijibani*, Vol. 1, Calcutta: Ananda Publishers, p. 220.

at around this time.[24] Commenting upon the literary development of the teenage Rabindranath in the year 1877, Pal says:

> From the point of view of fact [rather than of literary criticism] what is noticeable is that at the time Rabindranath's poetry, immersed in the vision of its own 'unclear shadowy image of itself', was engaged in travelling an imaginary dream-world of love and despair, while his prose came much closer to reality in order to capture the mystery of life and mind. There are reasons for this too. In poetry, he did not consider the example of Madhusudan worth taking, and although he liked Hemchandra's *Bṛttasaṃhār*, his poetic nature was such that he could not follow along that path; Biharilal's manner of composition did influence him, but was insufficient for the full flowering of his self-expression. As a result, apropos his poetic subject matter and style of expression, he had to find his own way through a variety of experimentation.[25]

Once again, we have the same formulation, in the same words, which are, as we have seen, Rabindranath's own words—'to find one's own way on one's own'—reiterated by poet and his critics alike in any discussion of the early formation of Rabindranath's poetic style.

The poem '*Hindumelāy upahār*' was composed and recited at the ninth edition of the Hindu Mela on 11 February 1875, and is Rabindranath's first publication signed in his own name. Subsequently, appearing in the bilingual *Amritabazaar patrika* on 25 February 1875, the poem rehearsed once more the formula made famous by Hemchandra in *Bhārat saṅgīt*:

Bhārat-kaṅkāl ār ki ekhan
Pāibe hāyre nūtan jīban;
Bhārater bhashne āgun jvāliyā
Ār ki kakhana dibere jyoti

Omār āñdhār āsuk ekhan
Maru hoye yāk bhārat kānan,
Candra surya hok meghe nimagan,
Prakṛti-sṛṅkhalā chiṅḍiyā yāk.

'Will skeletal India now find a new life, alas? Will flames ever rise from the ashes of the country, giving light? .... Let the darkest night come

[24] Ibid.
[25] Ibid., p. 270.

now / Let Bharat's gardens turn into desert / Sun and moon be covered in cloud, the order of nature be torn' was the general tenor of the questions asked and of the answers given repeatedly in the poem. The image of the arid landscape of the desert as a metaphor for the current condition of the country was used memorably by Hemchandra in *Bhārat Saṅgīt*, published five years earlier in 1870 in the pages of the *Education Gazette* edited by Bhudev Mukhopadhyay:

Hoyeche śmaśān e bhāratbhūmi
Kāre uccaiśvare dākitechi āmi?
Golāmer jāt śikheche golāmi!
    Ār ki Bhārat svajīb āche?

This land of Bharat has been turned into a desert
Who am I calling for so loudly?
A race of slaves has learnt slavery!
    Is Bharat still alive?[26]

Nabinchandra Sen wrote, in his autobiography, of seeing the teenage Rabindranath reciting a poem under a tree at the Hindu Mela; that poem, however, was not this one. That poem, called '*Dillī darbār*', was composed a couple of years later, and recited at the grounds of the Hindu Mela in 1877, following the Delhi Durbar organized by Lord Lytton in Delhi on 1 January 1877. The Hindu Mela ran into trouble with the police that year and could not be held as planned. Nevertheless, Rabindranath recited the poem and song he had prepared for the occasion under a large tree on the fair grounds. Nabinchandra recalled:

> I remember, while on holiday in Calcutta, I had visited a 'National mela' being held in a garden in some Calcutta suburb in 1876 or 1877. A year or so before that, my *Palasir Juddha* had been published and had then begun being enacted in a Calcutta theatre. A newly acquainted friend caught hold of me in the crush of the mela and said that somebody wished to be introduced to me. He took me by the hand and led me to the shade of an enormous tree in a corner of the park. I saw a good-looking young man wearing a loose white long-shirt and pants (*ijār-cāpkān*) standing there. About eighteen or nineteen years old, peaceful and still, as if a golden

[26] Hemchandra Bandyopadhyay, 1971, '*Bhārat saṅgīt*', *Hemcandra Racanā-Sambhār*, Calcutta: Mitra & Ghosh, p. 400.

> statue of a god had been erected under that tree. My friend said, 'This is Maharshi Debendranath's youngest son, Rabindranath.' His older brother, Jyotirindranath, was a fellow student with me in Presidency College. I looked, and saw the same good looks, the same style in clothes. After we had smiled and shaken hands, he brought out a 'notebook' from his pocket and sang a few songs and recited some poems in a singing voice. I was charmed at the sweetness, the tunefulness of his voice and at the talented spontaneity and sweetness of his poems.
>
> One or two days later, while visiting babu Akshaychandra Sarkar at his invitation at his home at Chuchura, I told him how I had heard the songs and poems of a wonderful young man at the National Mela, and that I believed one day he would be a talented poet and singer. Akshaybabu said, 'Who? Rabi Thakur? He is a sweet and sour green mango of the Thakur household.' After that, sixteen years have passed. Today it is 1893. My prediction has come true—today the unripe mango is a full-fledged '*phajli*'. Bengali literature and the Bengali people are made proud by the fragrance of his talent.[27]

This poem was so strident on the subject of British rule and on contemporary sycophants of the British that it was impossible for it to be published in any current newspaper or journal, and it was 'made to disappear' on the advice of well-wishers, who circulated it 'privately from hand to hand', Rabindranath later recalled.[28] A version of the poem, with the word 'Mughal' replacing all references to the British, reaches us due to its inclusion in Jyotirindranath's play, *Svapnamaẏī* (1882), where it starts:

> *Dekhicha nā aẏi Bhārat-sāgar, aẏi go himādri dekhicha ceye,*
> *Pralaẏ-kāler nibiṛ āñdhār, bhārater bhāl pheleche cheye…*
>
> [Do you not see there Bharat's ocean, there over the Himadri mountains
> The dark night of the storm has spread over Bharat's destiny…][29]

The period 1876-77 was also the time when Rabindranath composed a song whose first lines were '*Ek sūtre bāñdhiyāchi sahasrati man / Ek kārye sañpiyāchi saharsa jīban*' [We have tied a thousand minds with the same thread / We have dedicated a thousand lives to the

[27] *Āmār Jīban*, *Nabinchandra rachanabali*, Vol. 3, pp. 58–9.

[28] Rabindranath Tagore, letter to Sajanikanta Das from Mongpu, cited in Prashanta Pal, 2007, *Rabijibani*, Vol. 1, p. 240.

[29] Ibid.

same work], which remains famous to this day, still sung on national occasions with some regularity. Printed for the first time in the second edition of his brother Jyotirindranath's play, *Purubikram* (1879) only to be left out of the third edition, the rousing marching tune of this song had the words '*Bande mātaram*' added to its chorus when it was printed in Jyotirindranath's edition, *Saṅgītprakāśikā*, in 1905, perhaps because of the heated political background of the Swadeshi movement unfolding in the country at that time.[30] The complicated history of this song, as it was composed, and then appeared and reappeared in plays and performances in these years reflects quite accurately the national feeling that animated almost every thinking person in the circle around Rabindranath and in wider society at this time in Bengal. Recalling the rendition of this song to great patriotic feeling at the secret society called the *Sanjībanī Sabhā* that had been set up by Jyotirindranath around 1876, Rabindranth wrote, in a chapter titled '*Svadeśīkatā*' [Patriotism] in his *Jībansmṛti*, of an elderly Rajnarain Basu, 'eyes burning, heart suffused with feeling, waving his hands enthusiastically' as he joined all of them in singing—'not noticing at all if he was in tune or not'—*ek sūtre bāṅdhiyāchi sahasrati man*.[31]

In an article on Rabindranath's juvenilia, Prabodhchandra Sen points out that one of the first poems Rabindranath wrote in what he referred to as the 'hardbound Lets Diary' was a poem in the heroic style called '*Pṛthvirājer parājay*' [Prithwiraj's Defeat], written in February 1873. The valiant wars fought by the twelfth-century king, Prithviraj Chauhan, glorified in nationalist annals as the last Hindu king to sit upon the throne of Delhi, were a popular subject among nationalist poets, to the extent that even Michael Madhusudan—hardly only a nationalist—had written his first English verse tale, *The Captive Ladie* (1849), on the subject. All around him, Rabindranath's elder brothers too were engaged, in these years, in nationalist activity of every kind, from the organization of the Hindu Mela to the setting up of secret societies. The lurid description of the meetings of the *Sanjībanī Sabhā*, the secret society at which the song '*ek sūtre...*' was sung with some

[30] Prashanta Pal, 2007, *Rabijibani*, Vol. 1, p. 244. Both the notation (*svaralipi*) and the song were attributed to Rabindranath in this book.

[31] Rabindranath Tagore, *Jībansmṛti, Rabindra rachanabali*, Vol. 9, p. 465.

enthusiasm, gives a vivid indication of the attraction of the smoke and terror of underground extremist nationalist movements then:

> On the day that a new member was ordained into this society the president wore red linen and arrived at the *sabhā*. A manuscript of Vedic mantras had been brought from the Adi Brahmo Samaj Library and kept here wrapped in red silk. On both sides of the table were two skulls, within which two candles used to burn from the eye sockets. The skull was a sign of dead Bharat. The meaning of the lit candles was that we must infuse life into the dead country and open the eyes of its knowledge (*gṅyāncakkhu*). This was the basic idea behind this business.[32]

Speaking of the period between the writing of that first poem, '*Pr̥thvirājer parājay*' (1873) to that of '*Dillī Darbār*' (1876), Prabodhchandra Sen says that the note of patriotism that permeates most of the poems written by Rabindranath at this time was due to 'the contemporary just-aroused national consciousness', continuing, 'Everybody, including Rangalal, Hemchandra, Nabinchandra, Satyendranath and Jyotirindranath were uplifted by that patriotism. In fact, the Hindu Mela was merely the exteriorization of that national awakening'.[33] Rabindranath's contribution to his older brother's theatrical exploits at this time is enshrined in another song he contributed to Jyotirindranath's hit play of 1876, *Sarojini or the Attack at Chittor*, a fervent hymn glorifying the self-sacrifice of the Hindu widows who had jumped into the flames of funeral pyres after the Rajputs were defeated at Chittor, '*jval jval cita! dvigun dvigun*' [Burn, burn, pyre! twice as high]. The maddened response of the hysterical crowds to this scene on the stage as the song was sung, where an actual fire would be lit, and into which the actresses in red saris, wearing flowers or with garlands in hand, would jump, singeing their hair or clothes in the process, has been described by Binodini, the prominent actress who played the lead role in the play.[34]

Banishing the poems written for such occasions from his formal corpus of poetical works, Rabindranath sought to do what Pramathanath

[32] Ibid., p. 266.

[33] Prabodhchandra Sen, *Bhorer pākhi*, p. 57.

[34] Binodini Dasi, 1969, '*Āmār abhinetrī jīban*', *Āmār kathā o anyānya racanā*, Calcutta, pp. 106–7.

Bisi recalled the syllabus committee member doing, eliminating those poems from the canon that did not fit in with his notion of what poetry was. Disregarding the poems that are a testament to his early passionate involvement in the politically charged atmosphere of his teenage years would, however, be a disservice to literary criticism on the subject in two respects. First, it would, as was pointed out in the syllabus committee meeting then, 'create an enormous hole in the fabric of history', in that if we do not acknowledge the impact of poets such as Hemchandra upon Rabindranath's early poems, we do not get an accurate picture of the era, nor can we arrive at a proper estimation of the literary field as it was. Second, the distortion that results from such an altered picture of literary activity would be a disservice to a more complete understanding of Rabindranath's own achievement in wresting himself away from the overwhelming mood of the age to create, with the hard labour that accompanies consummate craftsmanship, the particular poetic achievements that he had to forge, as he repeatedly said, in his own way and on his own terms.

Early Style vis-à-vis Late Style

In his famous essay, 'Beethoven's Late Style', Adorno starts by pointing to a series of qualities that distinguish late style, qualities that seem equally applicable to the question of early style, or the style of the period, in a writer such as Rabindranath, that 'preceded the dawn':

> The maturity of a significant artist's late works is not like that of fruits. They are not usually round but, rather, furrowed, even ruptured; they tend to lack sweetness, and are prickly in their refusal to be merely tasted. They show none of that harmony which the classicist aesthetic is accustomed to demanding of a work of art, and the marks they bear are more those of history than growth.[35]

Speaking of a young Rabindranath, Akshaychandra Sarkar had used, similar to Adorno, the image of the fruit—the 'sweet and sour green mango'—not yet round, not ripe, not completely sweet. That

[35] Theodor Adorno, 2009, 'Beethoven's Late Style', in Rolf Tiedemann (ed.), *Night Music: Essays on Music 1928-1962*, translated by Wieland Hoban, Calcutta: Seagull, p. 11.

attainment of maturity and flavour in Rabindranath many years later is then compared by Nabinchandra Sen, with whom he had had that particular conversation, to the fully fledged ripe '*phajli*' variety of mango, known for its fragrance.[36] Showing 'none of that harmony which the classicist aesthetic is accustomed to demanding of a work of art', Rabindranath's early works are not yet representative of the poet's works in maturity, leading to a dissatisfaction within the poet himself as to their status. Adorno feels that Beethoven's last works, which are 'highly expressionless, distant formations', similarly, are not at all like the composer's magnificent middle period compositions, and he tries to find the key to a comprehension of the late style by closely scrutinising the formal element of these works, and their relation to convention.[37] Literary criticism on the subject of Rabindranath's early writings struggles with a problem similar to that faced in art theory when analysing Beethoven's late style, in that such criticism 'seldom lack[s] references to his life and fate', taking the works 'to the limits of art, and closer to the document'.[38] Adorno's thesis on late style, it seems, is also suited in most part to the early style of Rabindranath, whose early writings embody a personality not yet fully formed, still finding its way in terms of its relation to convention and creative self-expression, writings that are, in Adorno's words, 'prickly in their refusal to be merely tasted'.

If Rabindranath's first 'political' poems had been written in the hot flush of nationalist imaginings, in the style of Hemchandra Bandyopadhyay's more stirring patriotic poetry, then another fundamentally important impress upon his poetic composition at this time was that of English poetry and English literary convention. At seventeen, Rabindranath travelled to England for the first time in the September of 1878, and in preparation for his voyage, he was sent to his brother Satyendranath, who was district and sessions judge

[36] In Akshaychandra's own account of the incident, however, he recalled Nabinchandra as having expressed the feeling that the young Rabindranath was like a bud that would one day be transformed into a flower in full bloom, to which another friend interjected, 'one worries if in the end he turns out to be an unripe sweet-sour mango'. Nabinchandra's own account of that day, however, has Akshaychandra use the simile of the unripe mango. See Prashanta Pal, *Rabijibani*, Vol. 1, p. 240.

[37] Theodor Adorno, 2009, 'Beethoven's Late Style'.

[38] Ibid., p. 12.

at Ahmedabad at this time, where he embarked upon a self-inflicted crash course in English language and literature. Of this experience, he wrote:

> It was because my English was extremely raw that I sat down with a dictionary the entire day and began to read many books in English. From childhood, this was a habit I had, that even if I could not understand a language completely, it did not stop me from reading. From whatever little I did understand, I would construct something in my mind and make do with this quite well.[39]

(This was a policy that served him in his initiation into the French language as well, when he read and translated extensively from Victor Hugo. Translations preoccupied him deeply at this time; he was reading and translating from Tukaram, *Macbeth*, and Kalidasa's *Kumarasambhava*, publishing, within the next couple of years, translations of Edwin Arnold and Christina Rosetti, of Thomas Moore, Burns, Byron, Shelley, and Matthew Arnold, among others.) Worrying about his grasp of the English language, he characteristically jumped in at the deep end, asking his brother to bring him the reading materials that would enable him to 'write a history of English literature in Bengali'. In immediate response, he was presented with 'scores of books' on the subject, including one that he depended upon more than most, H.A. Taine's *History of English Literature*, published comparatively recently in 1871.[40] Out of these readings he then fashioned a series of essays that began to be published sequentially in *Bhāratī* in 1878 such as '*Syāksan jātī o ayṅglo-syāksan sāhitya*', which dealt with the Roman conquest and Anglo-Saxon presence in Britain, translating portions of *Beowulf* and Caedmon's *Genesis* and *Exodus* in the process. This was succeeded by '*Biyātrīce, dānte o tāhār kābya*' upon the nature of love in Dante, and '*Pitrārkā o larā*' [Petrarch and Laura], where he translated extensively from Petrarch, while an essay on Goethe ('*Gete o tāñhār praṇayinīgaṇ*') and another on the Norman Race and Anglo-Norman Literature in two parts followed, all in the same year.

[39] Rabindranath, *Jibansmṛti*, p. 358.

[40] H.A. Taine, 1871, *History of English Literature*, translated from the French by H. Van Laun, Vol.1, London: Chatto and Windus.

More important than any of these preliminary writings on the history of English and European literature were a series of essays that appeared at this time in *Bhāratī* that grappled with the issue that had so exercised Bankimchandra in his essay on Iswar Gupta's poetry: What is poetry? Volume Seventeen of the *Rachanabali* reprints thirty-one pieces in all that Rabindranath wrote at this juncture on the subjects of literature and poetry; the titles vary from '*Kābya: spashṭa ebaṃ aspashṭa*' [Poetry: Clarity and Obscurity] and '*Kabitār upādān rahasya (Mystery)*' [Poetry's Source: Mystery] to '*Sāhitya o sabhyatā*' [Literature and Civilization], '*Sāhityer saundarya*' [The Beauty of Literature], '*Sāhityer faurab*' [Literature's Pride] and simply, '*Sāhitya*' [Literature]. As is evident from the titles of the essays, the young practitioner is clearing a space for his own practice in the literary field of the age. In each of these brief excursions into the nature of poetry and literature, he is concerned with defending and establishing his domain critically from the attacks, both perceived and actual, of contemporary critics, while at the same time trying to formulate within his own mind the fundamental operations of these categories for himself.

Two essays among this welter of thoughts stand out clearly: '*Bāṅgālī kabi naẏ*' [The Bengali Is Not a Poet] and '*Bāṅgālī kabi naẏ kena*' [Why the Bengali Is Not a Poet], written in response to a debate around the subject in literary journals.[41] In the first essay, Rabindranath asserted that 'One does not become a poet just because one has a vivid imagination. It is necessary to have a well-educated, civilized and superior imagination', showing how a good poet might show a lack of proportion by quoting from Marlow's 'The Passionate Shepherd to his Love' ['Come live with me and be my love'], bringing to mind Rangalal's long excursion into Shakespeare's *Venus and Adonis* to show how it was coarse when compared to Bharatchandra in his essay of 1852 on Bengali literature.[42] In '*Bāṅgālī kabi naẏ kena*' the examples are taken from modern Bengali literature. Criticizing Nabinchandra Sen's *Abakāśranjinī*, he wrote that the poetry there was 'so lifeless and tasteless that one clearly sees that the poet has not felt

[41] These two essays were written in 1880 in response to an essay in the *Baṅgadarśan*, presumably by Bankimchandra, called '*Bāṅgālī kabi keno*' [Why the Bengali Is a Poet], and by Kaliprasanna Ghosh in the *Bāndhab*, called '*Nirab kabi*' [The Silent Poet].

[42] *Rabindra rachanabali*, Vol. 17, pp. 219, 221.

with his heart what he describes, he has only written it because he thought it necessary to write'.[43] Comparing it unfavourably with both Biharilal and with Shelley's *Epipsychidion* and 'The Woodman and the Nightingale', from which he quotes extensively, he lays out the poetic theories that were the backdrop of compositions such as *Bhagnahṛdaẏ* (1881).

The literary ideas that Rabindranath was grappling with in this period that came to him from the Western hemisphere were almost never taken ungrudgingly or in an uncontested manner. Always resistant to the language of colonial power, Rabindranath was still remarkable in his openness to what he responded to from within that corpus. Taking what he 'thought good and liked best' (which was what the native founders of the Hindu College had said they would take from Western education in 1816) from English and European literature, he repeatedly defended his right to do so, as a young Bengali writer, almost exactly in the manner Borges does in the famous essay 'The Argentinean Writer and Tradition'. In an essay in *Bhāratī* in 1882 written in response to his old friend, interlocutor and mentor, Akshaychandra Chaudhuri, he reacted impatiently to the former's idea that the influence of Western literature upon the Bengali language was too great, and that contemporary Bengali literature had become artificial because modern Bengali poetry had been displaced from its true indigenous context. Rabindranath wrote sharply:

> It is absolutely unnatural that our poetry should not reflect the furious change that has been felt in society, that we shall somehow overcome our present to cling to the cloth of our ancient poets, that when all around us everything is topsy-turvy, we should remain unaffected. The author [of the article] wishes to build a jailhouse of the imagination, but it is difficult to see why poets should willingly enter that jail just because its walls are made of this country's bricks.[44]

Rabindranath left for England for the first time from Bombay on 20 September 1878, with a desire to either appear for the ICS examinations or qualify as a barrister. In the event, he did neither. Returning to Calcutta in February 1880 after a year and a half

[43] Ibid., Vol. 17, p. 227.

[44] Ibid., p. 241.

without having accomplished a respectable passage into a respectable profession, having been suddenly recalled home by his father for no pressing reason that is apparent to the historian of these events, he resumed life at home in much the same situation as when he had left. Yet his life changed forever with the passage of these crucial months. Prashanta Pal writes that this trip to England

> created a fundamental change in his thinking. We know that although he went to England for further studies, he did not live his life there like a bookworm immersed in professional upliftment alone; he observed and analysed the gifts and particular character of the English with a very sharp eye and analytical insight; alongside this he entered deeply into the world of English literature mostly by his own efforts and partly due to the teaching prowess of Henry Morley.[45]

To Morley belongs the distinction of being the only teacher who ever inspired Rabindranath; Edward Thompson reported him speaking about 'the pleasure which came from reading the *Religio Medici* [1642, by Sir Thomas Browne, 1605-82] with Henry Morley. Also, I read *Coriolanus* with him, and greatly enjoyed it. His reading was beautiful. And *Antony and Cleopatra*, which I liked very much'.[46] Rabindranath spoke in *Chelebelā* [Boyhood] of how the visit to England changed him: 'I went to England, but did not become a barrister. I was not jolted out of the foundational structures of my early life, but I took into myself the handshake of East with West—I found the meaning of my name within my heart.'[47] This meeting of the East and West in Rabindranath's style, his persona, his form and his works has been, of course, remarked upon extensively by critics in a derisive (Dineshchandra Sen) or admiring (Buddhadeva Bose) way.

Although he was described by his biographer Prabhat Mukhopadhyay as having left as 'a shy boy' and having returned as a 'voluble youth', the publications of this period immediately after his return, between 1880 and 1882, bear testimony to the fact that although he was writing and publishing with regularity, this was still a

[45] Prashanta Pal, *Rabijibani*, Vol. 2, p. 70.

[46] Edward Thompson, 1979, *Rabindranath Tagore: Poet and Dramatist*, Calcutta: Riddhi, p. 31.

[47] Rabindranath Tagore, *Chelebelā*, p. 629.

period of some turbulence. It was in the year 1877 (identified as the end of his childhood period by Prabodhchandra Sen) that Rabindranath had begun to publish prolifically in the journal *Bhāratī* that had been set up at the initiative of his beloved older brother Jyotirindranath. The journal sought to find a permanent space. The journal sought for the many-sided literary productions of both his younger brother and his friend, Akshaychandra Chaudhuri, with whom the young Rabindranath cut his apprentice teeth in disputation, argumentation, and creative production.

The first issue of *Bhāratī* carried three items by Rabindranath—the poem '*Bhāratī*' [Of India], the short story '*Bhikhāriṇī*' [Beggar-Woman], and the first instalment of the critical essay, '*Meghnādbadh Kābya*'. This was followed by his first novella, *Karuṇā* [Pity], which appeared serially in the same journal, and remained uncollected in his *Rachanabali*.[48] Reference to the music of India having fallen silent in the poem *Bhāratī*, and its first lines, '*śudhāi ayi go bhāratī tomāy / tomār o bīṇā nīrab kena?*' [I ask you, o country / why is your *bīṇā* silent?], are immediately evocative of Derozio's famous sonnet, 'Harp of India', where the same question is asked, 'Thy music once was sweet—who hears it now?...Neglected, mute, and desolate art thou…'[49] Derozio's poem had already been translated famously into Bengali by his older brother, Dwijendranath Tagore, in 1874, and Rabindranath did not include '*Bhāratī*' in any of his published compilations as long as he lived. The critical essay on Madhusudan too suffered the same fate.[50] His career in *Bhāratī* continued unabated while he was in England, from where he sent home a series of letters

[48] Rabindranath called *Karuṇā* an example of 'what in rustic Bengali is called *jyāṭhāmi*'—an untranslatable word that is derived from the word *jyāṭhā* or elder uncle to denote a youth behaving authoritatively, as if he were much older than his age. Prashanta Pal, *Rabijibani*, Vol.1, p. 270.

[49] Henry Derozio, 1827, 'The Harp of India', *Poems*, Calcutta, in Rosinka Chaudhuri ed., 2008, *Derozio, Poet of India: The Definitive Edition*, Delhi: Oxford University Press, p. 96.

[50] Published serially over five numbers of *Bhāratī* in its first year of publication, this essay was not included by Rabindranath in any anthology as long as he was alive. He famously repudiated his own youthful stance in that essay later, writing in *Jībansmṛti* of how he had written it 'impelled by the force of youth… . When other abilities are not in evidence, then the ability to take a dig at something is sharper. I too had torn into that immortal poem in the hope of becoming immortal myself. I

published in it as *Ẏurop yātri kono baṅgiya yubaker patra* [Letters from A Certain Bengali Youth Travelling in Europe], later collected in book form as *Ẏurop-prabāsīr patra* [Letters from an Exile in Europe], comprising many essays in criticism as well as individual poems. His first publication in book form in November 1878, *Kabi-kāhinī* [Poet's Tales] (originally published in *Bhāratī* in the previous year), was produced just after he left for England in September 1878, and his second, *Banaphul* [Wildflowers], flagged his return, published in March 1880 as a welcome-home gift by his brother Somendranath. (These first-book publications were all subsidized by the accounts department at his family home, Jorasanko, paid for and produced by family and friends.) Yet despite this plethora of publications of every variety, among which were some achievements of lasting value, it would be fair to say that in poetry, Rabindranath had not yet found his metier in the style and form that became such a characteristic feature of his poetic vocation.

1881–82: Breaking Away

At the start of the year 1877, Rabindranath had lain down one day in the inner quarters of a corner room in Jorasanko, and written a line upon a slate: *gahana kusuma kunja mājhe* [Within the dense flowering woods]. In his recollection, 'It had one day become very cloudy at mid-day. In that cloud-darkened delight of leisure, lying on my stomach upon a bed in a room, I wrote upon a slate: *gahana kusuma kunja mājhe*. Writing it made me very happy.' And happy he should have rightfully been, for this line was one of the finest in the collection of poems/songs that appeared in every issue of *Bhāratī* save one between the years 1877 to 1878, and was later to be popularly known as *Bhānusiṃher padābalī*. The first line he wrote, however, was not the first poem he published in this collection. He had published the first poem of Bhanusingha in the *Áśvin* [Sept/Oct] issue of *Bhāratī* in 1877; in a different version from its later standardised form, which is how we now know it: '*śānan gagane ghor ghanaghaṭā / niśītha yāminī*

---

began my career in *Bhāratī* with this egoistical piece of writing.' *Rabindra rachanabali*, Vol. 9, p. 466.

re' [Splendidly dark with clouds is the monsoon sky / in the dead of night].

This was the start of the regular serial publication in *Bhāratī* of poems written under the pseudonym Bhanusingha, the name that meant Rabindranath, which appeared listed on the contents page of that periodical as '*Bhānusiṃher kabitā*' ['Bhanusingha's Poems'].[51] The story behind the publication of these poems by a sixteen-year old Rabindranath has been told many times and is well known. Like most of the reconstruction of his early work, this story too is heavily premised upon Rabindranath's own version of its composition as he presented it in *Jībansmṛti*. From 1874 onward, three years before the first line of *Bhanusingha* was written, Akshaychandra Sarkar, Saradacharan Mitra, and Barodakanta Mitra had edited and published a selection of poems they titled *Prācīn kābya saṃgraha* serially in the *Sādhāraṇī* periodical, edited by Akshaychandra. Here, the verses of the medieval Vaishnava poet Vidyapati were reprinted along with footnotes; Rabindranath has described how the volumes of the published periodical were purloined by him from his brother Jyotirindranath's collection. 'My elders were regular subscribers but not regular readers. Therefore, to collect and take them away was not too much trouble'.[52] Reading the poetry of Vidyapati enraptured him, and making a careful study of the use of language in this old dialect in self-made notebooks, he proceeded to fashion in that language a number of poems in the style of the medieval poet.[53]

It should not, perhaps, be surprising that Rabindranath first found his voice in poetry in the disguise of an imagined medieval poet long dead, in a language strangely obscure and archaic, tangentially placed within modern Bengali as it was spoken and written at the time in literary quarters. Inspired by the legend of Thomas Chatterton, whom

[51] The name Bhanusingha was derived from Bhanu, another word for the sun, or Rabi. The full name in both cases would then mean 'lord of the sun'. It has been speculated that the name was one given to him by Kadambari debi.

[52] *Jībansmṛti*, *Rabindra rachanabali*, p. 453.

[53] His mastery over the subject was so complete that a few years later, upon re-reading Akshaychandra's text, he wrote (no doubt goaded by that critic's unsparing criticism of his own poetry so far) a trenchant and unsparing critique of the lazy and slip-shod manner in which much of the work had been done in presenting Vidyapati in *Prācīn kābya saṃgraha.*

he had first heard about from his brother's friend, Akshay Chaudhuri, the person he credited with introducing him to much of English literature in this period, he set about replicating the achievement. 'Keeping aside the unnecessary part about his suicide', he writes, 'I rolled up my sleeves and began my endeavour to become the second Chatterton'.[54] The difficulty and ambiguity of the Maithili dialect (a mixture of old Hindi and Bengali prevalent in eastern India) that he simulated to write these poems appealed to him for precisely those very reasons: their half-hidden, half-revealed nature, similar, he said, to the attraction held by 'the seeds of trees, containing a mystery undiscovered underneath the earth'.[55] Those were seeds that contained embryonically within their encrypted code, in the disguise of Bhanusingha, the core of Rabindranath's poetic vocation, the musicality and mystery that his mature poetry would convey later with a direct intensity. Many other poems that were being published in *Bhāratī* at this time, apart from the ones that belong to this collection of the *Bhānusiṃher padābalī*, were signed with the initial letter 'Bh', revealing the extent to which the half-hidden half-revealed productions of this period shelter under the anonymity of pseudonyms and one-letter signatures, shy of proclaiming their nature and identity out loud and in the open.

Pretending that he had discovered an old and tattered manuscript of a medieval poet named Bhanusingha in the library of the Brahmo Samaj, he read his poems out to a friend. The friend, in turn, excited by their beauty, claimed they were better than anything written by Chandidas or Vidyapati, and wanted them for publication, at which point Rabindranath informed him that the poems were his own by showing him his exercise book in which they had been written. The friend reportedly became very grave, and had to concede, 'Not bad at all'. At the time that the poems were appearing serially in *Bhāratī*, Rabindranath wrote later, inaccurately, but with wry pride in *Jībansmṛti*, an academic called Dr Nishikanta Chattopadhyay had written a dissertation on these poems while in Germany, comparing them to European lyric poetry, thereby obtaining a doctorate on the subject.

[54] *Rabindra rachanabali*, p. 461.

[55] Ibid.

Nevertheless, this section on the Bhanusingha poems in *Jībansmṛti* ends with a disclaimer. While expressing his satisfaction with the language of the poems, which closely resembled the language of the medieval Vaishnava poets, he nevertheless concludes by saying that although their 'feeling was not artificial', they do not stand up to intense scrutiny, as their made-up nature is then revealed; 'they are not like the flowing heart-melting tune of the *nahabaṯ* (*shehnai* performance), but merely like the sound of the contemporary cheap English organ's ding-dong'. In later life too, he referred to this collection as 'an example of unlawful entry (*anādhikār prabeś*) into the precincts of literature', and it has been surmised that he might never have published the poems separately in book form if not for the shocking suicide in April 1884 of his beloved sister-in-law Kadambari Debi, wife of his older brother Jyotirindranath, close friend, childhood companion, and muse, at this time. In the dedication to *Bhānusiṃha ṭhākurer padābalī* he wrote: 'You had requested, many a time, that I publish the poems of Bhanusingha. At that time I did not grant your request. Today I have done so, and you are not here to see it'.[56] Yet his own attachment to these adolescent compositions can be seen from the fact that although he omitted almost every other poem he wrote at this time previous to *Sandhyā-saṅgīt* from the precincts of the *Rachanabali*, this group of poems were not conferred the same ignominy, but remain enshrined in his Collected Works in their rightful place.

In 1881, the year he turned twenty, Rabindranath had written and performed in his first dramatic production, *Bālmīki pratibhā*, at a meeting of the *Biddvajjan Samāgam* on 26 February. In the month of *Baiśakh* [April/May 1881], he then published a volume of lyric poetry called *Bhagnahṛday* [Broken Heart], whose first six cantos had appeared in the preceding issues of *Bhāratī*. *Bhagnahṛday* was a very long poetic drama in thirty-four parts that Rabindranath had felt himself very satisfied with at the time; as he remarks, 'At that time I developed an inordinate pride and tenderness towards this poem—there's no doubt about that'.[57] Its hazy murmur of love was pervasive and intensely felt, and its wistful air and rhythm made it something of a rage among impressionable readers. Khagendranath Chattopadhyay

[56] *Bhānusiṃha ṭhākurer padābalī, Rabindra rachanabali*, Vol. 1, pp. 137–60.

[57] Prashanta Pal, *Rabijibani*, Vol. 2, p. 104.

has remarked that 'with the publication of this book, Rabindranath's name began to be heard among students and youths. He became Bengal's "Shelley"—his dress, his hair, his spectacles, all began to be copied and became the fashion. "Rabibabu" was in the sky, in the air, and to poetry came a new metre and a melancholy air'.[58] But the prevalent dissatisfaction among Rabindranath's vociferous critics with the tone and language of his poetry also began with the publication of *Bhagnahṛdaẏ*. The indirection in his presentation was perceived as wilful, and the language obscure and unclear. Akshaychandra Sarkar wrote in the *Sādhāraṇī* with his usual sarcasm and directness:

> In trying to describe the mist in the heart of the heroine, the poet, in the first verse, has turned his language into a complete enigma. Such a use of mist may be praiseworthy when used sometimes by English poets such as Shelley and others—that does not mean that such vagueness is dear to the Bengali language. The poet Rabindra is inordinately fond of the half-bloomed nature of things. The moonlight that is present in page after page of his poetry is not a clear, bright moonlight; it is a flickering sleepy moonlight that the poet loves. And then on page 31 there is the indifferent impropriety of a phrase such as '*astamān yāminī*' [setting night]. In the first place, the night does not set; on top of that 'setting night' is another form of violence upon the language.[59]

Rabindranath himself was unsparing in his opinion of the poem when the issue of its re-publication in book form came up in 1908 when Manilal Gangyopadhyay had been reissuing some of Rabindranath's early work, such as *Sandhyāsaṅgīt* and *Prabhātsaṅgīt*, from the Indian Publishing House. Pulinbehari Sen writes that the first proofs of the reprints have been preserved in Santiniketan at Rabindra Bhavan; there, after correcting the proof, Rabindranath had written, in English, 'Rubbish!' on the proof pages, and, presumably to Manilal, 'For the love of God do not print this!!' Subsequently the plans to reissue it seem to have been dropped.[60] Early in 1882 he had then published a collection called *Sandhyāsaṅgīt* (of which he had said, as we have seen, in the introduction to the *Rabindra Rachanabali*, 'just as mist is not rain, so too, these poems are not poetry'), while all along, his first

[58] Ibid.

[59] Ibid., p. 105.

[60] Ibid., p. 104.

novel, *Bau-ṭhākurānīr hāṭ*, was being published serially across twelve issues of *Bhāratī* from *Kārtik* [October/November] 1881 to *Āśvin* [September/October] 1882.

It was only in 1882 that a poem appeared that he felt bore the stamp of his own individual voice with a certainty and clarity not evident so far, *Nirjharer svapnabhaṅga* [The Waterfall Awakens from a Dream], first published in *Bhāratī* on 2 December 1882. (When it was later incorporated into a book of poems, *Prabhātsaṅgīt* (1883), the poem had sixty-seven more lines added to the original two hundred and one lines; subsequently, it underwent many changes, and is currently available in the *Rabindra rachanabali* in one hundred and fifty four lines; however, the version in the *Sancayitā* is compressed to a mere forty-three.) When it was first published in *Bhāratī*, it had for company a twin poem by Akshaychandra Chaudhuri called '*Abhimāninī Nirjharinī*', which also accompanied it into the pages of *Prabhātsaṅgīt* because Rabindranath felt it could not be left out, as it had been written in response to '*Nirjharer Svapnabhaṅga*'. The two poems were therefore twinned at birth, and should be read together, he had felt then.

It was with the publication of *Prabhātsaṅgīt* that the tide of literary criticism turned substantially in his favour within the field of Bengali letters—critics and journalists across the spectrum, from Bhudev Mukhopadhyay in the *Education Gazette* to reviewers in the *Somprakāś* and the *Sanjībanī*—all published praise for the simple, unaffected marvel of language accomplished in some of the poems in this volume. Rabindranath grudgingly acknowledged as much of his own early work here: 'In the period of *Sandhyā-saṅgīt* my mind was taken over by a cloying articulation of my inner forceful feelings alone. With the season of *Prabhātsaṅgīt*, a few spontaneous forms began to be seen; that is, these productions were not the flowers but the fruit of harvest, although grown on uneducated, un-tilled farm land'.[61]

A long poem (in some versions perhaps too long), revised over and over again, the free flowing lyricism of *Nirjharer svapnabhaṅga* was contained in a metre and rhythm of astonishing suppleness; the words on the page quiver and tremble with an intensity captured almost entirely through sound and language, constituting a magnum leap

[61] Ibid., p. 132,

forward toward a form and style that was to become so distinctively his own. Revelatory and celebratory in its incantation of the beauty of morning, the poem's narrative resides entirely in language and sensation, capturing the wonder of the world as the poet sees it one extraordinary dawn. While his essays and letters of this period were self-assured, argumentative, and sometimes sharp and impassioned, his poetry was still afloat upon a vague inner turbulence. Returning home from England, he had published, in quick succession, four different volumes—*Bālmīki pratibhā*, *Bhagnahṛdaẏ*, *Rudracaṇḍa*, and *Ẏurop Prabasīr Patra*—each in a separate genre, and each accomplishing some element of success within its own precinct. Yet in the matter of poetry, although he had just published the collection, *Sandhyā-saṅgīt*, he was still to make the advance into his own domain, both in his own perception as well as in the reader's. With this poem, that breakthrough was finally accomplished.

One Extraordinary Dawn

Constructing the story of his beginning as a poet later in life, Rabindranath regarded his poetic accomplishments preceding *Nirjharer Svapnabhaṅga* as merely a prelude. This poem, he said, inaugurated his adult career as a poet, describing it as the Preface or Introduction to his entire poetic corpus ('*āmār samasta kābyer bhūmikā*').[62] Written in one sitting over the entire afternoon and evening of a day of extraordinary experience, Rabindranath has immortalized the poem not only on its own merit, but also upon the basis of the revelation on which it was based, an experience of whose importance he wrote repeatedly. Describing the sensation in *Jībansmṛti*, he wrote:

> At the place where the Sudder Street road came to an end one could see the trees in the garden of perhaps the Free School. One morning I stood on the veranda and looked in that direction. At that time, the sun was rising from behind the leaves of those trees. As I stood there and looked, suddenly, in a moment, the curtain fell from my eyes. I looked, and saw the world and this earth enveloped in an astonishing glory, everything swaying in joy and beauty. Piercing in one moment through the many layers of dejection in which my heart was covered, my entire inner self

[62] Ibid., p. 147.

was scattered in the light of the universe. On that day itself, '*Nirjharer Svapnabhaṅga*' seemed to flow out of me like a waterfall.[63]

This was not the only occasion that Rabindranath had felt such revelatory joy—he catalogues other instances in his childhood and life of a similar nature—but certainly it was the most sustained and powerful experience among them. 'Piercing the veil' was an expression he used repeatedly to indicate, as Dipesh Chakrabarty has pointed out, 'seeing beyond' the '*prātyahik*' or the everyday, which 'was "*anitya*", impermanent, subject to the changes of history. The realm of the poetic laced the everyday but had to be revealed by the operation of the poetic eye'.[64] The expression of wonder insists always upon that which cannot be understood but at the same time that which is undeniably premised upon the exigency of the experience. Ranajit Guha calls this heightened joy of wonder by its name in Indian aesthetics, '*camaṯkārā*', pointing out that it is usually rendered in English as 'supernormal rapture'.[65] Of the three similar childhood experiences cited by Rabindranath in the last essay of his life, *Sāhitye Aitihāsikatā* [Historicality in Literature], of glistening dew, gathering clouds, and a cow licking a foal, each occasion was in fact a repetition or premonition of that central experience on Sudder Street, which was 'a matter of seeing in a way Tagore claims to have been uniquely his own'. Guha then quotes Rabindranath himself in corroboration: 'It is in this [seeing] that one is a poet.'[66] To experience the world as an outsider was a feeling that animated other poems written at this time ('*Prabhāt uṯsav*', '*Ananta maraṇ*' and '*Ananta jīban*', '*Mahā svapna*', '*Sṛshṭi, Stithi, Pralay*'), but nowhere more clearly and extensively as in this one poem, '*Nirjharer svapnabhaṅga*'. The feeling had partly animated his composition of *Bālmīki pratibhā* as well, where, in language that was strangely reminiscent of his experience of writing *Nirjharer svapnabhaṅga*, he had said he wanted to capture how 'a deep

[63] *Rabindra rachanabali*, Vol. 9, p. 492.

[64] Dipesh Chakrabarty, *Provincilaizing Empire*, p. 168. Critic and poet Sankha Ghosh has written on the importance of '*dekhā*' [seeing] to Rabindranath in a special issue of *Deś* in May 2011.

[65] Guha, 2003, *History at the Limits of World-History*, Delhi: Oxford University Press, p. 67.

[66] Ibid., pp. 77, 80.

pity from within had pierced the dacoit's stern exterior. His natural humanity had been covered over by hard habit. One day, there was turmoil, and the inner man was suddenly impelled into the open'.[67]

Whatever the internal impulse of wonder upon which '*Nirjharer Svapnabhaṅga*' was composed, it is in its formal execution that the poem constitutes the rupture in relation to Rabindranath's entire poetic corpus. This might not be his finest poem, and is certainly not among the best poems of his career, but in it, he constructs, out of material he has already played with before in *Bhānusiṃher padābalī*, his particular poetic voice. Discarding the disguise of the Vaishnava poet, he assumes his own contemporary form, in the accomplishment of which there was at work not some mystical revelation alone but a hard fought attainment at a formal level. With this poem, the early style, prickly with the impediment of other poetic preoccupations and voices, largely disappears. If the Hindu mela poems had been written in imitation of Hemchandra and the nationalist feeling in the air at the time, and if the first lyric poems too were modelled in imitation of Biharilal, Shelley, and the other Romantics, then here, in this poem mainly, the tone and rhythm, the language and feeling that permeate his poetic voice—a voice so distinctively his own that it becomes instantly recognizable—are put into place for the first time. What is remarkable about the poem is also the manner in which the poet lets himself loose, sets himself free of all previous conventions and expectations:

Bahudin pare ekti kiraṇ
Guhāy diyeche dekhā,
Pareche āmār āñdhār śalīle
Ekti kaṇaka rekhā.
Prāṇer ābeg rākhite nāri
Thara thara kore kañpiche bāri,
Ṭala-mala jal kare thal thal,
Kal kal kari dhareche tān.
Āji e prabhāte ki jāni kena re
Jāgiyā uṭhece prāṇ.

[After many days has one ray
Appeared in the cave;

[67] *Rabindra rachanabali*, Vol. 1, p. 395.

Upon the dark waters   of my heart
        Has fallen a single trace of light.
    I cannot contain my heart's ardour
    The water trembles, it trembles,
    It quivers, sways and brims over
    It murmurs and warbles and sings.
Today in this morning   I don't know why
        My heart has awakened.]

The translation into English of Rabindranath's Bengali—not only here, but usually—fails on many levels, inevitably; but most of all, it fails to capture the repetition of the words and the rhythm of the lines as they are spoken aloud. In their content and subject matter they repeat the first words of poetry Rabindranath *thought* he read in Vidyasagar's children's primer, '*Jal paṛe, pātā naṛe*' [Water falls, the leaves move], which for him constituted the substance of all poetry. In their original spoken Bengali rhythm, the words work to constitute what Barthes famously called 'the rustle of language': 'to rustle is to make audible the very evaporation of noise: the tenuous, the blurred, the tremulous are received as the signs of an auditory annulation'.[68] 'Can language rustle?' Barthes asks, for it seems impossible, as in language, 'there always remains *too much meaning*' for that to happen.

> But what is impossible is not inconceivable: the rustle of language forms a utopia. Which utopia? That of a music of meaning; in its utopic state, language would be enlarged, I should even say *denatured* to the point of forming a vast auditory fabric in which the semantic apparatus would be made unreal; the phonic, metric, vocal signifier would be deployed in all its sumptuosity, without a sign ever becoming detached from it (ever *naturalising* this pure layer of delectation), but also—and this is what is difficult—without meaning being brutally dismissed, dogmatically foreclosed, in short castrated.[69]

Into that utopia of freedom—to paraphrase Rabindranath in 'Where the Mind is Without Fear'—has this poem awoken; and the poet is aware of the impossible nature of this attainment. Over and over again, in poems ranging from *Balaka* to *Sonār tari* to *Mānasī*, this would be

[68] Roland Barthes, 1989, 'The Rustle of Language', in *The Rustle of Language*, Berkeley: University of California Press, p. 76.
[69] Ibid., p. 77.

the unique character of Rabindranath's achievement, as he touched again and again with a surer and surer touch, this state of utopia where what he achieves in language is 'that meaning which reveals an exemption of meaning or—the same thing—that non-meaning which produces in the distance a meaning henceforth liberated from all the aggression of which the sign, formed in the "sad and fierce history of men," is the Pandora's box'.[70]

It is utopia, as Barthes points out, that often 'guides the investigations of the avant-garde', and it is to be found in many experimentations of the avant-garde. His own discovery of it is far removed from the world of Rabindranath, but has much to say in aid of pinpointing exactly the quality of the auditory that resides in Rabindranath's untranslatable poems. It was while watching, one evening, Antonioni's film on China, particularly a certain scene in which some children sit on a village street against a wall and read aloud together, but each from a different book, that Barthes discovers the rustle of language in the doubly impenetrable Chinese of different simultaneous readings. What he hears, however, in 'a kind of hallucinated perception', is what one hears in the poetry of Rabindranath: 'the music, the breath, the tension, the application'. Is that all one needs, Barthes wonders, 'in order to make language rustle, in the rare fashion, stamped with delectation'—'just speak all at the same time'? 'No, of course not; the auditory scene requires an erotics (in the broadest sense of the term), the élan, or the discovery, or the simple accompaniment of an emotion'. This was present for him in that moment in 'the countenances of the Chinese children', and it is present for the readers of Bengali, 'stamped with delectation', as Barthes felt, when they read the lines '*āji e prabhāte ki jāni kena re / jāgiyā uṇheche prāṇ*' in '*Nirjharer svapnabhaṅga*' above. (Other lines from other poems fulfil a similar function; so we can think of, for instance, the lines in the poem '*Duḥsamay*': '*tabu bihaṅga, ore bihaṅga mor, / ekhani, andha, bandha koro nā pākhā*'.[71]) What Barthes calls the 'erotics', the 'élan', or the 'simple accompaniment of an emotion' are an essential adjunct to the sound of the language in Rabindranath's best

[70] Ibid., p. 78.

[71] '*Duḥsamay*,' in *Kalpanā, Rabindra rachanabali*, Vol. 4, pp. 105–6. Translated imperfectly, the line means, 'And yet, O bird, O bird of mine, / Do not blind, don't close your wings just now.'

poetry, which accomplishes its effect upon these twin premises. The reader of poetry, especially the poetry of Rabindranath, must feel akin to the ancient Greek as described by Hegel that Barthes ends his brief essay with: 'he interrogated, Hegel says, passionately, uninterruptedly, the rustle of branches, of springs, of winds, in short, the shudder of Nature, in order to perceive in it the design of an intelligence'. To interrogate that shudder of meaning, Barthes says in closing, is to listen to 'the rustle of language', 'that language which for me, modern man, is my Nature'.[72]

Adorno, speaking of the apotheosis of Beethoven's accomplishment in the *Appassionata*, had said it was 'more compacted, closed, and "harmonic" than the late quartets', as well as 'in equal measure more subjective, autonomous and spontaneous'.[73] The same could be said of Rabindranath's mature poetry in comparison to the early poems written in what can be characterized technically as 'late style'. There, from *Nirjharer svapnabhaṅga* onward, in the mystery of his most beautiful poems, the 'subjectivist approach' predominates—'the rejection of all conventions, and the remoulding of those that prove inevitable in accordance with the requirements of expression'.[74] But in the early works, as in the late works of Beethoven, it is a very different Rabindranath that we find. To use Adorno's description of Beethoven's late style, 'in his entire formal language… one finds sprinklings of conventional formulae and phrases…. And often the convention becomes visible in a stark, unconcealed, unaltered form… that would hardly have been tolerated in the style of the middle period'.[75] If it is 'precisely in the thought of death' that the late works of Beethoven return to conventions, one could surmise that the early works of Rabindranath are suffused with the thought of immortality; death appears here as allegory. In fact, therefore, the subjectivity that created the mature works of perfection (works that are the 'products of a subjectivity or "personality" uncompromisingly articulating itself; which, for the sake of its own expression, breaks open the roundness

[72] Barthes, ibid., pp. 78–9.

[73] Theodor Adorno, 2009, 'Beethoven's Late Style', p. 13.

[74] Ibid.

[75] Ibid., p.14.

of conventional forms'[76]), now disappears from Beethoven's late style in the same manner as that subjectivity is yet to appear in the early work from our 'master's hand'. 'Heaps of material' that do not bear the shape of the force of subjectivity that would transform the best poems that are to follow, the early Rabindranath's political and romantic poems that we have been looking at are testimonies to 'the surplus of material', as Adorno called it, that are not 'penetrated or mastered by subjectivity but simply left to stand', as 'splinters' that will work toward the eventual expression of 'the solitary ego'.[77] Lacking 'the harmonic synthesis' of the mature works, the early style of a poet such as Rabindranath nevertheless lacks the poignancy and splendour that the late works of Beethoven manifested. It is its mirror opposite, alike in the technical similarities of an absence of subjective force and the presence of convention, but in its immaturity, its un-ripeness and its quality of the yet-to-come, utterly the obverse of the dissonance of suffering that characterizes late style.

[76] Ibid., p. 12.
[77] Ibid., p. 16.

Copyright Statement

A version of 'Disjunctions, Conjunctions' appeared as 'Reading Bharatchandra: Literary Language and the Figuration of Modernity in Bengal (1822–1858)', in *Interventions: International Journal of Postcolonial Studies*, Vol. 11, No. 3. Reproduced here with permission from the publisher, Taylor and Francis.

Portions of 'Reading Iswarchandra Gupta (1812–1859)' were originally published in Rosinka Chaudhuri's *Freedom and Beef Steaks: Colonial Calcutta Culture*, pp. 103–6 and 109–19, © Orient BlackSwan 2012. Reproduced here with permission from Orient BlackSwan Private Limited, Himayatnagar, Hyderabad.

'Michael Madhusudan Datta and the Marxist Understanding of the "Real Renaissance" in Bengal' appeared in *Economic and Political Weekly*, 7–13 November 2009. Reproduced here with permission of *EPW*.

'Hemchandra's "*Bhārat Saṅgīt*" (1870) and the Politics of Poetry: A Pre-History of Hindu Nationalism in Bengal' was originally published in *The Indian Economic and Social History Review*, Vol. 42, No. 2. Copyright 2005 © The Indian Economic and Social History Association. All rights reserved. Reproduced with the permission of the copyright holders and the publishers, Sage Publications India Pvt. Ltd, New Delhi.

'Cutlets or Fish Curry?: Debating Indian Authenticity' appeared as 'Cutlets or Fish Curry?: Debating Indian Authenticity in Late Nineteenth-Century Bengal' in *Modern Asian Studies*, Vol. 40 (2006), pp. 257–72, published by Cambridge University Press. Reproduced here with permission from the publisher.

'History in Poetry: Nabinchandra Sen's *Palāśīr yuddha* (1875) and the Question of Truth' was published as Occasional Paper No. 1 (2005) by the Centre of South Asian Studies, Cambridge University, and as 'History in Poetry: Nabinchandra Sen's *Palāśīr yuddha* and the Question of Truth' in *The Journal of Asian Studies*, Vol. 66, No. 4 (November 2007). Reproduced here with permission from the Centre of South Asian Studies, Cambridge.

'The Curious Case of Nabinchandra Sen and the Textbook Committee: An Investigation into Hindu/Muslim Representations' was originally published in *Studies in History*, Vol. 24, No. 1 (2008), copyright © Jawaharlal Nehru University, New Delhi. All rights reserved. Reproduced with the permission of the copyright holders and the publisher, Sage Publications India Pvt. Ltd, New Delhi.

A section of 'Rabindranath's Early Style and Reconstruction of the Past' appeared as 'The Rustle of Language' in *Journal of Contemporary Thought*, Special Number: Winter 2011, published by Forum on Contemporary Theory, Baroda, and University of North Texas, Denton, USA. Reproduced here with permission of *Journal of Contemporary Thought*.

Index

About the Author

Rosinka Chaudhuri completed her D. Phil. in English from the University of Oxford and has since been at the Centre for Studies in Social Sciences, Calcutta, where she is Professor in Cultural Studies. She has also been visiting fellow at the Southern Asian Institute, Columbia University, and Charles Wallace Fellow at Cambridge University.

A reputed scholar, Rosinka's areas of interests include poetry, criticism, literary history, nineteenth-century Bengal, and postcolonial studies. Her published works include *Gentlemen Poets in Colonial Bengal: Emergent Nationalism and the Orientalist Project* (2002), *Derozio, Poet of India: The Definitive Edition* (edited; 2008), *The Indian Postcolonial: A Critical Reader* (co-edited with Elleke Boehmer; 2011), and *Freedom and Beef-Steaks: Colonial Calcutta Culture* (2012).

Her articles have appeared in *Social Text*, *Journal of Asian Studies*, *Interventions*, *Studies in History*, *Indian Economic and Social History Review*, *Modern Asian Studies*, *Journal of Contemporary Thought*, *Seminar*, and *Economic and Political Weekly*; she reviews for *The Times Literary Supplement*. Currently, she has completed an introduction to and translation of Rabindranath Tagore's *Chinnapatrābalī*, titled *Letters from a Young Poet: 1887–1895*, for Penguin Modern Classics (2014). She has now been commissioned to edit and introduce *The Cambridge History of Indian Poetry in English*, the first such volume of its kind, and is working as well on the English writings of Buddhadeva Bose.

